The Political Economy of Capital Controls

Although globalization is seen by many as the key economic trend of recent times, restrictions on international capital movements remain the norm in international finance. In 1996, 144 out of 186 countries maintained capital controls (IMF). Yet the vast majority of economists object to most controls on capital movement, arguing that they distort the allocation of capital and allow opportunities for fraud.

What leads governments to impose restrictions on international capital movements? In this, the first study of capital controls, Günther Schulze uses a public choice model to explain this behavior. He considers the many aspects of capital controls, including quantitative measurements of capital controls, evasion, misinvoicing, the interaction between an investigating government and an evader, and the role capital controls play in helping governments meet their macroeconomic objectives. In addition to the theoretical and policy discussions the book also contains a comprehensive survey of the existing literature.

GÜNTHER SCHULZE is Assistant Professor at the Department of Economics, University of Konstanz. He has published widely in International Economics, including in *Journal of Economics*, *Public Finance Quarterly*, *Economic Inquiry*, *European Journal of Political Economy*, and *Public Choice*.

The Political Economy of Capital Controls

GÜNTHER G. SCHULZE

University of Konstanz,
Germany.

CAMBRIDGE
UNIVERSITY PRESS

PUBLISHED BY THE PRESS SYNDICATE OF THE UNIVERSITY OF CAMBRIDGE
The Pitt Building, Trumpington Street, Cambridge CB2 1RP, United Kingdom

CAMBRIDGE UNIVERSITY PRESS
The Edinburgh Building, Cambridge, CB2 2RU, UK   http://www.cup.cam.ac.uk
40 West 20th Street, New York, NY 10011-4211, USA   http://www.cup.org
10 Stamford Road, Oakleigh, Melbourne 3166, Australia

First published 2000

Printed in the United Kingdom at the University Press, Cambridge

Typeset in Times   [KWS]

A catalogue record for this book is available from the British Library

ISBN 0 521 58222 9 hardback

To my parents
Brigitte and Hermann

Contents

Figures

Tables

Preface

In a time of increasing integration of major core economies fears are mounting that globalization has gone too far, and books are written postulating that something should be done about the growing dependency on malevolent world market forces. Time and again, international trade and international capital movements have been blamed for unemployment, an "unfair" income distribution, sectoral decline, and economic downturns. If that diagnosis is to be believed, capital controls might be regarded as the solution at hand and the public outcry for restriction of capital movements would not be long in coming. Moreover, although economists understand and have uniformly advocated the efficiency gains from the international division of labor, politicians have frequently sought to restrict the free exchange of goods and factors. All liberalization efforts notwithstanding, capital controls are widely and persistently used. A majority of the world's population is currently living under a regime of capital controls of some sort. And, even in countries where capital is allowed to move freely across borders, some politicians have capitalized successfully on fears that globalization deteriorates individual well-being.

Are politicians just not listening? Of course, the answer is no. They use capital controls to their own ends which need not, and often will not, coincide with the interest of the population at large. This book attempts to explain capital controls – why they persist, how they function, and how effective they are. It details the features that appeal to politicians and explains who gains and who loses from those restrictions. In addition, it shows how controls are evaded and discusses the concepts to measure the effectiveness of capital controls. The book is designed for academics, graduate students, and advanced undergraduates. If economics is not your field, skip the technical parts and the book will work for you as well. All important results are also conveyed in a nontechnical way.

In writing this book I drew on many people's help and inspiration. It is a great pleasure to acknowledge the huge debt I have accumulated over the years. First and foremost, I am heavily indebted to Hans-Jürgen Vosgerau who has supported this book in every conceivable way. As speaker of the long-term research program "Internationalization of the Economy" (Sonderforschungsbereich 178) and as my academic teacher he created a stimulating research environment and provided me with guidance, valuable advice, constant encouragement, and all the resources necessary to make this book happen. Furthermore, I owe sincere thanks to Heinrich W. Ursprung, who introduced me to the theory of political economy and who greatly improved my understanding of economics. Arye Hillman has always been a great source of inspiration; he made me think twice when I wanted to think only once. Armin Gutowski (deceased) let me first understand how fascinating international economics is.

I have profited tremendously from numerous discussions with Karl-Josef Koch and I am very grateful to W. Jos Jansen with whom I worked on capital controls in Norway. Our joint work is included in the empirical part of the book. I have further benefited greatly from suggestions and discussions with Max Albert, Angelika Eymann, Bernd Genser, Andreas Haufler, Ronald I. McKinnon, Jürgen Meckl, Gerd Ronning, Agnar Sandmo, Guttorn Schjelderup, Albert Schweinberger, Birger Vikøren, and Hannelore Weck-Hannemann. Financial support of the German Research Foundation is greatly appreciated. I also thank the Department of Economics at the Norwegian School of Economics (Bergen) and the Department of Economics of Stanford University, and Professor McKinnon in particular, for their great hospitality during my stays. I am grateful to Patrick McCartan and Ashwin Rattan (Cambridge University Press) for their patience and competence.

My deepest thanks go to my parents Brigitte and Hermann. To them I dedicate the book. I owe it all to them.

1 Introduction

The control of international capital movements strongly remains the rule rather than the exception. More than two thirds of the world population live under a system of capital controls; merely 42 countries out of a total 186 allow free movement of capital. This constitutes a share of only 22.6 percent, which has hardly risen since 1975 (18 percent), all efforts to liberalize capital markets notwithstanding. Especially in developing countries liberalization has made little progress. (Table 1.1 summarizes the empirical evidence.) By the end of 1996, 144 countries out of a total of 186 had controls on direct investment, 128 countries controlled transactions with capital market securities, 112 countries controlled trade in money market instruments; still 103 countries regulated commercial credits (IMF 1997). Behind these aggregate figures hide a wide variety of restrictions; a closer look at the Annual Report on "Exchange Arrangements and Exchange Restrictions," published by the International Monetary Fund, reveals governments' interferences with the freedom of capital movements of an extraordinary coverage and intensity. This phenomenon obviously deserves our attention.

As a first reaction, economists most probably will object to capital controls. They hamper the efficient allocation of capital, reduce capital formation, disallow consumption smoothing when time preferences differ between countries, and cause huge administrative burdens, let alone ample opportunities for fraud and corruption that capital controls create. They should simply not be there! But the recognition that free capital movement is optimal for a society is of little help in explaining the existence, the permanency, the severeness, and the widespread use of capital controls. The question is blatantly obvious: What imperatives lead governments to impose restrictions on international capital movements, given that these restrictions are detrimental to economic efficiency? The answer to this question is the first central concern of this book.

Table 1.1. *Restrictions on capital account transactions, 1975, 1980, 1985, 1990 and 1993[a]*

	1975	1980	1985	1990	1993
Number of countries[b]	128	140	148	153	178
Separate exchange rate(s) for some capital transactions and/or some or all invisibles and restrictions on payments for capital transactions	22	26	32	32	40
Industrial countries[c]	2	2	–	–	–
Developing countries	20	24	32	32	40
Restrictions on payments for capital transactions only[d,e]	102	107[f]	116	120	98
Industrial countries	17	14	11	11	8
Developing countries	85	91	105	109	90
Separate exchange rate(s) for some capital transactions and/or some or all invisibles only	25	31	34	35	3
Industrial countries	3	3	1	1	0
Developing countries	22	28	33	34	3
Neither separate exchange rate(s) for some capital transactions and/or some or all invisibles nor restrictions on payments for capital transactions	23	28	30	30	37
Industrial countries	3	6	9	9	14
Developing countries	20	22	21	21	23

Notes: [a]The years indicate the publication year of the Report from which data are collected.
[b]Belgium and Luxembourg have been treated as one country.
[c]Grouping definition is based on the existing grouping presented in the latest issue of *International Financial Statistics.*
[d]Restrictions (i.e., official actions directly affecting the availability or cost of exchange, or involving undue delay) on payment to member countries, other than restrictions imposed for security reasons under Executive Board Decision No. 144-(52/51) adopted August 14, 1952.
[e]Resident-owned funds.
[f]Numbers for industrial and developing countries do not sum to the total because the position of two developing countries – Botswana and Haiti – is undetermined.
Sources: International Monetary Fund, Annual Report on *Exchange Arrangements and Exchange Restrictions* for 1975, 1980, 1985, 1990, 1993.

There is a body of literature on capital controls that tries to justify their use by identifying cases in which they may enhance overall efficiency as a second-best policy tool. As we will argue, this line of reasoning is inapt to explain the extent of capital controls that we observe. This empirical observation alone shows that it makes little sense to assume welfare-maximizing motives when explaining government behavior that leads to capital controls. Why should welfare-maximizing politicians impose restrictions that so constantly deteriorate "society's well-being"? Moreover, to dichotomize individuals with regard to their behavior (the altruistic selfless politician versus the egoistic utility-maximizing producer and consumer) is inconsistent with the methodological individualism underlying the economic paradigm. Politicians, like any individual, maximize their own utility. When explaining their behavior, it is decisive to understand under which constraints they operate.

It is against this background and in the face of the remarkable achievements of the modern political-economy approach in explaining international economic policy, notably trade protection, that we are very surprised that so little has been written on capital controls from a political-economic perspective, which we now adopt. To the best of our knowledge, only Alesina and Tabellini (1989), Schulze (1992a), and Alesina *et al.* (1994) analyze capital controls from a genuine political-economic perspective. This book is intended to help close this gap. We hope to contribute to a better understanding of the underlying motives for capital controls.

Thus, we analyze from a political-economic viewpoint how a government gains from the imposition of capital controls. Now we are able to understand why these restrictions are so popular: they have a revenue-generating and a redistributive function. Politicians seeking to extract more resources from the private sector will conveniently rely on capital controls to thwart induced tax avoidance. This holds true for various forms of taxation. Capital controls can also be used as a redistributive device: because capital can effectively be immobilized, controls make a politically desired shift of the tax burden to capital owners possible. In addition, by making the manipulation of domestic factor endowment ratios only possible, controls allow the government to alter factor prices in a political support-maximizing way. We will discuss in detail how controls work to these ends and to what extent they will be applied.

In the course of our analysis we will demonstrate that the severeness of capital controls imposed depends on the distribution of individual factor endowment ratios (capital relative to labor). Relevant to the determination of an individual's optimal restriction is only that part of individual capital that will *effectively* be subject to the controls. In other words, the extent to which an individual can evade controls will alter his or her preferences: evasion becomes relevant to the policy formation. A better understanding of capital controls must thus include a deeper insight into the possibilities to undermine these controls. It has frequently been argued (e.g., Bhagwati 1974, Petite 1987) that misdeclaration of international trade transactions opens the major window of vulnerability for the control system. For instance, the underdeclaration of export prices allows the exporter to retain a share of his/her export proceeds and to surrender only the declared amount. However, this has not been formalized thus far. We look at this omission in part II of the book where we deal with the evasion of capital controls, the second major concern of our book.

Now that we have determined the political calculus leading to the imposition of the optimal restriction and have investigated the major channel to undermine these very controls, the actual effectiveness is rendered an empirical question. As a consequence, measuring the effectiveness of capital controls is our third major concern. Here we present the traditional econometric approach, which relies on the comparison of on- and offshore interest rates, and investigate critically, for the first time, the usefulness of the saving–investment correlation for assessing the effectiveness of capital controls. Needless to say, that empirical results feed back to the process of policy formation. The circle is complete.

After we have stated our concerns we point out the limitations of the present study. We do not deal with specific forms of capital controls and do not provide a taxonomy of capital controls as such studies are already available (Swidrowski 1975, Krueger 1978, Phylaktis and Wood 1984). Here we have nothing new to add. We comment briefly, however, on the issue of financial versus real capital flows at the end of section 2.1 and argue that a restriction of financial flows will also effectively deter real flows, so that the fact that most controls apply to financial flows rather than to real flows is not an issue. Furthermore, we exclude the discussion of whether or not capital controls on volatile very short-term financial flows ("hot money") are needed to prevent speculation in order to stabilize the world currency system (Tobin 1978). We are concerned with restrictions that limit arbitrage persistently, and not only in the very short run.

Structure of the book

The arguments are organized as follows: Chapter 2, departing from the optimality postulate of free capital mobility first critically reviews traditional reasons for the efficiency and desirability of capital controls under certain conditions. It then reflects upon the relevance of a benevolent dictator's perspective and introduces the political-economic paradigm. Against this background, political-economic reasons for capital controls are presented. Here, our emphasis lies on a broad application of the political-economic paradigm to the analysis of capital controls rather than a formalization of the functional relations.

Chapter 3 elaborates on the distributional effects of restricting real capital flows in a small open economy. This is done in the framework of two general equilibrium models for the economic sector, the MacDougall–Kemp model and the specific factors model; the political sector is modeled as a majority voting process. The chapter concludes with a discussion of the pros and cons of a median voter model *vis-à-vis* alternative modeling strategies.

Chapter 4 extends the analysis of the preceding chapter by considering the two-country version of the model and by introducing unemployment. Section 4.4 concludes the first part of the book.

Chapter 5 acquaints the reader with the two strands of the literature, on tax evasion and on smuggling, that will be combined in our own approach to model evasion of capital controls through the misdeclaration of international trade prices.

In chapters 6 and 7 we present the models on misinvoicing import and export prices, respectively, and show that the problem is not symmetric for both cases. We explicitly model revenue-maximizing behavior on the part of the government, leading to a variable optimal auditing activity that depends on the declared price. It is then shown how the importer or exporter optimally misdeclares. We demonstrate how the result depends on tax and tariff rates, informational structure, the penalty and the arbitrage gain. To make this part easily accessible, mathematical derivations are relegated to appendix B as far as possible.

Chapter 8 introduces the reader to the problem of measuring the effectiveness of capital controls. Chapter 9 presents the traditional approach, pioneered by Dooley and Isard (1980), which looks at covered interest rate differentials. Subsequently, an empirical investigation is carried out for Norway, which until relatively recently had a comprehensive system of capital controls in place. Apart from covered interest differentials we look at differentials in bond and stock returns.

The correlation of saving and investment is the subject of chapter 10. First, we survey the extensive and ongoing discussion on the "Feldstein–Horioka puzzle" and criticize, second, the econometric specification. Third, we comment on the diagnostic power of this correlation for the mobility of capital and, last, investigate the Norwegian case. Here, very interesting results are derived which underpin our methodological statements. Data sources and test statistics are explained in appendix C, along with a relegated sensitivity analysis.

Summaries of the results are presented in the course of the discussion, and anticipated main findings are given in the various introductions. Chapter 11 concludes the analysis with an outlook on the future role of capital controls. Notation and abbreviations are summarized in appendix A.

Part I
The reasons for capital controls

2 Political-economic determinants of capital controls

2.1 The inefficiency of capital controls and their prevalence

It is an undisputed standard textbook result that, under rather general assumptions, free flow of capital is advantageous for both countries involved. For (otherwise identical) countries with different rates of time preference, capital mobility increases the welfare of all countries involved as it enlarges their choice sets. The country with the lower time preference shifts its consumption into the future, resulting in a present capital export, whereas the country with the higher time preference enjoys a higher present consumption at the expense of a lower consumption in the future: A capital import today is coupled with a capital export tomorrow, and *vice versa*. The amount of the international loan is such that the marginal rates of time preference are equal between the countries involved and thus equalized by the world interest rate. The (two) countries are on a higher utility level than they would be without capital mobility. This was discussed by Kindleberger (1967) and shown, in an overlapping generations model, by Buiter (1981).

An even stronger argument in favor of unrestricted capital movements can be made if capital's marginal product diverges between countries. Capital flows from the low-return countries to the high-return countries leading to an equal marginal rate of return. Since proceeds from capital installed abroad accrue to the capital-exporting countries, it is straightforward to show that, with rare exceptions to be explained below, capital movements lead to a Pareto improvement. Because this argument is so standard we do not elaborate on it here. Welfare is further improved for both countries if advanced technology is transferred, embodied in the exported capital. This has been demonstrated by Wang (1990), building on Findlay (1978), and elaborated by Wang and Blomstrøm (1992).

In other words, capital controls are welfare-deteriorating as they deny a country the opportunity to intertemporally optimize its consumption

9

path; moreover, they distort the efficient allocation of resources and hence reduce the national product. What is more, capital controls increasingly devour resources. Scarce human capital is absorbed in administering the controls, those engaging in foreign trade or international capital movements have to persevere in order to obtain the necessary permissions from the bureaucracy. If scarce foreign exchange is allocated according to some principle rather than auctioned, individuals will incur costs in seeking these rents.[1]

Capital controls exhibit an inherent tendency for a growing complexity. The regulation of certain transactions provokes a substitution of unrestricted transactions for restricted ones, so that controls have to be intensified and extended to an increasing number of transactions in order to fulfill their goal. In addition, permitted transactions also have to be monitored closely, because individuals find it profitable to evade controls and do so with increasing sophistication as controls persist. For example, current account transactions (which are normally permitted in principle) have to be scrutinized in order to prevent illegal capital flows through changed terms of payment or the misdeclaration of trade prices.[2] If financial markets come up with innovative instruments governments will have difficulties in keeping track and regulation will typically lag behind. No doubt, resources spent in attempting evasion and its prevention are socially wasteful.

For a small open economy it therefore pays to remove impediments to the free flow of capital even on a *unilateral* basis. Losers from the elimination of capital controls could be more than compensated by the gainers so that a removal of capital controls would lead to a Pareto improvement. Why is it then that the majority of the states resort to capital controls?

This is what we will investigate in this chapter. We will discuss a number of (alleged?) reasons for the imposition of capital controls and critically consider their explanatory power. In the course of this we will switch perspective: First, in section 2.2, we will review the traditional reasons for capital controls, seen from the standpoint of a welfare-maximizing social planner. We will argue that these reasons can by no means

---

[1] See Krueger (1974), the surveys by Nitzan (1994) and Tollison (1997), and the literature quoted in section 3.6 for the concept of rent seeking and the discussion to what extent the rent is dissipated.
[2] Gutowski (1972) and Hewson and Sakakibara (1975a) describe in detail the possibilities to – legally – circumvent controls and the need to extend the controls to previously unrestricted markets. Part II of this book is devoted to evasion of capital controls. Bhagwati (1978) and Krueger (1978) give an account of the increasing complexity of foreign exchange control systems. We will take up this point again in section 2.4.4.

account for the widespread and persistent prevalence of capital controls. In our quest for a more convincing answer we will then drop the assumption of an effective compensation of losers by the gainers, which implicitly underlies the benevolent dictator's perspective. Instead, we ask ourselves *who* profits from these controls. Reasons for that approach are provided in section 2.3. Next, in section 2.4, we will identify the gainers from this regulation – revenue-maximizing politicians, bureaucrats, lawyers, factor owners (depending on the restriction) – and show how the capital controls work to their benefit. Concluding remarks round off this chapter (section 2.5). In the following two chapters (chapter 3–4) we present formal models deriving the optimal degree of control and discuss the appropriateness of different modeling strategies for our problem. Section 4.4 provides a summary and concluding remarks for part I of this book.

Before we start our analysis on the reasons for capital controls, a clarification of the nature of (international) capital flows is in order. The term "capital" comprises two different notions – financial and real capital. *Financial capital* flows refer to processes of crediting: real resources are transferred today in exchange with a claim on real resources at some point in time in the future. In the international context, the export of financial capital means that a country acquires claims on future foreign output in the form of lending abroad, the purchase of foreign stocks, bonds, commercial papers, etc., or the holding of foreign currency. The capital export is mirrored by an equal surplus in the balance of trade in goods and services. This implies that the export of financial capital can be "effected" through the net export of any goods and services which the lending country may want; i.e., financial capital export can go together with the net export of bananas.

This is quite different from *real capital* flows which refer to capital as a factor of production. In the traditional comparative-static analysis an international flow of real capital reduces the productive capital stock in the capital-exporting country and augments the productive capacity of the capital-receiving country. In more sophisticated approaches this is modeled through investment–disinvestment processes in the countries involved.[3]

Note that real capital flows have to be distinguished from the *trade in capital goods*: the latter involves the exchange of goods and the transfer-

---

[3] It is the distinction between goods and factors that really lies at the heart of the difference between financial and real capital: Goods can be consumed directly whereas factors cannot. Although this distinction is not undisputable, it is commonly made in international economics.

ral of ownership, the capital goods add to the domestically owned capital stock of the country importing the capital goods. This does not reduce the capital stock of the exporting country compared to a situation in which no such trade would take place. The exporting country is not involved in any investment process taking place in the importing country. Hence, no domestic investment can be replaced by foreign investment and the political-economic reasons for locking in capital do not apply! In contrast, real capital exports imply that the capital goods newly installed in the foreign country are owned by domestic residents and thus create a flow of capital proceeds from the foreign country to the home country. The resident is accumulating productive capital and placing it abroad, whereas in the case of trade in capital goods the resident simply ships these goods to a foreign customer like any other good. The restriction of real capital exports may hence yield a higher capital formation at home whereas the restriction to export capital goods does not. As we are concerned with capital controls, not trade restrictions, the latter case is irrelevant to us.

An approach that includes real and financial capital flows must model, among other things, endogenous saving and investment decisions and international trade in assets in an intertemporal framework. Although such models exist (e.g., Sandmo 1977, Frenkel and Razin 1992), the literature on international economics remains largely dichotomized with respect to the type of capital mobility they study – and hence with respect to the effects of capital controls. The literature on trade and factor flows as well as most of the literature on international public economics (especially on tax competition) models only real capital flows[4] whereas the literature on international macroeconomics and international monetary economics mostly confines international capital movements to financial flows and disregards the real side. In this book we will look at both types of capital flows since there are political–economic reasons to restrict financial flows as well as real capital flows. To keep matters as simple as possible, however, we look at only one type of capital at a time; insofar we follow the classical dichotomy. It will become completely obvious which type of capital we will be dealing with.

One problem remains: capital controls predominantly restrict financial flows. Do these controls also restrict real flows? We will argue that under reasonable and fairly general assumptions they do.

Many restrictions apply directly to real capital flows, such as various concession requirements for direct investment, differential tax provisions

---

[4] For surveys see respectively Ruffin (1984) and, for instance, Bovenberg (1994) or Koch and Schulze (1998).

altering the after-tax rate of return for foreign-owned capital compared to domestically owned capital in case of capital import controls,[5] and other investment measures that affect the rate of return, like local content requirements etc. In as much as these measures are targeted to restrict capital flows, they have to be reckoned as capital controls. But the host of capital control measures apply to financial flows.[6] This includes the restriction of lending to, or borrowing from abroad; restrictions on cross-border sales or purchases of stocks, bonds, etc.; limits on the holdings of foreign exchange (in cash or in bank accounts), the prohibition to residents to open accounts abroad denominated in national currency and to non-residents to open domestic accounts in foreign currencies or ceilings on those accounts. The control system may also comprise regulations on the channels through which international payments may be effected and typically banks' operations are regulated and subject to close scrutinization. For example, limits on open positions for certain or all international transactions, or the total volume thereof, may be stipulated. Lastly, the import or export of cash, precious metals, art objects, etc. may be regulated.

If a country wants to restrict real capital imports it can do so effectively through restricting non-residents from buying stocks or other forms of equity capital and through concession requirements for the setting up of new firms or foreign subsidiaries.[7] If the government wants to prevent real capital outflow, it will restrict the export of financial capital as this effectively restricts real capital exports. Typically, the acquisition of foreign firms or the establishment of a subsidiary abroad is financed through foreign exchange holdings, a credit denominated in a convertible currency, or the sale of newly issued stocks abroad. This enables the resident to purchase from non-residents the stocks or equity shares in case of a foreign acquisition or the necessary goods and services (including land) to

---

[5] In the case of export controls, this will take the form of a differential tax on profits derived abroad.

[6] For a taxonomy of these see Phylaktis and Wood (1984).

[7] If capital imports are restricted the motivation is decisive. (Of course this applies in principle also to capital exports.) When capital controls are imposed to prevent speculative capital inflows (like in Germany in 1971–1973), real capital flows are normally not prohibited for establishing subsidiaries, setting up plants, or for buying resident companies, etc. Financial transactions to effect this direct investment are approved but monitored in order to prevent speculation. (For the case of German capital controls, see Schmidt [1977, esp. pp. 137–142].) Portfolio investment remains restricted. If real capital inflows are to be denied, authorities have forceful measures at hand to deter investors even on a case by case basis. Predominantly these comprise concession requirements and all kind of tax instruments. In developing countries governments and investors often negotiate the tax burden, Lewis (1984). Loopholes effecting real capital inflows when governments prohibit it are virtually non-existent.

set up a new firm abroad. If however the domestic currency is not fully convertible and borrowing from abroad is prohibited as is the holding of foreign exchange accounts and the cross-border sales of stocks, this channel for real capital exports is not open to the domestic investor.

For real capital exports to take place under these circumstances, it would be necessary for the resident to accumulate wealth abroad without involving a cross-border flow of financial capital (except for possible short-term trade credits which are typically permitted). This would be possible if a resident exported goods or services *and* could use the proceeds to purchase either stocks (or other types of equity) or goods and services needed to set up a firm.[8] This presupposes however that exporters are masters of their export proceeds. In most cases this does not hold: Out of 138 countries that had imposed restrictions of payments for capital transactions in 1993, 128 countries had imposed surrender or repatriation requirements on their export proceeds (IMF 1993: 590–596). At the end of 1996, out of 128 countries restricting portfolio investment, 115 required the repatriation of profits (IMF 1997: 946–952). It is clear therefore that this possibility is of minor importance, particularly in light of all the difficulties encountered by an investor who has to finance real investment only by export proceeds.

For these reasons it is fair to assume that effective restrictions on financial flows will yield effective restrictions on real flows.[9] We will proceed with this assumption in the following analysis. It is common practice of the literature on international trade and factor movements, to disregard the mechanics of capital controls and to assume their effectiveness. We will however investigate illegal ways to export/import capital in part II of the book. Having clarified the notion of "capital" and "capital controls" we can turn to the traditional reasons for capital controls next.

2.2 Traditional reasons for capital controls

The optimality of full capital mobility is easily proven in an "ideal" world, as is the optimality of free goods trade. Interferences with the freedom of capital movements can be justified (from a welfare-maximiz-

---

[8] Note that the balance of payments definition of imports and exports refers to the status of the trading partners (residents/non-residents), but not to the location of goods delivered. Thus, such transactions would amount to capital exports.

[9] Note that this is the opposite case to the discussion of the transfer problem, where it was noted that a financial flow need not result in a flow of real resources. Our argument is quite the reverse.

ing viewpoint) only with deviations from this "first-best world," such as externalities, market power, or other policy-induced distortions. The mere existence of such distortions, however, does not prove the case for capital controls – it must be shown in addition that capital controls are the best available measure to deal with the respective distortions. Below we will present the arguments most commonly adduced in favor of capital controls.

2.2.1 Diverging social and private return to capital

One reason for interfering with capital flows is that domestically installed capital may produce externalities. If the social return to capital exceeds the private return, then, according to the argument, it is sensible to tax capital outflow (or subsidize capital inflow) such that the socially optimal capital stock is installed at home. This capital stock is defined by the equality of the marginal social return to capital and the world interest rate.[10] The interest equalization tax (in case of a capital exporting country) would have to be levied at a rate that is equal to the difference between the marginal social and the marginal private rate of return *for* the socially optimal capital stock. Conversely, for negative externalities of domestic capital, capital exports should be subsidized or capital imports taxed, respectively. The arguments are detailed in Claassen (1985).

This argument, however, is flawed. First, it is not exactly clear what may lead to such externalities. Claassen (1985) does not provide any explanations. Caves (1976) states rigidities in the labor market and taxation of capital proceeds as examples: Capital exports may lead to unemployment and taxation of capital income drives the capital out of the country until the after-tax rate of return is equalized by the world rate. Both distortions drive a wedge between the social and the private return. (In the latter case this induces capital to leave the country only if the residents principle cannot be enforced, which may often be the case.)[11] Of course the best policy is to remove the causes of the externalities, whatever they may be. But even if this is not possible for certain reasons, capital controls are *not* the appropriate choice. A countervailing subsidy on domestic investment is superior because it does not reduce savings and leads to an efficient international allocation of capital. The equality of the domestic rate of intertemporal substitution and transformation is

---

[10] This is true because we take the position of the *national* welfare-maximizing social planner; otherwise the social returns would have to be equalized across countries.

[11] We will address the problem of unemployment in section 4.3 and discuss taxation as a motivation for capital controls in section 2.4.1.

restored. Moreover, insofar as capital exhibits externalities to different extents in various industries, or externalities are confined to certain investment projects, subsidization allows for specified assignment, whereas capital controls apply across the board and are thus inefficient in these cases.

2.2.2 Optimal tax argument

If a country is large enough to influence the world interest rate, it may be optimal for it to restrict capital outflows in the case of a capital exporter, or the inflows, if it is a capital importer. The argument is essentially similar to the optimal tariff argument and goes back to MacDougall (1960) and Kemp (1964, 1966). Since the optimal tax is derived analytically in section 4.2, only the gist of the argument is stated here.

Restriction of capital exports lowers the supply of capital on world markets thereby raising the world interest rate. While less capital earns income abroad, pre-tax earnings per unit of capital have risen, thereby changing the factor terms of trade in favor of the restricting country. At the optimal tax rate a country's marginal loss from capital misallocation is equal to its marginal gain from increased gross proceeds from exported capital. Conversely, for a large capital importer, curbing of capital inflows reduces the cost of foreign capital. At the optimal restriction, marginal gain from reduced cost is balanced by marginal loss from smaller capital imports. World welfare is reduced, but the large country's welfare is increased due to an international redistribution effect.[12]

The argument is correct, yet only relevant for those countries that have some market power in the world capital market. As Fieleke (1971: 4) notes, this has been argued in July 1963 in connection with the introduction of the US interest equalization tax on purchases of long-term securities from foreigners: "Much of the burden of the tax is likely to be shifted to the foreign seller [of securities]..." (1964 Senate Report 1267: 2). Fieleke remarks however that the optimum tax argument was considered "merely as ancillary dividend and not as an important justification for the tax" (p. 4). Chapter 4, therefore, embeds this consideration in

---

[12] This may induce other countries to retaliate if they are able to effectively cooperate with each other. Retaliation will typically reduce welfare of all countries below the level obtained without restriction, though this need not be the case, see Johnson (1953).

a political-economic framework, which provides a more convincing explanation of capital controls than the optimum tax argument alone.[13]

2.2.3 Immiserizing capital flows

Bhagwati (1958) points out that, under certain circumstances, growth may lead to immiserization. This is the case if the country's increased supply of exportables deteriorates its terms of trade so much that the effect of increased production possibilities is overcompensated. A related immiserization argument has been made in the context of capital inflows in less developed countries. The immiserization argument appears in two versions. In the first version, closely related to Bhagwati's (1958) original setup, immiserization is due to a deterioration of the terms of trade, which requires some monopoly power in world markets. In the second version, connected to the work of Johnson (1967a), immiserization results from increased distortion as a consequence of capital inflow in a tariff ridden (small) open economy.

Bhagwati (1958) demonstrates the possibility of immiserization in a two-country version of the standard 2×2 Heckscher–Ohlin model.[14] The initial world market clearing condition for importables is given by the equality of domestic supply thereof S_m, and imports M from abroad with the domestic consumption of importables C_m, where p denotes the relative price of the importable in terms of the exportable and α is a shift parameter, representing the effect of economic growth on the domestic production of the importable. Therefore, $S_m(p, \alpha) + M(p) - C_m(p) = 0$. Now suppose that the capital stock has grown exogenously and that due to a negative Rybczynski-effect the labor-intensive importable sector has declined at constant prices, i.e., $(\partial S_m/\partial \alpha)\, d\alpha < 0$. $\hat{p}$ (> 0) denotes the deterioration of the terms of trade (i.e., the relative change in the relative price for the importable) that exactly offsets the increased expansion of the national product at constant prices, so that we are able to disregard income effects. (Obviously, $\hat{p}$ is a function of the change in α as it is derived by totally differentiating the national income identity and setting

---

[13] These results are sensitive to the assumption of labor being immobile internationally in the following way. Building on Ramaswami (1968), Jones *et al.* (1986) show that it is welfare maximizing to prohibit capital outflow and to attract both foreign labor and foreign capital, *if* labor can be paid only the lower foreign wages. If labor has to be paid the higher home wages, however, total prohibition of immigration coupled with an optimal restriction of capital exports is optimal. The latter case seems relevant since an economy-wide discrimination of foreign workers is politically unlikely and hardly feasible.
[14] The exposition follows Bhagwati (1958: 204) and Findlay (1984). Koch (1992) provides an example of immiserizing growth in the framework of a growth model (which contrasts Bhagwati's comparative-static analysis).

it equal to zero.) Immiserization is then given if the following inequality holds (which is derived by total differentiation of the preceding equation)

$$C\left[\frac{S_m}{C_m}\sigma + \frac{M}{C_m}\epsilon + \eta\right]\hat{p} + \frac{\partial S_m}{\partial\alpha}d\alpha < 0,$$

where σ and ϵ are the price elasticities of the domestic supply of the importable and of the foreign supply of imports, respectively. η is the compensated price elasticity of domestic demand for the importable. The growing country suffers in real terms if, at a price increase of the importable that leaves income unchanged, the price-induced increase in domestic and foreign supply of importable plus the decrease in domestic consumption are insufficient to make up for the reduction in domestic supply at constant prices.[15]

For identical tastes and technologies (to keep matters simple) the home country would be worse off also if the foreign country's capital stock grew. World income would increase, raising demand for importables (assuming non-inferiority), but reducing production thereof (due to the Rybczynski effect). Terms of trade would deteriorate for the home country. In contrast, the pure transfer of capital between two countries with identical technologies would not change world production (if we exclude complete specialization). It would thus not lead to immiserization. Only under restrictive assumptions would foreign investment *as such* bring about immiserization of the host country. It is only the immiserization resulting from the mere *transfer* of capital that may establish a case for capital controls, not the capital augmenting growth as such.

Refering to Singer (1950), Brecher and Choudhri (1982) argue that less developed countries have a "technological superiority" in their capital-intensive resource-extracting export sector due to the natural resources at their disposal. This results in capital-intensive exports, although developing countries have a lower capital–labor ratio. The techological superiority in the production of these primary products leads also to a higher return to capital in developing countries which is the reason why capital is attracted to these countries. At constant prices, capital exports to the less developed countries (LDCs) lower production of labor-intensive importables there and raise it in industrial countries, but not by as much. This result is driven by certain conditions on the elasticities of factor substitution in both countries, which Brecher and Choudhri (1982: 188–189) assume to prevail. At the same time world income has increased, because capital now earns a higher return and, thus, demand for importables increases. The ensuing terms of trade deterioration which

---

[15] Note that we have excluded factor-intensity reversals.

reestablishes market clearing puts the host country on the receiving end: The nationally owned factors are fixed and hence the country's welfare depends only on the terms of trade.

Does this establish a case for capital controls? It hardly does for the following reasons: First, the result hinges on the assumption of capital-intensive exports on the part of LDCs. This may be true for some resource-extracting sectors, but for the total foreign trade of a developing country the pattern is less clear-cut. Furthermore, capital inflow is often essential for the resource-extracting sectors, because it goes hand in hand with the transfer of technology, without which the development of deposits is impossible (or much less efficient) for those countries. Restricting capital imports would harm the countries rather than prevent immiserization. Third, for restriction of capital inflow to be successful it is necessary that the restricting country be large enough to influence world prices. In particular, the capital outflow from the developed countries would have to be so huge that the import price level actually rose. This is hardly so for a single LDC; it is debatable whether it applies to the developing countries as a group. However, in that case a unilateral restriction of capital inflows would reduce a single LDC's production possibility set (at constant prices), but would not prevent the terms of trade deterioration – the loss would be twofold. As LDCs are not large countries, Brecher and Choudhri's analysis does not make a case for capital controls, even if it were true otherwise.[16]

The second argument against free inflow of capital seems more relevant as it does not require market power of the host countries. Johnson (1967a) shows that capital augmentation may produce immiserization for a small economy if the import-competing sector is protected and capital intensive. Again, the Rybczynski effect is at work expanding the import-competing sector and shrinking the export sector, however, according to the distorted domestic price signals. Immiserization occurs if the value of output at world prices declines, i.e., $dX/dK + p^* dM/dK < 0$, where p^* denotes the relative world price of the importable and $X(M)$ the domestic output of exportables (importables). Differently stated, $a_{LM} > a_{LX} p^*$ is sufficient for immiserization, where $a_{LX}(a_{LM})$ is the input coefficient for labor in the production of exportables (importables).[17] Graphically this means that the slope of the well-

---

16 It is now commonly acknowleged that this phenomenon has very little empirical relevance. All the more so in our context, since most countries have imposed capital *export* controls rather than general restrictions on inflowing capital.

17 This is derived from the full employment conditions which are differentiated with respect to K to yield $dX/dK = a_{LM}/(a_{KX} a_{LM} - a_{LX} a_{KM}) < 0$ and $dM/dK = -a_{LX}/(a_{KX} a_{LM} - a_{LX} a_{KM}) > 0$.

known Rybczynski line is flatter than the world price line in absolute terms with the importable on the ordinate. Reduction of exportable production is a necessary but not sufficient condition for immiserization, because the Rybczynski line could be steeper than the world price line, implying a suboptimal growth of GNP. This is not so in the case of capital inflows: they are always immiserizing if they increase output of the importable, because they earn the domestic rate of return which in this case exceeds the shadow price of capital (*viz.* the world rate of return). Hence they not only increase the distortive effect of the tariff, but are also rewarded by more than they contribute – immiserization is straightforward (see Brecher and Diaz Alejandro 1977, Findlay 1984).[18]

The literature on welfare effects of capital movements is now well-developed and well known.[19] The analysis has been extended to allow for more goods and factors, plus different production structures. We report only the main results. For a small open economy with free trade of goods, capital flows are unambiguously beneficial, whatever their size or direction (for a proof see Schweinberger 1989: 314–316). Welfare is also improved for a small open economy with given import tariffs, if a capital inflow increases the tariff revenue. This is a sufficient, but not necessary condition. It implies that the economy is specializing according to its comparative advantage. Schweinberger (1989: 316–319, esp. equation 16) points out that national welfare may improve, even if the tariff revenue falls, if the correlation between capital imports and the difference of pre-capital flow rentals to after-capital flow rentals is sufficiently large to offset the reduction in tariff revenue. In other words, capital flows follow the pattern of comparative advantage in factor trade closely.[20]

Grossman (1984) incorporates both sources for immiserization, as he analyzes a large tariff-ridden economy. The sufficient (but not necessary!, see footnote 20) condition for welfare-improving capital flows reads as follows

---

[18] Brecher and Diaz Alejandro (1977) analyze a two-good Heckscher–Ohlin model; their results are extended in Brecher and Findlay (1983) to a specific factors setting. In principle, foreign capital could be remunerated differently than domestic capital by means of a differential tax, thereby eliminating the welfare-deteriorating effect (Bhagwati 1973). See Shea (1997) for a general treatment of different remuneration schemes.

[19] *Inter alia* Markusen and Melvin (1979), Bhagwati and Brecher (1980), Grossman (1984), Neary and Ruane (1988). Schweinberger (1989) provides a comprehensive global analysis.

[20] The necessary condition for welfare improvement is given by $(K^1 - K^0)$ $[r(p, K^0) - r(p, K^1)] + t[M(p, u^1, K^1) - M(p, u^0, K^0)] \geq 0$, where p and K denote the domestic price vector and the vector of domestically installed mobile factors (capital), respectively. r stands for the corresponding rentals, u for utility, and superscript 0 (1) indicates the pre-capital flow (after-capital flow) situation. For a derivation see Schweinberger (1989).

$$e(p^1, u^1) - e(p^1, u^0) > \underbrace{(p^{*0} - p^{*1})M^0}_{\text{terms of trade effect}} + \underbrace{(p^1 - p^{*1})(M^1 - M^0)}_{\text{volume of trade effect}}$$

with e denoting the expenditure function, p the price vector, u the utility level, and M the import vector. The superscripts 0, 1, $*$ indicate pre-capital flow and post-capital flow situations and foreign variables. The first term on the RHS measures variation in the terms of trade (in the Paasche sense) and captures the Bhagwati-type of immiserization while the second term refers to the exacerbation of trade distortion due to factor movements. This reflects the Johnson-type of immiserization studied by Brecher and Diaz-Alejandro and Schweinberger.

No doubt, there are circumstances under which capital mobility may reduce national welfare and thus it may be suggested to resort to capital controls. These arguments, though logical, are, however, not very relevant in practice. As we have argued, terms of trade variations (e.g., due to large capital inflows into the LDCs) cannot be prevented by a single capital-receiving LDC. Either the capital-importing country must be large, which applies only to a very limited number of countries, or it calls for coordinated controls in the form of a cartel to restrict capital imports. This will not be sustainable (if at all attainable), given the heterogeneity of countries with respect to the factor intensities of their import-competing industries and the incentives to deviate from the agreement.

The second reasoning is not convincing either. If economic policy were in fact formulated by a benevolent dictator, tariffs leading to immiserizing distortions would be removed in the first place. However, reasons for trade protection are predominantly of political-economic nature;[21] therefore, it is inconsistent to argue that a benevolent Dr. Jekyll should react to trade distortions created by a selfish Mr. Hyde.

Still, even if we put this line of reasoning aside, immiserization due to increased distortions may be overcompensated by welfare gains thanks to superior technology "embodied" in the imported capital. Especially in this case, capital controls will have detrimental effects on long-run growth: Capital imports from a technologically more advanced country will put the capital-receiving country on a steady state growth path with a higher rate (Findlay 1978, Wang 1990, Wang and Blomstrøm 1992). Moreover, capital imports may alleviate labor market distortions, such as wage floors and resulting unemployment. But even if we account for such positive externalities and capital imports are still welfare deteriorating, controls can only be justified if immiserization through capital mobility

---

[21] See Ursprung (1987), Hillman (1989), Magee et al. (1989) and the literature quoted therein for a detailed argumentation on this point.

outweighs immiserization due to enormous efforts spent in administering and maintaining controls, on the one hand, plus outlays made in order to circumvent, evade, or overcome these restrictions, on the other hand. This waste is huge! Since capital controls exhibit a tendency to become a permanent feature with increasing coverage (see section 2.4.4), the management of it absorbs a growing amount of resources, especially the scarce skilled administrative staff that is lacking elsewhere. Because foreign exchange is in shortage due to the obligation to surrender it to the state and restricted reallocation thereof, its possession guarantees a windfall gain, in the form of either interest rate arbitrage or supernormal profits from the resale of scarce imports. Rent-seeking activities for scarce foreign exchange and efforts to camouflage evasion of regulations (through smuggling, misinvoicing, etc.) devour further resources.[22] Also legal, regular business activities like international trade are deterred as they become more costly. Additional bureaucratic regulations have to be adhered to; even if trade is free in principle, flexibility may be limited due to regulations on terms of payments, time-consuming monitoring, and approval procedures, which reduce competitiveness on international markets.

The balance shifts further in favor of free capital mobility.

2.2.4 Other reasons for capital controls

In the following, we list further arguments in favor of capital controls that have been raised, but are of minor importance in our context.

Limiting excess volatility in foreign exchange markets

Capital controls have been suggested as a short-term device to limit self-fulfilling speculative attacks. This has been done for fixed exchange rates by Johnson (1967b) as well as for flexible exchange rates by Tobin (1978) and Obstfeld (1986a), to name a few. The argument runs roughly as follows. Due to different speeds of adjustment in the financial and in the real sector of an economy, excess exchange-rate volatility may cause disruptions in real economic activity and, therefore, limiting short-term capital mobility will be beneficial. Capital controls in the form of a tax on foreign exchange transactions will "throw sand in the wheels" (Tobin 1978) and stabilize, but not disrupt, exchange mar-

---

[22] If rent-seeking activities take on the form of bribes only, it would merely result in a redistribution. Typically rent-seeking appears in a variety of forms notably including non-pecuniary transfers, which (as is commonly known) is inferior to cash transfers. Any resources spent to cover illegal activities apart from buying the inattention of government officials is a pure waste.

kets' activity. Though there may be something to this argument[23] we will not consider it here because it is not targeted at restricting international capital flows as such, but only short-term speculation. Capital controls are intended to be inefficient but for the very short run and, thus, the discussion lies in the realm of short-term monetary economics, which is not our concern.

Political default argument

If private investors tend to overlend or overinvest because they underestimate the political default risk, capital outflow should be curbed. Keynes (1924: 584) argues: "If a loan to improve a South-American capital is repudiated, we have nothing. If a popular housing loan is repudiated, we, as a nation, still have the houses." For this argument to make sense it must be assumed that the government is better informed about default risks than the private sector. This position can hardly be defended given the fact that the markets account for political risk, and demand an appropriate premium on top of the normal interest rate (see sections 9.2–9.3).

Crises, wars, stabilization policy

In times of war or crisis, it may be inevitable to impose capital controls in order to prevent capital flight and to allocate scarce foreign exchange to high priority needs. This is dictated by the extraordinary situation in which a credible economic policy to keep capital at home is infeasible – individuals will try to transfer their capital to safe havens, instead of surrendering it to the authorities, knowing that their possessions are most likely to be lost.

A related case can be made for the period of adjustment programs or structural reforms, when the credibility of the plan is lacking. This will typically cause capital flight which may hamper the stabilization success. By way of contrast, if a (at least partially credible) stabilization package includes austerity policy implying high interest rates, unrestricted capital inflows will contravene the tight monetary policy or lead to an appreciation which may counteract trade liberalization efforts and worsen the balance of payments.[24]

In these cases a transitory regulation of cross-border capital flows may be appropriate either to safeguard the stabilization success or for the

---

[23] This issue is widely debated. For instance, Dellas and Stockman (1988) argue that the thread of future capital controls in case of speculative attacks may exactly *cause* speculation even if macroeconomic policy is consistent and credible.

[24] For the latter argument see Dornbusch (1983) and also van Wijnbergen (1990).

duration of the war (and shortly afterwards). Both cases are exceptional and call for *temporary* impositions of controls – they cannot be made responsible for the persistence and widespread prevalence of capital controls.

This holds true also for capital controls in the process of economic liberalization. Controls should stay in place until appropriate institutions for a market economy, notably a fiscal system, have successfully been implemented. McKinnon (1993) has written an excellent book on that issue; we have nothing to add. His arguments do not establish a case for capital controls as such, but only for their late removal in the course of liberalization.

2.3 The relevance of a social planner's perspective and the political-economic approach

As we have seen in the previous section, there are *special* cases in which capital controls may be justified from a benevolent dictator's perspective who acts for the well-being of his (or her) subjects. We cannot exclude these cases on logical grounds. However, capital controls are the rule rather than the exception. For that reason, it is simply impossible to justify the existing amount and scope of capital controls in the world as the result of optimal policies for the society in the presence of some externality or market power. This is not surprising.

A benevolent dictator's perspective implies that the state provides public goods, internalizes externalities, and achieves a socially desired income distribution in a selfless way, only targeted at maximizing the welfare of the society as a whole. While the economic agents in the private sector seek to maximize their own utility, in the traditional approach "the state" pursues an exclusively altruistic policy – it lives in the clouds while its selfish subjects are struggling for their self-interest on earth. We know this is not so.

Methodological individualism, a foundation of modern economic theory, implies that the individual as the relevant economic agent (as opposed to organizations, the state, or other entities) acts in a rational way in order to maximize his or her utility. Though individuals' behavior according to this view is not inconsistent with some sort of altruism,[25] (s)he will maximize his/her utility predominantly in a self-interested way, given a set of constraints. As Adam Smith (1776) has written:

[25] See Frank (1988) for an excellent discussion of this point.

Man has almost constant occasion for the help of his brethen, and it is in vain for him to expect it from their benevolence only ... It is not from the benevolence of the butcher, the brewer, or the baker, that we expect our dinner, but from their regard to their own interest. We address ourselves not to their humanity but to their self-love, and never talk to them of our own necessities but of their advantages. (cit. after the 1937 edition, p. 14)

Are politicians any better than a butcher or a brewer? We rather doubt it. Firms maximize their profits, consumers their utility, and what makes politicians and bureaucrats tick? They maximize their utility all alike – the artificial dichotomy in the behavioral assumption of private and public agents is completely unjustified; it contradicts the concept of methodological individualism – and common sense.

This is why we adopt the modern political-economy approach.[26] It posits that the individual is the relevant agent (regardless whether he or she acts as a consumer, producer, voter, member of an interest group, politician, etc.), who behaves rationally in the following sense: the individual seeks to optimize his or her utility and reacts systematically (and hence predictably) to changing constraints under which (s)he operates. Collective decisions are based on individual preferences and aggregated according to some procedure, which may be very different across various groups, organizations, societies. Institutions matter in the sense that they determine the constraints under which individuals optimize; in particular, they determine how individual preferences are aggregated. However, organizations, collectives, and the like are not independent subjects as suggested in the organismic theories of the state.[27] Basically, this approach boils down to a consequential extension of methodological individualism (which has dominated economics since Adam Smith) to political decision-making. This approach suggests itself because it is incomprehensible why rational self-interested behavior should be limited to market decisions. Indeed, the "economic approach" has been adopted successfully for the analysis of a number of non-market activities such as crime, the legal system, marriage and family, charity, etc. (e.g., McKenzie and Tullock 1975 and Becker 1976, 1991).

How does this "new" approach change the way we look at the political process? Instead of maximizing the nation's welfare, the individuals form-

---

[26] This approach is also referred to as economic theory of politics or public choice theory. The classics are Arrow (1951, rev. edn. 1963), Downs (1967), Black (1958), Buchanan and Tullock (1962), Olson (1965) and Niskanen (1971). Mueller (1989) provides a comprehensive survey of this approach, Mueller (1997) contains a collection of up-to-date surveys of various areas in public choice theory.

[27] For a fundamental critique on the "organismic" approach to the state see Buchanan (1949).

ing the government use their power to their own selfish ends. The members of the government may have various and different aims, such as maximizing their income or prestige or translating their ideological conceptions into action, but their predominant goal is to remain in office because this is the prerequisite for accomplishing all the other aims. A politician out of power can achieve nothing, a politician in office has at least some possibilities of pursuing his or her own ideological views, to augment his or her wealth through bribes or regular income, etc. Staying in, or attaining power is the politician's supreme goal to which all other goals are secondary. This is true for all kinds of political systems; they differ only (but decisively so) with respect to the constraints under which their politicians act. Autocratic rulers may be constrained in their behavior by the threat of a revolution or by a minimum-political-support requirement on the part of the groups that secure their power (esp. the military or the ruling party) in order to prevent being overthrown.[28] In democracies, politicians are subject to a reelection constraint. Since political competition prevails, the incumbents use their power to enhance their probability of reelection as the challengers announce their policy platforms in order to defeat the incumbents.[29] Anthony Downs (1957: 28) notes:

Thus politicians ... never seek office as a means of carrying out particular policies; their only goal is to reap the rewards of holding office *per se.* They treat policies purely as means to the attainment of their private ends, which they can reach only by being elected. ... *parties formulate policies in order to win elections, rather than win elections in order to formulate policies.* (italics not in original)

The public choice perspective[30] focuses on the distributional impact of particular policies rather than on the impact they have on efficiency. The reason for this focus is the notion that (domestic) policy formation is largely dominated by distributional considerations rather than efficiency concerns. Leaving constitutional considerations aside, the state traditionally is assigned four major functions: to stabilize the economy, to internalize externalities, to provide public goods, and to achieve a "socially desirable" income distribution. All of these tasks have distributional

28 The public choice literature on autocracy is rather scanty. Notable exceptions are Tullock (1974, 1987a) and McGuire and Olson (1996); see also the literature quoted in Mueller (1989: 271–273).
29 The idea of vote-maximizing parties goes back at least to Schumpeter (1942: chapter 22).
30 The literature on the public choice approach is well developed and so well known that we refrain from explicating their premises and main results in detail. We only sketch the basic concept as far as it is relevant for our context. This seems justified as comprehensive surveys are easily accessible: Tullock (1987b), Buchanan (1988), Magee *et al.* (1989, esp. pp. 32–34), and Mueller (1989, 1997).

consequences and can be used to achieve distributional goals. Stabilization policies, the merits of which are highly disputed between the various schools of macroeconomic thought, have distributional consequences as for instance inflation or austerity programs affect different types of wealth and factor owners differently (cf., e.g., Edwards (1983) and also footnote 38). To be sure, there are government interventions that predominantly internalize external effects, e.g., in the realm of environmental policy. However, even in this field distributional considerations can be argued to play a major role, as the literature on ecoprotectionism shows.[31] Public goods provision has also clear distributional consequences, because public goods consumption or the valuation thereof differs between individuals.[32] This becomes even more evident when we consider the revenue-raising aspect of public goods provision: Taxation has obvious distributional effects. The distributional motivation for income transfers, subsidies, social security, and the like need not be argued. These redistributional schemes constitute the biggest item on the budget at least in most modern democracies. In short, nearly all government activity has distributional impacts, and the majority of government interventions simply *create* allocative deficiencies, so that efficiency cannot be argued to be the driving force behind government activity (cf. Aranson and Ordeshook 1981). On the contrary, most policies are motivated by their distributional consequences. This statement seems a good approximation to reality;[33] the rationale behind this perspective on policy is of course that redistribution can be designed in such a way that political support is increased. There are a number of reasons for this fact. Gains may be very concentrated and translate into support while losses may be widespread and hence for the individual too negligible to stir up opposition. Or opposing pressure groups may have different impacts on the political process in terms of the political support which they can offer to the politician in exchange for imposing, refraining

---

31 See for example Leidy and Hoekman (1994), Hillman and Ursprung (1993), Bommer and Schulze (1999). For a survey of the political-economic approach to environmental policy see Schulze and Ursprung (1999a).
32 This might not be true for very basic public goods such as a minimal juridical system and law enforcement (the provision of which is undisputed anyway), but holds for most publicly provided goods which, for the most part, are no *pure* public goods as congestion might occur. Roads benefit some people more than others just as museums, railroads, schools, and universities do.
33 We do not neglect policies that generate political support and are not primarily motivated through their distributional consequences. Examples are frequent on the constitutional level, such as establishing property rights and securing them via the provision of a judicial system, a minimum police force, etc. Once constitutions are established and implemented, however, these policies play a minor role in the political process.

from, or abolishing of a certain regulation. Group size, the ability to organize their interest, the stake, resources they can afford to spend on lobbying activity, access to the relevant information, and other factors determine the weight of a special interest in the political process.

Politicians in office possess a variety of redistributional tools. The choice of the regulative instrument and the way and the extent to which it is applied is determined in the political market for regulation. The outcome cannot be predicted without knowing the institutional setting relevant to both sides of the market. We name a few important determinants. The supply side: How competitive is the political system? Does the incumbent exclusively maximize votes or does (s)he enjoy discretionary scope, e.g., due to incumbency advantage, forgetfulness of the electorate in a representative system, or an autocratic system? How is the demand for regulation effectively channeled into the political system? In other words, is the issue decided in a referendum or in a representative democracy, or, in case of a non-democratic system, what are the groups on the support of which the incumbent's power is based? How high are information and participation costs and, consequently, how manipulable are voters? How are gains and losses from a certain regulation distributed, i.e., what are the relevant characteristics of the economic system (concerning factor mobility, factor ownership distribution, etc.)? The analysis of these characteristics of the economic system leads to the answers of the following important questions: What are the relevant interest groups, and: What is their relative power?[34]

Institutions matter – and differ between countries. As a consequence, there is no universally valid model for the political process leading to regulation. Yet, it has been analyzed how various institutional arrangements systematically influence the policy outcome. If, for instance, voters are rationally ignorant (e.g., owing to prohibitive information costs) they are manipulable and electoral-competition-cum-interest-group models are appropriate. In these models, interest groups support the candidates whose policies best serve their interests and the relative campaign contributions determine the electoral outcome; both policy platforms and contributions are endogenous to a maximization process. On the other hand, if voters are completely informed and vote in their self-interest, the median voter model is relevant. We will discuss this in detail in section 3.6.

Politicians operate under two further constraints, which are particularly relevant for the analysis of capital controls. First, the *administrative*

---

[34] A systematic overview of the institutional factors relevant for the political market of trade protection is given by Weck-Hannemann (1992a).

constraint denotes that the government must have the support of the civil service in order to put the policy effectively into operation. Apart from their ability to obstruct government policy, the public employees constitute a forceful group: they are well-informed and may be able to control the supply of information to both the government and the general public. Moreover, in implementing regulations, the bureaucrats pursue their own interests such as the enlargement of their budget and their staff. We will discuss this further in the context of capital controls in section 2.4.4. Second, most of the benefits the government allocates to maintain political support are costly.[35] Consequently, the *budget constraint* limits government's generosity. We will discuss how capital controls may ease this constraint in section 2.4.1.

It has now become clear that only by chance will the self-interested politician pursue a policy which is identical to the one a benevolent dictator would have pursued. Implicit behind this statement is the assumption that individuals are not identical and that non-distorting compensations do not take place. Otherwise distributional conflicts would not arise, as there would be no losers from implementing the efficient policy. Both assumptions are very reasonable. Except for politically inacceptable lump-sum taxes or transfers, all redistributive tools are distortive.[36] In most cases, compensation does not take place at all – consumers are not compensated for higher import prices due to trade protection, taxpayers are not reimbursed for higher liabilities caused by transfers and subsidies. It would simply run counter to the political objective on the respective policies. Moreover, individuals are different. If all individuals were identical with respect to interest and endowment, "there would be no organized economic activity to explain. Each man would be a Crusoe" (Buchanan and Tullock 1962: 5). We agree.

In contrast to the traditional approach, the political-economic approach is not only logically consistent with methodological individualism, it outperforms the former approach also on empirical grounds. It is no wonder that the explanatory power of the traditional approach is extremely limited when government activity is analyzed.

A prominent example is international trade protection. It is commonly agreed that free trade is optimal, though after the emergence of the new

---

35 There are important exceptions to this rule, e.g., tariff protection, and health and environmental standards which can be designed to favor the respective domestic industry.

36 Dixit and Norman (1980) show that the gains from trade can (partly) be redistributed to the losers from opening up trade not only by lump-sum transfers but also by a mix of factor and commodity taxes. A similar argument might hold in our context as well; nevertheless, such a redistribution is obviously distortive, quite apart from whether such a tax system is feasible or not.

trade literature this remains only as a good rule of thumb. The traditional arguments – infant industry, optimal tariff, and, lately, increasing returns and strategic trade policy – cannot justify the widespread prevalence of all kinds of protectionist policies. They are, however, perfectly explainable by political-economic considerations.[37]

Likewise, the political-economic approach to macroeconomic policy, focusing on the strategic role of credibility, reputation, and stability in the policy formation process, is able to explain policies which are suboptimal from a benevolent dictator's point of view. Political-economic optimization calculus determines also the dynamics of inflation and answers the question why stabilization programs are delayed. The existence of electoral cycles in monetary policy can be explained through reelection considerations on the part of the government and a myopic public (Nordhaus 1975).[38]

There are many more fields of government activity that have been approached successfully with the help of the political-economic paradigm. To list them lies beyond the scope of this book. It is all the more surprising that government interference with the free flow of capital has received almost no attention from scholars of public choice, their wide prevalence and importance notwithstanding. To the best of our knowledge the only exceptions are Alesina and Tabellini (1989), Schulze (1992a), and Alesina et al. (1994).

In the following section we will show how the politician, who possesses the monopoly of redistribution, uses capital controls to maximize political support. This includes the identification of gainers and losers from the restriction of capital mobility. First, in section 2.4.1 we argue that capital controls ease the budget constraint, then we show in section 2.4.2 how capital controls back up trade protection. Section 2.4.3 examines the direct distributional impact of the controls and, finally, we demonstrate how the controls please bureaucrats, lawyers, and the like.

---

[37] Classics of the new trade literature are Helpman and Krugman (1985, 1989); the strategic trade policy literature is surveyed by Laussel and Montet (1994). Krugman (1987) and Baldwin (1992), reviewing the results of the new international trade literature, support the free trade postulate as a good approximation and practical guideline. The political economy of protection is presented by Baldwin (1986), Hillman (1989), Magee (1994), Rodrik (1995), among others (see also footnote 34 on p. 78).

[38] Persson and Tabellini (1990) is a standard reference, they provide also a comprehensive survey of this literature; see Edwards (1993) for the political-economic approach to inflation and stabilization. The political business cycles theory was pioneered by Nordhaus (1975) who focused on monetary policy in a closed economy; Stephan (1994) applies his idea to exchange rate policies. See also the collection of articles edited by Persson and Tabellini, eds. (1994) and the survey by Gärtner (1994).

2.4 Political-economic reasons for capital controls

We have argued that politicians strive toward maximizing their political support and that they do so mainly through redistribution of resources. This transfer of benefits and burdens may appear in very different forms and its motivation may be camouflaged by alleged aims like "national security" (used regularly by right-wing dictatorships), and "in the nation's interest," or "social justice" (frequently adduced by left-wing governments).

We can classify redistributional tools according to the quality of government involvement. We call policy instruments *direct* if redistribution affects the government's budget. This includes all kind of taxes, income transfers, and subsidies. It also comprises all publicly provided private and public goods through its distributional effects on consumption and on production (through procurement policies), though distributional impacts may be less clear or less significant. We can distinguish the distributional effect on the expenditure side (provision of goods, transfers, procurement) from that on the revenue side (tax incidence). *Indirect* redistributional policies are those that affect individual income through non-fiscal means and redistribute income through a change of the economic environment, notably of goods and factor prices. Examples are import quotas, minimum wage directives, and social security regulations.

Capital controls work in both directions! They have a direct impact, because they ease the budget constraint. Restrictions on international capital flows allow for a shift in the tax burden toward the taxation of capital, since capital can no longer escape taxation through international reallocation. Capital controls serve also to increase seigniorage gains through an inflation tax and reduce the costs of budget deficit in that they secure the effectiveness of financial repression. Capital controls influence income distribution indirectly because they alter relative factor endowments and thereby, possibly, factor rewards. Moreover, they may deny or reduce tariff-induced foreign investment which would erode profits in the protected sector. This backs up the indirect redistribution effects of trade protection.

Last but not least, controls please bureaucrats as their administration increases their budgets, staff, and discretionary scope. Controls benefit government officials further as they offer decently paid jobs after retirement to pilot the business community through the jungle of regulations and procedures.

In the remainder of this chapter we will study these motivations in some detail in a nontechnical way. Thereafter, in the following two chapters, we will delve into selected aspects of importance, where we will present our arguments in a rigorous manner.

2.4.1 Capital controls and the power to tax

Government finances have been growing, and continue to do so, at a dramatic rate, which is constantly above the economy's growth rate. Not only is an increasing share of national product channeled through public bureaus for redistribution, but also government activity as such devours a rising portion of society's resources.[39] Though, as Mueller (1989: 346) notes, "little consensus exists in what the key determinants of the growth of government are," the phenomenon itself is undisputed and so is the consequence thereof: Governments over the years have sought to raise their revenue in order to finance their ever growing "needs."

Brennan and Buchanan (1980) take an extreme view on governments as they model them as Leviathans trying to exploit the private sector to the maximum amount possible. Though this is a rather radical perspective (and the authors themselves allow for the possibility that the governments act as Leviathans only at times), the underlying rationale is far from being unrealistic. It builds on the theory of bureaucracy as pioneered by Niskanen (1971).[40] Bureaucrats seek to maximize their utility in the same way as everyone else but they operate under different constraints. First, bureaus produce a monopoly output, which saves them from competitive pressure. By the very nature of their output, which is non-market and often difficult to measure (how much safety does a police force produce?), monitoring is very difficult. Information asymmetry, especially concerning the minimum cost necessary to achieve a certain mission, leads to severe principal–agent problems. Neither the general public, which is rationally ignorant, nor the legislative bodies can exert an effective control over the bureaus' outputs and prevent X-inefficiencies.[41] Second, bureaucrats are very limited in their ability to increase personal income (apart from through corruption). Almost the only possibility is to rise in the hierarchy of their bureau, which depends

---

[39] For ample empirical evidence see Mueller (1987, 1989: chapter 17) and the literature quoted.

[40] Precedents are Tullock (1965) and Downs (1967); for an overview of subsequent works, including empirical analyses, see Mueller (1989: chapter 14).

[41] Of course there are certain leverages available to contain inefficiencies, like the investigations by the General Accounting Office (USA), Court of Auditors (EU) or national equivalents, limited competition among government agencies, also for funds, etc. But they are all far from being able to eliminate large-scale inefficiencies.

positively on the size of the bureau. Non-pecuniary goals become very important. Niskanen (1971: 38) writes:

Among the several variables that may enter the bureaucrat's utility function are the following: salary, perquisites of the office, public reputation, power, patronage, output of the bureau, ease of making changes, and the ease of managing the bureau. All of these variables, except the last two, I contend, are a positive monotonic function of the total *budget* of the bureau during the bureaucrats tenure in office. (emphasis in the original)

Apart from the postulated monotony, this seems a reasonable description; budget maximization becomes the bureaucrats' intermediate goal for utility maximization. The strive for budget maximization translates into revenue maximization if the legislative body responsible for tax legislation is either accommodating bureaucrats' desire or is itself seeking to raise revenue. The first case may occur due to the principal–agent problem sketched above (the parliament is deceived about actual needs), the latter will occur if the politicians perceive a possibility of increasing their political support through income redistribution for reasons explained in the previous section.[42]   In their effort to maximize revenue the government might of course be limited by the reelection constraint. (Brennan and Buchanan argue that it is not binding with regard to taxation.)

However, not only revenue considerations, but also distributional motivations influence the design of tax policy! This is what Brennan and Buchanan neglect. If governments only want to maximize tax money taken from the private sector, they disregard the distributional consequences of their taxation policy. But, as we have argued earlier, most of the policies observed are driven by distributional objectives. It would be inconsistent if tax policy was any different. Indeed numerous tax concessions for certain groups or for certain activities support this claim.

---

[42] Of course, the interaction between the legislator and the bureaucracy is very complex in reality; it depends, among other things, on the – endogenous – degree of information asymmetry, the political system (democratic versus authoritarian), the design of institutions within the system (e.g., presidential or parliamentary democracy), the dimensionality of the issues, and whether there are multiple principals (see Moe 1997 for a survey of the issues). Moreover, bureaucracies may also strive for slack, prestige, and other goals which might at times conflict with pure budget maximization (Niskanen 1991, Wintrobe 1997). These caveats notwithstanding it remains true that increased budgets generally raise the utility of bureaucrats as this tends to increase their influence, their discretionary budget and in the long run also their career prospects and income and thereby makes their life more comfortable. See Wintrobe (1997) for a survey of modern bureaucratic theory.

Tax policy serves a dual purpose – to raise revenue and, at the same time, to optimally distribute the burden of taxation – but ultimately pursues the single objective of maximizing political support via redistribution. Governments solve a complex optimization problem: raising revenue up to a *level* where the marginal gain in terms of political support from spending/transferring the money is equal to the marginal loss from levying additional taxes, given that the taxes are raised in the political loss-minimizing way. The politically optimal tax *structure* equalizes the marginal political cost for all taxed activities. Ideally, this would imply interpersonally different tax rates, but administrative costs prohibit that. Tax brackets for different income categories can be seen as an approximation to the politically optimal differentiation (Hettich and Winer 1997).

In other words, the traditional public finance approach in the sense of Wicksell (1896) and Musgrave (1959) is at fault, because it assumes that governments levy a *given amount of revenue* (determined by the "need" for public goods provision, etc.) in the most efficient way. But also the Brennan and Buchanan approach, turning the traditional analysis on its head, is flawed because it assumes away political support maximization accomplished via a politically optimal redistribution policy – a motive that obviously governs most of today's policies.

Still, if derived revenue falls short of the politically optimal revenue government will look for possibilities to raise additional revenue. In the following subsections we show how capital controls serve to achieve the revenue goal as well as the distribution-of-tax-burden goal.

International capital mobility and the taxation of capital

Governments' ability to tax capital effectively is rather limited if investors are able to evade taxes by investing in low-tax countries. High capital mobility in the presence of international tax competition will erode revenues from taxing capital either by a dwindling tax base as capital relocates internationally or by forcing governments to lower tax rates in order to retain capital at home. In this situation capital controls can decouple the national capital market from international markets, thereby giving governments leeway to tax domestic capital more heavily. Giovannini (1988) reports that Italian capital controls, dating back from interwar years, were established in order to permit heavy taxation of domestic wealth.

Capital controls would be superfluous if domestically owned capital could be taxed on a worldwide basis. The superiority of residence-based taxation from an efficiency point of view is now well established (see, e.g., Giovannini 1989, 1991, Slemrod 1988). Each country taxes all capital owned by its residents wherever that capital is invested and exempts foreign-owned capital from domestic taxation. This leads to an efficient international allocation of capital since the tax wedge is independent of the location of capital. Savings are probably reduced owing to the distortion in the intertemporal rate of substitution, but it is usually argued that the interest elasticity of *domestic* investment (given international investment opportunities) is much higher than the interest elasticity of savings. Therefore, the distortions created by residence-based taxation are far less than the distortions created by source-based taxation (Malinvaud 1989).[43] Not only from an efficiency perspective, but also from a revenue-maximizing point of view, the residence principle is the first choice. Governments need not fear driving capital out of the country by high taxation, because residents are taxed wherever they place their possessions.[44]

But, alas, the residence principle cannot effectively be enforced! Bank secrecy laws, illegal channels like misdeclaration of international trade prices, and the lack of cooperation of low-tax countries which have a vested interest to (thereby) attract foreign capital make it impossible to tax income on a worldwide basis. Giovannini (1989) shows various instruments for successful tax avoidance, the contributions in Lessard and Williamson, eds. (1987) and Razin and Sadka (1991b) review substantial empirical evidence that governments encounter severe enforcement difficulties. Razin and Sadka (1991a) demonstrate the efficiency of zero taxation of capital for the case where the residence principle cannot effectively be enforced. They model two small countries which cooperate and a large third country (rest of the world), with infinitely elastic supply of, and demand for, capital. Their result is in accordance with the optimal tax literature, which states that elastic tax bases should be taxed at a low rate. With perfect capital mobility heavy taxation produces a high welfare loss due to the extent of the large tax avoidance reaction. The reason behind this zero taxation result as a welfare-maximizing policy is the production efficiency theorem by Diamond and Mirrlees (1971), which states that if all commodities and rents can be taxed optimal taxation never distorts production (see, however, Giovannini 1991 for an evaluation). In the context of international capital mobility this implies that mainly immobile labor is taxed. Needless to say such an efficiency-

---

[43] Source-based taxation distorts the allocation of capital, which is taxed according to the host countries' – differing – tax rates, but leaves savings unaffected. The response of savings are theoretically ambiguous under the residence principle due to income and substitution effects working in opposite directions. For an elaboration see Giovannini (1991).
[44] Governments may wish to tax foreign-owned capital as well, but if the country is small this is not feasible for perfectly mobile capital.

oriented tax policy would have severe distributional implications which may probably be undesired.[45] Razin and Sadka (1991b) show that if foreign source capital is not effectively taxable it will be efficient for the government to restrict capital outflow. Giovannini (1991, appendix B) demonstrates that in this case quantitative capital export controls can produce the same resource allocation as a system of residence-based taxation without tax evasion. This tax-induced capital flight is clearly also a major concern of revenue-maximizing governments because it severely limits their ability to extract revenue from capital proceeds. They may therefore also like to implement controls, but for different reasons and to different extents.

These results have been challenged, and rightly so, by arguing that capital may not react in such an elastic way as the above models imply. First, uncertainty produces portfolio diversification in an attempt to reduce risk; capital located at home and in various foreign countries are not perfect substitutes, because they will typically differ in risk for economic, political (default), and exchange rate reasons.[46] As a consequence, risk-averse individuals will adjust their portfolios as a reaction to a (tax-created) shift in after-tax returns, but they will not completely reallocate their capital (Slemrod 1988). Bovenberg (1986) shows that if financial capital is perfectly mobile internationally, but physical capital is inert, efficiency allows for positive tax rates on capital. These objections may alter the zero-taxation result for efficiency reasons in favor of a positive-tax result; they will not alter, however, the basic motivation of a revenue-maximizing government for the imposition of capital export restraints. There is substantial empirical evidence that capital flows are quite sensitive to tax incentives (for surveys see Kopits 1976, Alworth 1988). For example Dooley (1987) estimates that the USA may have experienced a capital flight up to US$ 250 bn in the period 1980–2. Bundesbank (1994) and Goulder (1990) show how sensitive markets reacted to the introduction of a withholding tax on interest income in Germany and the US. Cumby and Levich (1987) provide estimates on the enormous capital outflow from developing countries; Dooley (1988) estimates that for a large number of LDCs their capital flight in the period 1977–84 amounted to as much as one third of their external debt. This means clearly a large loss in revenues; in whatever manner portfolio considerations or immobility of physical capital may have an impact on the elasticity of the tax base.

---

[45] Moreover, as Gordon (1992) and Schulze and Koch (1994) have shown, tax competition in the presence of perfect capital mobility may lead to unstable situations.

[46] We will discuss the concept of risk in international asset trade in chapter 8.

Capital controls serve as a tool to increase capital taxation, as we have seen. Thereby, they enable the incumbent politician to place the burden of taxation in a political support-maximizing way. We will take up this point in section 2.5 and analyze the distributional issues concerning capital controls in greater depth in chapters 3 and 4. In these chapters the political process is modeled with the help of a median voter model for good reasons, as we will argue in section 3.6. It should be noted, however, that the rationale to adopt capital controls might be different (from the one to be described below) in a polarized society with high political instability. Alesina and Tabellini (1989) model two political parties, alternating in government, which are only obliged to their constituency (workers or capitalists) and tax the opponent's constituency at a confiscatory rate. Capital exports are the only way to escape exploitation, so that the capitalist government will deliberately refrain from controls in order to allow their constituency to insure against labor's expropriation. On the other hand, the labor governments will impose capital controls to a certain extent in order to increase domestic capital formation and to tax capital more heavily (at the costs of reduced capital exports of their own constituency). This model highlights the distributional conflict arising from the imposition of capital controls in a very drastic way. We will elaborate on this in section 3.

Inflation tax and seigniorage

Governments that raise a considerable share of their revenues through inflation tax have to prevent currency substitution in order to retain their tax base. They do this with the help of capital controls, which deny individuals the opportunity to escape from this sort of taxation by switching to a foreign, hard currency as means of payment and storage of value. Capital controls are important in this context because the seigniorage gain as well as the potential loss from currency substitution are quite substantial for many governments.

For less developed countries especially seigniorage constitutes a major source of government revenue, because LDCs typically have an inefficient tax system. They also lack a significant open market for primary securities, so that the government cannot sell bonds on a large scale (McKinnon 1993: chapter 5). During the 1960s and up to the late 1970s seigniorage amounted to between an average of 1 percent of GNP for industrial countries and 4 percent of GNP for non-oil-exporting Middle East countries, and contributed almost 6 percent and about 15 percent to the total government revenue for each group respectively. Table 2.1, a condensed version from Fischer (1982), provides a first impression on the significance of seigniorage as a source of government

Table 2.1. *Average annual seigniorage rates for selected country groups*

	Average of change of money reserves as a share of GNP	Average of change of money reserves as a share of total revenue
Industrial countries	0.010	0.057
Other Europe	0.021	0.080
Oil-exporting countries	0.023	0.068
Other Latin America and Caribbean	0.020	0.117
Other Middle East	0.041	0.153
Other Asia	0.016	0.093
Other Africa	0.013	n.a.

Source: Fischer (1982, table A2).

revenue. It covers the period of the 1960s to the end of the 1970s and shows the growth of reserve holdings as a share of GNP and total government revenue (i.e., normal tax revenue plus inflation tax revenue).[47]

Hidden behind these figures is a large variance of seigniorage revenues. Notably Latin American countries, experiencing hyperinflation, derived large parts of their revenues from inflation tax: They amounted to 17 percent for Colombia, 18 percent for Chile, 28 percent for Uruguay, and as much as 46 percent for Argentina – all countries known for having had capital controls in place. Fry (1995: 401–403) provides corroborating figures on total seigniorage revenue (cash and reserves) for a sample of 26 developing countries and the year 1984 (where possible): As percentage of GDP it produced on average a relatively modest contribution to overall tax revenues, but it was very unevenly distributed. For six countries seigniorage gains exceeded 5 percent of GDP, for ten countries it was larger than 2.5 percent of GDP. Seigniorage contributed more than 5 percent to overall tax revenue in 18 cases, in ten cases it exceeded 10 percent of total tax revenues. It was 42 percent of government current revenue for Mexico, 58 percent for Peru, and 133 percent for Yugoslavia. Some European countries also relied substantially on the printing press

[47] Exact figures, broken down by individual country, are provided by Fischer (1982, table A2). The reported figures should be regarded only as a first approximation to the order of magnitude, because the change in reserve holdings constitutes only one source of seigniorage, the change in cash being the other, though for LDCs the less important one (McKinnon 1993). The time span covered differs between countries and for a few countries one or other of the figures is not available.

to finance their budgets. Drazen (1989: 14) reports annual seigniorage as percentage of total tax revenue of 9.1 percent for Greece, 6.2 percent for Italy, 11.9 percent for Portugal, and 5.9 percent for Spain, averaged over the period 1979–1986. These figures are impressive and, therefore, revenue generation through seigniorage deserves a closer look.

Seigniorage gain is created through the provision of *additional* central bank money by the monetary authorities. This additional money constitutes a claim on real resources (goods, services, factors) of the economy which accrues directly or indirectly to the treasury.[48] The real value of these resources constitutes the seigniorage gain, which is, in essence, a rent from the monopoly to create money and can be used to squeeze the private sector. Strictly speaking, seigniorage is the difference between the purchasing power of this additional central bank money and the real costs of creating it, which is almost negligible in times of fiat money. Seigniorage is not exactly the same as inflation tax revenue; since the concept and the notation are somewhat blurred in the literature (see, e.g., Phelps 1973: 68), we will briefly set out the basic concept.[49]

The monetary base (B) consists of central bank money held by the public as cash (C) and reserves of the banks held with the central bank (R). Because these reserves typically (but not always) bear no interest, they are almost exclusively minimum reserves required by the central bank and levied on the deposits (D) at a rate r^M. Hence, the monetary base is calculated as

$$B = C + r^M D \tag{2.1}$$

and the corresponding money supply (M) is given by

$$M = 1/b\, B, \tag{2.2}$$

where $1/b$ is the money creation multiplier. It depends negatively on the minimum reserve ratio, $b = b(r^M) > 1$.[50] In the simplest conceivable

---

[48] Most central banks are dependent on the finance minister's decrees or are even a branch of the ministry of finance without separate budget. But also independent central banks (like previously the German Bundesbank) remit their profits to the treasury. The European Central Bank remits seigniorage gains to national treasuries according to the nations' shares in the ECB.

[49] For a more sophisticated model see Bruno and Fisher (1990).

[50] The maximum value for the money creation multiplier is given by $1/b = (1 + c^d)/(r^M + c^d)$, where c^d is the cash coefficient, i.e., $c^d = C/D$. An alternative way of writing this is $1/b = \tilde{c}^D + r^M(1 - \tilde{c}^D)$, where $\tilde{c}^D = C/M$. In reality, $1/b$ will be smaller as banks do not fully exploit their potential to create credit and thus money.

setup,[51] monetary equilibrium is restored when the following equilibrium condition is fulfilled

$$M/P = L(Y, r, \pi).$$ (2.3)

P is the aggregate price level; demand for real money balances (L) depends negatively on the real interest rate (r) and the inflation rate (π) as opportunity costs of holding money, and positively on the real national product (Y). The real value of seigniorage, S, from an increase of the monetary base of dB/dt (t being the time index) is given by

$$S = \frac{dB/dt}{P} = b\, g_M \frac{M}{P},$$ (2.4)

where we have made use of equation (2.2). g_M denotes the growth of the money supply. Totally differentiating equation (2.3) and dividing it by the same equation (2.3) yields

$$g_M = \pi + \varepsilon_{L,Y}\, g_Y.$$ (2.5)

g_Y denotes the real growth rate, $\varepsilon_{L,Y}$ the elasticity of demand for real money balances with respect to real income. In obtaining equation (2.5) the time derivative of the inflation rate is treated as zero, which means that we consider alternative steady states of inflation. In accordance with the Fisher hypothesis, we have assumed that the real interest rate remains constant, so that the additional term $+\varepsilon_{L,r}\, g_r$ has vanished. (In any case, variations in the real interest rate will be of much smaller order than the variables we focus on.) Moreover, we ignore any effect of inflation on the real growth rate, $dg_Y/d\pi = 0$. This is warranted since our task is to demonstrate how capital controls secure seigniorage and our results are not affected by this simplification. Extentions to richer formulations are straightforward, but do not provide new insights for our concern.[52]

Under these reasonable assumptions, and with the help of (2.4) and (2.5), seigniorage can be expressed as

$$S = b\frac{M}{P}[\pi + g_Y \varepsilon_{L,Y}].$$ (2.6)

---

[51] The exposition follows Friedman (1971), however in an altered version. For instance, Friedman does not distinguish between monetary base and money supply in the calculation of seigniorage, cf. his equation (4).

[52] Mundell (1965) analyzes the case of $dg_Y/d\pi > 0$ since he assumes that the government finances productive investment through an inflation tax. In reality, the long-run effect is the reverse: high inflation reduces real growth. There is mixed evidence for low inflation rates which seem to have no or even positive long-run effects on growth as they improve factor allocation in the presence of nominal price rigidities, but for double digit inflation rates the relationship is clearly negative: cf. Fischer (1996) and the literature quoted. If we assumed $dg_Y/d\pi < 0$, the revenue-maximizing inflation rate would be smaller.

For a stationary economy ($g_Y = 0$) with monetary expansion having no effect on real variables the rate of monetary expansion equals the resulting inflation rate. Seigniorage is identical to the revenue of the inflation tax, which is "levied" on the real balance M/P at a rate $b\pi$.[53] In all other cases seigniorage comprises a "growth tax" component, stemming from increased demand for money as a consequence of real growth.

We calculate the revenue-maximizing inflation rate by differentiating (2.6) with respect to π and setting it equal to zero. This yields

$$dS = b\frac{M}{P}\left[(1 + g_Y\frac{d\varepsilon_{L,Y}}{d\pi}) + (\varepsilon_{L,Y}g_Y + \pi)\frac{d(M/P)}{M/P}\frac{1}{d\pi}\right]\overset{!}{=}0,$$

and, hence, the inflation rate has to satisfy the following condition

$$g_Y\frac{d\varepsilon_{L,Y}}{d\pi} + \frac{\varepsilon_{L,Y}g_Y + \pi}{\pi}\varepsilon_{L,\pi} = -1. \tag{2.7}$$

For a stationary economy, the revenue-maximizing inflation rate is given by the unitary elasticity rule $\varepsilon_{L,\pi} = -1$. For a growing economy, this elasticity of demand for real money balance with respect to inflation rate must equal the fraction of π over $\pi + \varepsilon_{L,Y}g_Y$, if the income elasticity of real money demand is not affected by inflation. This smaller absolute value for $\varepsilon_{L,\pi}$ in the optimum (compared to a stationary economy) implies that π must be smaller. In other words, revenue maximization will produce lower inflation rates for growing economies because inflation reduces the demand for money and thereby reduces the seigniorage gain from the "growth tax." If the income elasticity of real money demand decreases as a consequence of inflation this effect is even more pronounced. With the optimal inflation rate so calculated, equation (2.5) gives the corresponding growth rate of money supply and equation (2.4) the maximum seigniorage gain.

There are other interesting aspects of seigniorage, not covered by our simple model of a revenue-maximizing inflation tax. For instance, inflation tax can tax underground activities indirectly (which largely rely on cash payments) when other taxes cannot. Therefore, from an efficiency perspective, the optimal inflation tax would positively depend on the relative size of the underground economy (provided that lump-sum taxes are not available, cf. Nicolini 1998). Political support-maximizing politicians may consequently use the inflation tax as a means to optimally

---

[53] Some authors, like Brock (1984), calculate the (total) seigniorage as $B(\pi + r)$ arguing that the central bank may either deposit their gain and earn interest or reduce the government deficit and thereby save interest payments. See Drazen (1984) for a discussion of different measurement concepts.

distribute the tax burden, also if they do not implement the revenue-maximizing tax rate: It may pay politically to limit the tax burden on the official sector (through taxes on income and consumption) and tax all sectors of the economy through a tax on cash holdings (and financial intermediation, see below), in particular because the politically influential groups typically belong to the official sector.

The incidence of this inflation tax is twofold. Increased supply of central bank money taxes cash holdings to the amount to which it produces inflation (which implies that $g_M > \varepsilon_{L,Y} g_Y$, a condition that is clearly met in the optimum, cf. equations (2.5), (2.7)). In developing countries the second component of the monetary base, the required reserves, constitutes a larger share than cash holdings as effective reserve ratios on bank deposits are considerably higher (McKinnon 1993: 56–57). This is a consequence of a deliberate policy of high minimum reserve requirements which increase the tax base for inflation tax. In other words, reserve requirements are a second policy instrument in order to maximize seigniorage revenues.[54] From the banks' perspective, required reserves establish a forced holding of a non-interest bearing asset, which increases the costs of loanable funds. These costs are passed on to the public and are shared by depositors who receive reduced yields and borrowers who incur higher costs.[55]

Most of the analysis on inflationary government finance has been carried out in the context of closed economies (e.g., Bailey 1956, Mundell 1965, Friedman 1971, Phelps 1973). It is, however, a well-known fact that inflation provokes currency substitution, as domestic currency serves increasingly less as unit of account, medium of transaction, and especially as a store of value. Examples are ample for this shift into hard currencies, predominantly known as "dollarization."[56] Obviously, this reaction squeezes government revenue and calls for countermeasures (though currency substitution may be welfare-improving as it disciplines governments and reduces the *effective* rate of inflation, since a growing share of transactions is settled in stable currencies). Fischer (1982) demon-

---

[54] See Brock (1989) for a general equilibrium analysis and Tamagna (1965) and Brock (1989) for a description of the reserve requirement policies in Latin America during high inflation. Brock (1989) shows for the period 1960–1984 that for a number of countries in Africa and Latin America increases in inflation rates were associated with increases in the reserve ratios. For many countries including the US, however, there are institutional ceilings on reserve ratios (see van Aarle and Budina 1997 for the recent Polish example).

[55] If the banking industry is imperfectly competitive, profits will decrease, cf. Siegel (1981).

[56] See Ortiz and Solis (1979) and Ortiz (1983) for the Mexican case, Clements and Schwartz (1993) for Bolivia, Ramirez-Rojas (1985) for Argentinia, Mexico, and Uruguay, and Melvin (1988) for the Latin American experience. Giovannini and Turtelboom (1994) provide a survey for the literature on currency substitution, including numerous empirical studies.

strates that the revenue loss from currency substitution is far from being trivial and that governments have therefore a strong incentive to effectively retain their own currency. Capital controls are assigned to defend the national monopoly over money creation. Indeed Alesina, Grilli, and Milesi-Ferretti (1994) find in their study of 20 OECD countries that inflation and seigniorage revenue are significantly higher in the presence of capital controls. This finding is corroborated by Grilli and Milesi-Ferretti (1995) for a larger set of countries, including 19 industrialized and 42 developing countries.[57] Controls need not be prohibitive. Brock (1984) shows that seigniorage may actually be increased in the course of partial liberalization of current and capital account transactions, if capital inflows are made subject to a reserve requirement, and prior import deposits are implemented. He also provides historical examples for prior import deposits and for reserve requirements on capital imports, which were implemented especially by Latin American countries, but the latter measure also by some OECD countries. Although capital movements may be possible, they are discouraged because they become more costly. All other capital flows are restricted to enforce the controls.

Capital controls may not only prevent the rush out of national currency, they may in addition shelter an inefficient banking system from international competition. This becomes especially important in the context of inflationary finance. As equation (2.1) shows, the monetary base consists of central bank money held by the general public (currency component) and minimum reserves held by the banking sector with the central bank (required reserve component). As noted earlier, monetary authorities can increase the demand for central bank money by increasing the required reserve ratio. Money supply is reduced *ceteris paribus* since the money creation multiplier is a function of r^M (cf. footnote. 50). Thus, the variation in these rates gives the government an additional lever for raising seigniorage revenue. This presupposes that domestic banks are the only financial intermediaries allowed to operate domestically because foreign competition would compel governments to reduce reserve ratios to international standards in order to keep the local banking industry competitive. Borrowing rates will be increased and deposit rates decreased, as reserve requirements function like a tax on financial intermediation driving a wedge between producer and consumer prices. This establishes incentives to borrow from, and to lend to abroad. Capital controls have to prevent this. High reserve requirements as well as high

---

[57] Their data set covers the period 1966–1989, country classification is made according to the IFS code. They also find that capital controls are more likely to be imposed in low-income countries, which have a less developed tax system.

inflation will most likely have detrimental effects on long-run growth as capital formation is discouraged (Drazen 1989), but since most politicians are myopic in their actions as they are bound by short-term constraints, this consideration may not play an important role in their calculus.

Financial repression and a cheap budget deficit

We have argued that capital controls must prevent domestic capital from flowing abroad when domestic interest rates are squeezed as a consequence of the government's drive to increase seigniorage revenue. Yet, low domestic interest rates may not only be a by-product of attempts to increase revenue through higher seigniorage, they can also be a direct means to reducing the costs of government finance as they decrease the treasury's interest bill. In this connection, capital controls are inevitable to maintain financial repression of an economy. Indeed, Grilli and Milesi-Ferretti (1995) show that capital controls are associated not only with higher inflation and a higher share of seigniorage in total taxes, but also with lower real interest rates (cf. footnote 57). This corroborates our claim that capital controls reinforce inflationary taxation and make financial repression possible.

The principle of financial repression[58] is very simple: The government pushes the domestic interest rate below the prevailing world interest rate, for instance by levying a tax on interest from foreign assets. This generates tax revenue, drives a wedge between lending and borrowing rates (the latter being determined by the world market), and reduces the debt service for government debt. It is easily shown (Aizenman and Guidotti 1990, Giovannini and de Melo 1993) that total tax revenue is the difference between the world interest rate and the domestic interest rate (tax rate) times the total stock of financial assets held by the private sector (tax base).

In reality financial repression is characterized by a large system of regulations, typically including the prohibition on, or the control of residents holding financial assets abroad, restrictions on the channels through which foreign assets may be acquired (authorized banks and brokers), and ceilings thereon. Domestic interest rates may directly be stipulated or depressed through an interest equalization tax on earnings from holding foreign assets. The system is regularly completed by the requirement that financial intermediaries hold a certain amount of gov-

---

[58] The classics in this field are McKinnon (1973) and Shaw (1973), who show the detrimental effect of financial repression on economic growth. Fry (1982) surveys the literature; for more recent work see, e.g., Giovannini and de Melo (1993) and the comprehensive work of Fry (1995).

ernment loans (which may even yield a lower interest rate than the pre-vailing domestic rate). Other elements include compulsory credit alloca-tions and differentiated interest rates according to the debtor or the financed project. Both regulations are a very direct means to cater to interest groups camouflaged behind the requirement to serve "priority needs." The basic mechanism however becomes already clear if we abstract from institutional details (for a description see McKinnon 1993 and Fry 1995) and assume a differential tax on foreign asset pro-ceeds.

It is now well established empirically that financial repression reduces financial intermediation, distorts allocation, and hampers economic growth.[59] Negative real interest rates or rates well below market levels do not discourage the level of saving too much as the propensity to save is rather inelastic with respect to the interest rate, if at all. It is the mis-allocation of funds that brings about detrimental effects on growth. The incentive to channel savings through the banking system to the investor are eroded by low or negative real interest rates; as a consequence finan-cial intermediation is low (as measured by the ratio of M3 to GDP), which in turn reduces real growth (Gelb 1989). Of course, financial depth is additionally determined by the inflation rate, which exerts a negative influence. Thus, the common package of financial repression and inflationary budget financing reduces growth performance twofold. The reason financial depth and high real interest rates stimulate growth is that the credit market is allowed to fulfill its allocative function through the price mechanism.[60] In the disequilibrium situation of financial repres-sion credit is allocated according to some (politically motivated) rule rather than according to the profitability of the investment project. As a consequence, raising real interest rates to market levels increases total factor productivity and the incremental output–capital ratio and hence fosters growth.

---

[59] See, for example, Gelb (1989) and the sizable literature surveys by Fry (1995: chapter 8). See Pagano (1993) and Levine (1997) for surveys on the – important – role of financial development for economic growth. Levine (1997) reviews considerable empirical evidence on a positive association and even causality between the degree and quality of financial inter-mediation and economic growth.

[60] Alan Gelb (1989) studies 34 LDCs for the period of 1965–1985 and regresses real growth rate ($\hat{Y}$) on the real (three to six month) deposit rate (RR), a measure of financial depth (M3/GDP), and a shift dummy (SHIFT) that is 1 for the post-Bretton Woods era (1974–1985) and zero otherwise. He finds

$$\hat{Y} = constant + 0.180\ RR + 0.034\ M3/GDP - 0.021\ SHIFT$$

$$(5.22) \qquad (2.13) \qquad (-3.91)$$

(t-statistics in parentheses), adjusted $\bar{R}^2 = 0.486$.

Nevertheless, the tax from financial depression has appealing features for governments, especially of developing countries. First, as for the inflation tax, it is a relatively inexpensive means to extract revenue from the private sector. Collection costs have to be incurred only for the tax on foreign assets; the larger share accrues costlessly to the government in the form of reduced debt service (Aizenman and Guidotti 1990). This cost advantage is especially pronounced for LDCs, which often have underdeveloped, and thus easily controllable, financial sectors and suffer from inefficient tax administrations, which make ordinary forms of revenue collection very costly. Second, the distributional consequence may be appreciated. Apart from generating revenue on outstanding government debt, financial repression redistributes income from creditors to debtors. Thus far it functions similarly to the inflation tax that reduces the real value of money holdings. The inflation tax can be (partly) evaded, however, by holding indexed bonds; this can be prevented by stipulating ceilings on nominal interest rates. Third, similar to the inflation tax, financial depression is a less transparent way to tax the private sector and may therefore arouse less opposition.[61] This form of taxation is indeed not too difficult to "justify," since it may be argued that low interest rates will stimulate investment (which is not true, though, because of the disequilibrium nature of financial repression) and may ease the interest burden malignant capitalists place on poor debtors.[62] Fourth, financial depression complements inflation tax and reinforces its efficiency.

Inflation tax and financial repression indeed exhibit many similar features: the former produces seigniorage gains on holdings of high-powered money whereas the latter produces seigniorage on holdings of government debt. While both instruments can be applied independently, they tend to reinforce each other. For given ceilings on nominal interest rates, inflationary finance decreases the real costs of government debt. Real interest rates have frequently been negative (see Giovannini and de Melo 1993). When holdings on both assets (money and bonds) are taxed, evasion from one sort of taxation will tend to increase the base for the other tax. If inflation is increased, demand for money will decrease *ceteris paribus* in favor of interest bearing assets. On the other hand,

---

[61] Tullock (1989) has argued that redistribution is greatly facilitated by a "smoke screen" that camouflages its real purpose.
[62] In Norway interest rate stipulation was *inter alia* motivated by the "assumption that such an interest rate policy would lead to a more equitable distribution of income" (Norges Bank, Annual Report 1977: 49–50). It was terminated because, among other reasons, empirical investigation had shown that low-income groups were holders of net financial assets, while high-income groups were benefiting from a low interest rate (ibid.: 50).

reduced real interest rates will increase the demand for money (e.g., Sussman 1991).

It is no surprise then that taxation from financial repression is an important source of government finance. Giovannini and de Melo (1993) analyze 24 developing countries with high foreign commercial debt incured by the central government for periods in the range 1974–1986. They calculate revenue as the difference between foreign borrowing costs and domestic borrowing costs times the average annual stock of central government domestic debt (held outside the central bank).[63] In seven countries (out of 24) the revenue exceeds 2 percent of GDP and averages to 1.8 percent of GDP over the whole sample. The average implicit tax rate amounts to almost 18 percent and the contribution to central government revenue (excluding financial repression revenue) averages 8.8 percent. Again, hidden behind these numbers is a large variance, spreading from 0 percent in Indonesia to 40 percent in Mexico. However, fluctuation over time is large and sample periods for a few countries are short, so that these figures must be viewed with some caution. Still it is fair to say that financial repression is a major source of revenue especially for highly indebted governments of less developed countries.

2.4.2 Capital controls and trade protection

This section notes a peculiarity of the literature on international political economy: It has not appropriately taken into account the importance of tariff-induced capital flows that might erode the very rents created through protection. Hillman (1992: 773) writes: "rents that might be sought by protection are eroded by the attraction of foreign capital. Hence industry specific interests that seek protection also have an interest in restrictions of capital inflow into their industry." This is true, but still most of the models disregard this interdependence. Exceptions include Findlay and Wellisz (1982), Findlay and Wilson (1987), Magee et al. (1989: chapter 12), and Schulze (1992a).

Typically, the basic story runs as follows. Sector-specific interests of import-competing industries lobby for protection. Interests are sector-specific because in the short run capital is installed and hence its return depends on the prevailing domestic price for industry's output and the wage rate. Labor's interest is sector specific to the extent it earns a lower wage in other industries owing to accumulated sector-specific human

---

[63] Thus they ignore possible revenue from taxation of foreign assets' interest earnings, which may be low in reality.

capital (Grossman 1983). Lobbying is successful because benefits are concentrated with a relatively small group and beneficiaries offer rewards in terms of political support (campaign contributions, etc.) in return for protection. Losses exceed gains but are spread over society and hence arouse no substantial opposition. Political support-maximizing regulators create the desired rents. End of story.

We do not object to the basic story – it is a plausible and empirically a very relevant portrayal of reality. Moreover, it has experienced many refinements that have increasingly taken into account the foreign dimension of the political process. For instance, Hillman and Ursprung (1988) incorporate foreign interests in the domestic political process, Hillman and Ursprung (1993) and Hillman et al. (1993) analyze the political interest a foreign direct investor will pursue, *once the foreign direct investment has taken place.*

We do claim, however, that the story on trade protection, correct though it is, needs amendment. This is where capital controls enter the stage. Trade protection that aims at creating sustained rents needs to be complemented by protection against foreign capital inflow.[64] Trade protection raises the rewards for factors specific to that industry, in particular for sector-specific capital, above world market levels. (In the long run, as factors become less industry specific, it raises the reward of the factor used relatively intensively in that industry.) This triggers the inflow of those factors which are internationally mobile, capital being the most prominent example, and leads to the erosion of the created rents. Trade protection would be inconsequential if not backed up by controls to prohibit tariff jumping. Because trade protection is industry-specific, this calls for capital import controls which are applicable on an industry-specific level. In the first place these controls consist of concession requirements and approval procedures for extending or expanding business activities. To safeguard the effectiveness of regulations, these controls may be supplemented by the requirement that the board of directors comprised a certain number of residents, certain information requirements and so forth. These regulations are well known in real life. The stipulation that foreign investment may only be made through joint ventures may be regarded as an extreme form of domestic industry protection that at the same time wants to take advantage of superior technology transferred through the foreign direct investment.

---

[64] We will analyze this point in more detail in section 3.5. Note that politicians' calculus for this kind of capital controls is not exactly the same as for trade protection. Industry-specific human capital will gain from trade protection, but not from capital import barriers as tariff-jumping foreign investment may create additional jobs, which will probably be paid higher wages since competition for scarce skills is intensified.

2.4.3 Capital controls and the distribution of income

In this section we are concerned with the distributional impacts of restrictions on the international mobility of real capital. We will argue that under reasonable and rather general assumptions the inflow of capital will reduce the domestic return to capital and increase the reward to labor. Consequently, capital export (import) controls serve to increase the reward to domestic labor (capital) and put domestic capital (labor) at the receiving end.

Capital controls are a binding constraint – and hence an interesting issue – only if the returns to capital, appropriately adjusted for differences in risk, differ between countries in the absence of free capital mobility. This presupposes in particular that factor price equalization does not obtain through trade in goods or other factors. This assumption is realistic. First, countries restricting capital flows typically restrict labor mobility as well; moreover, labor is much less mobile internationally than capital as the European Union shows. Albeit that labor is allowed to move freely within the EU, wage rates differ considerably between member states. If labor mobility cannot bring about equalization of its own factor price even if it is free to move as in the EU, it will not equalize capital returns. Second, goods trade will not equalize factor returns either, although this is theoretically possible. The factor price equalization theorem states that under certain – restrictive – assumptions factor price equalization can be brought about by trade in goods alone. Among these restrictions are the assumption of identical technologies, zero transportation costs and zero tariffs leading to equal goods prices, and not too different factor endowments (for details cf., e.g., Dixit and Norman 1980). This theorem is of little empirical relevance since these restrictions are not met in reality: especially goods' prices are not equal due to transportation costs and trade protection measures (Albert 1994, esp. section 4.3). It is therefore no surprise that factor price differentials constantly establish incentives for factor movements.[65]

---

[65] Other reasons for factor price differentials include different technologies and different government regulations such as taxes, environmental standards, etc. Albert (1994) provides an extensive and excellent analysis of the theoretical and empirical issues of the factor price equalization theorem. Leamer (1984) estimates differentials in good prices; Rogoff (1996) and Goldberg and Knetter (1997) provide recent surveys about studies on goods market integration. Chapter 8 discusses the literature on real interest rate differentials (as a proxy for differences in real rates of return). It is shown that real interest rates are different across countries, but tend to equate through capital flows (Modjtahedi 1988). Albert and Vosgerau (1990) demonstrate that factor price differences will occur during a time-consuming reallocation process toward the long-run equilibrium.

As we have pointed out in sections 2.2.2 and 2.2.3, factor movements may impact on the terms of trade and on the factor prices. To discuss in detail all possible effects of capital movements lies clearly beyond the scope of this book and is not necessary; interested readers are refered to the literature.[66] We point out the main effects. Variations in the terms of trade caused by international capital flows are relevant only for large countries. Dixit and Norman (1980: section 5.4) and Woodland (1982: section 13.4) analyze special cases but are unable to derive general results for the multi-commodity case (cf. section 2.2.3). Since most countries that have imposed capital controls are small and hence face exogenously given prices, terms-of-trade variation are a minor concern.

For a small open economy, factor flows will, at least ultimately, alter domestic factor prices. Initially factor flows need not have an impact on factor prices. This will be the case if factor prices are determined by goods prices. Because the factor price differential remains, the factor flow, say an inflow of capital, will continue and ultimately lead to specialization, i.e., at least the production of one good will be discontinued.[67] With the numbers of factors exceeding the number of goods produced, factor prices are no longer determined by goods prices but depend also on factor endowments. Then a capital inflow will reduce its return as it becomes more abundant and will increase the reward of factors that become relatively more scarce. The reaction of the other factor prices depends on the enemy–friend relationship investigated by Jones and Scheinkman (1977) and Diewert and Woodland (1977). A natural friend X of a factor Y gains from an increase in the endowment of Y, V_Y, through a higher return, R_X: $\partial R_X / \partial V_Y > 0$. The aforementioned authors have shown, for a small economy, that every factor has a friend if, of course, the number of factors exceed the number of goods. A capital inflow will favor capital's friends and hurt its enemies. In a model with two factors, capital and labor, capital inflows (outflows) will benefit workers (capital owners) and place capital owners (workers) at the receiving end. It goes without saying that this setup could be made more general allowing for more goods and factors, however only at the cost of the sharpness of results.

It has already become clear that politicians, having full information on the economy's technology, are able to achieve a desired distribution of

[66] Apart from the literature surveys by Ruffin (1984), more recent contributions include Grossman (1984), Svensson (1984), Neary (1985), Ethier and Svensson (1986), Schweinberger (1989), and Wong (1995).
[67] In a two-goods–two-factor setup, the capital-receiving country will ultimately specialize in the production of the capital-intensive good; for a formal derivation of the arguments see for instance Dixit and Norman (1980).

factor income shares by restricting the inflow or outflow of capital.[68] The reasons behind this desire to redistribute are of course of political support-maximizing nature, as we have already explained. Since we will analyze this redistribution technique in great detail in chapters 3–4, we will now round this section off with two remarks.

If labor is mobile, redistributional effects triggered by capital inflow may be dampened through induced emigration (Meckl 1994). This is obvious, because adjustment to increased capital endowment is not born by factor price variations alone, but additionally by factor movements. In the extreme case of perfect mobility of both factors, their rewards are determined by the world market. Though international migration is an important emerging issue, it seems fair to say that (unskilled) labor is still far from perfectly mobile. Moreover, most governments restrict immigration as they fear redistribution of social capital in favor of immigrants, which is perceived as detrimental to the political support they enjoy (Vosgerau 1992).

In this section we have stated the obvious: Restrictions of capital flows alter income distribution and that may be desirable for politicians. It is therefore astonishing that (with the exception of Schulze 1992a) the theory of international political economy has not addressed this policy instrument. Given the outstanding achievements of this theory in explaining trade policy formation, it is all the more astonishing, because restrictions on capital movements are nowadays much more prevalent than restrictions on trade.[69]

2.4.4 Capital controls, bureaucrats, and other rent-seekers

Capital controls please those who actually administer them. The pleasure is quickly increased as growing complexity is pathognomonical for controls – and capital controls are no different in this respect. In their studies on exchange control regimes Bhagwati (1978: 56–63) and Krueger (1978: 22–36, 38) discern five typical phases. In the first phase controls are implemented in a systematic and relatively simple way. This is quickly followed by a phase of intensification and proliferation of restrictions to other types of transactions, and growing complexity. While this development is observable in all cases, the subsequent stages may, but need not,

---

[68] Note that redistribution of personal incomes (as opposed to factor shares) will still have to rely on taxes and transfers unless the distribution of individual factor endowments are altered. This is politically much more difficult to achieve than an alteration of factor prices.
[69] Even Alesina *et al.* (1994) who do analyze capital controls from a political-economic perspective neglect the income distribution effect of managed factor endowments.

follow. The third phase may consist of a mere tidying-up of controls to make them more manageable or may launch a devaluation-cum-liberalization reform. If the latter is the case, phase four (continued liberalization) may follow, which could be succeeded by complete liberalization (phase five). However, cycling through phases two and three (and possibly phase four) was a typical feature for the countries analyzed by Bhagwati and Krueger.

The proliferation of controls has mainly three causes: Rent-seeking activities, evasion and avoidance, and bureaucratic self-interest (cf. Krueger and Duncan 1993). Capital controls create rents as they allow certain exceptions from general prohibitions. Licenses for approved, but restricted capital account transactions have an implicit market value (as they are not auctioned in most cases) and create rent-seeking activity through corruption, bribery, and political influence. If, for example, capital export is prohibited, but foreign trade is not to be hampered unduly, authorities may allow trade-related foreign investment (foreign-based marketing and sales branches, maintenance networks, etc.) within certain quotas. Guidelines will be set up for trade-promoting investment to be exempted from the general prohibition and foreign exchange will be allocated to applicants according to some principle. If funds are allocated, e.g., *pro rata* of foreign trade in a base year, rapidly growing companies or those with low sales in this particular base year may feel they are being treated unfairly and apply for exemption. Some firms may claim a larger share on the grounds that they are more "essential" than other firms since they serve high priority needs, and so forth. The same mechanism works for other restricted transactions like foreign trade credits, borrowing from abroad, purchasing foreign stocks (possibly for trade promotion), etc. Equity has always been a strong political argument and firms may succeed with their rent seeking. Once the dam bursts, the tide of additional claimants flood the bureaus. Those already enjoying the privilege will not oppose additional claims, those who do not *yet* enjoy it will regard additional claims, carried out successfully, as a justification to launch claims themselves. Bureaucrats will not be too unhappy with excemptions either, for reasons to be explained.

As capital controls prohibit profitable transactions, individuals will look for ways to circumvent restrictions. They can do this either legally, by switching to hitherto unrestricted transactions, or illegally through evasion. In order to maintain effectiveness of controls, authorities must close loopholes and also monitor unrestricted transactions closely. For instance, they may regulate the terms of payment for hitherto unregulated trade transactions in order to prevent illegal capital flows. They may stipulate periods within which export proceeds must be surrendered and they will check trade documents in order to thwart capital flows via misdeclaration of import prices. This adds to the complexity.

Last but not least, bureaucrats enjoy complexity! As we have argued earlier on page 33, bureaucrats' utility is an increasing function of the budget they control and the staff they command. Typically, salary rises with responsibility which is measured by the two aforementioned magnitudes, and so does reputation and power. Growing complexity establishes a welcome need for increased staff and thereby an increased budget (cf. Krueger and Duncan 1993).

Bureaucrats in charge of the administration of capital controls appreciate the enlargement of their tasks and, thus, of personnel as they become more senior. But also apart from this seniority and size effect, bureaucrats are charmed by complexity because it regularly increases the discretionary scope they enjoy. Whether somebody is eligible to a certain exception clause is always a matter of judgment; the more clauses there are, the more discretionary scope. Needless to say this discretionary scope provides power and reputation and, if appropriately handled, translates into convenient perquisites.

In many developing countries where poorly designed and enforced constitutional rules hardly limit the extent of government intervention, resource allocation is highly politicized and the civil service has replaced the marketplace as principal instrument for the allocation of resources. Mbaku (1996: 107) describes the African experience:

Civil servants are aware that lucrative monopoly rights created by the government regulatory activities provide their owners with enormous monopoly profits. As a result, bureaucrats try to capture rents by extorting bribes from entrepreneurs who request them. Where government regulation imposes significant costs on a business, the entrepreneur can minimize costs by paying bribes to members of the enforcement community.

Obviously, the allocation of scarce foreign exchange to a business or the exemption from restrictions on capital exports constitute such "windfall gains" given the existence of capital controls; or, stated differently, the compliance with criteria set up by the government to be eligible for a capital export license imposes a cost that can be avoided through corruption. In other words, complex regulations on economic activities, such as capital controls, make corruption of the bureaucracy possible (and often inevitable in order to stay in the market). It is a rent-seeking activity on the part of the ruling elite in government and the bureaucracy that is directly related to the extent of government interference with economic activity (Mbaku 1992).

Moreover, complexity is advantageous even if corruption is not an issue. The more complex a regulation, the higher the costs of compliance with the regulation. In turn, the higher the resources that have to be devoted to the interaction with the regulating bodies, the more rewarding specialization becomes. It is then economic for the regulatee to interact with the regulator through a hired "rule intermediary" (Kearl 1983) instead of acquiring the specific knowhow him- or herself. International trade lawyers, accountants, specialized consultants are frequent examples of such specialists. In other words, complexity creates vested interests in sustaining (and slowly growing) complexity as it induces and rewards specialization and deters outsiders from entry into the intermediation business. The natural candidates for this intermediation are former regulators, because they have optimally invested in the necessary specific human capital by having created and administered the very regulations they advise on. For this reason, bureaucrats – in anticipation of higher-paid job opportunities in the future – have an additional incentive to maintain a complex and fairly stable set of regulations.[70]

2.5 Concluding remark

In our quest to answer the question, "why have governments implemented capital controls so frequently, so persistently, and to such an extent?" we have come thus far. We have discarded efficiency reasons as incapable of explaining the extent of prevailing controls. We have lodged reservations against this line of reasoning instead, because of suspected inconsistencies in this perspective with methodological individualism and because of observation.

We believe we have identified the main reasons for the resort to capital controls. It is no wonder that convincing explanations for these regulations are to be found in the realm of the political-economic paradigm. They fall into two categories.

First, capital controls have a government-financing function. They serve to enhance revenue by immobilizing mobile, and hence untaxable, capital and by increasing seigniorage. They ease the debt service by making financial repression possible. Apart from pleasing the bureaucracy by the process itself, taxation ultimately enables the government to redistribute resources through various policies, not analyzed in this book.

[70] Stability is required, because otherwise the acquired human capital depreciates too quickly and the incentive to specialize is eroded. Some variations may be desirable, because they increase investment costs in human capital for outsiders and deter market entry, but can easily be learnt on the job (Kearl 1983: 220).

Capital controls have also immediate distributional consequences. They constitute the second category of explanations. Only by making capital taxable do capital controls allow governments to distribute the tax burden in a desired way. Moreover, by changing relative factor endowments installed domestically, capital controls alter the factor prices and thereby redistribute income indirectly. It is obvious that the incumbent's calculus to derive his/her optimal distribution is (almost) identical for the two forms of distributive policies. In other words, the considerations governing the politician's optimization of the factor–price ratio are also applicable to the design of relative tax burdens on labor and on capital. This analogy allows us to confine the subsequent analysis to the influence of capital controls on factor rewards, and the political calculus ruling the design of optimal control. More specifically, we will inquire *to what extent* capital controls will be implemented as a consequence of political optimization. Now that we have identified gainers and losers from restrictions of capital movements we want to know by how much they lose and gain. This is what we will investigate in the next two chapters.

3 Capital controls in a small open economy

3.1 Introduction

Restrictions of capital movements affect factor earnings and thus individual incomes. Because the controls suppress the freedom of capital flow, and thereby factor–price arbitrage activities, the relative factor endowments in the country imposing the controls are different from what they otherwise would be – marginal productivities are altered. As individuals differ with regard to their factor endowments, they are disproportionately affected by these controls: a conflict of interests arises with respect to the severeness of the controls to be adopted, if any.

We dwell on these issues in the present chapter. Specifically, we analyze how, and to what extent, factor prices are altered by the imposition of capital controls and in what way the individual factor endowment determines the individually optimal degree of restriction. Lastly, we study how restrictive the capital controls will be if individual preferences are aggregated via a majority voting process.

We use the MacDougall–Kemp model (MacDougall 1960, Kemp 1964, see also Ruffin 1984) as well as the Specific Factors model (Jones 1971, Mussa 1974), the former because of its analytical simplicity which already serves to demonstrate the main issues.[1] The latter is applied not only because it allows for a third factor (and makes the extension to n factors straightforward) but also because it has been given strong attention in the theory on political economy of (trade) protection, as it formulates the sector specificity of interests (Hillman 1989). In contrast to sector-specific interests with regard to trade policy it turns out that in the context of capital controls the owners of the specific factors would side against the

---

[1] A key feature of both models is that factor–price equalization cannot be brought about by trade in goods alone but only by factor movements. For a more precise elaboration on this point see Dixit and Norman (1980: 122–125): The probability of factor–price equalization through trade alone has zero dimension.

intersectorally mobile labor. Moreover, the focus is on capital *export* restrictions as the by far more prevalent form of capital controls (cf. IMF various issues). Since a competitive environment is assumed, quantitative restrictions on capital exports are modeled by means of a discriminatory tax on income from exported capital.

We remove the classical dichotomy of capitalists and workers (since this is obviously very often an unrealistic and restrictive portrayal of real life) and instead allow individuals to own different amounts of capital and labor.[2] We show that within the premises of the MacDougall–Kemp model there exists for each individual factor–ownership ratio a unique optimal tax (subsidy) on foreign capital earnings which maximizes individual income by changing factor rewards. In the absence of voting costs it is the median voter's optimal tax rate which is adopted by majority voting. Since the median voter model does not describe the complete political market for protection but rather portrays the aggregation procedure on the demand side in that market, this chapter does not claim to explain the ultimate level of capital export restrictions but to provide insights into the individual's interest and the decision-making process. The final outcome depends on the institutional setting, which certainly differs across countries.[3] We elaborate on this point in section 3.6. The recognition that individual factor endowments differ across individuals was introduced into the literature on the political economy of protection by Mayer (1984). This chapter follows insofar Mayer's line of argument.

---

[2] Alesina and Tabellini (1989), however, analyze capital controls in a polarized society (capitalists versus workers) with alternating governments (see p. 46).

[3] There is just one paper that assumes a particular institutional setting. Checchi (1996) analyzes the capital controls setting of a political support-maximizing government in a stage game with four types of agents. In the first stage the government sets the restrictions on capital exports, i.e., a share of the representative investor's wealth that he is allowed to invest abroad, then the investor chooses his optimal portfolio from risky domestic industry loans and foreign bonds and riskless government bonds. In the third stage the union sets a wage rate and subsequently the manager hires workers and borrows domestic capital to produce a commodity the price of which is subject to stochastic fluctuations. While the investor always favors the abolition of capital export controls, the union favors capital export restrictions if they lead to higher domestic credit, which is the case if the yields from domestic loans and foreign bonds are positively correlated. The manager favors capital controls if in the case of a positive (negative) correlation between domestic and foreign credit the resulting higher (lower) credit to the firm leads to higher profits. This depends on the parameters of the model, because higher credits lead to higher production and also to higher wages and employment, according to the union's wage setting.

Although his setup is very rich in allowing different types of assets and different types of agents, it is very special at the same time – the results depend crucially on the staging of events, the exogenous weights assigned to the different interest groups by the government, the union's objective function, among other things. Also, it does not allow for interpersonally different endowments, but assumes a representative investor/manager and disregards voting or electoral competition.

He demonstrates that for every capital–labor ownership ratio there exists a *tariff* that maximizes individual income. He *implicitly* assumes that factors of production do not move across borders, since, if they did, international factor–price differentials would instantaneously give rise to capital movements or migration. Initial differences in factor earnings (e.g., caused by trade protection) would be eliminated, and trade would be brought to a standstill.[4]

The analysis of capital controls in a specific factors setting, with capital internationally mobile but sector specific, yields somewhat different results. As a starting point it is shown that industry-specific factors no longer seek tariff protection if capital is internationally mobile. Under this assumption, specific factors' interests are parallel across industries – Mayer's (1984) result of the conflict of interests between industries (i.e., the specific factors thereof) no longer holds.[5] Instead, restrictions on capital exports reduce the rewards from all specific factors, though to differing extents. The mobile factor, assumed to be labor, is better off. It turns out that the result of majority voting depends not only on the factor ownership distributions of the different industries but also on their relative size in terms of the number of individuals owning a specific factor of the respective industry. Voting costs and characteristics of the industries, such as labor intensity and the distributive share of labor in production, also influence the outcome of the voting process.

The chapter is organized as follows. In section 3.2 a small open economy which exports capital is modeled according to the MacDougall–Kemp approach. The impact of capital controls on national, as well as on individual income, is analyzed and the individually optimal tax is derived in section 3.3. Section 3.4 is devoted to individual voting behavior and the result of majority voting. Subsequently, in section 3.5 capital controls are analyzed in a Specific Factors model. We discuss the appropriateness of the median voter model and alternative ways to model the political process in the concluding section 3.6.

3.2 A simple model of international capital movements

Consider a small open economy producing one homogeneous good X, called output, by means of two homogeneous factors, capital (K) and

---

[4] See Mundell (1957). This result hinges on the assumptions that, in a Heckscher–Ohlin setting, production functions are internationally identical and linear homogeneous, countries are not specialized, and factor intensity reversals can be excluded.
[5] For a critical survey of international trade policy under different assumptions about factor mobility see Ursprung (1987), Hillman (1989), and Weck-Hannemann (1992a,b).

labor (L).[6] The production function is assumed to be linear homogeneous and the labor force is fixed. Output is produced under perfect competition so that factors will earn their marginal product. The price level is defined at unity. The economy is endowed with a constant stock of capital $(\bar{K})$ which is allocated to production at home (K^h) and abroad (K^*)

$$\bar{K} = K^h + K^*. \tag{3.1}$$

The production function can be written as

$$X = F(K^h, L) \quad \text{with} \quad F_K = \frac{\partial F}{\partial K^h} > 0 \quad \text{and} \quad F_{KK} = \frac{\partial^2 F}{\partial K^{h2}} < 0. \tag{3.2}$$

Capital invested at home and capital invested abroad are assumed to be perfect substitutes – the allocation of capital depends solely on the rentals received from foreign and domestic investments. Foreign capital earnings are repatriated. Due to equation (3.2) and perfect competition, we have

$$r = F_K \quad \text{and} \quad \frac{\partial r}{\partial K} < 0 \tag{3.3}$$

with r being the prevailing interest rate on the domestic capital market. Capital controls are introduced via a discriminatory tax on dividends earned abroad (t), applicable to residents in the case of a capital-exporting country or to foreigners if the country imports capital. Although capital controls often also take the form of quantitative restrictions, it is justified to model them this way since we assume a competitive environment. Hence the equivalence proposition (concerning taxes and tariffs) holds.[7] Subsequently we will confine our analysis to capital exports. The analysis of capital import restrictions runs *mutatis mutandis* parallel to that set out here. Since we consider a small open economy with a given foreign interest rate r^*, investors will ensure via arbitrage that

$$r = (1 - t) r^*. \tag{3.4}$$

National income Y is then defined by

$$Y = F(K^h, L) + r^* K^* = wL + r\bar{K} + tr^* K^* \tag{3.5}$$

---

[6] Note that this economy is small with respect to capital markets; otherwise it could benefit from a positive factor terms of trade effect (see chapter 4); however, it is also small with respect to goods markets in the following sense: the inflow or outflow of capital, and the resulting restructuring of the production sectors, does not affect the world market prices for the goods traded and hence the country's terms of trade.

[7] See Kindleberger (1958), Bhagwati (1965, 1968) for a discussion.

with $w = \partial F/\partial L$ being the wage rate and $tr^*K^* = T$ the tax revenue. Following Mayer (1984), this revenue is distributed in such a way that an individual's share of tax revenue T^i equals his or her income share from factor ownership Ψ^i, i.e.

$$T^i = \Psi^i T \tag{3.6}$$

and

$$\Psi^i = \frac{wL^i + rK^i}{wL + r\bar{K}} . \tag{3.7}$$

Every individual owns a positive amount of labor, L^i, and a non-negative amount of capital K^i. Hence, individual income y^i can be calculated as

$$y^i = wL^i + rK^i + T^i = \Psi^i Y. \tag{3.8}$$

This tax redistribution scheme is introduced not because we consider it to be particularly realistic but because we want to focus on the variation of factor rewards as the motivation for capital controls. Other redistribution schemes can be introduced without altering the basic results of the model. Equations (3.6) and (3.8) would change accordingly.

3.3 Individual's optimal tax rate

Because factor endowments differ across individuals a change in the tax rate (i.e., a variation in the intensity of capital export control) benefits some and hurts others.[8] This is demonstrated in figure 3.1 which depicts the marginal productivity of domestic capital as well as the (constant) marginal rental from foreign investment.

The distance OD depicts the economy's capital endowment $\bar{K}$. With no capital controls in place, equality of real interest rates implies that OB is invested at home and the remainder BD is invested abroad. If a tax $t > 0$ is imposed, the domestically owned foreign capital stock is reduced from BD to CD. Capital loses by $EGMH$ while labor gains by $EFIH$. The tax revenue is represented by $FGMJ$ and the "social loss" amounts to FJI which is always non-negative for small open economies. Hence it follows that if all individuals were endowed with

$$k^i := K^i/L^i \quad = \quad k := \bar{K}/L$$

any taxes on dividends from foreign investment would unanimously be rejected. Capital controls can only be explained if a redistribution of

---

[8] The formulation of the problem follows Mayer (1984). The interpretation is somewhat different.

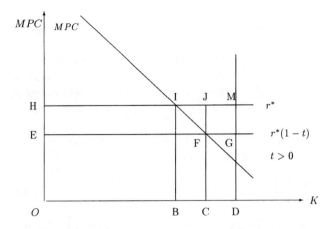

Figure 3.1 Capital export controls in a small open economy

income takes place, i.e., if some lose and others gain from capital controls. Under majority voting, the restriction of capital exports can only happen if the distribution of capital ownership is skewed to the right. In the following, this argument will be worked out in detail. Subsequently we assume for notational convenience: $L^i = 1$.[9]

Since we are considering a single-good economy, an individual's utility exclusively depends on the level of individual income – utility maximization is equivalent to the maximization of y^i. From (3.8) follows

$$\frac{\partial y^i}{\partial t} = Y \frac{\partial \Psi^i}{\partial t} + \Psi^i \frac{\partial Y}{\partial t}. \tag{3.9}$$

From (3.5) and (3.4) and the fact that $\partial K^h / \partial t = -\partial K^* / \partial t$ follows

$$\frac{\partial Y}{\partial t} = -tr^* \frac{\partial K^h}{\partial t} \tag{3.10}$$

which is negative. Differentiating (3.4) with respect to t and using (3.3) yields

$$\frac{\partial K^h}{\partial t} = -\frac{r^*}{\partial r / \partial K^h} = -\frac{1}{1-t} K^h \xi > 0 \tag{3.11}$$

with $\xi < 0$ being the elasticity of demand for capital (i.e., the reciprocal of the elasticity of the marginal product curve of capital). Thus

---

[9] Results, however, would not be altered if allowance were made for $L^i \neq 1$. The capital-labor endowment *ratio* is decisive.

$$\frac{\partial Y}{\partial t} = \frac{tr^*}{1-t} K^h \xi < 0. \tag{3.12}$$

Restrictions of capital exports lead to a reduction in the national income. This affects all individuals negatively according to their personal income share Ψ^i. A second source which alters individual income is the change in the personal income share, depending on the individual factor endowment.

Returning to equation (3.9) and using (3.10), we can now calculate the optimal tax rate of agent i denoted by t^i_{opt}

$$t^i_{opt} = Y \frac{\partial \Psi^i}{\partial t} \frac{1}{\Psi^i} \frac{1}{r^*} \frac{1}{\partial K^h / \partial t}. \tag{3.13}$$

Since $\partial K^h / \partial t$ is positive, t^i_{opt} is positive if and only if the individual income share rises as a consequence of a tax increase

$$\text{sign}(t^i_{opt}) = \text{sign}\left(\frac{\partial \Psi^i}{\partial t}\right).$$

To work out the relationship between factor ownership and economic interest (concerning capital controls), we calculate

$$\frac{\partial \Psi^i}{\partial t} = \frac{L}{[wL + r\bar{K}]^2} (rw' - wr') \{k - k^i\}. \tag{3.14}$$

w' stands for $\partial w / \partial t$ which is positive from the properties of the production function and $r' = \partial r / \partial t = -r^* < 0$ which follows from (3.4). The expressions in square brackets and parenthesis[10] are positive. It is thus in the interest of an individual to restrict capital exports if and only if he or she is underproportionally endowed with capital ($k^i < k$). Furthermore, from (3.13) and (3.14), it is clear that it will be purely accidental if free movement of capital is in the individual's interest, that is if his or her factor endowment ratio coincides with the ratio of the economy. Otherwise the individual will favor either taxation or subsidization of capital exports.

Individuals with a relatively poor (rich) capital endowment will profit from taxation (subsidization) of earnings from investment made abroad the more their factor endowment ratio differs from the figure for the economy. But while their slice becomes larger in the course of increasing taxation (subsidization) the cake shrinks. Hence, the individual capital endowment determines economic interest, i.e., the individual optimal tax

---

[10] Note that $(rw' - wr') = r^*(1 - t)\partial w' / \partial t + wr^*$, which is evidently positive.

rate and thereby voting behavior.[11] These relationships will be detailed in the following section.

3.4 Formation of capital controls via majority voting

First, we consider the voting behavior of an individual i who has to vote on the increase, the decrease, or maintenance of an *existing* tax on capital exports. This tax is optimal for exactly one capital–labor endowment ratio, say k^j. Equation (3.13) can thus be written as

$$
\begin{aligned}
t_{opt}^j &= Y \frac{\partial \Psi^j}{\partial t} \frac{1}{\Psi^j} \frac{1}{r^*} \frac{1}{\partial K^h / \partial t} \\
&= \frac{YL(rw' - wr')}{(wL + rK)(w + rk^j)r^* \partial K^h / \partial t} (k - k^j) .
\end{aligned}
\tag{3.15}
$$

Individual i gains from a tax increase if and only if $\partial y^i / \partial t > 0$. Using (3.9) and (3.14) and substituting t_{opt}^j from (3.15) for t, some standard transformations yield

$$
\begin{aligned}
\frac{\partial y^i}{\partial t} &= Y \frac{\partial \Psi^i}{\partial t} + \Psi^i \frac{\partial Y}{\partial t} \\
&= \frac{1}{[wL + rK](w + rk^i)} (rw' - wr')(k^j - k^i) .
\end{aligned}
\tag{3.16}
$$

Equation (3.16) shows that an individual will favor a tax increase only if his or her capital–labor ratio is below the one for which the existing tax is optimal. Otherwise he or she will support a reduction of capital controls. Figure 3.2 depicts the relationship between economic interest EI (i.e., the variation of individual income resulting from a tax increase) and the individual capital–labor endowment ratio. Each curve describes the situation of a particular existing tax rate which is optimal for the individual capital–labor ratio at which the curve intersects with the abscissa. Free movement of capital (EI_0-curve) is optimal only for $k^i = k$ whereas people with $k^i < k$ will be better off if taxes are levied. EI_1 describes the same relationship for a positive tax on capital exports.

With increasing taxes (graphically a shift of the EI curve to the left) the number of individuals benefiting from a *further* increase becomes smaller. Since the above relationship (3.16) holds for any value of k^j, equation (3.16) implies that individual preferences are single peaked. The indivi-

---

[11] It can be shown by substituting (3.14) into (3.9) that even prohibitive tax rates cannot be excluded from being individually optimal.

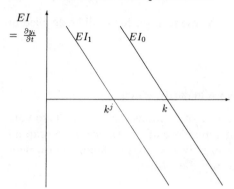

Figure 3.2 Individual income variation and factor endowment

dual i will strictly support a tax increase (reduction) as long as $k^i < k^j$ $(k^i > k^j)$.[12]

Now individual preferences are aggregated via majority voting. Equilibrium is reached when no majority can be obtained for a tax, other than the existing one. Since the median voter theorem is standard in economics, we do not study it here, but refer the reader to the literature. Building on the work of Hotelling (1929), the median voter theorem was elaborated by Black (1948) and Downs (1957).[13] According to Black's (1948) famous contribution, the median voter's optimal tax rate will be the final outcome of a majority voting process. Hence "society" will restrict capital exports if the median voter's factor ownership ratio $k^m < k$, that is the distribution of factor ownership, is skewed to the right.[14]

This result, however, hinges on the presupposition that every factor owner is eligible to vote and that no costs of voting exist. To obtain more realistic results, eligibility rules have to be taken into account. If we assume that the representative young factor owner who is not yet eligible to vote has a lower-than-average capital endowment, the relevant distribution is less skewed to the right and hence k^m may increase. Furthermore, if gains from a proposed tax variation fall short of parti-

---

[12] As above $k^j = k^j(t)$ is the capital–labor ratio for which the prevailing tax is optimal.
[13] Long before Hotelling, Marquis de Condorcet (1785) showed the possibility of cycling if preferences are not single-peaked. Arrow (1951, rev. edn. 1963) shows the incompatibility of (*inter alia*) the majority rule with a set of fundamental axioms. For a comprehensive review of the theorem see also the classic Black (1958), and more recently, Enelow and Hinich (1984), Ordeshook (1986), and Mueller (1989, chapters 5, 10).
[14] This is a typical at least for Western industrialized countries, but it may also be true for a number of developing countries.

cipation costs (defined in the broadest sense) it is rational to abstain from voting.[15] It seems reasonable to assume that the probability of voting depends on the expected net gain from voting. Since Mayer (1984) has modeled this hypothesis in a similar context the reader is referred to his article.

3.5 The specific factors model

In this section we show how the industry-specific interest in tariff protection disappears if we allow for international mobility of the respective specific factor. Rents (of the specific factor) created by tariff protection cannot be sustained due to the influx of foreign capital, unless capital import controls are in place. What is more important, we demonstrate that the results derived in the one-sector MacDougall–Kemp model basically carry over to the multi-sector case; we show how the results derived above must be amended to account for the richer economic structure. The restriction of capital import establishes a vehicle to increase the rewards of the specific factors.

We assume capital to be sector-specific and internationally mobile. Labor is internationally immobile, but mobile between sectors. These assumptions on factor mobility, though they may seem restrictive, make good economic sense: most countries severely restrict migration; differences in language, culture, education profile, etc. constitute further obstacles for prospective migrants. Workers are hired or made redundant relatively easily as sectors expand or contract. Capital, including human capital, is sector-specific in the short run, because processes to adjust to new products, production technologies, and markets are very time consuming as they require the acquisition of new skills, product-specific and market-specific know-how. Compared to these adjustment requirements, it is relatively easy to (partly) relocate the production of an already produced good abroad. Since political decisions are motivated by short-term considerations, our assumptions on factor mobility are justified.[16] For simplicity we adopt the standard two-sector model as in Jones (1971) and Mussa (1974). The extension to the multi-commodity case is straightforward.

Mayer (1984) has shown that a sector could obtain tariff protection via majority-voting though only the specific factor of that industry would

---

15 For a detailed analysis of the impact of voting costs on voting behavior see, e.g., Mueller (1989).
16 Magee (1980) provides evidence on the sector-specificity of interests in the context of trade policy, which points to the appropriateness of our model.

gain and all other specific factors would lose. He assumed the respective good to be "unbiased with respect to labor" in the Ruffin and Jones sense.[17] This result was due to an uneven distribution of gains and losses from protection together with the existence of voting costs. Hence, voting participation rates were apt to be different between losers and gainers. How this result would be altered if the specific factor of the protected industry is assumed to be internationally mobile, though intersectorally bound, is investigated next.

Consider a small open economy producing two goods, the first of which, say the industrial commodity, is produced by means of capital (V_1) and labor (V_{N1}). The second good, the agricultural commodity, is produced by a fixed amount of land (V_2) and the residual labor (V_{N2}). As Mussa (1974) has noted, different interpretations of factors and commodities are conceivable. The intersectoral mobility of internationally immobile labor equalizes the wage rate (R_N) across sectors. We assume a linear homogeneous production technology, perfect competition, and international mobility of capital. Following Jones (1971), this economy can be described by the following zero profit conditions (3.17)–(3.18) and the full employment conditions (3.19)–(3.21)

$$a_{11}R_1 + a_{N1}R_N = p_1 \tag{3.17}$$

$$a_{22}R_2 + a_{N2}R_N = p_2 \tag{3.18}$$

$$a_{11}X_1 = V_1 \tag{3.19}$$

$$a_{22}X_2 = V_2 \tag{3.20}$$

$$a_{N1}X_1 + a_{N2}X_2 = V_N. \tag{3.21}$$

R_1 (R_2) denotes the rental rate for capital (land), X_1 (X_2) stands for the production of the first (second) commodity and p_1, p_2 are the respective commodity prices. a_{ij} represents the quantity of factor i $(i = 1, 2, N)$ required per unit of commodity j $(j = 1, 2)$, and is a function of the relative price of the respective factors $(a_{ij} = a_{ij}(R_j/R_N))$.

In a small open and capital-importing economy, which by assumption exports the agricultural product (X_2), prices are related to world market prices (superscribed by "*") in the following way

$$p_1 = p_1^*(1 + \tau_1) \tag{3.22}$$

---

[17] "Commodity j is said to be unbiased with respect to labor if the relative change in the wage rate . . . brought about by an increase in p_j is precisely the average for the changes in all factor prices" Ruffin and Jones (1977: 339).

$$p_2(1 + \tau_2) = p_2^* \qquad (3.23)$$

$$R_1^* = (1 - t)R_1. \qquad (3.24)$$

τ_1 (τ_2) denotes an import (export) tariff whereas t represents either a discriminatory tax on the return from foreign investment accruing to foreigners or is the result of a quantitative restriction of the inflow of foreign capital (in a competitive environment). At the outset, we set $\tau_1 = \tau_2 = t = 0$.

From the above formulation it is seen that a tariff on the imported commodity will trigger off an inflow of capital V_1 which will drive down the rental rate of capital to its initial value, i.e., the world market level. We denote a relative change of a variable with "$\hat{\ }$", the share of labor used in the first (second) industry with λ_{N1} (λ_{N2}) while θ_{kj} is the distributive share of factor k in industry j, $\theta_{kj} = R_k V_{kj}/(p_j X_j)$. σ_i is the elasticity of substitution between factors in industry j, $\sigma_j = (\hat{a}_{jj} - \hat{a}_{Nj})/(\hat{R}_N - \hat{R}_j)$.

The relative influx of capital $\hat{V}_1$ induced by a relative price increase of the first commodity ($\hat{p}_1$) is given by

$$\hat{V}_1 = \frac{\lambda_{N1}\frac{\sigma_1}{\theta_{11}} + \frac{1}{\theta_{11}}\lambda_{N2}\frac{\sigma_2}{\theta_{22}}}{\lambda_{N1}\frac{\theta_{N1}}{\theta_{11}}}\hat{p}_1. \qquad (3.25)$$

where we used equation (10) from Jones (1971). While the rental rate of capital, R_1, remains unchanged the rental rate of the specific factor in the second industry will decline due to the inflow of V_1

$$\hat{R}_2 = -\frac{\theta_{N2}}{\theta_{22}\theta_{N1}}\hat{p}_1. \qquad (3.26)$$

Only the mobile factor gains unambiguously

$$\frac{\hat{R}_N}{\hat{p}_1} = \frac{1}{\theta_{N1}} > 1. \qquad (3.27)$$

Even in a specific factors model the classical conflict of interests between labor and capital is prevailing if capital is assumed to be internationally mobile! This conflict, however, differs from that in the Heckscher–Ohlin–Samuelson model since owners of specific factors are differently affected by "protection" of a distinct sector – depending on the *type* of the specific factor they own. In this model the owners of capital will lose insofar as national income decreases[18] and p_1 rises. Owners of land will lose *in*

[18] This decline equals zero if in an initial situation of free trade only marginal tariffs are levied. For the analysis of the general case see Mayer (1984: 973).

addition to that from the reduction of the rental rate of land (R_2). The inflow of specific capital to one sector has made labor relatively scarcer in all sectors, thereby increasing its return and depressing the returns of all specific factors other than the protected, but internationally mobile one. Its return stays put at the world level due to its free mobility. Since individuals, by assumption, also own labor the net effect of gains from an increased wage rate and the losses described depends on the factor endowment ratio. In the presence of capital mobility, however, Mayer's suggestion that a specific factor could obtain rents via tariff protection does not hold: rents cannot be sustained in the absence of barriers to entry!

If capital inflow is restricted the specific factor will gain as compared with a situation where capital is allowed to move freely between countries. Consider a quantitative restriction on capital imports in a competitive environment (with free trade of commodities). This restriction is modeled via a discriminatory tax t on returns on foreign capital (cf. Bhagwati 1965, 1968). We assume, in accordance with section 3.3, that individuals own one unit of labor and can be endowed additionally with a quantity of specific factors of at most one *type*.

We apply Mayer's analytical approach (Mayer 1984: 978–983) to the case of capital control as far as it is appropriate for our problem. Individuals seek to maximize their (indirect) utility function which is given by

$$U^i = U^i(p_1, p_2, \Psi^i Y). \tag{3.28}$$

National income Y is defined by the sum of factor rewards and tax proceeds

$$Y = R_1 V_1^h + R_2 V_2 + R_N V_N + t R_1 V_1^*. \tag{3.29}$$

Capital in the home country consists of domestically owned capital (V_1^h) and capital from abroad (V_1^*)

$$V_1 = V_1^h + V_1^*.$$

Again, Ψ^i denotes the individual income share

$$\Psi^i = \frac{R_N + R_l V_l^i}{R_N V_N + R_1 V_1^h + R_2 V_2}; \quad l = 1, 2, \tag{3.30}$$

where l indicates the type of the specific factor that individual i owns. Ψ^i is an (indirect) function of t: all other exogenous parameters constant, a variation of t will alter Ψ^i through an induced change of the equilibrium values of the factor rewards. The change in individual's utility by a restriction of capital imports is seen from a differentiation of (3.28) with respect to t

$$\partial U^i/\partial t = \partial U^i/\partial y^i[\Psi^i \partial Y/\partial t + Y \partial \Psi^i/\partial t]. \tag{3.31}$$

A quantitative restriction of the import of foreign capital V_1^* that causes a relative reduction of (domestically installed) capital of

$$\hat{V}_1 = dV_1^*/(V_1^h + V_1^*)$$

results in relative increase of R_1

$$\hat{R}_1 = -\frac{1}{\Delta}\lambda_{N1}\frac{\theta_{N1}}{\theta_{11}}\hat{V}_1; \quad \Delta = \lambda_{N1}\frac{\sigma_1}{\theta_{11}} + \lambda_{N2}\frac{\sigma_2}{\theta_{22}}. \tag{3.32}$$

This result follows from differentiation of (3.17)–(3.21), the definition of λ_{Nj}, θ_{ij}, σ_j ($j = 1, 2$; $i = N, 1, 2$), and the fact that a_{ij} are chosen in order to minimize unit costs.[19] For the derivation of this result see Jones (1971: 4–7). Analogously

$$\hat{R}_2 = -\frac{1}{\Delta}\frac{\theta_{N2}}{\theta_{22}}\lambda_{N1}\hat{V}_1 \tag{3.33}$$

and

$$\hat{R}_N = \frac{1}{\Delta}\lambda_{N1}\hat{V}_1. \tag{3.34}$$

Though both specific factors are better off if restrictions on capital imports are imposed, the factor specific to the industry, with the higher distributive share of labor, gains also *relatively* to the other specific factor, i.e. $| \hat{R}_1 | > | \hat{R}_2 |$ iff $\theta_{N1} > \theta_{N2}$.[20]

Differentiating (3.29), substituting (3.32)–(3.34) in the resulting expression, and after some manipulations we get

$$\partial Y/\partial t = R_1 t \partial V_1/\partial t. \tag{3.35}$$

National income declines if capital import restrictions are tightened up. The variation of individual income share is calculated by differentiating (3.30)

---

[19] That means that $\theta_{jj}\hat{a}_{jj} + \theta_{Nj}\hat{a}_{Nj} = 0, j = 1, 2$, cf. Jones (1971: 6).
Stated in terms of t, the domestic rental rate of capital can be raised via an increase of t : $dt = (1 - t)\hat{R}_1$ which is seen from the differentiation of (3.24) and the condition of a given R_1^*. Hence

$$\partial t = -(1 - t)\frac{1}{\Delta}\lambda_{N1}\frac{\theta_{N1}}{\theta_{11}}\hat{V}_1.$$

[20] $\hat{R}_1 - \hat{R}_2 = \frac{1}{\Delta}\frac{1}{\theta_{11}\theta_{22}}(\theta_{N2} - \theta_{N1})\lambda_{N1}\hat{V}_1, \quad \hat{V}_1 < 0$. Jones (1971 : 7).

$$\frac{\partial \Psi^i}{\partial t} = \frac{R_l V_l^i}{[R_N V_N + R_1 V_1^h + R_2 V_2]}(\hat{R}_l - \hat{R}_N)$$
$$- \frac{(R_N + R_l V_l^i)(R_1 V_1(\hat{R}_1 - \hat{R}_N) + R_2 V_2(\hat{R}_2 - \hat{R}_N))}{[R_N V_N + R_1 V_1^h + R_2 V_2]^2}.$$

Substituting in the equilibrium reaction of the factor rewards triggered off by variation of V_1, (3.32)–(3.34), yields

$$\frac{\partial \Psi^i}{\partial t} = \frac{1}{[R_N V_N + R_1 V_1^h + R_2 V_2]} \frac{1}{\Delta} \lambda_{N1} \hat{V}_1 \{ R_N - \frac{\theta_{Nl}}{\theta_{ll}} R_l V_l^i \}$$
$$= \frac{1}{[R_N V_N + R_1 V_1^h + R_2 V_2]}[R_l V_l^i \hat{R}_l + R_N \hat{R}_N]. \tag{3.36}$$

As seen from the term in braces in (3.36) and the definition of θ_{Nl} and θ_{ll} individuals' income share will increase as a result of tighter restrictions on capital imports only if

$$V_l^i > V_l / V_{Nl}. \tag{3.37}$$

In other words, individual i's relative factor endowment must exceed the factor employment ratio for the respective industry ($V_N^i = 1$, see above). Changes in individual income y^i stem from two sources – the reduction of national income and the variation in the individual's income share.

$$\frac{\partial y^i}{\partial t} = \frac{1}{[R_N V_N + R_1 V_1^h + R_2 V_2]}\{ Y \underbrace{(R_l V_l^i \hat{R}_l + R_N \hat{R}_N)}_{\geq 0 \text{ or } < 0} + \underbrace{(R_l V_l + R_N)R_1 t dV_1^*}_{\leq 0} \}. \tag{3.38}$$

Assuming initially free trade of goods and factors ($t = 0$) this expression is reduced to

$$\partial y^i / \partial t = [R_l V_l^i \hat{R}_l + R_N \hat{R}_N] = \frac{\partial \Psi^i}{\partial t}. \tag{3.39}$$

Hence

$$\left. \frac{\partial U^i}{\partial t} \right|_{t=0} = \frac{\partial U^i}{\partial y^i} \frac{\partial \Psi^i}{\partial t}.$$

Individuals are assumed to vote in their economic interest, i.e., according to the effect on their real income through the restriction of capital imports ($\partial y^i / \partial t$). Consider fixed per capita voting costs c. Individuals will participate in voting only if the potential gain from a tax (subsidy) will

exceed voting costs. With initially free movement of capital this condition
is given by

$$\partial y^i / \partial t = |\ R_l V_l^i \hat{R}_l + R_N \hat{R}_N\ | > c. \tag{3.40}$$

Alternatively stated, individuals with a factor endowment of

$$V_l^i \in \left[\frac{V_l}{V_{Nl}} \left(1 - c \frac{\Delta}{\lambda_{N1} \hat{V}_1 R_N} \right) ; \frac{V_l}{V_{Nl}} \left(1 + c \frac{\Delta}{\lambda_{N1} \hat{V}_1 R_N} \right) \right] \tag{3.41}$$

will not participate in voting.[21] All individuals for whom

$$V_l^i > \frac{V_l}{V_{Nl}} \left(1 + c \frac{\Delta}{\lambda_{N1} \hat{V}_1 R_N} \right)$$

will vote in favor of a restriction on capital imports. Individuals with an
endowment of the specific factor less than the lower bound of interval
(3.41) will vote against an imposition. The range of the interval depends
not only on the magnitude of voting costs but also on the characteristics
of the respective industry. The final outcome of the majority voting process in turn depends on the factor ownership distribution and the range
and the position of interval (3.41) for both industries as well as on industries' relative size in terms of the number of individuals owning the specific factor of that industry.

Specifically, if there were no voting costs and both factor ownership
distributions were skewed to the right, restrictions on capital imports
would not be imposed.[22] If both factor ownership distributions were
symmetric with the median voters' endowment of the specific factor,
$V_l^{med} = V_l/V_{Nl}$, majority voting would result in free movement of capital.
If, however, capital is concentrated (with a factor ownership distribution
skewed to the right), whereas land is distributed with a density skewed to
the left, parameter values have to be taken into account to derive the
restriction resulting from a majority voting process.

If capital controls are voted for, these restrictions will generally not be
prohibitive since the group of gainers diminishes (and losers increase in

---

[21] It is a rather strong assumption that individuals will not vote *if and only if* their V_l^i lie
within this interval. We could introduce voting probabilities that depend on the magnitude
of $\partial y^i / \partial t$ without altering the results basically. We have adopted this approach from Mayer
(1984). For critical reflections on this approach see section 3.6 and the literature cited there.
[22] This result still holds unambiguously if the interval is such that median voter's V_l^i, i.e.,
V_l^{med} is left of the interval (3.41)

$$V_l^{med} \overset{!}{<} V_l/V_{Nl}(1 - c\Delta/(\lambda_{N1} \hat{V}_1 R_N)).$$

number) as national income declines (see (3.38)). An individual will not vote for a *further* increase of restrictions if

$$\partial y^i / \partial t \leq c,$$

where $\partial y^i / \partial t$ is given by (3.38). Again, the individual optimal tax rate t_i^{opt} is reached when the marginal reduction in national income equals the marginal increase in individual's income share, so that $\partial y^i / \partial t = 0$.

3.6 On the relevance of the median voter model

3.6.1 Voting behavior and the paradox of voting

In this chapter we have identified the parameters determining the level of capital controls and have demonstrated *how* these parameters influence the outcome of majority voting. The factor endowment *ratio* determines individual interest concerning the severity of capital controls. In the simple MacDougall–Kemp model the median voter's optimal capital control is selected (if we line up individuals according to their relative factor endowment). In the framework of the Specific Factors model, results are less clear-cut: apart from the distribution of relative factor endowments, the outcome depends also on the characteristics of the two industries such as size and labor intensity.

The results derived rest upon two assumptions. First, if individuals vote, they vote in their self-interest. That means that they will support every policy which raises their individual income and oppose any other policy, regardless of what effect this has on the income of others. Second, individuals participate in voting. In section 3.4 we have implicitly assumed that all individuals vote; in section 3.5 we assumed that individuals participate in voting if the possible individual benefit b from the adoption of their preferred alternative exceeds voting costs c. In our context the parameter b denotes the gain in individual income if the supported policy is adopted.

The second assumption (in either version), however, is inconsistent with the idea of a self-interested, rational voter. In a narrow sense, a rational voter would participate in voting only if his or her *expected* utility from voting is greater than the incurred voting costs, i.e., $pb - c > 0$, with p denoting the probability that *his or her* vote will decide the result of the poll. It is clear, however, that in general elections pb will always fall short of c – except under very strange assumptions. The probability of casting the decisive vote is very close to zero (and roughly of the same size as the probability of being killed in a car accident on the way to the polling station, Skinner 1948: 265). Still a vast number of people do vote, even if economists say it is not rational do so. Does this fact render the median voter model (MVM) void of explanatory power? We will argue that it does not.

The paradox of voting has been the subject of extensive debate, which is well documented,[23] so that we are able to confine our discussion to the issues most relevant to our context. Ample empirical evidence of considerable voter participation implies that motivations other than narrow self-interest account for the decision to vote. Riker and Ordeshook (1968) introduce a direct intrinsic benefit from the act of voting itself,[24] d, unconnected with the result of the poll so that the voter will participate if $pb - c + d > 0$. This boils down to $d > c$, because pb will be negligibly small. As d remains exogenous, the aforementioned formulation is close to a tautology; moreover, variations in the voter turnout are not explained by this approach.[25]

Ferejohn and Fiorina (1974) try to resolve the paradox by assuming a minimax regret strategy on the part of the voters. This approach is theoretically so unconvincing (see Aldrich 1997: 379–381) and empirically refuted (Struthers and Young 1989: 9–11) that we will disregard it. Again, the probability that the individual's vote will decide an election is simply far too small to matter. A regret from not having cast the decisive vote is as likely to occur as is a regret from having crossed the neighborhood street and being hit by a car. Do people stop crossing streets?

Palfrey and Rosenthal (1983), Ledyard (1984), Austen-Smith (1984), and others portray the voter turnout as a mixed strategy equilibrium: A rational individual will abstain from voting as long as a considerable number of fellow countrymen are expected to participate. Yet, if all other individuals abstain on these grounds, it is rational to cast a vote, because it will then be decisive. For this reason, if all voters are rational, each individual will pursue a mixed strategy of voting and abstaining. This model, though theoretically appealing, does not explain the existence of regular voters – empirical evidence shows contrary to the model's prediction that most individuals do not switch from voting to non-voting. More importantly, voter turnout should be very much lower in equilibrium.

---

[23] Comprehension surveys of the literature on (majority) voting, including the voting paradox, can be found in Struthers and Young (1989), Mueller (1989), and more recently in Aldrich (1997) and Fiorina (1997).

[24] Downs (1957) had a related idea arguing that individuals would vote out of fear that high abstention could put democracy at risk.

[25] See also Barzel and Silberberg (1973) who posit that individuals derive utility from fulfilling their duty as responsible citizens.

From the above argument it is clear that the high level of voter participation cannot be explained by narrowly defined self-interested behavior; rather sociological factors account for the high turnout (Kirchgässner 1980: 428–431, Tollison and Willett 1973). Ashenfelter and Kelley (1975) find that education and a sense of obligation to vote have a significant positive impact on the decision to cast a ballot, whereas indecision on whom to vote for reduces participation significantly.[26] Fiorina (1976) reinterprets the the intrinsic value of the voting act itself d (Riker and Ordeshook 1968), or the utility for fulfilling the citizen's duty (Barzel and Silberberg 1973). He argues that people derive utility from expressing their preferences at the ballot box. What motivates people to participate in voting is not the expectation that they might decide the election in their favor, but rather to express their preferences regardless the inconsequential nature of voting. What looks as mere relabelling of the d term at first sight differs from previous concepts like citizen's duty in that it might explain changes in voter turnout. The stronger the preferences for a certain alternative over the other(s), the higher the utility derived from expressing these preferences and, thus, the more likely participation in the election. Likewise, the higher the costs of voting the smaller the net utility derived from expressing one's preference through voting, the more likely abstention.

In fact, individuals do react to variations of p, b, and c. There is considerable empirical evidence that the "closeness" of the race increases voter turnout (e.g., Barzel and Silberberg 1973, Silberman and Durden 1975, Filer and Kenny 1980, Capron and Kruseman 1988, Cox and Munger 1989, Kirchgässner and Schimmelpfennig 1992).[27] Tollison et al. (1975) demonstrate that information provided by mass media influence the perceived closeness and thereby the turnout. Likewise, Filer and Kenny (1980) find that participation in polls rises with the absolute value of the mean gains resulting from an electoral outcome, whereas increased costs of voting reduce the turnout. Brody and Page (1973) confirm the former result: indifference provokes abstention. The latter result is in accordance with the findings of Riker and Ordeshook (1968), Silver (1973), Ashenfelter and Kelley (1975), and Squire et al. (1987). The costs (and also the benefits) of voting depend, among other things, on

[26] For a survey of empirical studies of voter participation see Mueller (1989: 354–361) and Struthers and Young (1989: esp. tables I and II). Weck-Hannemann's (1990) study of referenda for industry protection in Switzerland supports the view that voter *participation* cannot be explained by pure individual self-interest.

[27] The evidence has not gone unchallenged; see also Foster (1984) and Mueller (1989: 358–360) for a critical review and Grant (1998) for a recent contribution also covering the latest contributions to the controversy.

institutional factors, such as the obligation to register or alternative possibilities for direct legislation through referenda; they significantly influence voter turnout (Jackman 1987, Merrifield 1993).

To summarize, the high *level* of voter turnout cannot be explained by means of a purely self-interested voter, but instead through sociological (and psychological) factors, especially the moral obligation to participate in voting as the duty of a responsible citizen and the utility from voicing individual preferences. The *variations* in voter turnout, however, can be explained reasonably well by the variables entering the economic model of self-interest, i.e., the costs of voting and the expected benefit derived from a favorable outcome. (The latter may yet be a proxy for the intensity of preferences.) Hence, the violation of the second assumption on voter participation as stated on page 72 is not destructive to our results. Instead of having a sharp cut-off value for possible gains, below which individuals will not vote, abstention will become more likely, the more this gain shrinks.[28]

A more serious objection has been raised to the assumption that individuals cast their vote exclusively to raise their utility (i.e., the first assumption mentioned on page 72). Given the insignificance of their vote why should people cast their vote on the basis of their economic interest? The perceived irrelevance of the individual's vote produces a "logical gap between voter action and voter preference" (Brennan and Buchanan 1984: 199), people may or may not vote according to their preferences – they may also simply pull the levers they prefer (p. 194).[29] Therefore, other motivations such as ideological attitudes, party identification, social concern, or simply a misperception of individual's economic interest due to a lack of information (rational ignorance) may lead to "unreasonable," i.e., not exclusively self-interested, casting of votes.[30]

---

[28] As long as abstaining is only correlated with the expected gain from a favorable election outcome, results will be identical to those set out above. If, however, abstention is influenced by other factors which in turn are correlated with the factor endowment *ratio*, the result of majority voting may be biased – provided that individuals vote according to their self-interest. (Ashenfelter and Kelley [1975], for example, found each year of schooling increased the probability to vote by 3 percent. If better educated people tend to have a higher relative capital endowment, this could bias the results.)

[29] Brennan and Buchanan (1984) draw an analogy of voters to spectators of sports events: They care about the outcome of the match and cheer in the stadium or even in front of the TV screen knowing that their behavior does not affect the outcome. Brennan and Pincus (1987) regard voting as a speech-act rather than a choice: in the Carter–Reagan election people in the Western states kept going to the poll even after the Eastern results had been known and had been decisive for the overall outcome. Individuals derive utility from expressing their preferences that need not be purely economic.

[30] There is empirical evidence for the US that the electorate as a whole is relatively good at estimating the various policy positions of candidates or parties (Brady and Sniderman 1985; see also Fiorina 1997).

Kliemt (1986) argues that people are inclined to vote according to their moral sentiments even if those conflict with their economic interests. The reason for this is that the "external costs" in terms of reduced net income will, if at all, accrue to them irrespective of their single voting behavior, whereas they will have to bear the "internal costs" (i.e., psychological costs of acting against one's moral convictions) if they vote against what they perceive as morally good.

This decoupling of individual voting behavior and self-interest on *logical* grounds renders the identification of the forces determining the voting behavior an empirical question. The widespread practice of tactical voting (supporters of small parties vote for candidates of the big parties when representatives are elected by majority voting) shows that people do not simply toss a coin in the polling booth or wish to express their preferences regardless of the election's outcome, as Brennan and Buchanan (1984) seem to suggest (Tsebelis 1986). Instead they try to support a preferred candidate who has a real chance of winning, however small their contribution may be. Another example for tactical voting occurs in countries such as Germany with a constitutional clause laying down that only parties with more than 5 percent may be represented in parliament. Smaller parties are frequently found to "borrow" votes from bigger parties with which they have agreed on a coalition. (This voting behavior may be deemed to make no rational sense, but it describes a real world phenomenon: Voters may vote in their self-interest even if this is individually irrational.)

Not surprisingly, there is some empirical evidence showing that voting behavior is not *exclusively* self-interested (Mueller 1989: 367–369 and the literature cited). Since voter *participation* cannot be explained solely by individual self-interest in a narrow sense, it would be strange if the *actual casting* of the ballot was to be traced back exclusively to this motivation. But there is systematic empirical evidence that people do vote in favor of their economic interest. Holcombe (1980) and Munley (1984) find the outcome of referenda to be consistent with the median voter model. Pommerehne (1987) surveys 14 studies on referenda on tax-financed schooling expenditures in municipalities in the USA and finds that polls on the variation of school expenditures support the view of self-interested voting behavior. Bloom (1979) provides corroborating evidence for a referendum on a tax reform in Massachusetts. (See also McEachern 1978 for a supportive test of the median voter model.) Also Weck-Hannemann (1990) finds that voters do vote in their self-interest – however, not in a deterministic way as assumed in our model (see Holcombe 1989 and Mueller 1989 for further empirical studies). Holcombe (1989: 121) concludes: "In short, there have been a number of empirical tests of the model over the years, all taking very different approaches, and most have found the evidence to be consistent with the model."

3.6.2 Majority voting and the process of policy formation

While the median voter model portrays reality very well in a direct democratic setting, this is less so in a representative democratic context. Nevertheless, Pommerehne and Frey (1976) show that the median income outperformed the mean income in explaining local public expenditures. Analyzing data from 111 Swiss municipalities, Pommerehne (1978) demonstrates that the superiority of median income over the mean income as explanatory variable for local public expenditure is more pronounced in municipalities with direct legislation than for those with representative legislation. The reason for this is the obvious neglect of interest groups' influence in the political process. Due to this omission the explanatory and predictive power of the presented models for representative democracies must be viewed with some caution.

Nevertheless we have deliberately disregarded interest groups in our formal setup for various reasons. First, as we will argue below, the MVM serves as an appropriate benchmark case – it portrays the demand side of the political market for protection from factor mobility, if this market side is atomistic. Second, the existing models on interest groups have shortcomings which, for our context, are at least as grave as those of the MVM. Third, capital controls occur in very different political systems (direct and representative democracies, traditional monarchies and dictatorships, left-wing and right-wing authoritarian states[31]) and in very different institutional environments, even within a class of political regime. This alone makes it impossible to model the political process leading to the imposition of capital controls in a way which is both generally applicable and sufficiently realistic. Hence, we have decided to portray a MVM as a convenient point of departure for more specific analyses of particular groups of countries, in which the prevailing institutional factors can be given explicit consideration.

Without question, interest groups play a major role in Western democracies and the public choice literature has taken account of that. We do not survey the huge literature on interest groups' influence in the political

---

[31] For a political-economic classification of the regimes see Findlay (1990).

process, as comprehensive surveys are readily available,[32] but point out their main shortcomings insofar as they are relevant to our context. To state a major critique at the outset, most of the literature on interest groups either completely ignores the influence of voters on the decision-making process or models it in such a rudimentary fashion that can hardly be regarded appropriate.[33]

In the traditional rent-seeking literature following the seminal papers by Tullock (1967) and Krueger (1974), lobbying activity is only modeled as a strategic interaction of (mostly two) pressure groups. The government reacts mechanically to the lobbying outlays of the interest groups as modeled by a contest success function: it is neither explained *how* the influence is exerted nor what the government optimization calculus might be; voters are disregarded completely.[34] Rent-seeking models of this type might appropriately portray the allocation process of a *given* rent that is too small to affect the whole economy in a perceptible way, but it cannot describe properly the process leading to the design and adoption of a macroeconomic policy. Hence, rent-seeking models will definitely be unsuited to analyze the determination of the overall degree of capital controls; but they may aptly describe the allocation of the scarce foreign exchange or the capital import quota (e.g., license to borrow abroad) once the degree of capital export or import has been decided upon.

A related approach models interest groups' behavior as attempts to influence the policy platform of the candidates rather than their probability to win. Though these models (e.g., Ben-Zion and Eytan 1974, Bental and Ben-Zion 1975, Aranson and Hinich 1979, Welch 1980) acknowledge the existence of elections, they take the candidate's probability of being elected as given and assume rather than explain that

---

[32] Mueller (1989, chapters 11, 13–15), Mitchell and Munger (1991), Potters and van Winden (1994), and the articles collected in Hillman, ed. (1991) and Mueller (1997). For surveys focusing only on rent seeking see footnote 34, for the analysis of the international trade policy see Baldwin (1985), Hillman (1989), Magee *et al.* (1989), Weck-Hannemann (1992b), Magee (1994), and Rodrik (1995). Leidy (1994) surveys the recent literature on trade policy and *prospective* protection.

[33] Nice exceptions are Mayer and Li (1994), Baron (1994), and Grossman and Helpman (1996), to be discussed below.

[34] To be fair it must be noted that the bottom line for these works is the determination of the social loss by rent-seeking activities, given that the rents exist, rather than explaining the amount of rents that are sought – a task which is very satisfactorily accomplished. Examples are Becker (1983), Hillman and Katz (1984), Delorme and Snow (1990), Stephan (1994), and the collection of articles in Buchanan *et al.*, eds. (1980) and Rowley *et al.*, eds. (1988). The rent-seeking literature is surveyed by Tollison (1982, 1997), Brooks and Heijdra (1989), and, very comprehensively, by Nitzan (1994).

campaign contributions alter policy platforms. Again the political process is demand-determined – and a black box.[35]

The above approaches focus on the strategic interaction of interest groups seeking to influence government policy via their financial outlays; they assign the politician a perfectly passive role. Quite opposite to this, the "theory of regulation," pioneered by Stigler (1971) and Peltzman (1976), deals with the politician's optimization calculus. In short, the politician is striving to maximize political support provided by the various interest groups and will therefore design the policy such that political support (and opposition) for this special regulation is balanced at the margin. The influence of interest groups remains largely implicit; it is described by a political support function, which the regulator maximizes: this function contains the interest groups' utilities weighted by the (marginal) political influence they exert. Examples for this approach are Hillman (1982), van Velthoven (1989), van Long and Vousden (1991), and Bommer and Schulze (1999). These models are very helpful in explaining government behavior in response to a shift in exogenous parameters as they show how the regulator spreads windfall gains or losses accruing to one group across society in order to reestablish the political support-maximizing equilibrium. However, since the political process leading to such an equilibrium remains a black box (in particular, the interaction among the relevant interest groups and with the government is not modeled), this approach does not lend itself naturally to the analysis of such a political equilibrium.

Recently, Grossman and Helpman (1994, 1995a,b) and Dixit, Grossman and Helpman (1997) have shed light on the political process that is hidden behind the political support function approach. They apply the common agency approach by Bernheim and Whinston (1986) to the political economy of protection: Organized interest groups announce contribution schedules that map the possible tariff-subsidy vectors to their financial contributions to the incumbent. The incumbent politician

---

[35] "[T]he relevant purpose and impact of political investment is not the election of an unpopular and less desired candidate, but rather the adoption of a less desired policy by a leading and popular candidate" Ben-Zion and Eytan (1974: 9). To be precise, the aforementioned authors do assume that campaign contributions produce additional votes and that candidates deviate from the median voter's policy position in exchange for campaign contributions such that the marginal loss of votes from deviation is equalized by the marginal gain of votes from spending campaign funds. They implicitly assume, however, that these activities do not change the overall probability of election in a significant way and they do not model strategic interaction between candidates. A related approach is by Findlay and Wellisz (1982), who portray interest groups lobbying for and against tariff protection. (Rodrik 1995 terms this the "tariff-formation function approach.")

(potential challengers are disregarded) maximizes the weighted sum of overall contributions and the aggregated welfare, taking the pre-announced schedules into account. While a major merit of Grossman and Helpman's contribution lies in the endogenization of the political weights that the politician attaches to the interest groups involved[36] and in the explanation of the resulting *structure* of protection, it is not entirely clear that the political process functions as the authors posit. In particular, the announcement of complete contribution schedules in advance for all lobbies requires a huge transfer of information. Information problems will presumably be hard to overcome in practice. Moreover, as in the whole political support function approach, electoral competition is only very indirectly modeled.

The interest-group-cum-electoral-competition models represent a far more elaborate approach than the simple political support function approach[37] to analyzing the political process. They are neither completely demand-side determined nor completely supply-side oriented, but model the strategic interaction of both sides of the market, i.e., the interest groups and the candidates for a political office. In this process, campaign contributions as well as the probability of being elected are endogenized: Candidates announce as Stackelberg leaders' policy platforms in order to maximize their (re)election probability; interest groups in turn contribute funds for their favored candidate's campaign according to their stakes, which are a function of the difference in policy platforms. The relative campaign contributions then determine the probability of election. Since all relevant players are completely informed and anticipate accordingly, the game is solved recursively. In contrast to the traditional rent-seeking literature, interest groups influence policy outcomes not directly, but through the probability of election (which depends indirectly on the respective policy announcement). Prominent examples for such models are Brock and Magee (1980), Young and Magee (1986), Hillman and Ursprung (1988), Magee, Brock, and Young (1989), Ursprung (1990, 1991). Though these models are very rich with respect to the strategic aspect they do not exactly explain *how* (relative) campaign contributions

---

[36] There have been earlier attempts to endogenize and assess the power weights of the interest groups; however since this is done in a cooperative context (by means of the Shapley-value, cf. Roth, ed. [1988]) it is not particularly convincing. See for example Aumann and Kurz (1977).

[37] This excludes, of course, the sophistication thereof by Grossman and Helpman.

translate into vote production or into the probability of election.[38] Though it is quite plausible and appealing, the standard contest success function put forward by Tullock (1980) lacks a sound microeconomic foundation. In its basic (and most commonly used) version this function equates the probability of being elected to the fraction of own resources spent in the campaign as a share of total resources spent. Hirshleifer (1989), criticizing the "Tullock-function," makes the probability of winning dependent on the *difference* in the respective efforts and thereby derives different, new equilibria. This demonstrates the sensitivity of results with respect to the contest success function chosen[39] – a sad result, given the lack of theoretical foundation for this function.

The deficiencies described do not at all render these models void; instead it is one of their outstanding merits that they portray the strategic interaction between lobbies with opposing interest and competing candidates. They stress the role of interest groups in the political process and, moreover, acknowledge the importance of elections for the politicians' calculus. However, voters' behavior is only *very* rudimentarily modeled! As described by the "Tullock-function," voters cast their votes in accordance to the (relative) propaganda of the candidates, but not at all according to their economic interest! Elections degenerate to lotteries in which the two candidates buy tickets in the form of concessions to interest groups, and thereby in the form of campaign spendings. The rationale behind this setup is the assumption that the herd of voters is (rationally) uninformed and hence completely manipulable. As we have seen above,

---

[38] A notable exception is Austen-Smith (1987), who shows in a probabilistic voting model with risk-averse and incompletely informed voters how interest groups' contributions may clarify policy positions and thereby increase the number of votes for the advertising candidate. However, he wrongly equates a party's probability of being elected with its expected share of votes. This mistake is removed in Mayer and Li (1994) who provide the microfoundations of the Magee, Brock and Young (1989) model by analyzing tariff setting in a rich probabilistic-voting, specific-factors framework. Their model contains uncertainty of the risk-averse voters about (tariff) policy platforms and uncertainty on part of the candidates about non-policy biases of the electorate. Campaign contributions help to overcome the former uncertainty and hence increase the probability of being elected. Mayer (1993) analyzes tariff lobbying and probabilistic voting in a Heckscher–Ohlin framework.

[39] His class of contest success functions, however, is likewise assumed instead of derived. See also Körber and Kolmar (1995) for a more general treatment. Hirshleifer and Riley (1978) and Hillman and Samet (1987) apply an alternative contest-success function in which the highest outlay gains the rent. Though this rule seems intuitively more appealing it comes about likewise as *deus ex machina* instead of being the result of an optimization process on the part of the politician distributing the rent. Here is scope for future research: The contest-success function itself should result from game-theoretical analysis in which the rent-setter maximizes the contributions received. Hillman and Riley (1989: 36–37) point out briefly that the highest-bidder-gets-it-all rule can be transformed into the Tullock function if a stochastic element is added.

empirical evidence contradicts this extreme assumption! Voters do vote in their self-interest, though not exclusively so, and not in a deterministic fashion; not all of them are completely uninformed.

Once we remove this extreme informational assumption, the consequences for economic modeling become severe. McKelvey and Ordeshook (1985) have shown that "with any positive fraction of informed voters, any equilibrium extracts all available information: all participants – voters and candidates alike – act as if they were fully informed" (p. 55). The reason for this is that uninformed voters, only knowing their ideal point in relation to the society's distribution of ideal points, will gather, from repeated poll and interest group endorsement data, what their position on the issue would be if they had incurred the costs of information. Informed voters reveal their information to the uninformed through the polls and this leads to an informationally stable equilibrium: Candidates, taking this process into account, adopt the position of the median of the entire electorate. The existence of a share of informed voters and the availability of such "low cost data" relating the position of uninformed individuals to those of the informed ones make a strong point in favor of the traditional median voter model applied in this chapter: The uninformed voters behave *as if* they were fully informed.

In a recent paper, Baron (1994) also analyzes electoral competition with both informed and uninformed voters, but assumes, different from McKelvey and Ordeshook (1985), that uninformed voters are manipulable by means of campaign expenditures. He distinguishes two types of policy: first, a *particularistic* policy, which provides benefits to a particular interest group and denies them to non-contributors, but spreads the costs so widely that no opposition is aroused. The second, *collective* policy benefits some interest groups significantly while at the same time imposing significant costs on other interest groups, regardless of whether they have contributed or not. For particularistic policies both candidates will adopt the median position as long as a critical value of uninformed voters is not exceeded. Beyond this value, candidates will increasingly deviate from the median in order to attract campaign contributions with which they can attract more (uninformed) voters than they may lose informed ones. In other words, the median voter model is a good portrayal for particularistic policies at issue if the electorate is relatively well informed. This is even more so in the case of collective policies! The competition for the informed voters dominates and, consequently, both candidates locate themselves in the median position. This result is obtained because both interest groups contribute according to their stakes, which are represented by the difference in the policy platforms. A candidate's movement toward the median position increases his or her votes from the informed voters, but decreases the contributions to *both* candidates. Thus, in equilibrium both candidates adopt the median position and interest groups do not play a role. The existence of interest groups notwithstanding, we are left with the median voter model.

To summarize, the median voter model though having been criticized heavily (see esp. Rowley 1984) establishes a very convenient point of departure for the analysis of the political process in democracies leading to regulation. It is the adequate portrayal if a sufficiently large share of voters is informed or if the uninformed voters link themselves to those that are informed. It is moreover the reduced form of an interest-group-cum-electoral-competition model, if interest groups offset each other's influence as in the case of Baron's collective policies.

The imposition of capital controls is clearly a collective policy in the sense that everybody will be affected and that – depending on the level of control – some individuals will significantly benefit from it whereas others will be significantly hurt. Whether the issue of capital controls will lure interest groups onto the scene, and whether they will have an offsetting influence, depends *inter alia* on the distribution of relative factor endowments and on industry characteristics, as we have seen in section 3.5. It is an achievement of the models presented in the preceding sections that they have identified the parameters determining individuals' interest and thereby an important subset of parameters determining the formation of interest groups. If the scenarios in which the MVM is directly applicable do not prevail, we are left with the task of identifying the strength of the factors that lead to a *bias* in the result.[40] This can only be done on a case-by-case basis, taking institutional factors explicitly into account. At any rate it seems doubtful that any other existing model could establish a likewise appropriate (and general) point of departure, given the short-comings described above.

One qualifying remark, however, must be added. While the MVM may serve as a good yardstick for political systems that are either democratic or have an effective electoral system, politicians in authoritarian systems will operate under very different constraints and therefore other para-digms may become relevant.[41] The Public Choice literature on non-demo-

---

[40] In that case the MVM still serves as a benchmark – as an analogon to the perfect competition models for the political market: "In microeconomics, the competitive model provides the polar case upon which imperfections are added to form more realistic models. In public choice theory, the median voter model can provide a similar polar case of majority rule decision making under ideal 'competitive' conditions" Holcombe (1989: 122).

[41] There are many intermediate systems between democracy and autocracy, in which elections play a major role. For example, Mexico and South Korea are by no means pure democracies, but their presidents have to cope with elected legislatures. Both systems have capital controls in place.

cratic regimes is rather scarce, Tullock (1987a) being a notable exception,[42] and hence not very much will be said here. Though reelection is not an issue for the autocratic ruler his (or her) predominant goal is also to stay in power and prevent this power from being eroded. The major difference between a democratic and an autocratic ruler is that the former has to please the majority (even with the help of interest groups) whereas the latter must please the small number of people who secure or who may effectively jeopardize his (or her) position. These groups tend to be identical (the military, the bureaucracy etc.) considering that general revolutions are relatively rare, although not unheard of, compared to *coups d'états*. If these are the dominant constraints under which an autocratic ruler optimizes *with respect to capital controls*, then the MVM is inappropriate. If, however, the revolution constraint rather than the threat of being toppled by his own people is binding, or if people may erode his (or her) power by emigrating ("voting with the feet") as a consequence of the – lacking? – restrictions on capital mobility leading to wage differentials *vis-à-vis* the neighboring countries, then the MVM may serve as a yardstick. The same holds true if *this* economic policy, the restriction of capital movements, is intended to secure minimum political support by the general public. Still the ruler's discretionary scope will tend to be larger than the one his (or her) democratic counterpart enjoys.

Especially in autocratic regimes, politicians may be able to appropriate in part interest-groups contributions, so that income maximization would be an additional goal, in which case models would have to account for corruption.[43] Formally this has been done only in traditional rent-seeking models (Appelbaum and Katz 1987) and election-cum-interest-group models (Ursprung 1990), which suffer from the described deficiencies.[44] Again, since there is as yet no coherent model for autocracy, we are left with the MVM or, in case the general public has no role to play, with traditional rent-seeking models.[45]

As we hope to have shown, the MVM serves as an appropriate benchmark which is widely applicable, however with necessary caution. It must

---

[42] See also Findlay (1990), Mueller (1989: 271–273), Frey and Eichenberger (1994) and the literature quoted therein.

[43] Corruption is dealt with in Rose-Ackerman (1978); see Shleifer and Vishny (1993) and Kurer (1993) for recent work and a survey of the – scanty – literature.

[44] Note that personal corruption must be distinguished from official corruption. In the former case the politician can appropriate part of the contribution made by the relevant interest groups, after the policy platform has been announced. In the latter case the sequencing is reversed: the interest-groups offer bribes in exchange of the desired policy, cf. Ursprung (1991: 8).

[45] In this case election-cum-interest group models are inappropriate since elections do not take place.

be amended by institutional factors when analyzing a concrete case. But this is all the more so for alternative models. Eventually, it is an empirical question which model portrays best the political process for a given country and a given policy issue. Instead of refining the model of the political sector for various different institutional settings, we have decided to address two shortcomings of the economic sector. In the next chapter we will consider a large country and hence include factor terms of trade effects and we will analyze how the existence of unemployment, a major problem for many economies, alters the results.

4   Extensions: Large open economy and unemployment

4.1 Introduction

This chapter builds on the analysis of the previous chapter by two major issues. First, we analyze to what extent the results derived carry over to the large country case. Second, we allow for unemployment to prevail or to be created through capital exports. It is obvious that unemployment is a major concern in many countries and that capital controls may be adopted to lock in capital in order to enhance employment. We inquire how this motivation fits in with our theoretical framework and how it alters the results derived. Would voters vote for an export of (a part of) their jobs? How tight would the optimal restriction be?

We confine our analysis of these questions to the two-country version of the MacDougall–Kemp model of international capital movements introduced in sections 3.2–3.4 for reasons of simplicity. We have shown in section 3.5 that the basic results carry over to a multi-sectoral specific factors model and must only be amended by industry-specific variables. The reason for this is that owners of the various specific factors all profit from the export of one specific factor, such as certain sector-specific capital, because labor becomes more abundant in all industries. As a consequence, labor is worse off. Owners of different specific factors are not affected to the same extent, but in the same direction, and we have shown in section 3.5 how to account for that. However individuals are affected differently by the regulations as their endowment ratios differ. Because this basic conflict of interest is already portrayed by the MacDougall–Kemp model and the analysis of the two new issues in the specific factors model will not provide any other insights beyond those to be presented, we will concentrate the exposition of our arguments on the MacDougall–Kemp model.

Again, we look at the restriction of capital flows from two perspectives. First, we start with the assumption that either individuals are identical with respect to their economic interests toward capital controls, or that sophisticated (and costless) compensation schemes are effectively implemented, so that losers make up for incurred losses through transfers from gainers. A distributional conflict does not exist. Therefore, voters will vote for the restriction which maximizes the national product.[1] Underlying this concept is the idea of a "benevolent dictator" who kindly maximizes the welfare of "the society as a whole" and achieves a fair distribution by lump-sum transfers. This serves as a benchmark.

Yet, individuals are not equal with respect to their factor endowments, and compensations, if they exist at all, are designed to mitigate some of the worst consequences of a certain policy rather than to fully compensate the losers. Pareto improvements are rare exceptions, not the rule.[2] Because the above assumptions underlying the social welfare approach are not met in reality, a conflict of interests arises between the individuals differently endowed with factors of production. In our second approach we allow individuals to own different amounts of capital and labor and aggregate individual preferences via majority voting. As in chapter 3 we compare optimal tax rates according to both criteria and we compare for each criterion the optimal values for the large economy with and without unemployment with each other and with the value optimal for the small economy.

It turns out that the optimal restrictions are tighter in the case of a large economy due to a positive factor terms of trade effect. They are even tighter if unemployment prevails. As in the previous chapter, individuals' optimal restrictions deviate from the national product-maximizing one according to the individual factor endowment ratio. Individuals relatively well endowed with capital will always favor a less-than-GNP-maximizing restriction and *vice versa*.

This chapter proceeds as follows. In section 4.2 we analyze a large open economy with flexible factor prices. First we show how capital export restrictions affect the national income (section 4.2.1), then we derive the individually optimal restriction and, subsequently, the result of the majority voting (section 4.2.2). The impact of capital export controls in the presence of unemployment is dealt with in section 4.3, in which we proceed in the same steps as in the previous section (subsections 4.3.1–4.3.3). This part of the book will be rounded off with

[1] They still have to decide how to share the overall gain from adopting the optimal – national income maximizing – policy, but there is no disagreement about the level of capital controls as such.

[2] This is the consequence of political support maximization as the predominant motive of politics as explained in section 2.3.

section 4.4, in which a brief summary of the results and some concluding remarks are offered.

4.2 Two-country model with full employment

In what follows we drop the previous assumption of a small open economy and consider the diametrically opposed case of two large open economies. All other things remain equal so that equations (3.1)–(3.8) continue to apply. In particular, it is assumed that the foreign production function is also linear homogeneous, though it need not be identical to the domestic one. The foreign capital stock is likewise fixed and amounts to $\bar{K}^*$.[3] Without loss of generality, we assume that the home country is capital exporting so that the capital stock installed in the foreign country amounts to $K^* + \bar{K}^*$. Now restrictions of capital exports not only lower the domestic interest rate but also raise the foreign interest rate. Equation (3.4) still holds via arbitrage, but r^* varies according to $\partial r^*/\partial K^* < 0$.

Kemp (1964) has demonstrated that from an efficiency point of view there exists an optimal tax t_{opt}^S on capital exports for the home country as a whole which amounts to

$$t_{opt}^S = -\xi^{*-1}\mu^*; \quad \mu^* = \frac{K^*}{\bar{K}^* + K^*}; \quad \xi^{*-1} = \frac{\partial r^*}{\partial K^*}\frac{\bar{K}^* + K^*}{r^*} \tag{4.1}$$

with $\bar{K}^*$ being the capital stock in the foreign country which is derived from internal sources of the foreign country, and hence ξ^{*-1} is the elasticity of the foreign marginal product curve of capital and μ^* the proportion of capital stock that the foreign country has borrowed from the home country. This finding is a result of maximization of total national income (including tax revenue) that ignores redistributional effects. How is the tax that results from majority voting related to this reference point?

4.2.1 Capital export restrictions and the national income

Redistributional effects of an *increase* in capital controls are demonstrated in figure 4.1. The resulting decrease of capital exports affects both the amount of national income and its distribution. The home country's origin is denoted by O and the downward sloping curve MPC depicts the marginal productivity of capital invested at home.

---

[3] The superscript * denotes the foreign country; the home country carries no superscript unless otherwise indicated. Again K^* denotes capital export by the home country; the world capital stock amounts to $\bar{K} + \bar{K}^*$.

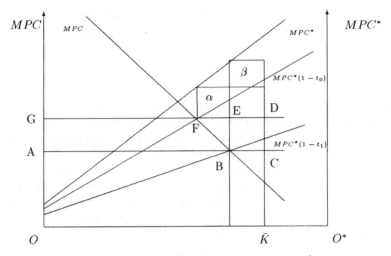

Figure 4.1 Capital export restrictions in a two-country setting

Analogously, O^* denotes the foreign country's origin, MPC^* stands for the gross marginal product, and $MPC^*(1 - t_0)$ and $MPC^*(1 - t_1)$ for the net marginal product from investment in the foreign country before and after the tax increase ($t_0 < t_1$). The national capital inputs are measured from O to the right and from O^* to the left, respectively. The distance $\overline{OK}$ depicts the home country's fixed capital endowment $\bar{K}$ that can be allocated to investment at home and abroad whereas $\overline{O^*\bar{K}}$ depicts the capital stock owned by foreigners, i.e., $\bar{K}^*$. If the tax t is raised from t_0 to t_1 the domestically owned foreign capital stock is reduced from FD to ED and the domestic rental rate of capital is depressed from OG to OA.

Home capital loses (represented by the rectangle ACDG) while domestic labor gains (ABFG); society's change in tax revenue amounts to BCDE $- \alpha + \beta$. "(Home) society's loss" consists of BEF $+ \alpha - \beta$ which can be negative, i.e., "society as a whole" may well be better off after a tax increase. In order to derive the individually optimal tax rates from (3.9) we calculate the variation in national income due to a change in the tax rate by differentiating (3.5) with respect to t

$$
\begin{aligned}
\frac{\partial Y}{\partial t} &= \left[-r^* t - \frac{\partial r^*}{\partial K^*} K^* \right] \frac{\partial K^h}{\partial t} \\
&= [-r^* \mu^* \xi^{*-1} - r^* t] \frac{\partial K^h}{\partial t}.
\end{aligned}
\tag{4.2}
$$

In contrast to a small open economy we do not obtain clear-cut results since national income can move in either direction depending on the relative effects of misallocation and international redistribution.[4]

$$\frac{\partial Y}{\partial t} \gtreqqless 0 \iff t \lesseqqgtr |\xi^{*-1}| \mu^*.$$

Setting equation (4.2) equal to zero and solving it with respect to t gives us the Kemp result, equation (4.1).[5] The larger the home country, i.e., the stronger the influence of domestically owned capital on the foreign country, the more restrictive is the home country's optimal policy.

Furthermore, capital flows react less to a (given) increase in the tax rate because a reduction in the net marginal product of investment abroad triggers off redistribution of capital which not only depresses the marginal product at home but also raises the gross marginal product abroad. This is seen from comparing (3.11) with (4.3)[6]

$$
\begin{aligned}
\frac{\partial K^h}{\partial t} &= -\frac{r^*}{(\partial r/\partial K^h) + (\partial r^*/\partial K^*)(1-t)} \\
&= -\frac{1}{1-t} \frac{1}{\xi^{-1}(1/K^h) + \xi^{*-1}(1/(\bar{K}^* + K^*))}.
\end{aligned}
\tag{4.3}
$$

In other words, for a large economy the adjustment to the new equilibrium of equal net returns is not borne by the domestic factor price variation alone, but shared between domestic and foreign prices. This makes only a smaller relocation of capital necessary compared to the case of a small open economy. Factor rewards are changed less (which can be seen by differentiating (3.4) with respect to t for $\partial r^*/\partial K^* = 0$ and $\partial r^*/\partial K^* < 0$). Moreover, due to a positive factor terms-of-trade effect increased capital controls have a less negative or even positive impact on national income.

4.2.2 Individually optimal restriction and majority voting

For these reasons the individual optimal tax rate (which is assumed to be the sole instrument for achieving individuals' optimal factor price ratio) must be higher the larger the economy in which the individual

---

[4] Note that (3.10) is a special case of (4.2) since for a small open economy $\xi^{*-1} = 0$. This makes capital export restrictions unambiguously unprofitable for the small country case.
[5] Though Kemp (1964) does not analyze uniqueness of t^S_{opt} (note that $-\xi^{*-1}\mu^*$ is an implicit function of t) it is straightforward to show that at least for Cobb–Douglas functions t^S_{opt} is unique.
[6] For $\xi^{*-1} = 0$, (4.3) reduces to (3.11).

lives. This is shown by maximizing (3.8) with respect to t and substituting (4.2) for $\partial Y/\partial t$, in the same manner as in section 3.3. And, indeed, the individually optimal tax rises with $-\mu^*\xi^{*-1}$, which is higher the larger the country is.

$$t^i_{opt} = Y \frac{\partial\Psi^i}{\partial t} \frac{1}{\Psi^i} \frac{1}{r^*} \frac{1}{\partial K^h/\partial t} - \mu^*\xi^{*-1}. \tag{4.4}$$

Moreover, a comparison of (4.4) with (3.13) demonstrates that the sign of t^i_{opt} is not necessarily equal to the sign of $\partial\Psi^i/\partial t$ if $\partial\Psi^i/\partial t < 0$ since $-\mu^*\xi^{*-1} > 0$! It may well be that a person relatively well endowed with capital ($k^i > k$) will support a tax increase though his or her income *share* would diminish. This is due to an international redistribution effect: though his diminished income share from factor ownership gives him a smaller slice after the tax increase, the cake has increased due to a positive factor terms-of-trade effect. The latter effect more than offsets the former as long as $t < t^i_{opt}$. In the small country case ($\xi^{*-1} = 0$), the sign of an individual's optimal tax is equal to the variation of his or her income share from factor ownership, $\partial\Psi^i/\partial t$. For a large economy, we have to take into account the "correction term" $-\xi^{*-1}\mu^*$.

As in the case of the small open economy, the "socially optimal" restriction serves as a reference point. An individual will again favor an even tighter restriction than a benevolent dictator would impose, if (s)he were to exist, if and only if the individual's income share would increase as a consequence of a tax increase. Again, this will take place only if his or her relative capital endowment exceeds the amount of the economy, as we will show below.

It is also easy to see that in this case the variation of Ψ^i due to a tax change is given by (3.14). Other things being equal the individual income share from factor ownership will be altered more by a marginal tax increase the more the individual factor endowment ratio differs from the figure for the economy as a whole. Equations (4.4), (3.14), and (4.1) yield

$$t^i_{opt} = t^S_{opt} + Y \frac{L}{[wL + r\bar{K}](w + rk^i)} \frac{(w'r - r'w)}{r^*\partial K^h/\partial t}(k - k^i). \tag{4.5}$$

This equation demonstrates that individuals will almost always find it profitable to deviate from the "socially optimal" policy and will agree to such a policy if and only if their factor ownership ratio coincides with the economy's capital–labor ratio. Individuals *relatively* well endowed with capital will favor a less restrictive policy or even a policy supporting capital exports, i.e., a negative tax rate t_{opt}^i.[7] Conversely, individuals with less capital relative to their labor endowment than the economy's figure will be in favor of capital export restrictions that still exceed t_{opt}^S. Presumably this group will constitute a majority in at least most of the Western countries.

The assumption of a large open economy does not change individual voting behavior on principle. A person will still support a (further) tax increase if and only if his or her capital–labor ratio falls short of the one for which the existing tax is optimal. This can be shown by calculating $\partial y^i / \partial t$ which yields the identical result as (3.16). Again, individual preferences are single-peaked, and the median voter theorem applies. The final outcome of majority voting, the median voter's optimal tax, will be higher in contrast to a small open economy. That means, if we can presume that small countries have a similar distribution of factor ownership, large countries will pursue a more restrictive policy toward capital exports.

How are the results altered if we allow for the possibility of unemployment? It has been argued frequently that unemployment is due to an insufficiently large capital stock *given* that the labor market is rigid. A prospective capital export would of course aggravate the burden of unemployment.[8] Next, we will investigate how voters change their voting behavior if they anticipate that capital exports create or increase unemployment.

4.3 Capital export and unemployment

When capital exits the domestic economy, labor becomes relatively more abundant, diminishing labor's marginal product. If prices are flexible, labor is paid a lower wage rate; however, if there exists an institutional "floor" value below which the wage rate is not allowed to fall, then

---

[7] In reality such subsidization of capital exports can take a variety of forms (in part not covered by this model): tax exemptions of the parent company for the profits of its foreign subsidiary, loss carryforwards, tax holidays applying to foreign activities, and the like. Moreover, governments can provide guarantees for risks connected to the foreign direct investment.

[8] This view is very appealing and underlined by frequent complaints that capital export would mean the export of jobs. We will analyze it formally in the subsequent section. However, there is an alternative view to this issue: capital exports may instead create employment by allowing foreign countries a loan which will result in (foreign) higher demand for domestic goods (cf. Preiser 1950). If at all, this will work only in a Keynesian situation of a demand-constrained economy, a situation which calls for deficit spending on part of the government rather than for crediting foreign demand which will only partly be effective at home. We will disregard this line of reasoning in the following.

capital export generates unemployment. In this section we show how this "waste" of productive factors will affect national product and income distribution and, thus, individual voting behavior.

4.3.1 Capital controls, unemployment, and national income

One of the most important reasons for persisting unemployment are rigidities in the labor market, especially a downwards inflexibility of the wage rate.[9] Unemployment results if the shadow wage rate falls below the wage floor because the capital–labor ratio has decreased. Such wage floors can be caused by a number of institutional arrangements as for example the level of unemployment benefits or welfare, wage bargaining of unions and employer federations, or legal restrictions on the wage level. These institutional arragements are the result of a political process in the past which we consider exogenous to the problem at hand.[10] Because we want to focus on the interaction between capital mobility, unemployment, and the level of capital controls and not on the microeconomics of the labor market, we use the simplest institutional arrangement that already serves our purpose and assume an exogenously given minimum wage rate $\bar{w}$.

Perfect competition requires that unit cost $b(w, r)$ equals the commodity price (which we have set at unity). This implies that every wage rate is associated with a unique rental rate of capital. Consider a situation of domestic capital export such that the minimum wage rate $\bar{w}$ (and the associated rental rate of capital $\bar{r}$) prevails exactly at the full employment level $\bar{L}$, which we now have to distinguish from the actual level of employment L. Now t is reduced at the margin, leading to a further capital outflow. This is depicted in figure 4.2.

The left-hand panel shows the international capital allocation as known from figure 4.1, whereas in the right-hand panel the unit cost curve for the home country is depicted. A reduction in the tax rate from t_0 to t_1 turns the after-tax marginal product curve from $MPC^*(1 - t_0)$ upwards to $MPC^*(1 - t_1)$. With full flexibility of factor

---

[9] Another aspect, not dealt with in this chapter, is the lack of mobility of labor between sectors. This causes unemployment especially if the rate of structural change is high.

[10] In principle, we could think of a simultaneous determination of the levels of the wage floor and capital controls, but typically institutional arrangements in the domestic labor market are much more persistent than foreign economic policy which reacts to changed economic conditions at home. Therefore, these institutional arrangements have to be considered exogenous to the determination of foreign economic policy such as capital controls.

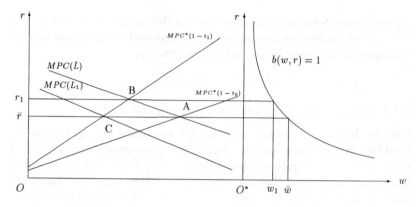

Figure 4.2 Capital export and minimum wage constraint

prices, capital would exit the country to the extent of $\overline{r}A - r_1 B$ according to (4.3), the domestic rental rate of capital would increase by $r_1 - \overline{r}$ (see (3.4)), at the same time the foreign rental rate of capital would diminish due to the influx of capital.[11] The wage rate would be lowered accordingly from $\overline{w}$ to w_1. The equilibrium would be shifted from A to B.

With a rigid price in the domestic labor market and capital remuneration given by the arbitrage condition (3.4), the domestic adjustment is borne by factor movements alone (instead of variations in the quantity of domestically used capital *and* in factor prices).[12] Capital will exit the country until the foreign net-of-tax rate of return has been depressed to $\overline{r}$, the domestic "maximum rental rate." Graphically this is described by the intersection between $MPC^*(1 - t_1)$ and the horizontal line going through $r = \overline{r}$, i.e., point C in figure 4.2. The outflow of capital will generate unemployment as the shadow price of labor falls short of the minimum wage ($w_1 < \overline{w}$). Labor is displaced to such an extent that its marginal product equals the minimum wage. With a linear homogeneous production function this implies that at the boundary factor prices ($\overline{w}, \overline{r}$) the factor input ratio must be same for all employment levels. In figure 4.2 this is represented by a downward shift of the MPC curve so that the new marginal product curve of capital runs through point C.

We turn to the formal presentation of the argument made above. Starting from a situation of full employment at $\overline{w}, \overline{r}$ we calculate the

---

[11] This could be shown graphically by depicting the gross rental rate of capital for the foreign country which lies unshifted above $MPC^* (1 - t_1)$.

[12] Of course *gross* rental abroad will change, but the domestic rental $\overline{r}$ is given by $b(\overline{w}, \overline{r}) = 1$.

capital outflow resulting from marginal decrease in the tax rate t. From the total differential of (3.4) and the fact that $dr = 0$ follows

$$\frac{\partial K^*}{\partial t} = \frac{1}{1-t}(\bar{K}^* + K^*)\xi^*.$$ (4.6)

Reformulating (4.6)

$$\frac{\partial K^h}{\partial t} = -\frac{1}{1-t}\left[\frac{\xi^{*-1}}{\bar{K}^* + K^*}\right]^{-1} = -\frac{\partial K^*}{\partial t}$$ (4.7)

shows that the capital flow owing to a tax variation is higher in the case of a binding minimum wage restriction than if factor prices are flexible, which is given by the subsequent equation (4.8), also derived from (3.4)

$$\frac{\partial K^h}{\partial t} = \frac{1}{1-t}\left[\frac{\xi^{*-1}}{\bar{K}^* + K^*} - \frac{\xi^{-1}}{K^h}\right]^{-1} = -\frac{\partial K^*}{\partial t}.$$ (4.8)

It is well known that for linear homogeneous production functions factors' marginal products depend on the factor input ratio. Hence, for $w = \bar{w}$ the outflow of capital must be accompanied by a proportional reduction of employment to ensure a constant factor input ratio

$$\frac{\partial L}{\partial t} = \frac{L}{K^h}\frac{\partial K^h}{\partial t} = -\frac{L}{K^h}\frac{\partial K^*}{\partial t}.$$ (4.9)

In other words: capital export triggers off unemployment or aggravates this problem. (Note that L stands for the actual employment; it equals $\bar{L}$ only if the shadow price of labor coincides with, or exceeds, the minimum wage rate.) We assume that the individual has no a priori information about the distribution of (reduced) labor and thus takes the expected average wage rate as the relevant decision variable.[13] The expected wage rate $w^e = \bar{w}\frac{L}{\bar{L}}$ and the wage bill $(\bar{w}L)$ then change accordingly

$$\frac{\partial w^e}{\partial t} = -\bar{w}\frac{1}{1-t}\frac{1}{K^h}\frac{L}{\bar{L}}\xi^*(\bar{K}^* + K^*)$$ (4.10)

$$= \frac{1}{\bar{L}}\frac{\partial(\bar{w}L)}{\partial t} \quad > 0 \,\forall\, \xi^* \neq 0.$$ (4.11)

---

[13] One could argue that an individual knows whether he or she is employed and thus earns $\bar{w}L^i$ or he or she earns nothing. At this stage of the analysis, however, we are concerned with a fictitious situation optimal for an individual i who does not know who will be laid off. The veil of uncertainty and the assumption of risk-neutrality justify the above formulation.

Clearly, labor will be worse off if the restriction on capital exports is lessened whereas capital remains unaffected since $\bar{r}$ constitutes a ceiling on the rental rate of capital;[14] a reduction in the tax rate will eventually only affect the geographical distribution of domestic capital but not its net return.

Still we cannot exclude that national income is increased due to a positive factor terms-of-trade effect that more than offsets labor's loss. For this purpose we calculate the variation of national income due to a marginal change in the tax rate for $w = \bar{w}$ (and any level of employment $0 \le L \le \bar{L}$). National income is given by

$$Y = \bar{w}L + \bar{r}K^h + r^*K^* \tag{4.12}$$

and so is the first derivation of Y with respect to t[15]

$$\frac{\partial Y}{\partial t} = \underbrace{-\bar{w}\frac{L}{K^h}\xi^*\frac{1}{1-t}(\bar{K}^*+K^*)}_{\text{employment effect} \ge 0} + \underbrace{tr^*\xi^*\frac{1}{1-t}(\bar{K}^*+K^*)}_{\text{capital reallocation} \le 0} + \underbrace{\frac{1}{1-t}r^*K^*}_{\substack{\text{change in earnings} \\ \text{from existing FDI} \ge 0}}.$$

$$\tag{4.13}$$

Rearranged, this yields

$$\frac{\partial Y}{\partial t} = \left[\bar{w}\frac{L}{K^h} - tr^* - \mu^*\xi^{*-1}r^*\right]\frac{\partial K^h}{\partial t}. \tag{4.14}$$

Setting (4.14) equal to zero and solving for t yields the optimal tax on earnings from exported capital for the case of a binding minimum wage constraint as follows

$$t^S_{opt^{ue}} = \bar{w}\frac{L}{K^h}\frac{1}{r^*} - \mu^*\xi^{*-1}. \tag{4.15}$$

Comparing (4.15) with (4.1) shows that the "socially optimal" degree of restricting capital exports is higher in the presence of unemployment than if labor is fully employed. This makes good intuitive sense, because in the former case a curbing of capital exports not only improves the terms of factor trade at the expense of capital misallocation, but also prevents a loss of employment and, thus, of output.

A priori it is not possible to determine whether t^S_{opt} from (4.1) or $t^S_{opt^{ue}}$ from (4.15) applies. This depends on the production functions and the minimum wage rate, the latter of which in turn determines $\bar{r}$ via the

---

[14] Capital may earn higher gross profits abroad, but capital will exit the home country until the arbitrage condition holds thereby equating the after-tax rates of return.
[15] FDI stands for foreign direct investment, K^*.

condition $b(w, r) = b(\bar{w}, \bar{r}) = 1$ ("unit costs equal price"). Equation (4.15) applies if

$$\bar{r} < r^* + r^* \mu^* \xi^{*-1}. \tag{4.16}$$

So far we have shown that for a large open economy there exists a positive restriction of capital exports that maximizes national income. If factor prices are flexible, capital exports benefit capital whereas labor is worse off. If factor markets are rigid, capital exports lead to a proportional reduction of employment and the optimal restriction is tighter than in the case of full employment. Labor suffers from capital export while capital does not profit since the improvement in the factor terms of trade is siphoned off via the tax. However (increased) tax proceeds are redistributed according to Ψ^i which favors capital, see pages 98–99.

Again, this result of "social welfare" maximization[16] serves as a reference point, to which we relate individually optimal policies. The distributional conflict is clear – labor loses from a tax reduction as it becomes increasingly unemployed, capital gains from a higher share of the tax proceeds at the expense of labor, and the factor terms-of-trade effect shows in changing tax proceeds. Starting from a prohibitive tax on capital export proceeds, a reduction of the tax first increases national income and then leads to a declining income beyond $t^S_{opt^{ue}}$, which might be still be optimal for capital-rich individuals as their shares of the tax proceeds increase. Next we analyze how this distributional conflict between factors translates into individual optimal policies when unemployment prevails and individuals have different endowments.

4.3.2 Individual's optimal tax rate

We calculate an individual's optimal tax rate by totally differentiating (3.8) with respect to t and substituting (4.14)

$$t^i_{opt^{ue}} = \left[Y \frac{\partial \Psi^i}{\partial t} \frac{1}{\Psi^i} \frac{1}{r^*} \frac{1}{\partial K^h / \partial t} \right] - \mu^* \xi^{*-1} + \bar{w} \frac{L}{K^h} \frac{1}{r^*}. \tag{4.17}$$

As in the case of full employment, the individually optimal tax rate is linked to the "socially optimal" tax rate in the following way

[16] Social welfare is only maximized *given* that a minimum wage exists. A truly benevolent dictator would remove the minimum wage in the first place.

$$t^i_{opt^{ue}} = t^S_{opt^{ue}} + Y \frac{1}{\Psi^i} \frac{1}{r^*} \frac{1}{\partial K^h/\partial t} \frac{\partial \Psi^i}{\partial t}. \tag{4.18}$$

The direction of the deviation from this reference point $t^S_{opt^{ue}}$ is given by the sign of $\partial \Psi/\partial t$. In case of unemployment we have to be aware that in (3.7) w has to be interpreted as the expected wage rate $w^e = \bar{w}L/\bar{L}$ and that factor prices are fixed. Equation (3.7) can thus be written in this context as

$$\Psi^i = \frac{w^e L^i + \bar{r}K^i}{\bar{w}L + \bar{r}\bar{K}}, \tag{4.19}$$

where we have allowed for individually differing amounts of labor endowment $L^i \geq 1$. Again, Ψ^i is a net-of-tax concept and has now to be interpreted as *expected* factor income share. Totally differentiating (4.19) with respect to t and considering (4.10) yields

$$\frac{\partial \Psi^i}{\partial t} = \frac{L^i L}{[\bar{w}L + \bar{r}\bar{K}]^2 K^h} \bar{r}\bar{w} \frac{\partial K^h}{\partial t} \{k - k^i\}, \tag{4.20}$$

and hence the sign of (4.20) is equal to the sign of $(k - k^i)$. This result is evident: Capital cannot increase its after-tax earnings by lessening the restrictions on capital exports, and labor will be worse off because of increased unemployment. Since tax proceeds are redistributed to individuals according to their income share from factor ownership, a person relatively scarcely endowed with capital, $k^i < k$, will encounter a decline in his or her share due to a reduction in the tax rate. A person relatively well endowed with capital will experience an increase of his or her part of the tax proceeds, which may still increase individual income even if the absolute amount of tax proceeds falls; hence, $t^i_{opt^{ue}} < t^S_{opt^{ue}}$ cannot be excluded a priori

$$t^i_{opt^{ue}} = t^S_{opt^{ue}} + \frac{YLL^i\bar{r}\bar{w}}{[\bar{r}\bar{K} + \bar{w}L](w^e L^i + \bar{r}K^i)K^h r^*} (k - k^i). \tag{4.21}$$

To summarize, in the case of a binding minimum wage constraint, the optimal degree of curbing capital outflow from an efficiency point of view is tighter than if full employment prevails and so is the individually optimal restriction. This latter restriction differs from the former reference point of a nation's product-maximizing restraint depending on the relative factor endowment ratio. Those well endowed with capital per unit of labor (relative to the capital–labor endowment ratio of the whole economy) favor a less-restrictive policy, whereas the opposite applies to persons relatively poorly endowed with capital.[17]

4.3.3 Voting on capital export restrictions

To establish voting behavior in the case of unemployment consider again an individual i who votes on the variation of an *existing* tax t that is optimal for a factor endowment ratio k^j and implies the existence of unemployment, i.e., $t = t^j_{opt^{ue}}$ (cf. equation (4.17)). The basic result derived in sections 3.4 and 4.2.2 continues to be valid if unemployment prevails. From (3.9), (4.14), and (4.20) and the substitution of $t^j_{opt^{ue}}$ from equation (4.21) for t, we obtain after some standard transformations

$$\frac{\partial y^i}{\partial t} = Y \frac{L}{K^h} L^i L^j \frac{\bar{r}\bar{w}(\bar{r}k + w^e)}{[\bar{w}L + \bar{r}\bar{K}]^2 (w^e L^j + \bar{r}K^j)} \frac{\partial K^h}{\partial t} (k^j - k^i). \qquad (4.22)$$

Save for $(k^j - k^i)$ all terms are necessarily positive so that

$$\text{sign}\left(\frac{\partial y^i}{\partial t}\bigg|_{t = t^j_{opt}}\right) = \text{sign}(k^j - k^i).$$

Since this relationship holds for all values of k^j it implies that preferences are single-peaked and the median voter theorem applies. The results of section 4.2 basically carry over to the case of unemployment: An unrestricted capital outflow neither would be optimal in the traditional sense of social welfare maximization, nor would it be backed by self-interested voters with different factor endowments if they could vote on the capital export restrictions. The prevalance of unemployment, however, makes both the benevolent dictator's and the median voter's optimal tax rate tighter. If individual preferences were aggregated through majority voting, the resulting restriction would be tighter than the national-income-maximizing one – provided that factor ownership distribution was skewed to the right.[18] This is typically so at least for Western industrialized economies. Capital exports might nevertheless

---

[17] Note that capital cannot increase its reward directly through more lenient capital export restrictions as its return is fixed at $\bar{r}$; its gain from less restrictive policies is due to the redistribution scheme for the tax proceeds. But even if tax proceeds were distributed equally independent of factor ownership ratios, a distributional conflict would arise. A switch from restriction at which full employment prevails to a national income-maximizing restriction with unemployment would benefit all individuals, but hurt those relatively well endowed with labor more than proportionally, such that they might lose on net terms. This case could also be analyzed along the lines set out here.

[18] That means that the median voter's factor ownership ratio $k^m < k$.

create domestic unemployment under both a social-welfare-maximizing government and under majority voting.

4.4 Conclusion

In this part of the book, which we now conclude, we have demonstrated the motives that make governments impose controls on international capital flows. Not surprisingly, it has turned out that capital controls serve as a useful tool for support-maximizing politicians to exert their power to their own ends.

A closer look at the traditional reasons for restricting capital flows has failed to explain the persistence and widespread prevalence of these controls. Instead of healing distortions, capital controls have only created further distortions. Though second-best arguments in favor of capital controls cannot be refuted on logical grounds, we have discarded them as being empirically irrelevant and as being inconsistent with methodological individualism. Since there is no such creature as a welfare-maximizing benevolent dictator and economic theory tells us that *all* individuals are predominantly motivated by self interest, it seems inconsistent to assume self-interested people in the marketplace, but to explain policy outcomes by politicians' striving for efficiency and the maximization of the nation's welfare.

Instead, capital controls have been shown to be a convenient (and often inevitable) device for politicians seeking to increase government's revenue. They safeguard revenue extraction from financial repression and inflation tax, and they enable the treasury to tax mobile capital more heavily. Moreover, capital import controls make the sustained success of trade protection only possible as they prevent the created rents from being eroded by foreign investment. Increased revenue enhances the scope of possible redistribution, which, as we have argued, translates into increased political support (if appropriately designed). Capital controls have also an immediate impact on income distribution. Not only do they allow for other distributions of the tax burden, but they also influence factor prices as relative factor endowments can be managed with their help. Capital controls please politicians – and bureaucrats – as we have shown.

The deeper reason behind all that is that the controls reestablish the national politicians' monopoly power of coercion, which they have lost in a world of increasing international interdependence. Individuals can escape government authority to a growing extent: they can relocate their wealth in order to escape taxation or to gain higher profits, they can opt against national money when it becomes too unattractive, and so forth. By constraining individuals' behavior through capital controls, politicians lift a constraint on their policy space, imposed by international arbitrage possibilities. This is a basic insight this part of the book wants to convey.

How much discretionary scope politicians actually enjoy depends of course on the political-economic system, whereby politicians' behavior is constrained. If the policy outcome is demand determined, the median voter model is appropriate to portray the political process. We have extensively reviewed the critique levelled against the median voter model and surveyed existing alternative modeling strategies. It turns out that alternative families of models suffer from shortcomings which are, for our context, at least as severe as those encountered by the median voter model. Moreover, we have argued that basic objections to the latter are either exaggerated or unjustified. Given the difficulty in modeling the political process both generally applicable and sufficiently realistic and taking into account that the control of capital flows is a macroeconomic policy, the benefits of which do not accrue only to a small particularistic interest, we have decided to adopt the median voter model. We believe it serves, for our problem, as the best yardstick available.

As for the economic model, we have allowed for individually different factor endowments and applied both the classical MacDougall–Kemp and the Specific Factors model. The results are as follows. Individual's interest concerning capital controls is determined by his or her factor endowment *ratio*. An individual with a lower (higher) capital–labor endowment ratio than the economy as a whole will favor a tighter (less tight) restriction on capital exports than the national-product-maximizing restriction. Since preferences are single peaked, it is the median voter's optimal capital control that is finally adopted. It will only coincidentally be identical to the welfare-maximizing capital control (which is zero for a small economy), but probably tighter; if relative factor ownership distribution is skewed to the right. Individuals' optimal restrictions are tighter if the country is large owing to a positive factor terms-of-trade effect. They are even tighter if unemployment is an issue, as capital outflow creates or aggravates "the export of jobs." Nevertheless, it may still be optimal, in the traditional sense as well as for the median voter's interest, to encounter a loss in employment and production to some extent – depending on the level of the minimum wage – because of a positive factor terms-of-trade effect.

In the preceding analysis we have determined the individually optimal restriction on capital outflow. It was derived under the presupposition that the restriction will be enforced and, therefore, that capital is either locked in the country or the stipulated tax must be paid by all capital-exporting individuals alike (or the equivalent quantitative restriction is effectively enforced and licenses are auctioned off). Of course, this individually optimal tax rate so derived is not really the best possible solution for the individual. Ideally, (s)he would like to export all of his/her capital unrestrictedly in order to earn higher returns abroad and completely lock in all other capital, thereby benefiting from a high domestic wage rate. But even though this will be possible only in theory every individual has an incentive to evade controls, whatever the existing level of capital controls, because the rest of the world is offering a higher return. At the same time (s)he hopes that nobody else will escape the control, because that would reduce his or her wage rate, the return to his or her only domestically retained factor endowment. It is a classical prisoner's dilemma.

We thus have a situation in which every individual wants to evade the controls; but given that this is only partly possible for reasons to be explained, the individual seeks a level of capital controls that is optimal for him or her after the expected evasion has been taken into account. In other words, the individual's optimal restriction will be determined by the endowments ratio of the factors that *effectively remain* located in the home country or are subject to a controlled (i.e., taxed) capital outflow. To the extent that capital-rich individuals can escape controls better than others, the distribution relative factor endowments have to be corrected for that. This would make the level of capital controls stricter (but not more effective) than if evasion did not take place. This line of reasoning implies that individuals take into account the extent of their evasion when forming their preferences. Evasion becomes relevant to the formation of capital controls. Hence, we will study it.

Part II
The evasion of capital controls

5 Ways and means to escape the restrictions

5.1 Introduction

Restrictions necessarily bear the seeds of their own erosion: Since they deny individuals the opportunity to carry out transactions which would be profitable, they inevitably establish an incentive to be circumvented. Maintaining an interest rate differential *vis-à-vis* the rest of the world is a distinct political economic goal of a rational government imposing capital controls, as we have seen in part I of this book. At the same time it is rational for economic agents to arbitrage away the unexploited profit opportunities by evading or avoiding these controls. The government anticipates these activities and tries to enforce its regulations by closing loopholes in the law, auditing potential evaders, and making evasion subject to severe punishment. The evader in turn seeks to escape detection.

How do the two rational players interact? What parameters are decisive for the degree of control enforcement? What are the optimal strategies for the two players? These issues are the concern of the second part of this book. In the subsequent chapters we present two models which for the first time incorporate the inevitable interdepence of evading taxes, tariffs, and capital controls, and which at the same time explicitly model the evader's individual profit maximization as well as the authorities' revenue-maximizing enforcement policy. By analytically deriving the optimization behavior of the two players and in accounting for additional important factors relevant to the evader's decision, we believe we have built more comprehensive and realistic models than those existing for individual decision-making on evading capital controls.

There are a variety of ways to escape capital controls (cf. Walter 1987). Capital export restrictions, for instance, can be evaded via the international payment mechanism, if bank officials and the monitoring civil servants are bribed. Illicit capital exports can furthermore be effected through hidden cash movements, i.e., by taking foreign or domestic currency, traveler's checks, cashier checks, or other bearer-type monetary instruments out of the country. The export of small and easily moveable stores of value, such as jewellery, precious stones and metals, or art objects, serves the same purpose. These documents and objects are typically brought out of a country by residents or foreign tourists and business travelers, through legal ports of entry. A different channel lies in smuggling in the original sense – merchandise is loaded aboard ships at remote points along the coastline or driven across the border at unobserved locations in the dead of the night. The sale proceeds are then deposited outside the domestic jurisdiction in clear violation of the repatriation requirement for export proceeds, which goes together with capital export restrictions. All these practices involve the risk of (physical) search, confiscation, and punishment.[1]

We do not consider such practices here; not that they are insignificant (Walter 1987: 113), but they do not represent a theoretical challenge. Risk-neutral individuals will smuggle as long as the expected marginal return from evading the controls exceeds the expected marginal costs (punishment plus confiscation multiplied by the probability of being caught in addition to the costs of camouflage); authorities will expand investigative activity until their marginal return equals their marginal costs. Since the parameters involved are basically exogenous,[2] there is not very much to be said from a theoretical perspective about the optimal degree of this kind of smuggling. Furthermore, these situations, although special cases, are part of the analytical problem we are concerned with: The *faking of foreign trade prices*. Because, as we will show below, the probability of being caught faking invoices depends on the degree of misdeclaration, the evader faces a portfolio choice problem: By deciding the degree of misdeclaration (s)he determines the risk and the expected yield of his or her assets simultaneously, out of a range of possible combinations. The decision whether or not to smuggle in the pure sense as described above (i.e., to physically conceal the documents or goods exported) boils down to the choice between a risky and a non-risky asset, with no possibility to select a combination of the two assets. Analytically speaking, that choice problem is more restricted than the

---

[1] Travelers are typically restrained in the amount of domestic and/or foreign exchange they may take out of a country in order to prevent illegal capital export.

[2] These are for the evader the tax and tariff/subsidies rates, the interest rate differential, the increased transportation costs due to the clandestine character of this transaction, the probability of detection, and the severity of punishment. The authorities additionally have to consider the costs of investigation and the likelihood that monitoring the border prevents successful smuggling – either through deterrence or through capture.

one we are analyzing. Thus, the tools that will be developed can also serve to analyze these simpler problems.

Our formulation of the problem is not only less restrictive analytically, it shows also a broader coverage of real-life situations.[3] Misdeclaration of international trade prices can still take place, if the authorities are in a position to effectively prevent smuggling in the original sense: Imported or exported goods cannot physically be disguised, if for example ports of entry (harbors, airports, etc.) are few, easily controllable, and cannot be circumvented. This is especially true for bulk cargos and other spacious commodities.

Our analysis also covers smuggling through misdeclaration of the traded volume, instead of prices, if the detection probability is a function of the ratio of smuggled goods to legal trade, an assumption often made in the literature on smuggling (e.g., Pitt 1981, 1984, Martin and Panagariya 1984, Thursby et al. 1991). The legally traded volume serves to camouflage the "extra" quantity imported or exported.

In order to enforce capital controls, the administration must monopolize the domestic supply of, and demand for, foreign exchange. Export proceeds have to be repatriated and surrendered to the central bank in exchange for domestic currency at the official exchange rate, while foreign exchange is allocated to importers through a licensing procedure. These licenses could be granted in accordance with a development plan, ranking import priorities, but they will also be distributed in response to rent-seeking activities of various kinds.[4] Even if current account transactions are unrestricted and therefore foreign exchange earnings need not be surrendered, the government will have to monitor trade closely to prevent the illegal flow of capital.[5]

In the case of capital export restrictions, illegal capital export can be effected through overinvoicing of imports and underinvoicing of exports. In the former instance the importer remits foreign exchange in excess of the amount due and deposits the difference abroad at a higher interest rate; in the latter instance the exporter surrenders less than the actual proceeds and deposits the surplus abroad, or sells it on the black market at a premium. A countervailing effect arises from an import tariff or an export subsidy: overdeclaration of imports increases tariff liabilities while

---

[3] According to a study on illegal trade practices in southeast Asia by Naya and Morgan (1969). "The major channel for illegal transfer of wealth between countries is underinvoicing of exports and overinvoicing of imports" (p. 132 of the reprint in Bhagwati, ed. 1974).

[4] Surveys on rent seeking are Buchanan et al., eds. (1980), Tollison (1997); in the international context see esp. Hillman (1989); see also page 78.

[5] This is a rare case: restrictions on capital transaction go hand in hand with the requirement to repatriate and to surrender export proceeds, see IMF (1997), esp. pp. 946–952.

underdeclaration of exports reduces transfers from the state. This trade-off has been noted by Bhagwati (1967) and Alleyne (1987) but not analytically treated. In addition to these effects, the overdeclaration of imports reduces the stated profits and thereby income taxes are evaded. The reason for this is the requirement to consistently state transaction prices to both customs and tax authorities because these branches of the finance minister's portfolio cooperate. To this effect it does not matter whether imports are used as inputs or resold on the domestic market – the declared profit margin is reduced. The same holds true for the under-declaration of exports. In other words, faking international trade prices affects tax payments, tariffs or subsidies, and capital controls at the same time! This has not hitherto been noted in the literature that we will now sketch.

5.2 The existing literature

Our focus is on the optimal misdeclaration of the individual importer and exporter in the presence of an optimizing investigative behavior on the part of the authorities. We are not concerned with social welfare considerations, because we do not view the government and the bureaucracy as benevolent dictators maximizing society's welfare, but as pursuing their own self-interest. This has become clear in part I of this book. Instead, we want to adequately portray the interaction of the cheater and the one cheated. This will also give us some clues as to how the government may approach its enforcement deficiencies, by altering those magnitudes which are treated parametrically in the subsequent models and in the literature. From this perspective we will briefly review the existing literature on the evasion of capital controls, on smuggling, and on tax evasion.

At the outset of this section it must be noted that a body of empirical literature on trade misinvoicing has developed. Building on Morgenstern's (1950) seminal contribution, Bhagwati (1964) and Naya and Morgan (1969) have developed an estimation technique, which relies on partner-country-data comparisons, making adjustments for transportation costs and insurance fees. (Imports are usually measured on cif terms, while the trading partner country's exports are reported on a fob basis.)

Bhagwati (1964) shows, for disaggregated Turkish trade data of 1960–1961, that the high import tariffs led to large-scale underinvoicing of imports even in spite of capital controls. Importers saved more money through reduced duties than they had to spend on the black market for the foreign exchange in addition to the officially allocated amount, neccessary to pay the true import bill. Naya and Morgan (1969) find significant underinvoicing of exports and overinvoicing of imports for Southeast Asian countries; however, the picture differs considerably from country to country. This is not surprising, as the decision whether or not over- or underinvoicing of imports is optimal depends on taxes, the interest rate differential, and the tariff: the former are country specific, whereas the latter is item specific.[6] Besides, the countries' enforcement policies may differ in effectiveness, so that the degree of faking is unequal. We will analyze this in detail in chapters 6 and 7. Bhagwati *et al.* (1974) find that underinvoicing of exports was used much more as vehicle of illicit capital exports than overinvoicing of imports, since high tariffs reduced the profits of overinvoicing and made sometimes even underinvoicing profitable. This is confirmed by Bhagwati (1978: 72–76) who also shows that faking occurs predominantly with manufactured goods, because their invoices are more easily faked thanks to the differentiated character of the goods involved. A correct reference price is harder to establish.[7] Sheikh (1973) observes substantial underinvoicing of imports for Pakistan. Gulati (1987) using 1970–1985 trade data for Latin American countries finds simultaneous underinvoicing of imports (to evade tariffs and quotas) and underinvoicing of exports (to export capital), so that the net effect on the capital account was less clear-cut than in Bhagwati *et al.* (1974) – in many instances even resulting in capital import. Cumby and Levich (1987) review other concepts to measure capital flight; they also find lacking correspondence between partner countries' trading data, which they attribute partly to data problems and partly to misdeclaration of international trade.[8]

Although there is a huge body of literature on macro-monetary models which analyzes the effects of capital controls on macroeconomic variables, the analysis of llegal activities linked to these restrictions has received relatively limited, though not insignificant, attention. For the most part, these studies have focused on the determination of the black market exchange rate, like Dornbusch *et al.* (1983) and Phylaktis (1992), or the effectiveness of macroeconomic policies in the presence of black

---

[6] All these partner-country-data comparisons suffer from an inevitable deficiency: Since tariffs are commodity specific, it may be optimal to overinvoice one import, but underinvoice another so that huge misdeclaration may cancel out in the aggregate.

[7] Bhagwati (1978: 67–70) also reports on country studies in the framework of an NBER project on exchange control regimes that found widespread faking of trade declarations.

[8] Concept and measurement of capital flight is analyzed *inter alia* in Lessard and Williamson, eds. (1987) and in Varman (1989). There is also an extensive body of literature on the empirical analysis of pure smuggling, e.g., Richter (1970), Simkin (1970), Cooper (1974), Dercon and Ayalew (1995).

markets and restrictions on current and capital account transactions, like Bhandari and Decaluwe (1986) and Pinto (1991). This literature is concerned with the welfare implications of the controls and the triggered black markets, not with the determinants of individual fraudulent behavior. Further prominent examples are Greenwood and Kimbrough (1987), Macedo (1982), and Nowak (1984). Huizinga (1991) to a certain extent bridges the gap between the smuggling literature and monetary models, by explaining the coexistence of legal and illegal trade through risk aversion, and by determining the black market premium in a setting of multiple exchange rates. Though helpful for the understanding of the influence of capital controls (and thus black markets) on variables like real exchange rates, inflation, etc., these works provide little insight into the individual trader's evasion decision, i.e., into the microeconomic foundation of the phenomenon, the macroeconomic effects of which they are investigating.

A second strand of literature closely related to our problem is the economic analysis of smuggling pioneered by Bhagwati and Hansen (1973). They show that smuggling may be welfare decreasing since it involves real resource costs; however, the coexistence of legal trade and smuggling is tied to very restrictive assumptions. The per-unit real resources devoured by the smuggling must exactly equal the tariff rate! Sheikh (1974), introducing a third non-traded good, shows that smuggling can be welfare improving. Pitt (1984), Martin and Panagariya (1984), and Thursby et al. (1991) explain the observed coexistence of legal and illegal trade by the fact that legal trade cloaks smuggling activities. Pitt (1984) provides reasons for the perceived positive disparity of the tariff-inclusive legal import price and the domestic price and shows that this is welfare enhancing. These results are confirmed by Deardorff and Stolper (1990), who analyze smuggling in Africa from an institutional and theoretical perspective. Dercon and Ayalew (1995) test the Bhagwati and Hansen (1973) model against the model by Pitt (1981). Bhagwati and Hansen assume that the probability of detection is a function only of the quantity smuggled with the consequence that in equilibrium smuggling and official sales generate the same marginal net revenue. Therefore, total output depends only on the official price, not the black market price; the black market premium determines merely the fraction sold in this market. Contrastingly, Pitt assumes that official sales cloak sales on parallel markets and, therefore, total output reacts to price movements in the official and the parallel market. In their study on coffee smuggling in Ethopia they find a supply response to changes in the black market price which supports Pitt's model.

The fact that overdeclaration of imports may be optimal was not realized by authors dealing with smuggling and related phenomena. This highlights the general perspective that is taken by this literature: Smuggling is seen as a reaction to trade taxes rather than foreign exchange restrictions. Only very few authors try to incorporate the black market into their models; Bhagwati (1964, 1967) and Sheikh (1976) raise this point, but do not formalize the interdependence of black markets and illegal trade. In Pitt (1984) the black market is a mere reflection of illegal trade: both imports and exports are underinvoiced to reduce import and export taxes. The non-declared export proceeds are channeled on to the black market. They finance the difference between the actual and the underinvoiced import value, for which no foreign exchange is officially allocated. Though being a path-breaking work, it disregards capital controls as a motive for smuggling and hence ignores the possibility of overinvoicing of imports.

Alleyne (1987), following up Martin and Panagariya (1984) in his modeling strategy, reverses this "one-sided" perspective and views exchange control regulations as motive for smuggling. Alleyne's work and all other literature on the economic approach to smuggling suffers from two major deficiencies. First, they do not consider the effects of smuggling on the income tax liabilities. For example, smuggled inputs cannot be filled in on the tax return, and therefore tax liabilities are higher than in the case of legal trade. Instead, smuggling is regarded as an isolated problem, not linked to other economic activities. This is a shortcoming we will address in our approach. Second, the probability of being caught remains exogenous; it does not stem from an explicit optimization behavior on the side of the authorities. The evader optimizes, but the government does not.

Moreover, the prevailing approach to the analysis of smuggling (Johnson 1972, Bhagwati and Hansen 1973, Sheikh 1974, 1977, 1989, Falvey 1978, Ray 1978, Pitt 1981, Deardorff and Stolper 1990 among others) does not explain the degree of smuggling, but is concerned with its welfare implications. The choice problem of an individual firm is not addressed. With the exception of Martin and Panagariya (1984),[9] Alleyne (1987), and Norton (1988), the literature on smuggling lacks a rigorous microeconomic treatment in the sense that the outcome of smug-

---

[9] Their model is essentially a refinement of Pitt's (1981) work. They use the same detection function, and are concerned with explaining the price disparity between domestic and tariff-inclusive world market price and analyzing the welfare implications of smuggling.

gling is *ex ante* uncertain and that, consequently, its degree depends upon the authorities' law enforcement policy.[10]

As we have pointed out earlier and will discuss below in depth, misinvoicing of international trade involves the evasion of either trade taxes, or income taxes, or both; therefore it is obvious that our anaysis is closely linked to the tax evasion literature. The foundations of this literature have been laid by the seminal paper of Allingham and Sandmo (1972), which has inspired a fast growing body of theoretical and empirical work. These studies analyze the determinants and the optimal degree of the individual tax evasion.[11] The only clear-cut relationships are the negative relationship between tax evasion and penalty, and that between the former and the probability of detection. The influences of tax rate and real income are ambiguous – they depend on assumptions about (absolute and relative) risk aversion or risk neutrality. Various aspects of tax evasion have been studied, such as the interdependence between tax evasion and tax avoidance pointed out by Seldon *et al.* (1979), Cross and Shaw (1982), Geeroms and Wilmots (1985), Alm (1988), Alm and McCallin (1990), Cowell (1990a), and others, or the effect of tax evasion on labor supply (Sandmo 1981, Cowell 1985b), and on the tax revenue (Waud 1986, 1988). The tax evasion literature comprises a huge number of theoretical papers, numerous empirical studies, and also a few tax evasion experiments. The vast majority focus on income tax evasion and the United States, but there are also empirical studies on other countries (e.g., Pommerehne and Weck-Hannemann 1996) as well as contributions on the evasion of indirect taxes, e.g., Virmani (1989), Gordon (1990), Cremer and Gahvari (1993). In the context of this book, it is impossible to review the huge body of tax evasion literature adequately. Yet it is not necessary, rather we can limit our overview to some relevant key features, because there are excellent surveys readily

[10] For example, Bhagwati and Hansen (1973) regard smuggling as risk free, but attribute special resource costs to it. Sheikh (1974, 1977) assumes that a firm faces constant risk costs per unit, thereby leaving the individual level of smuggling indeterminate. Pitt (1981) does not *explicitly* model risk either, though he introduces a smuggling function that relates the volume of illegal trade to the volume of legal trade. Hence, contrary to Sheikh (1974, 1977), Pitt (1981, 1984) as well as Martin and Panagariya (1984) relate positively the risk of being caught to the *ratio* of illegal to legal trade, and not to the *level* of smuggling. Sheikh (1989) is the first to explicitly introduce risk aversion; however, the government's investigative activities are only very crudely modeled: a fixed amount is spent per time period in an unspecified way, regardless of the consequences (p. 1943, fn. 16). Authorities' behavior does not depend on the evaders' behavior.

[11] *Inter alia*: Srinivasan (1973), Kolm (1973), Yitzhaki (1974, 1987), Nayak (1978), Pencavel (1979), Fishburn (1979, 1981), Koskela (1983), Kesselmann (1988), Alm and McCallin (1990), Cowell (1990a), Yaniv (1990b), Macho-Stadler and Pérez-Castrillo (1997), and Chander and Wilde (1998).

available such as Cowell (1985a), Pyle (1991), and Myles (1995: chapter 12). A very extensive and excellent analysis of evasion, including an extremely comprehensive review of the literature, is found in Cowell (1990b); Andreoni *et al.* (1998) provide an excellent, comprehensive, and up-to-date overview.

The economic approach to tax evasion which emphasizes the individual decision problem rather than being exclusively concerned with the welfare implications of tax evasion, provides us with useful insights equally relevant to the issue we are analyzing.[12] The sound microeconomic foundation of this approach serves as the basis for the analysis of our problem: by amending it with the neccessary features it portrays the evasion of capital controls through misinvoicing of international trade.

With the exception of Schulze (1994) and Genser and Schulze (1997), there is not a single paper that links individual evasion of income taxes to the evasion of any other kind of taxes, like trade taxes (tariffs, subsidies) or indirect taxes.[13] It is obvious, when authorities cross-check tax declarations for different sorts of taxes, that such a link exists; and in fact such cross-checking of import declarations (on which duties are based) and income tax returns is a well-established practice for some countries.[14] Schulze (1994) has established that link, but analyzes only misdeclaration of import prices, not of export prices, which is the more prominent vehicle for evading capital controls. The reason for this confinement is that capital controls are disregarded altogether, thereby making import price faking the more relevant case. As we have noted on page 108, the literature on smuggling has not established this link either, although it is evident: smuggled inputs cannot be declared to the tax authorities, declared costs are thereby inevitably reduced, and thus taxable declared profits are increased. Smuggled exports reduce declared profits and thereby taxes.

---

[12] Of course there are also quite a few articles on the effect of tax evasion on social welfare, e.g., Weiss (1976), Stiglitz (1982), Yitzhaki (1987), Spicer (1990).

[13] The literature on transfer pricing notes taxes and tariffs as determinants for price-setting behavior of multinational firms (Horst 1971); however the focus is quite different. For example, it disregards completely the possibility of detection and is therefore not in line with the economic approach to crime and punishment.

Gordon and Bo Nielsen (1997) analyze the optimal mix of VAT and cash-flow income tax given that individuals evade both taxes through cross-border shopping and income shifting to abroad. They do not, however, analyze the interdependence of evasion activities from the perspective of the individual evader.

[14] For instance in the Federal Republic of Germany this cooperation between tax authorities and the Customs is required once misdeclaration has been revealed by either authority; cf. footnote 8 on p. 122.

On the other hand, the interdependence between capital controls evasion and tariff evasion has insufficiently been dealt with (cf. p. 108). It lacks a rigorous analytical treatment. Needless to say that also the interdependence between the evasion of capital controls and tax evasion has not been noted so far. These missing links establish the point of departure for our approach, which we will present now.

5.3 Our approach

Using two related models, we will analyze the optimal invoicing behavior of an importer and an exporter, respectively, who are confronted with income tax, capital controls, and possibly trade taxes, and who are facing an optimal investigation on the part of the authorities. Our approach takes into account the existing interdependences relevant to the individual firm's decision to evade capital controls. Thereby we also connect smuggling and tax evasion, two well-investigated aspects of the economic approach to crime and punishment, pioneered by Becker and Stigler.[15]

The following two models do not only portray the choice problem facing a potential evader of capital controls more realistically, they may also contribute to each separate body of literature they connect. They give that part of the smuggling literature that focuses on the individual choice whether or not to smuggle, and if so how much to smuggle, a sounder theoretical foundation than it currently enjoys. The effects of smuggling on tax liabilities simply cannot be neglected! It contributes to the tax evasion literature by analyzing a channel to evade taxes on business income by misinvoicing traded inputs. Last but not least, we provide a first theoretical analysis of the optimal evasion of capital controls, which up to now has lacked a thorough analytical treatment incorporating all relevant decision parameters.

For the analysis of the tradeoff between capital controls, income taxes, and trade taxes, various combinations are conceivable. We could consider restrictions on capital exports or on capital imports, and we could assume tariffs or subsidies on exports as well as on imports, or free trade. We have chosen *capital export restrictions* because they are more prevalent (see IMF 1997).[16] In the case of import misdeclaration we assume an

---

[15] Becker (1968), Stigler (1970), Becker and Stigler (1974). See also Stern (1978) for a critique on Becker (1968).

[16] The picture has not been that clear-cut for the OECD countries in the 25 years up to 1990; but since the member countries agreed to major expansions of their liberalization obligations on capital movements in May 1989, the remaining capital controls in both directions are negligible. See OECD (1990, esp. diagram 1 on p. 64).

import tariff to be in place. This is done because import tariffs are more common, for countries imposing capital controls, than import subsidies or free trade (IMF 1997). The exporter faces neither an export subsidy nor an export tax. This is realistic for a wide variety of commodities and a large number of countries. Besides, the analysis of an export subsidy would run parallel to that of an import tariff: both instruments have a countervailing effect to that of tax liabilities in case of misinvoicing. For example, overdeclaration of imports reduces income taxes, but increases duties. The analysis of an export tax or an import subsidy in turn does not enrich the theoretical analysis: Trade-related payments react in the same direction as the income tax. The underdeclaration of exports reduces income taxes along with the export taxes; the overdeclaration of imports reduces income taxes and simultaneously increases import subsidies. More importantly, the lack of an export subsidy or an import tariff alters authorities' investigative behavior. Hence, any other conceivable case can be solved with the analytical tools developed for the two cases analyzed. We briefly sketch these two cases.

We model an importer of an intermediate product facing both an *ad valorem* tariff and an income tax. The firm declares the same import price to both the customs and the tax authorities. Authorities audit so as to maximize revenue. As a result, the probability of auditing depends on the declared price of the imported good. The firm in turn maximizes its profits with respect to the declared price. It turns out that it is optimal for the firm either to *under*state the import price or to *over*state it, or even to be honest – depending on the relative magnitudes of tax and tariff rates and the gain from illicitly exporting capital. Since taxes are levied on after-tariff profits, underdeclaration reduces tariff liabilities and *simultaneously* increases tax liabilities; for overdeclaration the case is reverse. Overdeclaration of import prices results in an illicit capital export, whereas underdeclaring forces the importer to resort to the black market and to buy foreign exchange at a premium. The extent of misdeclaration of the import price, and hence the extent of evasion of capital controls, hinges solely on the probability of detection and the penalty. The extent of tax and tariff evasion, however, is additionally determined by the tax and tariff rates; it may even be negative.

This model shows how the government can induce honest declaration by setting tax and tariff rates appropriately (for a given interest arbitrage gain from exporting capital). All the authorities have to do is to check the consistency (but not the correctness) of separate declarations. Even if relative rates can only be manipulated within certain bounds, due to some political constraint, the government can limit its overall loss from evasion of capital controls through increased tax and tariff revenue, or reinforce capital controls at the expense of revenue by requiring that taxable objects be declared consistently. This gives the government an additional edge in tackling evasion other than the traditional tools of auditing and punishment.

For the exporter, who is not granted export subsidies, only underdeclaration comes into consideration whatever the tax rate is: taxes are reduced and an illicit capital export is effected. Since the authorities take into account that overdeclaration will unambiguously make them better off, in terms both of revenue and of enforcement of the capital controls, they will now investigate only supposed underinvoicing. As a result of this, the possibility of multiple equilibria cannot be excluded a priori.

Revenue-maximizing auditing behavior of the authorities[17] results in a likelihood of detection that is a strictly increasing function of the amount of misdeclaration.[18] This crucial result is derived under rather general assumptions in a qualitative response model of government investigative behavior.[19] That the detection function is derived from an optimization calculus makes our approach different from many other contributions to the tax evasion literature. Either a fixed probability of detection is assumed (*Inter alia* Nayak 1978, Crane and Nourzad 1985, Cowell and Gordon 1988, Gordon 1990, Huizinga 1991) or a variable detection probability depends – unrealistically – on magnitudes that are unobservable for the authorities, such as true income (Srinivasan 1973) or the ratio of undeclared income to true income (Koskela 1983). This is true also for the smuggling literature, in which the probability of being caught depends either on the level of smuggling (Sheikh 1974, 1977, 1989) or on the ratio of the smuggled quantity to the one legally traded. Such assumptions obviously ignore the interaction between taxpayers/potential evaders and authorities; it is simply suboptimal to treat all individuals alike.

---

[17] Quite a few authors have analyzed optimal auditing and punishment under the assumption of a social welfare-maximizing government: Kolm (1973), Srinivasan (1973), Fishburn (1979), Kemp and Ng (1979), Polinski and Shavell (1979), Sandmo (1981). In contrast, the approach taken here is in line with Niskanen (1971), who argues that utility-maximizing bureaucrats will seek to maximize their budgets. This is in accordance with a number of studies, which assume revenue maximization of the revenue-raising arm of the government, cf. Andreoni *et al.* (1998).

[18] As noted above in the export case only underdeclaration is investigated and therefore the probability of detection is a strictly decreasing function of the declared price and reaches zero at the true price.

[19] I am grateful to Gerd Ronning for inspiring me to study authorities' investigation behavior in a threshold model.

There has been a growing body of literature, in which the auditing probability depends on individual taxpayer's decisions. The first were Allingham and Sandmo (1972) who assume that authorities group taxpayers according to their profession and audit higher declared income with diminishing probabilities.[20] Landsberger and Meilijson (1982) and Greenberg (1984) make investigation probability contingent on past information (such as possible conviction), but disregard the current information the taxpayer supplies to the authorities, i.e., the declared income. Reinganum and Wilde (1985, 1986), Graetz *et al.* (1986), and Cremer *et al.* (1990) explicitly model the optimization problem of both the taxpayer and the authority. Chander and Wilde (1998) analyze the interplay of optimal enforcement (auditing and penalties) and optimal taxation, i.e., the government has three instruments at its disposal. All these contributions are only concerned with income tax evasion.

These approaches are appealing, because it is apparent that not only the evasion, but also the investigative behavior stems from an optimization of rational economic agents. We follow this logic in our model: the probability of investigation is not imposed exogenously but depends on the *signal*, i.e., the declared price that the individual firm gives to the authorities. This has intuitive appeal: the more "unrealistic" a price seems to be to the authorities, the higher the probability of detecting evasion activity. Obviously, a greater deviation from the true price is more likely to arouse suspicion and will make detection easier. Moreover, we give special attention to the fact that investigation does not necessarily lead to detection and conviction – a fact that (though commonly known) has not been incorporated into formal analyses so far.[21]

Some qualifying remarks seem appropriate. First, we do not deal with the welfare implications of tax and tariff evasion. Instead, we focus on the individual decision-making process of authorities and the evader who faces an avenue for a combined tax and tariff evasion, but from opposite sides. Second, we exclude the possibility that tariff payments could be reduced by misstating the nature of the goods so that a lower/higher tariff rate would apply.[22] From a theoretical perspective, this form of misde-

---

[20] They assume in an extension of their basic model that authorities have "some ideas about normal incomes in the various professions" (p. 331) and audit with a different probability function for each profession, which depends negatively on the declared income. However, this function is exogenous and does not stem from an explicit optimization calculation.
[21] It has been incorporated into empirical analyses though as "detection controlled estimation." See Feinstein (1990) and the literature cited in Andreoni *et al.* (1998: 849–850).
[22] For a related analysis in the context of tax evasion (income source misreporting for the case of differential taxation) see Yaniv (1990a), for smuggling see Cooper (1974).

claration is closely related to the form of misdeclaration which we are concerned with. If misdeclaration of the quality of the goods traded does not entail any misdeclaration of the value, it is simply smuggling and does not include any illicit capital movement. This is not our concern. If however a different quality entails the declaration of a different price, we have the same situation as before – declaration of a higher quality of the imported goods increases tariff liabilities, reduces income tax liabilities, and results in an illegal capital export. Since this analysis runs parallel to the one to be presented in the subsequent chapters we need not deal with it explicitly.[23] Furthermore, our analysis ignores the fact that additional public goods can be financed out of tax and tariff revenues paid by the firm considered. This is justified on the grounds that a single firm considers overall tax and customs revenue as given, because the number of taxable entities is huge; its contribution to the financing of the public goods from which it profits is therefore negligible.[24]

The remainder of part II is organized as follows. Chapter 6 deals with the misdeclaration of imported inputs in four steps: first, we model optimal investigation activity for cross-checking authorities; second, we derive optimal evasion activity for individuals who take authorities' behavior into account and we look, third, at the comparative-static properties of the solution. The last section offers policy considerations. Export misinvoicing is the subject of chapter 7. At the outset we sketch the differences to the case of import misdeclaration, then derive the different detection function stemming from the same optimization rationale, and subsequently characterize the solution. Comparative statics and policy reflections round off this analysis. Proofs and lengthy derivations of functional forms are relegated to appendices B.1–B.3. As before, a synopsis of the notation used in this part is given in appendix A.2.

---

[23] The only difference may be that there are only a discrete number of qualities, whereas the price can almost be continuously varied.
[24] The relation between public goods provision and tax evasion has been analyzed by Kolm (1973), Cowell and Gordon (1988), and Falkinger (1991).

6 Misinvoicing international trade: Imports

We analyze the case of capital export restrictions targeted at keeping domestic interest rates at a low level and assume consequently that the world interest rate level exceeds the domestic one. This interest rate differential constitutes an incentive to evade capital controls and to realize arbitrage gains.

One of the most prominent and most important avenues for doing so is the misinvoicing of international trade transactions. Such misinvoicing will have implications for the effectiveness of capital controls (this is analyzed empirically in part III), but it will also affect the tax payments and possibly the duties of the evader. In this chapter we study misdeclaration of import prices. This activity will always affect tax and tariff payments, but will result in an illicit capital export only if imported inputs are overinvoiced. The importer is granted the foreign exchange necessary to pay the imports at the declared price, but he or she uses only part of it to actually pay the imports and transfers the difference to a "safe haven," thereby realizing the arbitrage gain. When considering overdeclaration, the importer must weigh the arbitrage gain and the reduced tax payments (owing to a diminished tax base) against increased tariff payments. It may turn out that evading capital controls becomes an unprofitable venture; instead, underdeclaration may increase the expected net profit.

The questions which this chapter answers are the following: Under what parameter constellations of tax and tariff rates and the interest rate differential does the importer overdeclare or underdeclare and to what extent? What is the authorities' optimal investigative behavior and how does it translate into conviction? Lastly, in which way does different government behavior (probability of detection, punishment, restrictiveness of capital controls, alteration of relative tax and tariff rates) influence the importer's optimal choice?

We proceed as follows. Section 6.1 derives the probability of detection as a function of the declared price in two steps. First, the authorities' investigative behavior as a consequence of revenue maximization is analyzed; second, it is discussed how investigation translates into conviction. Subsequently, the optimal misdeclaration of a profit-maximizing firm is derived in the presence of auditing and punishment. Section 6.3 contains comparative-static results. Finally, section 6.4 summarizes the results and offers policy conclusions.

6.1 Investigation and detection

The firm under consideration imports an intermediate good, which is needed to produce the finished product x. Of course this will not be the only input the firm uses, but we assume for simplicity that it is the only one *imported*.[1] The firm pays a (*t*rue) price, p^t, for the intermediate good to the foreign supplier, but *d*eclares a different price p^d to the tax, customs, *and* exchange control authorities. The assumption that the declared price is identical for tax authorities, the Customs, and the authority enforcing the capital controls (usually a branch of the ministry of finance or the central bank)[2] is crucial for the analysis, because it links the illicit realization of arbitrage gains, tax evasion, and tariff evasion. Otherwise the importer would understate the import price at the customs to save duties, overstate it in his or her tax return to reduce taxable profits and overstate it to the exchange control authorities to obtain more foreign exchange than needed to pay for the import.

In almost every country imposing capital controls there is some cooperation between the control of trade administered by the Customs and the foreign exchange control, but the intensity of cooperation differs sizeably from country to country (Swidrowski 1975: 19–21). On the other hand, tax authorities and the Customs closely cooperate in a number of countries. Legal obligation to cooperate or a unified administration will foster the exchange of information or joint investigations.[3] However, one goal of this paper is to demonstrate that such a cooperation is a useful instrument for the authorities in their attempt to curb overall evasion.

[1] To allow for more than one imported input would simply mean replicating the analysis.
[2] Though institutional regulations have differed considerably across countries, there is almost always some division of administrative power between a central exchange control administration and authorized banks or agents. The central control power is often delegated from the ministry of finance to the central bank, which establishes a special department for the administration of the controls (Swidrowski 1975: 23).
[3] For example in Germany both authorities belong to the Minister of Finance's portfolio and are legally obliged to cooperate. This is laid down in §§6, 116 Abgabenordnung, the German Fiscal Code; cf. also footnote 8 on p. 122.

Therefore, we make this assumption even if for some countries it does not describe the current practice.

The tariff on imports is levied *ad valorem* with a constant rate of τ ($\tau \geq 0$); and income is taxed at the fixed rate t ($1 > t > 0$). Overdeclaration of the import price, if undetected, will increase tariff payments while simultaneously reducing tax liabilities, whereas for underdeclaration the case is reversed. The arbitrage gain depends on the interest rate differential, looked upon as exogenous in this part (in contrast to part I) and the amount of overdeclaration. This is justified because we want to study individual evasion behavior, for which tax and tariff rates are given. Whether over- or underdeclaration is optimal depends on the relative tax and tariff rates and the arbitrage gain per currency unit evaded, as we will see in section 6.2. Since the importer takes authorities' auditing into account we first analyze the optimal degree of investigation, which will turn out to depend on the declared price p^d. We postulate that this declared price cannot fall below zero or rise beyond the domestic price of the finished product P, which is known to the authorities: $p^d \in [0; P]$.[4]

For clarity of exposition the notation used is summarized in appendix A.2 on page 218.

6.1.1 Informational structure and investigation

Economic theory of politics argues that bureaucrats seek to maximize their own discretionary budget (Niskanen 1971). Moreover, they will enforce regulations like capital controls in such a way that they secure their own discretionary scope and importance. We share the basic behavioral postulate of public choice theory that man is a self interested, rational utility maximizer – regardless of whether (s)he is an economic agent, a politician, or a bureaucrat – and assume, consequently, that authorities examine tax declarations, applications for foreign exchange, and customs documents in order to increase their net revenue and to keep evasion of capital controls within narrow bands. There is some empirical evidence supporting this hypothesis (Wertz 1979) – as opposed to a social welfare-maximizing government as presumed by many authors dealing with tax evasion (see footnote 17 on p. 116).[5] Authorities expand their

---

[4] It is assumed that tax liabilities cannot become negative; in other words losses are not even in part borne by the government.

[5] Even if one assumed the government to maximize social welfare, it would still be reasonable to assume that the revenue raising arm of the government maximizes revenue when auditing individuals or firms, given its auditing budget provided by the government; see Andreoni (1998: section 7.1) on this.

investigation activities as long as the expected marginal gain exceeds the marginal cost of investigation.[6] This in turn leads to an investigation activity that depends on the extent of misdeclaration. Many authors dealing with evasion have assumed fixed probabilities of detection.[7] Obviously, it is much more realistic to assume that a large misdeclaration will more likely be investigated than just a slight deviation from the true price. We will derive this next from an optimizing government behavior.

In the following we do not distinguish between customs investigation service, the investigation branch of the ministry of finance, and the investigative body of the central bank. In many countries these are different authorities, auditing independently. However, this does not invalidate our analysis: All we need to assume is that once one authority detects misdeclaration it automatically informs the other authorities. This is realistic for a number of countries,[8] it is desirable for the others, as we will show (cf. p. 120). In an environment with more comprising regulations cooperation tends to be even more important since the possibilities and incentives to evade controls are higher.

Officials do not know the true import price p^t with certainty (otherwise evasion could never be successful),[9] but they have (a priori) a density function of the latent variable $\tilde{p}^t$, $q(\tilde{p}^t)$ attaching the true import price the highest probability. (The tilde indicates the random variable – from the standpoint of the authorities.) In other words, government officials do

---

[6] In this context tax and tariff rates are looked upon as exogenous because we consider the revenue raising arm of the bureaucracy as being distinct from the government as an actor in the political market for protectionism and for determining the tax rate, respectively. Parameters t, τ are predetermined by the legislator as a result of a political market process. The political economy of taxation is analyzed by Brennan and Buchanan (1980) and Hettich and Winer (1990, 1997). By the same token the restrictiveness of capital (export) controls, as measured by the interest rate differential is given for the investigating authorities: As we have shown in part I, it is also determined by the political market. In section 6.3 we will however analyze how results vary with changing values for t, τ.

[7] For example, Nayak (1978), Crane and Nourzad (1985), Cowell and Gordon (1988), Gordon (1990).

[8] For tax search and customs investigation this applies to a lot of countries not restricting capital flows. In Germany, companies are checked regularly by tax authorities, with a lower frequency for smaller firms (Tipke and Lang 1996; section 22, IV). A regulation issued by the Ministry of Finance requires exchange of information between tax and customs authorities and explicitly gives overinvoicing of imports as an example for a relevant offense (Blumers et al. 1997: 122ff).

[9] They do not permanently follow the price fluctuations on world markets for all import goods, but they will analyze the particular market if a stated price has aroused their suspicion. For differentiated products (especially services like consulting, management contracts) it *may* be particularly hard to assess a "normal" price since the product may be firmspecific or even transactionspecific. Thus, it is very plausible to assume that authorities do not *know* the true import price a priori, but have a reasonable idea about what it could be.

not have a systematic misperception of the true price p^t, but are facing uncertainty.[10] Clearly, this density function depends on the quality of the imported good: the more homogeneous the good and the better established the world market for it, the lower will be the variance of $q(\tilde{p}^t)$.

Let us assume that $q(\tilde{p}^t)$, depicted in figure 6.1, has the following properties:

1 $q(\tilde{p}^t)$ is continuous and defined on $[0, P]$.

2 $q(\tilde{p}^t)$ is twice continuously differentiable and strictly concave for $\tilde{p}^t \in (\tilde{p}^t_l, \tilde{p}^t_u)$ with $dq(p^t)/d\tilde{p}^t = q'(p^t) = 0$. That means that the modus of the distribution coincides with the actual (true) import price p^t.

3 $q(\tilde{p}^t) = 0$ for $\tilde{p}^t \notin (\tilde{p}^t_l, \tilde{p}^t_u)$.

Note that symmetry concerning the vertical axis at p^t (i.e., $p^t = P - p^t$) is not required. It is understood that other classes of functions are also conceivable, e.g., bell-shaped functions. One special case would be the normal probability distribution, however in a truncated version since the domain of the function is bounded.[11] Adopting this class of functions would not change the subsequent analysis fundamentally. Since there is no a priori information about the knowledge of the authorities and since requirements for strict concavity and differentiability of $q(\tilde{p}^t)$ within $(\tilde{p}^t_l, \tilde{p}^t_u)$ are rather general, assumption 2 is justifiable.

The authorities observe the declared price p^d. Given this price p^d, the extent of misdeclaration $M = p^d - \tilde{p}^t$ is also a random variable with the same properties as $\tilde{p}^t$ due to the linear transformation of $q(\tilde{p}^t)$. Authorities investigate *under*declaration as well as *over*declaration, the reason for this being that, for example, overdeclaration raises the tariff revenue but undermines the effectiveness of capital controls while simultaneously reducing the tax revenue.[12] In practice, investigative activities may be split between various government agencies: customs officials look for possible underdeclaration whereas tax auditors and the authority enforcing the capital controls (finance ministry or central bank) investigate possible overdeclaration of imports. Each agency will start investigating a case when the suspected amount of misdeclaration warrants the

---

10 Moreover, authorities do not expect everybody to cheat on them – for instance about two thirds of all income taxpayers in the US intended to pay their taxes correctly (Andreoni *et al.* 1998: 820). This figure need not carry over to our case, but it is clear that not everybody intends to evade controls; social norms, guilt, and the fear of shame may prevent people from evading. We will take up this point on page 154.

11 From the following analysis it can be deduced that a bell-shaped function $q(\tilde{p}^t)$ would result in an inverted bell-shaped investigation function. This would parallel the standard probit analysis. For further reference see Ronning (1991).

12 As we will see in section 6.2, the net effect depends on the relative tax and tariff rates.

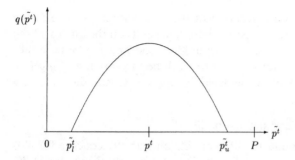

Figure 6.1 Density function of $\tilde{p}^t$

auditing outlays. As soon as one agency has initiated an investigation, the different agencies cooperate. (In the following therefore we will not distinguish between various agencies.) If the absolute value of misdeclaration falls short of a critical value a, investigation is not rewarding because the costs of investigation exceed the expected gain from detection, including the gain made by the prevention of undermining capital controls. a is determined by the investigation technology and the efficiency of the legal system. Hence, it follows that authorities' probability of investigation must be identical with the probability that $\mid M \mid = \mid p^d - \tilde{p}^t \mid \geq a$.[13]

The probability that investigation is not rewarding, i.e., $-a \leq M \leq a$ depends on the the declared price p^d. With $Q(\tilde{p}^t)$ being a primitive of $q(\tilde{p}^t)$ this probability is given by

$$\text{prob}(M \leq a) - \text{prob}(M \leq -a) = \text{prob}(\tilde{p}^t \geq p^d - a) - \text{prob}(\tilde{p}^t \geq p^d + a)$$

$$= 1 - \int_{-\infty}^{p^d - a} q(\tilde{p}^t)\, dp^d - 1 + \int_{-\infty}^{p^d + a} q(\tilde{p}^t)\, dp^d$$

$$= Q(p^d + a) - Q(p^d - a). \tag{6.1}$$

The probability that authorities do investigate is correspondingly

$$i(p^d) = 1 - Q(p^d + a) + Q(p^d - a). \tag{6.2}$$

---

[13] Investigation need not imply that evasion is uncovered with certainty. The economic calculation focuses on expected detection. Consequently, a is not only determined by the costs of investigation, the tax and tariff rate, which link the evaded amount to the extent of misdeclaration, and by the – political – costs of undermining the capital controls; it is also influenced by the probability that investigation produces detection. This probability in turn depends on the amount of misdeclaration, since a huge over- or underdeclaration will be proved more easily than a small one.

For convenience we make a further assumption on $q(\tilde{p}^t)$:

4 $\tilde{p}_l^t \le a$, and $\tilde{p}_u^t \ge P - a$, i.e., the regions in which p^t occurs with zero-probability are limited from the bounds of the domain of $q(\tilde{p}^t)$ by the critical value a.

Assumption 4 is not indispensable, it is made to ensure strict convexity of $i(p^d)$ for $p^d \ne p^t$. It can be shown that for $p^d \in [0, P]$

$$i(p^d) = 1 \quad \text{if} \quad \begin{cases} p^d \le \tilde{p}_l^t - a \\ p^d \ge \tilde{p}_u^t + a. \end{cases}$$

In other words, if assumption 4 was removed the probability of investigation would reach unity for some $p^d \in (0, P)$.

The derivation of the investigation function is illustrated in figure 6.2. The vertical difference between the two functions $1 - Q(p^d - a)$ and $1 - Q(p^d + a)$ represents the probability that for a given p^d authorities do *not* investigate (i.e., $1 - i(p^d)$). This strictly concave function is depicted by a solid line. The dotted graph depicts the investigation function $i(p^d)$.

From (6.1), (6.2), and assumptions 1–3 on $q(\tilde{p}^t)$ it follows that $i(p^d)$ is a strictly convex function with the vertex $(p^t, i(p^t))$.

6.1.2 Detection and conviction

An investigation does not bring conviction with certainty. First, evasion must be discovered. This is more likely the greater the difference between the true and the stated price, because small over- or underinvoicing can be explained by (unobservable) price fluctuations, special discounts or surcharges, and the like. Even if in the course of an investigation authorities find a reference price for the imported product on the world market, they may falsely trace back a small price differential to legal transaction-specific costs or benefits. This probability of misinterpretation, however, will diminish with rising price differentials and the deal will become more suspicious.

Second, in order to prove the evasion and to convict the importer, authorities have to collect evidence with probative force and to charge him or her. Then, proceedings against the importer must be instigated. Scrutiny and legal proceedings incur costs so that it makes sense to dismiss the case if the expected gain falls short of the costs.[14] The expected

---

[14] For instance, under German law a case can be dismissed on its merits according to section 398 AO (Abgabenordnung, i.e., German Fiscal Code).

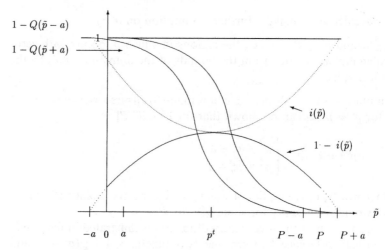

Figure 6.2 Derivation of the investigation function $i(p^d)$

gain consists of the evaded tax and tariff liabilities plus penalty, on the one hand, and the avoided (political) costs of undermining the capital controls, on the other hand, both being multiplied with the probability of condemnation. Obviously the expected gain rises with an increasing price differential.

Hence, the probability that an investigation leads to a conviction $l(p^d - p^t)$ is an increasing function of the price differential. It is zero for $p^d = p^t$ and assumed to be a non-negative and strictly convex function of $(p^d - p^t)$. Connecting multiplicatively $i(p^d)$ and $l(p^d - p^t)$ results in a function f that describes the probability that for a stated import price p^d tax and customs declarations will be scrutinized, evasion will be detected, and the importer will be sentenced. This "detection function" f is relevant for the importer's calculations. As follows from the above analysis f has the following properties

$$f = f(p^d - p^t) \tag{6.3}$$

and, being a probability

$$0 \le f \le 1. \tag{6.4}$$

Clearly

$$f(0) = 0. \tag{6.5}$$

Furthermore, f is twice continuously differentiable and a strictly convex function of $p^d - p^t$. This can be expressed as

$$\partial f/\partial p^d \overset{\text{def}}{=} f' \overset{>}{\underset{<}{=}} 0 \quad \text{iff} \quad p^d \overset{>}{\underset{<}{=}} p^t. \tag{6.6}$$

$$\partial^2 f/\partial p^{d^2} \overset{\text{def}}{=} f(p^d - p^t)'' > 0. \tag{6.7}$$

Different assumptions about $l(p^d - p^t)$ are conceivable. We have assumed that the probability of detection and condemnation f is *strictly convex* with minimum zero at $p^d = p^t$, i.e., $f(0) = 0$. Alternatively, one could assume that marginal evasion would also lead to discovery and condemnation with a probability distinctly greater than zero. For example, if every investigation led to discovery and condemnation for $p^d \neq p^t$, the resulting probability distribution for condemnation would coincide with $i(p^d)$ for $p^d \neq p^t$ and would have a discontinuity at $p^d = p^t$, since correct declarations cannot be punished.

The qualitative result of the model – the existence of a unique optimal point of misdeclaration – is not altered for this class of detection functions. Only a critical value for the rate of penalty exists, above which misdeclaration will not take place at all. This can be concluded from Schulze (1992b), in which tax and tariff evasion is also analyzed with a lump-sum penalty.

It is the importer's economic calculation that we turn to now. We assume that he is aware of the authorities' detection function as well as the penalty he has to face if detected.

6.2 The importer's optimal evasion

Since we focus on the evasion activity of the domestic importer we model the production sphere as simply as possible. In addition to the assumptions made on page 120, we postulate that the firm sells its finished product in a competitive market at a given price P. Without loss of generality the input coefficient for the imported good is set equal to unity. The firm's total costs consist of the true costs for the imported input $p^t x$, (further) production and marketing costs, $K(x)$, which are assumed to be linear in quantities with factor k, and the payments to the government.

By overdeclaring the import price to the foreign exchange authority the importer is given $p^d - p^t$ of foreign exchange per unit of imports in excess of what he or she needs to pay the foreign supplier. The importer remits $p^d x$ to the foreign business partner, who in turn transfers $(p^d - p^t)x$ to an account of the importer in a safe country. The capital was raised domestically at an interest rate of r_θ^h (or could have been invested alternatively at r_θ^h); now it earns $r_\theta^* > r_\theta^h$, where θ is the time index. We set the exchange rate equal to one and assume stationary expectations. Of course, if the evader expects a devaluation of the domestic currency, the arbitrage gain becomes bigger and the incentive to evade stronger.[15] This arbitrage gain is realized in each period beginning with the period after the successful evasion, so that we can write for the arbitrage gain per unit of import and per currency unit of overdeclaration

$$g = \sum_{\theta=0}^{\Theta} \frac{E(r_\theta^* - r_\theta^h)}{(1 + \iota)^\theta}. \tag{6.8}$$

Θ stands for this calculation's final point in time, at which, for example, the account is liquidated or the importer expects his or her life to end; it can also become infinity (bequest motive). $1 + \iota$ is the person's individual discount factor and the expectation operator $E(\cdot)$ indicates that the future interest rate development is uncertain. The value of g is given at the time at which the importer decides on the misdeclaration. The arbitrage gain per unit import (or output) is given by $(p^d - p^t)g$. If the undetected importer underdeclares his or her liabilities to the foreign supplier (s)he has to cover his or her foreign exchange gap either via the black market or by raising a loan abroad. (This gap opens up because under the control regime foreign exchange is allocated on the basis of the declared needs, i.e., declared price multiplied by the quantity imported.) In both cases he or she will incur costs $(\bar{g})$ exceeding g, because he or she will have to pay a black market premium or find costly ways to serve a foreign loan despite the exchange controls.[16] Arbitrage payments due to the misdeclaration are thus calculated as

$$\text{Arbitrage gain} = (p^d - p^t)\beta g \quad \text{where} \quad \beta = \begin{cases} \bar{g}/g \geq 1 & \text{iff } (p^d - p^t) < 0. \\ 1 & \text{otherwise} \end{cases}$$
$$\tag{6.9}$$

Tariff liabilities are based on the declared import price and the taxes are calculated on the basis of the declared profit. This quantity in turn is the difference between sales proceeds and costs for domestic inputs plus the declared costs for the imported input including the duties paid. When misdeclaration is brought to light, a proportional penalty is imposed, tax and tariff being based on the true price p^t. The allocation of foreign exchange is corrected to the amount actually paid to the supplier and

---

[15] Cuddington (1987) shows in an empirical study of seven Latin American countries that an overvalued currency is a major determinant of capital flight as eventually the domestic currency must be devalued.

[16] Moreover, borrowing rates exceed lending rates (even without controls), which also contribute to the differential.

in case of evasion (i.e., overdeclaration) the importer is fined proportionally to the extent of overdeclaration. The importer is assumed to be risk neutral in the relevant range. Thus, his or her objective is to maximize the expected true profit with respect to the declared price p^d. All parameters are given for the firm, except for p^d and the probability of detection, which in turn is a function of p^d. By choosing p^d appropriately the importer determines the extra profit he or she makes if the evasion goes undetected and, simultaneously, the probability of being detected. Since costs, gains, duties, and taxes are linear in quantities, magnitudes are calculated per unit output. The expected profit per unit is given by[17]

$$E(\Pi^t(p^d)) = P - k - p^t - [\underbrace{p^d\tau + t\{P - k - p^d(1+\tau)\}}_{\text{declared pre-tax profit}}](1-f)$$

$$- [\underbrace{p^t\tau + t\{P - k - p^t(1+\tau)\}}_{\text{true pre-tax profit}}]f + \underbrace{\{\beta g(p^d - p^t)\}}_{\text{arbitrage gain}}(1-f) - Sf. \quad (6.10)$$

The (per unit) penalty S is tied to the net amount of taxes and tariffs that the importer unsuccessfully attempted to evade. This kind of punishment is chosen because income tax evasion is punished this way in the United States of America (Andreoni *et al.* 1998), Israel (Yitzhaki 1974), and the Federal Republic of Germany,[18] as well as in other countries. In addition, overdeclaration as an attempt to evade capital controls is punished as a separate offense and again the penalty is proportional to the extent of misdeclaration.[19]

As can easily be verified, the penalty equals

$$S = s(p^d - p^t)\{\alpha[t(1+\tau) - \tau] + \gamma\} \quad (6.11)$$

with s being the non-negative and constant rate of penalty (surcharge). γs represents the additional surcharge per unit currency for evading capital export controls: γ is positive for $p^d > p^t$ and zero otherwise. If $[t(1+\tau) - \tau](p^d - p^t) < 0$ (i.e., the importer has paid too many taxes and

---

[17] The arguments of the detection function $f = f(p^d - p^t)$ are omitted for notational convenience.

[18] Sections 71, 370 AO (i.e., Abgabenordnung, German Fiscal Code). All major results continue to apply if a lump-sum penalty is added to, or substituted for, the proportional penalty; cf. Schulze (1992b).

[19] The same reasoning applies: The severity of the offense increases with the misdeclaration, and, thus, so does the fine. Underdeclaration is not punishable *under this offense* because it does not contradict the objective of the capital controls, but it is punishable if taxes and tariffs have been evaded (i.e., $\alpha = 1$). In contrast to the tax and tariff evasion the penalty for evading capital controls cannot be made proportional to the gain from this activity, since the latter depends on individual expectations as equation (6.8) shows.

tariffs), we reasonably assume that no reward is made by the authorities for his or her stupid misdeclaration. This is ensured by defining α such that

$$\alpha = \begin{cases} 1 & \text{iff } [t(1+\tau) - \tau](p^d - p^t) > 0 \\ 0 & \text{otherwise.} \end{cases} \tag{6.12}$$

For notational convenience we define

$$A \stackrel{\text{def}}{=} (P - k)(1 - t) - p^t , \tag{6.13}$$

which is not affected by the evasion decision, and

$$z \stackrel{\text{def}}{=} t(1+\tau) - \tau . \tag{6.14}$$

z indicates the relative importance of the tax and tariff burden: $z > 0$ implies that the tax burden exceeds the tariff burden whereas the opposite applies for $z < 0$. In other words, if the importer increases p^d *without detection*, he or she will be better off for $z > 0$: the reduction in the tax base and, hence, in tax liabilities due to the increased costs for the imported input outweighs the increased tariff payments. In order to judge whether over- or underdeclaration is advantageous to the importer the gains or losses (in case of underdeclaration) from evading capital controls must be added to the reduction of payments to the state due to over- or under-declaration ($z < 0$). We turn to this next.

Substituting (6.11) into (6.10) and simplifying it according to (6.13) and (6.14) yields

$$E(\Pi^t(p^d)) = A + zp^d + (p^t - p^d)[z + \beta g]f + (p^d - p^t)\beta g - s(p^d - p^t)\{\alpha z + \gamma\}f. \tag{6.15}$$

The expected total gain from misdeclaration is calculated as

$$E(\Pi^t(p^d)) - \Pi(p^t) = (p^d - p^t)(1 - f)(z + \beta g) - Sf. \tag{6.16}$$

Equation (6.16) shows that misdeclaration can only become fruitful if $(p^d - p^t)$ and $(z + \beta g)$ have the same sign (since $1 - f \geq 0$).[20] Recall that βg is always positive whereas z can have either sign. We distinguish three cases.

I We consider $z + g > 0$. If furthermore $z > 0$, this implies that over-declaration reduces the tax payments by more than the increase in tariff payments. Additionally the importer realizes the arbitrage gain from illegally exporting capital. Overdeclaration is still advantageous if

[20] In appendix B.1.2 we explicitly take into account the penalty function S and make the above statement even more obvious.

$z < 0$, but $z + g > 0$: The rise in overall payments to the state is more than offset by the gain from capital export. In other words, the existence of capital export restrictions creates a bias toward overdeclaration compared to the "simple" tax and tariff evasion case.

II If $z + g < 0$, but $z + \bar{g} > 0$, then misdeclaration does not pay off. Overdeclaration is unprofitable because the arbitrage gain cannot outweigh the loss due to higher payments to the state ($g < z$). On the other hand, underdeclaration is not worthwhile either. The reduction of overall tax and tariff liabilities falls short of the costs to cover the foreign exchange gap ($| z | < \bar{g}$), which are higher than the gains from an illicit capital export (cf. equation (6.9) on page 128: $\bar{g} > g$.) The fact that correct invoicing may be the best strategy stems from the asymmetry between the gains from illicitly depositing foreign exchange (g) and the costs of illicitly obtaining foreign exchange ($\bar{g}$). This assumption makes perfect sense: The black market traders demand a reward for their service[21] in excess of what they could otherwise earn by depositing the foreign exchange abroad. Inasmuch as competition between black market traders reduces the difference between $\bar{g}$ and g, the region of truthfulness will shrink.

III If $z + \bar{g} < 0$, underdeclaration is optimal. The decrease of tariff payments will not only more than cover the increased tax liabilities ($z < 0$), it will additionally more than offset the costs for obtaining the necessary foreign exchange.

Figure 6.3 shows the three different regions in the (z, g)-space.

We analyze in detail the functional form of $E(\Pi(p^d))$ for the different cases in appendix B.1 on pages 221–227. We also prove there the optimality of correct invoicing for the parameter constellation $z + g < 0 < z + \bar{g}$ (appendix B.1.2, pp. 224–227).

We derive the optimal point of misdeclaration next.

Calculating the first derivative of (6.15) we obtain[22]

$$\partial E(\Pi')/\partial p^d \stackrel{\text{def}}{=} \Pi' = (1-f)[z+\beta g] + (p^t - p^d)[z + \beta g + s\{\alpha z + \gamma\}]f' - s\{\alpha z + \gamma\}f$$

$$(6.17)$$

and the first-order condition for a maximum yields

---

21 Their service either consists in obtaining the necessary foreign exchange and bringing the money into the country and selling it to the importer or in directly paying the foreign supplier the difference between true and invoiced price. Both activities incur costs and the risk of being caught, and hence a compensation will be demanded.

22 Note that Π' is not differentiable at $p^d = p^t$ and hence $\Pi(p^t)'$ is not defined. The same applies to $\Pi(p^t)''$. This is due to the fact that $\bar{g} > g$, cf. appendix B.1.

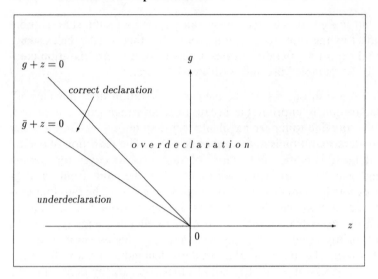

Figure 6.3 Parameter constellation for over- and underdeclaration

$$p^{d\star} = p^t + \frac{1 - f(p^{d\star} - p^t)\left(1 + s\frac{\alpha z + \gamma}{z + \beta g}\right)}{f(p^{d\star} - p^t)'\left(1 + s\frac{\alpha z + \gamma}{z + \beta g}\right)}. \tag{6.18}$$

Obviously no p^d can establish an extremum for which

$$f(p^d - p^t) \geq \left(1 + s\frac{\alpha z + \gamma}{z + \beta g}\right)^{-1}.$$

This follows straightforwardly from the properties of f': for $p^d > p^t$, $f' > 0$ and hence the numerator has to be positive.

Recall that we distinguish three cases: $z + g > 0$ (I), $z + g < 0 < z + \bar{g}$ (II), and $z + \bar{g} < 0$ (III). We exclude case II (no misdeclaration) from the following analysis; it is studied in depth in appendix B.1.2. Instead, we are concerned with (interior?) optima of misdeclaration.

From the calculation of the second derivative of $E(\Pi^t)$

$$\partial^2 E(\Pi^t)/\partial p^{d^2} \overset{\text{def}}{=} \Pi'' = (p^t - p^d)[z + \beta g + s\{\alpha z + \gamma\}]f'' - 2f'[z + \beta g + s\{\alpha z + \gamma\}] \tag{6.19}$$

it follows that for $z + g > 0$

$$\Pi'' \gtrless 0 \quad \Longleftrightarrow \quad p^d \lessgtr p^t \tag{6.20}$$

whereas for $z + \bar{g} < 0$ the case is reversed.[23]

We confine the formal exposition of our argument to the case of $z + g > 0$, because this is the case which involves the evasion of capital controls. For $z + \bar{g} < 0$, the argument runs *mutatis mutandis* parallel to that set out below.

As follows from (6.20), in the case where the tax burden and the possible gain from illicit capital export dominate the tariff burden, an interior solution which maximizes $E(\Pi')$ – if existing – is found only in the range of overdeclaration. The qualitative shape of $E(\Pi'(p^d))$ is depicted as shown in figure 6.4. For a detailed qualitative analysis see the appendix B.1.1.

So far, the global maximum could either be a boundary or an interior solution. Without specifying the respective parameters and the concrete detection function, f, it is impossible to know whether $E(\Pi')$ reaches a local maximum in the interior of the interval $[0; P]$.

First, we exclude that $E(\Pi')$ takes on its maximal value at $p^d = 0$. For this purpose the expected true profits for $p^d = 0$ and $p^d = p^t$ are compared. From (6.15)[24]

$$E(\Pi'(0)) - \Pi'(p^t) = -[z + \bar{g}]p^t(1 - f) - s\alpha z f \leq 0. \tag{6.21}$$

Equality holds only if the probability of being detected equals unity and $z > 0$, and so overall tax and tariff liabilities are based on the true import price – obviously, this misdeclaration does not make any sense at all. In all other cases the importer is worse off when underdeclaring. Consequently, $E(\Pi'(0))$ cannot establish a global maximum for $z + g > 0$.

Understating makes sense if and only if $z + \bar{g} < 0$, i.e., the tariff burden exceeds the tax burden and the burden of illegally obtaining foreign exchange.

The condition for an interior solution is investigated next. Since $E(\Pi)$ is not differentiable at $p^d = p^t$ (see appendix B.1, page 223), we compare $\lim_{\epsilon \to 0} \Pi(p^t + \epsilon)'$ (where $\epsilon > 0$) with $\Pi(P)'$ according to the mean value theorem. From (6.6), (6.12), and (6.17) it follows that

---

[23] If $z + g > 0$, then for $p^d > p^t : \alpha = 1$, $z, \gamma > 0$ and hence the term in square brackets is also positive. f' is positive for $p^d > p^t$ and f'' is positive throughout $[0,P]$ anyway (analogous for $p^d < p^t$ and for the case III).

[24] As z can have either sign, the penalty may either be zero ($z > 0$) or sz in case of detection.

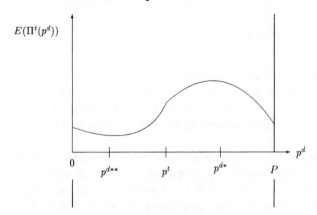

Figure 6.4 Expected true profit function for $z + g > 0$

$$\lim_{\epsilon \to 0} \Pi(p^t + \epsilon)' = z + g > 0. \tag{6.22}$$

Hence, for an interior maximum

$$\Pi(P)' = (1 - f(P - p^t))[z + g] + (p^t - P)[z + g + s\{\alpha z + \gamma\}]\cdot$$
$$\cdot f(P - p^t)' - s\{\alpha z + \gamma\}f(P - p^t) \overset{!}{\lessgtr} 0 \tag{6.23}$$

$$\Rightarrow f(P - p^t) \overset{!}{>} \underbrace{(p^t - P)f(P - p^t)'}_{<0} + \underbrace{\frac{z + g}{z + g + s\{\alpha z + \gamma\}}}_{>0 \text{ but } \leq 1} \tag{6.24}$$

As a sufficient, but *not* necessary condition an interior solution is obtained if $f(P - p^t)$ equals unity because $f(P - p^t)' > 0$ (cf. (6.6)).[25] In other words, an interior solution is guaranteed if we assume that the probability of detection equals unity when the importer declares the price of his intermediate good to be as high as his finished product. How realistic this assumption is depends on the fraction of the intermediate good of the total value, i.e., p^t/P. If it is well below unity it seems justifiable to assume that $f(P - p^t) = 1$.

For $z + g > 0$, some possible $E(\Pi^t(p^d))$ and corresponding Π' curves are shown (in the relevant range) in figure 6.5.

The government's policy goals are affected by the misdeclaration of import prices on two counts.[26] First, the illicit capital export undermines

---

[25] By analogy $f(-p^t) = 1$ is a sufficient condition for the existence of an interior solution in the case of $z + \bar{g} < 0$.

[26] We still confine our arguments to the case of $z + g > 0$.

the government's target to keep domestic interest rates a distinct amount below the world level by locking capital in the country. The expected illegal capital export per unit of import, Cex, amounts to

$$Cex = (p^d - p^t)(1 - f(p^d - p^t)) \qquad (> 0 \text{ for } z + g > 0). \qquad (6.25)$$

Second, misinvoicing imports alters the tax base and the tariff base; in case of $z > 0$ overdeclaration reduces government's overall revenue. As follows from (6.15), the expected net evasion (after deduction of surcharges in case of detection), Eva, yields[27]

$$Eva = (p^d - p^t) z \{1 - f[1 + s\alpha]\} > 0. \qquad (6.26)$$

For $z + g > 0$, evasion can have either sign, since z can take on negative values, but overdeclaration will always be profitable on an overall basis. For $z > 0$, tax and tariff evasion is positive because overinvoicing is also rewarding without the arbitrage gain.

Note that the loss in revenue and the undermining of capital export restrictions are not the total costs of misinvoicing to the government, because auditing devours resources. Moreover, this possibility of extra – illegal – profits through misinvoicing imports will *ceteris paribus* create a distortion in favor of foreign suppliers. Given the fact that domestic suppliers were protected by the tariff ($\tau > 0$), this illegal activity may enhance efficiency by mitigating the distortive effect of the tariff;[28] in any case it will cause political costs to the government, because the tariff is the result of government maximization behavior in the political market for protection.[29]

Summarizing the above findings we can conclude: Only if the tariff burden exceeds the tax burden plus the gain from illicit capital export is it optimal to understate the value of imported intermediate goods, whereas if the case is reversed overstating makes sense. The amount of misdeclaration, of illegal capital exports, and of overall tax and tariff evasion is dependent on the relation between tax and tariff rates (z), the probability of being detected (f) and the magnitude of the surcharge

---

[27] We could add also the surcharge for the evasion of capital controls because they contribute to the net revenue, but do not reduce expected capital exports directly since the surcharges are due in domestic currency and not in foreign exchange. If we included this fine as well, the term in brackets of (6.26) would change into $[1 + s(\alpha + \gamma/z)]$. We do not do this here, because we want to keep the two – interlinked – effects separate for reasons of analytical clarity. However, in appendix B.2.1.2 we point out the modifications to the results that would arise from such an inclusion.

[28] Since there is more than one distortion in this economy (tariff, tax, and capital controls) a conclusive statement can only be reached within the context of a general equilibrium model. This is what the theory of the second best teaches us.

[29] For a detailed analysis and survey of the literature see Weck-Hannemann (1992a,b).

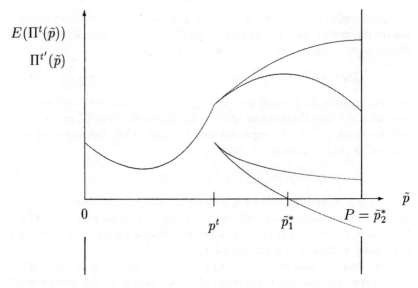

Figure 6.5 Interior and boundary maximum of $E(\Pi^t(p^d))$ for $z + g > 0$

levied in case of detection (s and $s\gamma$, respectively). Honesty is rational only if the relative tax and tariff rates lie within a narrow bound which is in essence the black market premium:[30] $\bar{g} > -z > g$.

6.3 Comparative static results

In this section we shall examine how the optimal declared price $p^{d\star}$ depends on the parameters s, $f(p^d - p^t)$, t, τ, and βg. It is self-evident that for a meaningful analysis we must exclude the case in which honest declaration is the optimal strategy; in other words we exclude $z + g < 0 < z + \bar{g}$. To begin with we study the influence of the rate of penalty s. Restating the first-order condition (6.18) we obtain after some simple manipulations

$$0 = \left(1 + s\,\frac{\alpha z + \gamma}{z + \beta g}\right)[(p^t - p^{d\star})f' - f] + 1. \qquad (6.27)$$

Note that the term $(\alpha z + \gamma)/(z + \beta g)$ is always positive: For $z + g > 0$ overdeclaration is optimal and therefore either $\alpha = 0$ in case of $z < 0$ or z is also positive (for overdeclaration, $\gamma > 0$ per definition). For

---

[30] The black market premium is equal to $\bar{g} - g$, cf. page 128.

$z + \bar{g} < 0$, z needs to be negative and underdeclaration is optimal. Consequently, $\alpha = 1$, $\gamma = 0$, and thus the numerator is negative. Since the denominator is negative as well, the fraction is again positive.

Since in equation (6.27) the term in parentheses is positive, the term in square brackets must be negative. The total differential of the first-order condition (6.27) is solved with respect to $dp^{d\star}/ds$

$$\frac{dp^{d\star}}{ds} = \frac{\frac{\alpha z + \gamma}{z + \beta g}\{f - (p^t - p^{d\star})f'\}}{[(p^t - p^{d\star})f'' - 2f'](1 + s\frac{\alpha z + \gamma}{z + \beta g})}. \tag{6.28}$$

We now see that the numerator of (6.28) is unambiguously positive, since the term in braces is the negative value of the term in brackets of equation (6.27). As for the denominator, the term in parentheses is positive as we have seen, while the sign of the term in brackets depends on the direction of misdeclaration: it is negative for $p^{d\star} > p^t$ and positive for the opposite case. As the direction of misdeclaration depends on the sign of $z + g\beta$ we conclude that

$$\text{sign}\left(\frac{dp^{d\star}}{ds}\right) = -\text{sign}(z + \beta g).$$

The same qualitative result is obtained for a variation of the penalty for evading capital controls, γ. Note that γ is positive only in case of over-declaration. Thus

$$\text{for } z + g > 0 \qquad \frac{dp^{d\star}}{d\gamma} = \frac{\frac{s}{z + \beta g}\{f - (p^t - p^{d\star})f'\}}{[(p^t - p^{d\star})f'' - 2f'](1 + s\frac{\alpha z + \gamma}{z + \beta g})} < 0. \tag{6.29}$$

This negative relationship between misdeclaration and penalty is very much in line with the results in the (tax evasion) literature[31] and with economic intuition: other things being equal, higher penalties lower the expected profits from illegal activities.

This may raise the question of why the government does not eliminate the problem of tax and tariff evasion without incurring any costs by maximal punishment. Though the government could not eliminate evasion totally,[32] it could reduce it to an arbitrarily small amount by threatening potential evaders with the loss of their total wealth or life. If these penalties deter effectively they will almost never have to be applied, so the

---

[31] *Inter alia* Allingham and Sandmo (1972: 330), Cowell (1990b). Dubin and Wilde (1988) provide empirical evidence for the deterrent effects of auditing and punishment.

[32] Because $\lim_{\epsilon \to 0}\Pi(p^t + \epsilon)' = z + g > 0$ for $z + g > 0$ and $\lim_{\epsilon \to 0}\Pi(p^t - \epsilon)' = -(z + \bar{g}) > 0$ for $z + \bar{g} < 0$ (see (6.17)), honest declaration is suboptimal also in case of maximal punishment, except for the case $\bar{g} > -z > g$ (> 0) as has been discussed.

authorities do not "even have to incur the small cost of paying the wages of the hangman" (Cowell 1985a: 181). We do not want to argue along these lines although there are also economic counterarguments (see Cowell 1985a: 180–182 and the literature quoted). We regard maximal punishment of evasion as contradicting the basic principles of law and thus incompatible with the legal systems in at least all Western countries: therefore ethical considerations alone constitute a ceiling for the surcharge.[33]

For given $p^{d\star}$ the probability of detection will increase, *ceteris paribus*, either if the auditing technology or the effectiveness of the legal system is improved or if the expected gain from detection increases. In the notation of section 3.1 this means that the critical value a decreases (see page 124). This in turn will raise the probability of investigation for every $p^d \in [0, P]$ as can be seen from (6.2): Because $Q(p^d)$ is *ex definitione* a monotonically increasing function, $Q(p^d + a) - Q(p^d - a)$ will decrease as a falls.

If the auditing costs are lowered, the detection function will be substituted by one which attributes a higher probability of detection to each $p^d \neq p^t$, because the investigation probability $i(p^d)$ will have increased. If the legal system is improved, the probability of detection $f(p^d - p^t)$ will *additionally* be enhanced via a "higher" function $l(p^d - p^t)$.

In order to provide insights into the way in which $p^{d\star}$ depends on the probability of detection we substitute

$$e(\kappa, p^d - p^t) = f(p^d - p^t) + \kappa\eta(p^d - p^t)$$

for f. The function η is arbitrary but fixed and has the same properties as f (strict convexity in $(p^d - p^t)$ and minimum at $p^d = p^t$ with $\eta(0) = 0$). The parameter κ is a (non-negative) scalar such that $e(\kappa, p^d - p^t) \in [0, 1]$. Thus, $e(\kappa, p^d - p^t)$ establishes a one parameter family of functions with the same geometrical properties as f.

The first-order condition (6.27) is altered to

$$0 = \left(1 + s\frac{\alpha z + \gamma}{z + \beta g}\right)[(p^t - p^{d\star})(f' + \kappa\eta') - (f + \kappa\eta)] + 1. \tag{6.30}$$

Because $1 + s(\alpha z + \gamma)/(z + \beta g) > 0$, the term in brackets is negative (cf. pp. 136–137).

---

[33] See also Stern (1978) and Cowell (1990b, chapters 7, 8) for further discussion. Individuals might evade taxes and tariffs by mistake. This possibility makes extreme penalties unjustifiable. Moreover, maximal punishment also for relative small offenses reduces effective deterrence for major offenses – "one might as well be hung for a sheep as for a lamb" Cowell (1990b: 150).

We analyze the impact of a variation of κ on the optimal declared price. An increase (decrease) in κ implies that for every $p^d \neq p^t$ the value of e is increased (decreased), $\partial e / \partial \kappa = \eta$. Totally differentiating (6.30) with respect to $p^{d\star}$ and κ yields

$$\frac{\mathrm{d}p^{d\star}}{\mathrm{d}\kappa} = \frac{-(p^t - p^{d\star})\eta' + \eta}{(p^t - p^{d\star})(f'' + \kappa\eta'') - 2(f' + \kappa\eta')}. \qquad (6.31)$$

From (6.30) and the properties of f and η it can be seen that the numerator is always non-negative while the denominator is positive (negative) for $z + \bar{g} < 0$ ($z + g > 0$). Thus

$$\mathrm{sign}\left(\frac{\mathrm{d}p^{d\star}}{\mathrm{d}\kappa}\right) = -\mathrm{sign}(z + \beta g).$$

The optimal declared price shifts toward the true price if the probability of detection is increased. Again, this negative relationship between the probability of detection and the extent of misdeclaration is in accordance with the familiar results of the literature, which are quite plausible for the same reasoning as noted above.

A higher probability of detection or a higher penalty will reduce the evasion of capital controls – if existing – it will furthermore drive down net tax and tariff evasion when it is positive. If the net tax and tariff evasion is negative, i.e., the importer pays too much to the state because the gain from illicit capital export via overinvoicing outweighs this loss, an increase in f or s will reduce the capital export but also the overpayment of tax and tariff liabilities, cf. equations (6.25) and (6.26).

A variation of <u>tax or tariff rates</u> changes the amount of misdeclaration only via the effect of the penalty, as long as z does not change its sign. This is seen from (6.18) or (6.27), the F.O.C. for a maximum of $E(\Pi^t(p^d))$, in which z occurs only in combination with the rate of penalty s. If s were zero, or the base for the penalty was strictly proportional to the net gain from misdeclaration, i.e., $\alpha z + \gamma = c(z + \beta g)$ where c is constant, then misdeclaration would not change at all. (The reason for this is the assumed risk neutrality of the firm, leading to expected profit maximization.)

If z varies such that $z + \beta g$ changes its sign, misdeclaration will be superseded by honest declaration and if z continues to vary in the same direction it will eventually be replaced by misdeclaration of the opposite sign. This has been shown on pages 130–131 and depicted in figure 6.3. Within either region of misdeclaration, the amount of misdeclaration rises if the variation of z reduces the penalty base relative to the gain from (undetected) misdeclaration. Since this finding is not central to our further analysis, we relegate its derivation and precise formulation to appendix B.2.1.1.

In any case, the amount evaded will be greatly influenced by an alteration of t and τ. In appendix B.2.1.2 we show the following: An increase in z further increases the amount evaded when $z > 0$ (overdeclaration); less clear-cut results are obtained when overdeclaration is optimal on an overall basis ($z + g > 0$), but overdeclaration implies that the cheating importer has to pay too much taxes and duties (i.e., $z < 0$). The loss of extra payments to the state per currency unit of overdeclaration is reduced, but the overdeclaration rises. Lastly, an increase in z reduces the evaded amount if underdeclaration is optimal ($z + \bar{g} < 0$). (The opposite holds *mutatis mutandis* for a reduction of z.) These results are quite intuitive: The higher the profit per unit of misdeclaration from successful evasion (z), the higher the overall amount evaded.

Setting tax and tariff rates does not only determine total liabilities, but their relation to each other will at the same time determine the fraction of those liabilities that will actually be paid.

The variation of the interest rate differential or the individual time preference yields unambiguous results. For negative z however, $z + \bar{g}$ must not change its sign; otherwise underdeclaration would be replaced by honesty and, if g continues to rise, eventually by overdeclaration (see pp. 130–131 and figure 6.3). We differentiate the first-order condition (6.27) with respect to the optimal declared price and the arbitrage gain g. We assume that the variation of g goes in tender with the variation of $\bar{g}$, i.e., that the black market premium remains constant. If this was not true, we would have to write down a separate equation for $\bar{g}$, which would yield the same qualitative result as (6.32)[34]

$$\frac{\mathrm{d}p^{d\star}}{\mathrm{d}g} = - \frac{\beta(1 + \{(p^t - p^d)f' - f\})}{\{z + \beta g + s(\alpha z + \gamma)\}[(p^t - p^d)f'' - 2f']}. \tag{6.32}$$

For a positive penalty rate s the numerator is always positive as we can see by comparing it with equation (6.27): since $s\frac{\alpha z + \gamma}{z + \beta g} > 0$ as we have shown, the term in brackets in equation (6.27), which is identical with the term in braces of the numerator of (6.32), must be negative but greater than -1. The denominator is always negative because the term in braces and the term in brackets carry the opposite sign.[35] Therefore, $\mathrm{d}p^{d\star}/\mathrm{d}g > 0$. Misdeclaration is increased in case of overdeclaration, but is

---

[34] For this reason, we can use the general form βg instead of g.
[35] The denominator is identical with the denominator in (B.13), see pages 228–229 for the detailed argument.

reduced if the importer underinvoices his or her imports. If overdeclaration is increased, illegal capital export is increased as well. We prove this intuitive result with equation (B.18) (appendix B.2.2, page 233). Again we see from the comparison of (6.27) and the numerator of (6.32) that the alteration of misdeclaration hinges on the existence of a positive penalty: if $s = 0$, misdeclaration would remain the same. The unambiguity of the above results is due to the assumption that profits from a given misdeclaration have risen whereas the penalty has not. This is not realistic.

Economic crimes are normally fined proportionally to the potential gain from the illegal activity. This is clearly so for a number of countries in the case of tax evasion (see page 129) and likewise for the evasion of capital controls. We should therefore expect an increase in γ when g rises. Moreover, if controls are tightened up thereby increasing the interest rate differential, the punishment is usually increased in order to enforce the more restrictive allocation of capital export licenses and to deter potential evaders from realizing an enhanced arbitrage gain. The effect of an increased arbitrage gain and that of a raised penalty work in opposite directions.[36] In appendix B.2.2 we analyze the interesting case in which the government is able to raise the rate of penalty by as much as the arbitrage gain has risen, $d\gamma = dg$. The result is that overdeclaration increases if $\gamma > g$ in case of $z > 0$ or if $\gamma > z + g$ for $z + g > 0$ but $z < 0$, respectively. This is identical to the statement that overdeclaration increases if the potential gain from overinvoicing increases *relatively* more than the penalty base.

6.4 Policy implications

Overinvoicing of intermediate imports effects an illicit capital export, whereas underinvoicing requires the importer to supply himself or herself with foreign exchange on the black market at a premium. This misdeclaration moreover affects the payments to the state: Overinvoicing reduces taxes, but increases tariff liabilities. In this chapter we have shown that for every combination of (linear) import tariff, (linear) income tax, and a given interest arbitrage gain there is one optimal point of (mis)declaration. This is true because the probability of detection and punishment depends positively on, and is convex in, the amount of misdeclaration, which in turn is a consequence of the authorities' revenue-maximizing behavior, as has been derived formally in a qualitative response model.

---

[36] Of course this is only true for the case of overdeclaration since otherwise $\gamma = 0$.

The *sign* of misdeclaration depends solely on the relative magnitudes of tax and tariff rates and the arbitrage gain from evading the capital export restrictions, whereas the *amount* of under- or overdeclaration is determined by the detection function and the form of punishment. The higher the penalty rate or the detection probability, the smaller the amount of misdeclaration. The extent of evasion is jointly determined by the five parameters mentioned.

We have argued that the traditional instruments are of limited use: Investigative activity reaches its cutoff point when it becomes unprofitable. As shown in section 6.1.1, profitability of investigative activity is mainly determined by investigative technology and the effectiveness of the legal system, which in the short run cannot be significantly improved. On the other hand, punishment of evasion is restrained by the required consistency of the criminal law as well as ethical considerations, even aside from economic considerations.

The requirement that import prices be stated consistently to the tax authorities, the customs office, and the body monitoring the exchange regulations opens another avenue of approach to this problem. For one thing, the loss of revenue due to the evasion of taxes is (partly) offset by the increased duties levied on overinvoiced imports, and vice versa. Equation (6.26) on page 135 demonstrates that the evaded liabilities are a function of the relative tax and tariff rates. Setting these rates such that $\tau = t/(1 - t)$ would entirely eliminate evasion of this kind. The evasion of capital controls, however, would remain. To remove the incentives to evade those controls the increase in (tax and tariff) liabilities to the state due to overdeclaration would have to outmatch the arbitrage gain. In other words, for a targeted interest rate differential the tax system would have to be designed with high tariffs and relatively low tax rates, so that $z + g < 0$. Under this parameter constellation, underdeclaration may still be profitable: capital export restrictions are reinforced by illicit capital imports, but the government's revenue is eroded (cf. case III on p. 132).

Ideally, to eliminate both kinds of evasion, tax and tariff rates and the interest rate differential should be set so that $z + g < 0 < z + \bar{g}$ (this is case II as on p. 132 and appendix B.1.2). This would lead to the declaration of the true import prices; the government could accomplish either the revenue goal or the interest differential goal, because both sets of policy variables would then be interlinked. This linkage would not only abolish evasion, it would moreover save the government huge outlays for auditing. All the authorities would have to do is to check the consistency of tax, customs, and foreign exchange declarations.

Yet, this scenario is not so easy to implement. First, governments have to know the black market premium, which is not too difficult, and must adjust at least one of their policy parameters to the fluctuations thereof. Second, since time preference may differ across individuals, the arbitrage gain g may differ likewise. The government or, more precisely, the legislator must consider a "medium" value of g and accept misinvoicing of some individuals. Third, and most important, the elimination of evasion is not the predominant goal when setting (tax and) tariff rates; generating revenue and protecting domestic industries are the ruling targets. Analogously, capital controls are aimed at obtaining a certain interest rate differential *vis-à-vis* the rest of the world for distributional reasons as we have seen in part I; therefore they will not be subject to major deviations from their target value in order to fulfill the above requirement for honesty.

The above considerations may nevertheless be valuable for governments confronted with huge evasion of taxes, tariffs, and exchange controls by internationally operating firms subject to domestic taxation and foreign exchange regulations. In particular less developed countries continuously suffer from an inefficient tax and foreign exchange administration, which makes evasion an extremely profitable and riskless venture. This may be especially pronounced for subsidiaries of multinational enterprises trying to shift domestically generated profits to low-tax or high-interest countries by misinvoicing goods and services delivered to them by their parent companies.[37]

Even if taxes and tariffs or the interest rate differential cannot be manipulated freely because of conflicting targets or other constraints, z may be changeable to some extent in order to enhance the degree of goal accomplishment. For instance, if the incentive to overstate import prices could not be removed (i.e., $z + g > 0$), the affected countries could reform the structure of their levies by granting special tax reliefs to the internationally operating firms and introducing tariffs on imports so that z would become (more) negative. Evasion of capital controls would then partly be compensated by payments to the state which exceed the importer's true liabilities. In other words, if the incentive to illegally export capital cannot be removed for some reason, tax design cannot reduce the size of the capital export[38] (see (6.25)), but it can foster the revenue

---

[37] They can misstate the prices for transactions within their hierarchy more easily because market prices for those activities often do not exist, and reference prices are difficult to calculate (the so-called "transfer pricing" problem). The same applies to market transactions involving highly specialized goods and services, for which a well-established market (with easily observable reference prices) does not exist.

[38] This can be accomplished by the traditional means of auditing and punishment only.

goal. Correspondingly, if the tax system was designed such that $z + \bar{g} < 0$ and hence underinvoicing was optimal, z could be made less negative. This would reduce evasion, but the capital import (which in this case reinforces the capital controls) would remain the same. The reform could be designed in such a way that the overall (nominal) tax and tariff burden of the domestically residing subsidiaries would remain unaltered, but revenue would be increased through reduced evasion or excess payments.

7 Misinvoicing international trade: Exports

This chapter is devoted to the second important avenue for circumventing capital export restrictions: the misdeclaration of export prices. An internationally operating firm can export capital illicitly by *overinvoicing* its *imports* and depositing the foreign exchange abroad that it was granted in excess of the amount actually due to the foreign supplier. It can also effect the capital export by *underinvoicing exports*. This reduces the foreign exchange that the exporter has to surrender to the authorities in exchange for domestic currency; the difference between the actual export proceeds and the amount invoiced (and thus transferred to the authorities) is remitted by the foreign customer to an account outside the exporter's country. In doing so the exporter earns a higher interest than at home, where interest rates are kept low by the capital controls.

We analyze this possibility in a framework similar to the one set out in the preceding chapter, assuming a profit-maximizing exporter and revenue-maximizing authorities. The formal resemblance notwithstanding, marked differences emerge compared with the case of faked import prices. First, the misdeclaration of exports affects the gain from reduced payments to the state and from the illegal arbitrage activity in the same direction. Successful underinvoicing produces (or increases) the interest arbitrage gain while at the same time reducing income tax payments and export duties (where they exist).[1] Second, since only underinvoicing is lucrative authorities will exhibit a different investigation pattern. We show by what mechanism the evasion of capital controls becomes poss-

---

[1] Export duties are especially prevalent in developing countries at a very low stage of their development, because they are easy to implement and to enforce. Export activity is often concentrated on a few specific locations such as harbors and airports and carried out by a small number of relatively well-organized companies so that export duties as well as import levies serve as a major source of revenue when sales taxes or direct taxes cannot effectively be implemented; Hinrichs (1966).

ible: it is the existence of investigation costs and the probability that investigation leads to conviction, which is convex in the amount of misdeclaration.

The chapter is in three sections. The first section introduces the economic problem, the following section describes the auditing behavior and derives the detection function and the ensuing equilibrium. Finally, the third section is devoted to comparative statics and policy implications.

7.1 The economic problem

We formulate the problem, as far as it is possible, along the same lines as set out in chapter 6. A domestic profit-maximizing exporter sells his or her product on the foreign market at a price P^t, but declares a price P^d to both the tax and the foreign exchange control authorities. If the misdeclaration goes undetected the difference between the true and the declared price is remitted to a foreign account and the exporter realizes an arbitrage gain of $(P^t - P^d)g$ per unit of output where g is defined by equation (6.8). To keep matters not directly related to the evasion activity simple, we assume once more constant per unit costs of production k. Again, the firm is subject to a proportional income tax levied at the rate t. We do not consider an export tariff in this context as it functions in the same way as the income tax[2] and is by far less frequently found than an import tariff.

Revenue-maximizing authorities audit invoices with an endogenous probability $\tilde{f}(P^t - P^d)$ which will be derived in section 7.2. (The " ˘ " indicates a variable similar to the one in chapter 6, but with a different functional form or a modified definition. If not mentioned otherwise the notation introduced in the preceding chapter is maintained.) In the case of exports overdeclaration is unambiguously unprofitable: it increases tax payments and requires the exporter to supply himself or herself with costly foreign exchange on the black market in excess of the export proceeds. Authorities take this into account and thus, as we will see, the detection function $\tilde{f}(P^t - P^d)$ is monotonically decreasing in P^d. Lower declared prices are more likely to be faked. In case of detection, taxes and the surrender of foreign exchange are based on the true profit and true sales proceeds, respectively, and the evader is fined proportion-

---

[2] Underinvoicing reduces export duties as well as income taxes. If export subsidies were granted, the analysis would parallel the one set out in chapter 6.

ally to the misdeclaration:[3] $S = \alpha \check{s}(P^t - P^d)$. Again α ensures that paying too much taxes, bringing foreign exchange into the country and surrendering it to the authorities is not fined: $\alpha = 1$ for $P^d < P^t$, zero otherwise.

Assuming risk neutrality the importer maximizes his or her expected profit with respect to the declared price P^d

$$E(\Pi^t(P^d)) = P^t - k - t(P^t - k)\check{f} - t(P^d - k)(1 - \check{f})$$
$$+ \beta g(P^t - P^d)(1 - \check{f}) - \alpha \check{s}\check{f}(P^t - P^d). \tag{7.1}$$

β is defined as above (p. 128); it is introduced only for the sake of completeness: in the irrelevant case of overdeclaration, the exporter has to surrender more foreign exchange than he or she has earned and must therefore turn to the black market.

The first-order condition is given by

$$P^{d\star} = P^t + \frac{t + \beta g - \check{f}(t + \beta g + \alpha \check{s})}{\check{f}'(t + \beta g + \alpha \check{s})}. \tag{7.2}$$

From (7.2) we can see that overdeclaration is not optimal. The numerator is greater or equal to zero since $(t + g)(1 - \check{f}) \geq 0$ and $\alpha = 0$ for $P^d > P^t$, the denominator is negative since $\check{f}' < 0$. At most correct declaration is possibly an optimal strategy; otherwise it is found in the range of underdeclaration. We calculate the second derivative of the expected profit function (7.1), Π''

$$\Pi''(P^d) = (t + \beta g + \alpha \check{s})[2\check{f}' - \check{f}''(P^t - P^d)] \overset{?}{\lessgtr} 0. \tag{7.3}$$

The sign of the RHS of (7.3) is undetermined. The term in parentheses is positive whereas the term in brackets may have either sign also if calculated only for $P^d = P^{d\star}$. It is negative only for a "sufficiently convex" (part of the) detection function and, thus, an interior maximum can only exist if this condition is met.[4] To assess whether an interior maximum of the expected profits exists we need to know the functional form of the detection function. This is what we discuss next.

---

[3] The reasoning behind equation (6.11) also applies here. In many countries tax evasion is punished proportionally to the evaded tax; as in chapter 6 we assume that illegal capital export is also fined proportional to the severity of the offense, i.e., proportional to the amount of misdeclaration. In this chapter we need not distinguish between the penalty for evasion of capital controls and the one for tax evasion since both are proportional to the misdeclaration and run parallel. In the notation of chapter 6: $\check{s} = st + \gamma$.

[4] The S.O.C. for a maximum of $E(\Pi^t(P^d))$ is met if and only if $f''(P^{d*} - P^t) > 2\check{f}'(P^{d*} - P^t)/(P^t - P^{d*})$.

7.2 The probability of detection and the equilibrium misdeclaration

7.2.1 Authorities' investigative behavior

The same rationale as in section 6.1.1 applies. Authorities do not know the true export price, but they have a reasonable idea of what it could be: They form a unimodal density function q for the latent variable of the export price, $\tilde{P}^t$, which attaches the highest probability to the true export price. Assumptions 1–4 made for $q(p^t)$ on pages 123–125 apply *mutatis mutandis* also for $q(\tilde{P}^t)$.[5] Again, assuming bell-shaped density functions, like a truncated normal probability distribution, instead of the assumed concave function, would not alter the analysis significantly.

Authorities investigate imports with a probability that is identical to their subjective probability that at the declared import price the *absolute* value of the misdeclaration exceeds a certain critical value (cf. p. 124. In other words, they consider both over- and underdeclaration. The reason for this is that overdeclaration undermines capital controls and reduces the tax base while underdeclaration squeezes the tariff revenue.[6] Contrastingly, misdeclaration of exports affects both capital export restrictions and government revenue in the same way[7] – underdeclaration erodes government revenue and undermines the capital controls. For that reason authorities are concerned only with underdeclaration and investigate with a probability identical to the probability that the extent of underdeclaration exceeds a critical value a. We recall that this critical value represents the expected net costs of an investigation (cf. footnote 13 on p. 124). Hence, the probability of investigation for a given declared price P^d, $i(P^d)$, is given by

$$
\begin{aligned}
\breve{i}(P^d) &= \mathrm{prob}(\tilde{P}^t - P^d > a) = 1 - \mathrm{prob}(\tilde{P}^t < P^d + a) \\
&= 1 - \int_{-\infty}^{P^d+a} q(\tilde{P}^t)dP^d = 1 - Q(P^d + a).
\end{aligned}
\tag{7.4}
$$

$Q(P^d + a)$ denotes the primitive of $q(\tilde{P}^t)$. The graphical illustration runs parallel to the one in chapter 6. Therefore we sketch only the differences to the analysis on pp. – . The primitive of the density function $q(\tilde{P}^t)$ of the kind shown in figure 6.1 on p. 124 is depicted in figure 7.1 below. Note

---

[5] The only exception is that q is now defined on $[0, \infty)$.
[6] From a procedural point of view the reason for this is that each government agency (customs, internal revenue service, and the central bank) initiates investigations of suspicious declarations independently from each other, but once one agency detects misdeclaration they cooperate. They do, however, check for consistency of declarations in any case.
[7] For capital *import* restrictions the conflict between the realization of arbitrage gains and the minimization of payments to the stage reemerges.

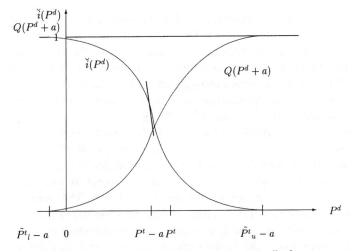

Figure 7.1 Derivation of the investigation function $\check{i}(P^d)$ for export prices

that the inflection point of $\check{i}(P^d)$ is at $P^d = P^t - a$. In contrast to $i(p^d)$ in chapter 6 the investigation function in case of exports, $\check{i}(P^d)$, is – at least in part – concave.

7.2.2 The detection function and the sort of equilibria

An investigation does not necessarily amount to a conviction; instead as we have argued in section 6.1.2 the probability that an investigation leads to conviction is convex in the price differential $P^t - P^d$. In the context of misinvoicing exports this holds of course only for positive differentials since overinvoicing is not an offense but stupidity. In what follows we confine our arguments to $P^d \in [0, P^t]$ as the relevant interval.

The probability of detection, i.e., the probability of being audited, convicted and punished, is the product of $i(P^d)$ and $l(P^t - P^d)$, the probability of being convicted and punished once investigations are installed. The latter function is assumed to have the same geometrical properties as $l(p^d - p^t)$ in section 6.1.2 on p. 126. We show the derivation of $\check{f}$ in figure 7.2.[8]

---

[8] In figure 7.2 it is assumed that conviction is never certain, $l < 1$. This need not be the case, $l(P^t - P^d)$ could also reach unity for some value $P^d > 0$. The same holds for $i(P^d)$ if we removed assumption 4 on page 125. In the former case, the detection function would be unambiguously concave for small values of P^d, in the latter case, it would be unambiguously convex in the respective range.

Figure 7.2 shows the dilemma concerning the functional form of the detection function. For the interval $(P^t - a, P^t)$, $\check{f}$ is convex, but for $[0, P^t - a)$ no conclusive statement can be reached without the knowledge of the concrete functions $\check{i}$ and l. Anything can happen: $l(P^t - P^d)$ may dominate $i(P^d)$ so that $\check{f}$ is convex throughout the interval $[0, P^t - a)$, the case may be reversed, or the function may pass through various forms when P^d is lowered, beginning with $P^d = P^t - a$.

We are able to show that *interior maxima for the expected profits (equation (7.1)) will only exist if* $\check{f}(P^t - P^d)$ *has a convex part in* $[0, P^t)$.[9] If that is *not* the case, either honest declaration or maximal underdeclaration will be optimal strategies. Since the proof of this statement is somewhat lengthy, we relegate it to appendix B.3 on pp. 234–239. The intuition behind these findings is as follows. A rise in misdeclaration has two opposing effects – on the one hand, the gain from *undiscovered* evasion increases while, on the other hand, the probability of detection and punishment grows. Starting from $P^d = P^t$ we increase the extent of underdeclaration: For the concave $\check{f}$ either the increase in $\check{f}$ is so small from the outset that augmentation in profits from unrevealed misdeclaration (due to reduced taxes and the arbitrage gain) outweighs the enhanced probability of being detected. If this is true for $P^d = P^t - \epsilon$ with $\epsilon \to 0$ and positive, it is true throughout the interval $(0, P^t)$ because $\check{f}$ increases at decreasing rates whereas the gain from undetected misdeclaration is linear in $P^t - P^d$. This case yields a corner solution: It is optimal to state $P^d = 0$.

The second possibility in case of a concave $\check{f}(P^t - P^d)$ throughout the interval $[0, P^t)$ is that $\check{f}(\epsilon)$ is sufficiently high to ensure that an increase in misdeclaration will drive up the detection probability to such an extent that the expected profits decrease despite the increase of profits from *undiscovered* evasion. Expected profits will diminish with rising misdeclaration, however at a decreasing pace since $\check{f}$ is concave. The function $E(\Pi^t(P^d))$ may reach a local minimum and increase thereafter. If such an interior minimum exists, then for large misdeclarations beyond this minimum the detection probability rises only slightly whereas profits from undiscovered misinvoicing rise at a constant rate which more than offsets the increased probability of being caught. For this second possibility either honesty or audacity ($P^d = 0$) is the optimal strategy.

In contrast to a concave $\check{f}$, convexity produces inner solutions: For small misdeclarations the effect of an increased probability of detection is more than offset by the constant rise of profits from successful evasion because $\check{f}$ grows only slowly in the beginning. Since $\check{f}$ accelerates to grow

---

[9] See also the discussion of equation (7.3) on page 147.

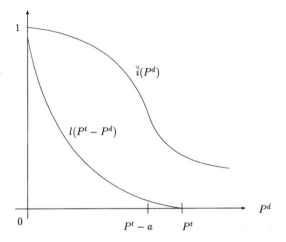

Figure 7.2 Derivation of the detection function $\check{f}(P^t - P^d)$ for export prices

as the misdeclaration rises the relative importance of both effects shifts up to a turning point, beyond which misdeclaration becomes an unprofitable venture. We show some possible slopes of the function $E(\Pi'(P^d))$ in the relevant range in figure 7.3. Note that interior maxima need not exist. For an exact derivation of these, the reader is referred to appendix B.3.

The analysis of appendix B.3, the results of which were reported above, clearly demonstrates the importance and correctness of two assumptions made on authorities' investigative behavior. If there was no critical value of misdeclaration (a), below which investigation is not rewarding and if investigation brought about conviction with a constant probability, e.g., with certainty, rational investigative behavior would imply the boundary solutions of either honesty or maximal underdeclaration.

Clearly, this is not what we observe. In the presence of capital controls there *is* a lot of faked invoicing going on, but we observe misinvoicing rather than smuggling; Bhagwati (1978: chapter 4). This observation reinforces the idea of a threshold consideration on the side of the auditing arm of the fiscal authorities and the observation that a large misdeclaration is easier to detect, to prove, and to convict (and it is more rewarding to do so) than a small one. The assumption of convexity of $l(P^t - P^d)$ seems justified; the assumption constantly made in the literature[10] that

---

[10] Among many others: Allingham and Sandmo (1972: 324), Koskela (1983: 71), Reinganum and Wilde (1985), Alm (1988: 36), Cowell and Gordon (1988), Mookherjee and Png (1989); most authors, however, do not distinguish between investigation and conviction and assume a constant probability of detection. This is a severe oversimplification!

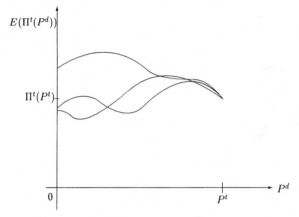

Figure 7.3 Possible slopes of $E(\Pi^t(P^d))$ for the underdeclaration of exports

once an investigation is installed it will produce conviction with certainty is shown to be a dubious one.

7.3 Comparative statics and policy considerations

In this section we show that misdeclaration and hence the evasion of both taxes and the capital controls increase, *ceteris paribus*, with the gain per unit of successful misdeclaration, i.e., with the tax rate or the arbitrage gain. On the other hand, misinvoicing declines if the probability of detection, or the surcharge rise. We consider only marginal variations of t, g, s, and f; this ensures that the optimal point of misdeclaration is altered continuously with the varying parameters. Discrete parameter variations may cause the point of optimality to jump from one maximum to another when there is more than one local maximum. Likewise, the global maximum may jump to the boundary, or from the boundary to an interior maximum, if the parameters are changed in discrete steps.[11] We exclude this possibility.

We reformulate the first-order condition (equation (7.2))

$$\partial E(\Pi(P^{d\star}))/\partial P^{d\star} \overset{\text{def}}{=} \Pi'(P^{d\star}) =$$

$$= (t+g+s)\underbrace{\left[\frac{t+g}{t+g+s} - \breve{f}' + \breve{f}(t+g+s)(P^t - P^{d\star})\right]}_{=0} = 0. \quad (7.5)$$

---

[11] This can also happen with marginal changes in s, t, g, f, however with a probability of the dimension zero.

First, we consider a variation of the *tax rate t*. Differentiating totally (7.5) with respect to $P^{d\star}$ and t yields

$$\frac{\mathrm{d}P^{d\star}}{\mathrm{d}t} = \frac{1 - \check{f} + \check{f}'(P^t - P^d)}{(t+g+s)[2\check{f}' - \check{f}''(P^t - P^{d\star})]} \tag{7.6}$$

The numerator of (7.6) is positive as can be seen from a comparison with the term in square brackets of (7.5). Since we are analyzing the variation of the global interior maximum only the denominator is negative: this is implied by equation (7.3). In other words, optimal underdeclaration rises if the tax rates are increased. That is intuitive since underdeclaration has become more profitable.

A variation of the *arbitrage gain* per unit of underdeclaration, g, yields the same result: $\mathrm{d}P^{d\star}/\mathrm{d}t = \mathrm{d}P^{d\star}/\mathrm{d}g < 0$. Once more these results are immediately clear: If the gain per unit of successful underdeclaration rises while punishment and the probability of detection, which depend both positively on the amount of underinvoicing, remain unaltered, the expected value of profits is maximized at a higher degree of cheating.

Stiffened sanctions decrease cheating. A variation in the *rate of penalty*, s, yields the following effect

$$\frac{\mathrm{d}P^{d\star}}{\mathrm{d}s} = -\frac{\check{f} - \check{f}'(P^t - P^d)}{[2\check{f}' - \check{f}''(P^t - P^{d\star})]} \quad > 0. \tag{7.7}$$

The numerator is positive since $\check{f}' < 0$ throughout the relevant interval (cf. section 7.2.2 and appendix B.3, esp. figure B.9) and underdeclaration is optimal. The denominator is negative for the same reason as above. Other things being equal, stricter punishment reduces the extent of criminal activity.

The same is true for the *probability of detection*. To analyze this we substitute $\kappa\check{f}$ for $\check{f}$ with κ positive. The first-order condition becomes

$$-(t+g) + \kappa\check{f}(t+g+s) - \kappa\check{f}'(t+g+s)(P^t - P^{d\star}) = 0.$$

Differentiating this new F.O.C. with respect to κ and $P^{d\star}$ yields[12]

$$\frac{\mathrm{d}P^{d\star}}{\mathrm{d}\kappa} = -\frac{\check{f} - \check{f}'(P^t - P^d)}{\kappa[2\check{f}' - \check{f}''(P^t - P^{d\star})]} \quad > 0.$$

In the absence of export subsidies, underdeclaration of export proceeds is the only sensible strategy – it diminishes taxes and, at the same time,

---

[12] $\kappa > 0$ and such that the altered detection function satisfies the condition $0 \geq \kappa\check{f} \geq 1$ for all $P^d \in [0, \tilde{P}^t_u - a]$.

effects a clandestine capital export thereby realizing an interest arbitrage gain. The authorities take this into account in their investigative behavior; this leads possibly to multiple maxima of the exporter's expected-profit function. Under reasonable assumptions we can exclude corner solutions. Without knowing the relevant parameter values and thus the specific detection function, it is impossible to determine how many interior maxima will exist and, if applicable, which one will be the global maximum.

In this setting, the authorities' scope for fighting evasion is limited. Punishment can be stiffened only within certain bounds as we have argued on page 137. The probability of detection is a result of an optimizing behavior: if the determinants of this optimization do not alter, the detection function will not either. In turn, these determining parameters, which influence the critical value a, can be changed only gradually over time (see page 124). They reflect the costs of investigation and the probability that investigation leads to conviction. Investigation technology and efficiency of the legal system can be improved only slowly in the course of time; they may even become worse if cheaters become more sophisticated and it therefore becomes more difficult to prove their guilt.

Other avenues of approach are an improvement on the a priori information and international cooperation. The former measure would reduce the variance of $q(\tilde{P}^t)$ (cf. p. 123) and thereby enhance the investigation probability for each $P^d < P^t - a$. The latter measure could make use of the interests of the domestic exporter and the foreign importer which may become opposed *if* their tax declarations are checked for consistency. As we have seen, the exporter seeks to understate the value of his or her goods whereas the foreign importer wants to overstate it if z is positive, i.e., the tax burden exceeds the tariff burden.[13] These conflicting interests are especially likely if the trading partner resides in an OECD country: duties are comparatively low whereas income tax rates or corporate tax rates, respectively, are substantial (i.e., $z > 0$). Moreover, international cooperation with more advanced countries "imports efficiency" from the tax administration of the partner country, which enhances the effective probability of detection.

A qualifying remark seems appropriate. As with most of the literature on the economics of crime, the results of the models presented have to be taken with a pinch of salt. In the preceding two chapters only economic variables have been considered. Empirical studies, however, provide strong indications that the models should also include psychological

---

[13] We have assumed that the trading partner does not face capital controls; otherwise the argument would have to be modified accordingly as set out in chapter 6.

and sociological variables as determinants of evasion.[14] People feel guilty when evading and shame in addition when detected which may deter them from evading taxes. Moreover, they may incur psychic costs which depend on the number of people who likewise evade taxes (Gordon 1989, Myles and Naylor 1996). Lastly, tax compliance may also be influenced by the degree of satisfaction with the government: If the taxpayer's beliefs coincide with those of the powers that be then he is less inclined to evade taxes and tariffs.[15]

Because further factors determine whether an individual will cheat the government or not, there will be two groups: the cheaters, or free-riders, and the "irrational" compliers, i.e., those loyally meeting their obligations to the state.[16] This observation, however, reinforces the government's case for curbing individuals' cheating: Investigation and punishment and the system of mutual checks on evasion activity, as outlined in chapter 6, will not only bring about increased effectiveness of government policy, but also reduce inequity between these two groups.

Yet, one of the most promising ways to reduce evasion in the long run is to pursue a policy that is supported by the people who are governed and burdened by controls and taxation. But this is already a different topic.

---

[14] For example, Geeroms and Wilmots (1985) and Alm *et al.* (1992) for an extensive discussion and Cowell (1985a: 178–180) and Pommerehne and Weck-Hannemann (1992: 445–461) and Andreoni *et al.* (1998: 850–852) for surveys of the literature.

[15] The influence of equity considerations and the belief in existing laws and institutions on the attitude toward tax evasion is analyzed in Baldry (1987), Geeroms and Wilmots (1985), Spicer (1986), Spicer and Becker (1980), and Webley *et al.* (1991), among others. Weigel *et al.* (1987) elaborate a social-psychological model of tax evasion behavior.

[16] Thurman (1991) provides evidence for the US that 75 percent of income taxpayers do not at all anticipate engaging in non-compliance. Andreoni *et al.* (1998: 819–821) come to a similar conclusion – two thirds of all US income taxpayers intend to pay their taxes correctly. Of course, this empirical finding need not and typically will not carry over to the case of a firm evading taxes and capital controls in a regulation-ridden developing economy. It underscores however the importance of factors other than purely economic ones.

Part III
Empirical measurement of the effectiveness of capital controls

8 The effects of capital controls – unexploited profit opportunities?

Capital controls, if they are biting, prevent otherwise profitable arbitrage operations and thus establish yield differentials between home and abroad. That is their intended effect. Economic agents subject to these controls try to realize this arbitrage gain nevertheless. They effect the desired capital export or import either legally by resorting to hitherto unrestricted transactions[1] or illegally by evading the controls, as we have seen in the previous part of this book. The government typically reacts by reinforcing the controls and broadening their coverage in order to close legal loopholes and to deter evasion more effectively, for these (illegal) arbitrage activities feed back to their cause – they tend to eliminate the intended yield differential. How effective are the controls in the end? This is the question we will address in this part of the book. It seems natural to look at the yield differential in order to assess the effectiveness of capital controls. If there are no unexploited profit opportunities the capital controls were not biting, however restrictive the regulations may have been.

Gros (1987) maintains that *quantitative* restrictions, as opposed to controls based on the differential tax treatments, may be effective in the short run, but will prove ineffective in the long run. The reason for this is that quantitative controls apply to flows rather than to entire stocks of particular assets; over time these controls can be evaded entirely, as evasion incurs costs which are assumed convex in the amount evaded. In the short run, however, it may be too costly to evade them to a

---

[1] Hewson and Sakakibara (1975b) provide examples for such circumventions for the US: The imposition of the Interest Equalization Tax, the Voluntary Foreign Credit Restraint and the Foreigh Direct Investment Program induced US banks to divert a considerable part of their activities to the unregulated Euromarket, thereby severely undermining the US regulations.

substantial extent.[2] This notion of long-run ineffectiveness is supported by empirical evidence: e.g., Giavazzi and Pagano (1985) show the Italian controls to be effective only during crises in the EMS, i.e., in times of expected realignments, but to be ineffective in calm periods.

Gros' results rest on the assumption that evasion which is sufficiently small is costless, so that over time any amount can be evaded. While this has certainly been the case for Italy in the 1980s and for other countries and for different periods as well, it is not an iron law which applies to any case. Italy is a very open economy with an import share of some 30 percent of GDP and millions of tourists crossing the borders every year. This opens many windows to circumvent controls in the medium term. Moreover, the effectiveness of capital controls will diminish with the development of the financial sector, as investors can switch to a close substitute if and when a control is imposed on a specific asset. Therefore, the same control may be effective in a financially less developed economy, but have no effect in a developed one. Phylaktis (1990) for instance provides evidence for the long-term effectiveness of Chilean capital controls; the French capital controls also have some effect even during calm periods of the EMS (Giavazzi and Pagano 1985). Empirical evidence is apparently mixed: the effectiveness of capital controls depends on specific circumstances and has thus to be established on a country-by-country basis.

In principle there are four avenues of approach when trying to assess the degree of capital mobility, or the effects of controls thereon; each approach tackles the problem from a different angle. One could look at the transaction impediments themselves, the price differentials created by them, or on their impact on capital flows and stocks. All routes have been taken to different extents and with different degrees of success.

The most direct approach looks at the capital controls themselves. In the simplest form capital controls are represented by a dummy variable that takes on the value one when capital controls are in place and zero otherwise. This approach has been taken for example by Alesina *et al.* (1994) and Grilli and Milesi-Ferretti (1995), who analyze the determinants of capital controls. The obvious shortcoming of this measure is that it does not account for different degrees of intensity of controls, but reflects their mere existence. This holds true for more "refined"

---

[2] Gros (1987: 622) suggests that differential tax treatments like withholding taxes on profits from exported capital may be permanently effective, because they refer to outstanding *stocks* rather than flows. This argument however is flawed because if controls of capital flows can be evaded, with the passage of time they will constitute stocks abroad, which authorities cannot monitor and, thus, their proceeds cannot be taxed.

approaches such as that used by Quinn and Inclan (1997) or Quinn (1997). They use the IMF classification of financial restrictions, i.e., restrictions on exchange payments and on exchange receipts, both for goods, invisibles, and capital, and they code each of the six classes from 0 to 2. Zero means that the transaction is prohibited, 2 means that it is unrestricted; the code can take on values between 0 and 2 in steps of 0.5 for each class of transaction. These values are added up and augmented by a variable (0–2) reflecting whether a country has entered legal agreements limiting its ability to restrict its financial flows. This results in a 0–14 dummy. This procedure might look impressive, it is however based on the extent of *stipulated* regulations only; in addition, the assignment of the dummy value for each category of transactions is somewhat arbitrary. It is not clear that this aggregated value reflects the true intensity of controls. First, it does not capture different degrees of enforcement. Second, restrictions of a certain class of transactions might cover a wide range of transactions within this category leading to a high dummy value. Yet, if they leave out some transactions within this category which constitute an efficient loophole, the stipulated restrictions might not be effective at all. The same rationale might apply across categories. If capital account transactions are tightly restricted, but some current account transactions are not (and they are not monitored either), the capital account restrictions might not be effective at all due to misinvoicing of the unrestricted transactions. An additive dummy does not account for the interdependency between transaction categories; it does not measure the effects of the controls but their existence.[3] It may serve as additional information explaining the findings of more reliable measures especially in time series studies when controls vary over time. Yet, a measurement concept that tries to assess the *consequences* of controls therefore captures much better the stringency of controls than this dummy variable approach.

A second approach looks at existing stocks and asks whether portfolios are optimally diversified or whether there is a diversification benefit from investing abroad. In particular, assets with perfectly correlated rates of return should have the same price regardless of the location if markets are integrated. A test on the effects of capital controls presupposes, however, specifying an asset-pricing model with and without restrictions, where the

---

[3] Edwards (1995a: 3) writes: "Ample historical evidence suggests that there have been significant discrepancies between the legal and the actual degree of controls. In countries with severe impediments to capital mobility ... the private sector has traditionally resorted to the overinvoicing of imports and underinvoicing of exports to sidestep legal controls on capital flows." The massive capital flight in Latin America in times of debt crisis underscores that. The dummy variable approach would just not capture these effects.

asset-pricing models depend on the restrictions imposed (Stulz 1981). Moreover, since portfolios are not optimally diversified, in countries that do not restrict capital movements (see Tesar and Werner 1995 for evidence on the US), it is difficult to assess which part of observed unexploited gain from portfolio diversification is due to capital controls and not to other (informational or institutional) barriers, individuals' attitudes, or irrationality. Moreover, as Stulz (1994: 32) puts it "The problem with using asset pricing models to test for the existence of barriers to international investment is that such tests typically lack power. The estimates are sufficiently imprecise that tests that use market integration as null hypothesis cannot reject the existence of economically significant barriers." We therefore do not pursue this approach here much further.[4] This is not to say that this approach does not have its merits; for the analysis of capital controls, however, the following two approaches are more suitable.

Because effective capital controls prevent arbitrage from taking place, it is natural to look at return differentials of assets which exhibit the same economic characteristics, but differ in the political jurisdiction under which they are issued. In other words we analyze covered interest rate differentials. This can be done by comparing the onshore and offshore (Euro-) rates of otherwise identical assets. Alternatively, assets may also differ in currency denomination, but are made comparable by a spot transaction in the market for foreign exchange and its countertransaction in the forward exchange market (covered interest rate differential in the original sense). This eliminates uncertainty about the future exchange rate and, therefore, assets differ again only with respect to the country in which they are issued. Consequently, any return differential can be traced back to government interference with the free movement of capital or to the risk of future interferences.

The last approach, pioneered by Feldstein and Horioka (1980), looks at capital flows rather than price differentials. Feldstein and Horioka argued that with mobile capital, domestic savings should be uncorrelated with domestic investment, because the former would go to a world-wide pool of funds and be allocated according to the marginal rate of return on a world-wide basis. Hence an increase in domestic savings should not

---

[4] For a survey see Stulz (1994); on the conceptual difficulties of measuring capital controls with stock market data see Gultekin *et al.* (1989); they provide an event study of the Japanese financial liberalization, where controls were dismantled in one step in December 1980. See Jansen (1995: chapters 6–7) for an analysis of German capital controls in this context and Claessens and Rhee (1994) for selected developing countries.

result in increased domestic investment for a small open economy. The authors consequently interpreted the correlation of saving and investment to be a measure of international capital mobility. This concept has not been used for the analysis of capital controls hitherto, but since it is claimed to be a test on the degree of capital mobility it seems straightforward to adopt it as a test on the restriction thereof, i.e., for the measurement of capital controls. The interpretation of the correlation of domestic saving and domestic investment as a measure for the degree of capital mobility has been seriously criticized on various grounds. We review and assess this critique and put forward our own methodological critique on the various econometric specifications used so far, before we discuss whether the correlation of saving and investment can serve as a suitable measure for the effectiveness of capital controls. Chapter 10 is devoted to this issue.

We refrain from reporting on the number of empirical studies which have analyzed the effects of capital controls for particular countries. This would entail lengthy descriptions of the country-specific institutional details; the effectiveness of capital controls is very dependent on the specifics of the particular case. For convenience, however, table 8.1 gives an overview of selected empirical studies of capital controls in various parts of the world.[5] In addition, Marston (1995: chapter 3) provides an excellent integrative survey of the British, French, German, Japanese, and US capital controls and their impact on interest differentials.

In the following two chapters we also present the results of empirical studies on Norwegian capital controls. They serve to underpin theoretical arguments and constitute new findings of the hitherto barely analyzed Norwegian capital controls. These studies are based on joint work with my colleague Willem Jos Jansen from The Tinbergen Institute, Rotterdam (Jansen and Schulze 1996a,b), to whom I am very much indebted. Why did we study Norway of all countries (apart from being able to present new results)? Norway constitutes a particularly interesting case: It had imposed a set of very restrictive regulations on transborder capital movements and was one of the very last West European economies to open up its credit markets. Capital controls were phased out as late as July 1, 1990! Moreover, the structure of the Norwegian economy

---

[5] The list can hardly be exhaustive, but we have tried to cite the most important pieces. We include only analyses which econometrically test for the effectiveness of capital controls, although descriptive (as opposed to econometric) analyses can be very informative as well. See Edwards (1995b) and Ito and Krueger, eds. (1996) for a number of such insightful studies.

Table 8.1. *Selected empirical studies, by region*

Asia	
Japan	Otani and Tiwari (1981)
	Ito (1986)
	Fukuda (1995)
Korea	Reisen and Yeches (1993)
	Chinn and Maloney (1996)
Taiwan	Reisen and Yeches (1993)
	Chinn and Maloney (1996)
Europe	
EU countries	Holmes and Wu (1997)
France	Claassen and Wyplosz (1982)
	Frankel (1982a)
	Giavazzi and Pagano (1985)
	Giavazzi and Giovannini (1986)
Germany	Herring and Marston (1976)
	Dooley and Isard (1980)
Ireland	Browne and McNelis (1990)
Italy	Giavazzi and Pagano (1985)
	Giavazzi and Giovannini (1986)
Norway	Jansen and Schulze (1996a,b)
Latin America	
Argentina	Phylaktis (1988)
	Phylatkis (1990)
Chile	Phylaktis (1990)
Colombia	Edwards and Khan (1985)
Mexico	Melvin and Schlangenhauf (1985)
	Spiegel (1990)
Uruguay	Phylaktis (1990)

was (and still is) remarkable. A very outward oriented shipping sector contributed an average 2.6 percent to GDP, but 16.6 percent to total exports in 1980–1989. What is more important, the oil sector has become very dominant since the second oil price shock, producing an average of 14 percent of the GDP, 20 percent of total exports, and around 20 percent of domestic capital formation.[6] These two sectors were granted free access to world credit markets, but banned from domestic markets, while the picture was reversed for the rest of the economy. This dichotomy in

---

[6] Data taken from the *Statistical Yearbook*, Norwegian Central Bureau of Statistics (various issues).

regulation makes the system of Norwegian foreign exchange controls even more interesting. The controls, designed to "insulate the domestic credit market and the domestic interest rate level from external influence" (Norges Bank 1989: 43) were gradually liberalized during the eighties, the year 1984 marking a major liberalization step.

Did the controls achieve their intended goal? Had there been unexploited profit opportunities in the past? This is what we will investigate next, comparing yields of otherwise identical assets traded in and outside Norway.

9   Return differentials

9.1 Introduction

This chapter presents the common approach to measuring the impact of capital controls and it briefly surveys the main empirical studies on this subject, all of which rely on a comparison of domestic and foreign interest rates. It furthermore analyzes empirically the effectiveness of Norwegian capital controls in the eighties. We do this by comparing return differentials of various assets, i.e., loans, bonds and stocks, between the onshore and the offshore market or between Norway and the rest of the world, respectively.

As we have pointed out, the analysis of Norway's capital controls seems promising. It is rather surprising though that, apart from Vikøren (1993), the financial integration of the Norwegian economy has not been studied hitherto. Yet, even Vikøren does not explicitly test for the effectiveness of capital controls as we do, following the standard Dooley and Isard (1980) approach; furthermore our coverage is broader, comprising also bond and equity returns.

We proceed as follows. The next section (9.2) is devoted to the analysis of covered interest rate differentials in the context of capital controls. We first survey the literature on the covered interest rate parity, identifying the reasons for covered interest rate differentials; then we present briefly an approach pioneered by Edwards and Khan (1985), which assesses the degree of financial openness if data for either forward exchange rates or market determined domestic rates are not available so that a test on covered interest rate parity is not feasible. This is a common difficulty for developing countries, where these rates are only established after liberalization has made major progress and a sufficient degree of capital mobility has been established. In section 9.3 we present the Dooley and Isard approach for measuring the impact of capital controls, which we subsequently adopt for the analysis of Norway's capital controls. In section 9.5, we turn to differentials of bond returns and equity returns. Lastly, we offer some concluding remarks.

9.2 Capital controls and the covered interest rate parity

The covered interest rate parity (CIP) theorem states that, in integrated capital markets, the yields of assets with identical economic characteristics, *viz.* the same default risk, should be equal across national financial markets: the interest rate differential should equal the forward discount of the two currencies involved. Algebraically stated, CIP implies

$$\frac{f - s}{s} = \frac{i - i^*}{1 + i^*},$$ (9.1)

where s denotes the spot rate, f the forward rate for a maturity equal to the holding period of the assets, and i (i^*) the domestic (foreign) nominal interest rate of this asset. In the absence of capital controls, deviations from the CIP are attributable to either transaction costs, government regulations such as minimum reserve requirements, or less-than-infinite elasticities of demand and supply for foreign exchange or securities. These costs constitute a neutral band around the parity, within which arbitrage is not profitable (for the derivation, see Frenkel and Levich 1975). It is now well established that in the Euromarket, in which government regulations are absent, transaction costs account for almost all of the deviations from the parity line (Frenkel and Levich 1975, 1977, 1981), though there is some debate as to the size of this band (McCormick 1979, Clinton 1988).[1] When comparing assets in different national markets, covered interest differentials have to be adjusted for divergent minimum reserve requirements and/or taxation of interest earnings and capital gains to appropriately measure the effective yields (or costs of funding).[2] The overwhelming result of these empirical studies implies that there are no systematically unexploited profit opportunities, either in the Euromarket or between national markets – the covered interest rate differentials fall, almost always, within the neutral band. This result holds true if onshore interest rates are compared with offshore rates in the same currency, i.e., appropriate rates in the Euromarket. In the absence of

[1] Unlike Frenkel and Levich, Clinton (1988) and Taylor (1989) show that there are occasional deviations, especially in times of turbulence, which however are very small.
[2] Levi (1977) models deviations due to differences in taxation, Lizondo (1983) estimates these effects for the dollar–peso differential; Herring and Marston (1976) adjust the US rates for minimum reserve requirements.

controls, interest rate differentials are due to minimum reserve requirements.[3]

Capital controls drive a wedge between onshore and offshore rates just as they cause the interest rate differential to deviate from the forward discount. This has been demonstrated by many empirical studies, *inter alia* by Herring and Marston (1976) for German domestic and Eurorates, by Frankel (1982a) for France, by Giavazzi and Pagano (1985) and Giavazzi and Giovannini (1986) for France and Italy, by Melvin and Schlangenhauf (1985) for Mexico, and by Ito (1986) for Japan. Capital controls bring about the covered interest rate differentials through two channels: the *existing* capital controls and the political risk. The existing capital controls, if they are biting, have an effect comparable to a tax; in the case of capital export controls they function like a tax on earnings on foreign-placed funds. The interest rate in the Euromarket exceeds the domestic interest rate by more than the transaction costs because the controls inhibit arbitrage.

Aliber (1973) argues, the threat of *future* capital controls will make two (otherwise identical) assets imperfect substitutes, if they are issued under different political jurisdictions. They will differ in political risk, which he defines as

the probability, that the authority of the state will be interposed between investors in one country and investment opportunities in other countries. (p. 1453)

By the very nature of risk, the political risk has nothing to do with the level of existing regulations. For example, even if capital controls were not in place and onshore rates were initially equal to Eurorates, capital would exit the country if people began to fear the imposition of controls to lock in domestic capital at lower future rates. This anticipatory avoidance of future capital controls alone would thus establish a yield differential. By the same rationale, foreigners may be willing to hold additional domestic assets only if they are compensated by an interest rate premium, especially if they anticipate that the repatriation of profits or funds could be jeopardized by future capital controls. We will discuss the determinants of the political risk premium in section 9.3.

---

[3] See for example Giavazzi and Pagano (1985) for the Dutch Guilder. See also Taylor (1987) for corroborating evidence on the CIP and Levich (1985) and MacDonald and Taylor (1990) for surveys. Leaving transaction costs aside, which are minimal in the Euromarket, the neutral band is now defined by the following inequalities: $i(1 - m) \le i^e \le i$, where i^e denotes the Eurorate of the respective domestic currency and m denotes the minimum reserve requirement rate.

The interest differential becomes particularly large if a devaluation[4] is expected. An expected devaluation of the domestic currency will increase the forward discount as the forward exchange rate rises. If capital moves unrestrictedly as in the Euromarket, investors will switch their capital to other currency-denominated assets, until the interest rate differential in favor of the domestic currency makes up for the devaluation loss. CIP is reestablished. While this equilibrating mechanism works in the Euromarket, residents do not have the option to buy foreign assets, as capital controls inhibit these transactions efficiently at least in the short run. The interest rate on assets denominated in the domestic currency is rocketing in the Euromarket, but remains fairly stable in the domestic market. Giavazzi and Pagano (1985) illustrate this point.

In order to separate the tax effect from the political risk effect on the covered interest differential (CID), it is necessary to assess the rigor of the capital controls independently of the covered interest differential. A common, yet crude approach to this is to portray the varying tightness by dummies for discrete changes or a polynomial for a continuous variation. Frankel (1982a) shows that the intensification of controls after the election of a socialist president and a socialist majority in France had considerable effect on the covered interest differential: his "Mitterrand dummy" (beginning 1981) is sizeable and significant. Dooley and Isard (1980) use a step-function for dummies, as well as a third degree polynomial, to portray the varying tightness of German capital import controls. They furthermore explain the political risk premium by means of a portfolio balance model and are thereby able to explain 80 percent of the observed CID. Their approach has been used frequently for the analysis of capital controls. Claassen and Wyplosz (1982) for instance adopt the Dooley and Isard method to analyze the French capital export controls, making use of the Mathis scale to measure the tightness of capital controls. Mathis (1981) proposes a three-step scale, distinguishing restrictions on banks and non-banks. Other papers using the Dooley and Isard method of investigating the effects of capital controls are Phylaktis (1988) for Argentina, Phylaktis (1990) for Argentina, Chile, and Uruguay, and Spiegel (1990) for Mexico.

We also follow the approach developed by Dooley and Isard (1980) in order to investigate the impact of Norwegian capital controls in the eighties. Before we present their approach, however, we note one major shortcoming. Covered interest rate differentials rely either on the com-

---

[4] In the case of capital export controls, which we are considering here, a revaluation is very unlikely. Dooley and Isard (1980) analyze the opposite case, i.e., German capital import controls in the early seventies when a revaluation was anticipated.

parison of onshore and offshore rates for identical assets or on domestic interest rates being made comparable to foreign interest rates of otherwise identical assets by means of a spot and a matching forward transaction in the market for foreign exchange (cf. equation (9.1)). This requires however that either an offshore (Euro-) market for assets denominated in this currency exists or that a forward market for the domestic currency exists and that a market-determined domestic interest rate is available. While these requirements have been met by most advanced countries with capital controls, for many developing countries the respective markets come into existence only after a considerable degree of capital mobility has been established. Hence the estimates of covered interest rate differentials are not generally feasible.

Edwards and Khan (1985) suggest a framework for measuring the degree of capital mobility for this case. It has been modified by Haque and Montiel (1990). It is based on the notion that the observed domestic interest rate (i) is a weighted average of the interest rate that would prevail if the economy were completely closed (i^c) and the interest rate of a completely open economy (i^o)

$$i + \psi i^o + (1 - \psi)i^c; \quad 0 \leq \psi \leq 1. \tag{9.2}$$

ψ is a structural parameter of the economy and measures the degree of openness. The open economy interest rate is given by the uncovered interest parity, i.e., $i^o = i^* + \Delta s^e$, where i^* is again the world interest rate and Δs^e denotes the expected rate of change of the exchange rate.[5] The interest rate for a closed economy is derived from the domestic money market equilibrium in the absence of private transborder capital flows. Money supply (M) is the sum of the stock of domestic credit (D) and foreign exchange reserves (R) which is the sum of last periods stock of reserves (R_{-1}) and the change in reserves, which in turn consists of the balances of the current account (CA), the public sector capital account (KA_G), and the private sector capital account: (KA_P)

$$M = R_{-1} + D + CA + KA_G + KA_P. \tag{9.3}$$

The money stock that existed in the absence of capital mobility (M') is then – following Haque and Montiel (1990) – given by $M' = M - KA_P$. That allows them to estimate the – fictitious – market clearing domestic interest rate in the absence of capital mobility

$$\ln(M'/P) = \alpha_0 + \alpha_1 i^c + \alpha_2 \ln y + \ln(M/P)_{-1}. \tag{9.4}$$

---

[5] Note that this is an approximation, the exact formula is given by equation (9.1) when the forward rate f is replaced by the future expected spot rate s^e_{t+1}.

The right-hand side of (9.4) is the logarithm of the real money demand which depends on the fictitious interest rate i^c, the real output y, and the previous period's real money supply. (P denotes the price level.) The parameter ψ then provides information about the degree of capital mobility; the closer it is to unity, the higher the degree of capital mobility.

This approach has been used for developing countries, e.g., by Reisen and Yeches (1993) for Korea and Taiwan, Dooley and Mathieson (1993) for the Pacific Rim, and Dooley (1995) for Korea. It is of course not without problems: First, there are persistent systematic deviations from the *un*covered interest rate parity also for countries with free capital mobility, so that estimates may be biased. Second, this approach makes the strong assumption that there is no contemporaneous interaction of private capital flows with either public capital flows or the current account. Endogeneity problems however are frequent in such settings, for instance they occur if government borrowing abroad is a substitute for private borrowing. Moreover, Dooley (1995) shows that the results for the degree of capital mobility are highly sensitive with respect to the selection of "the" domestic interest rate (regulated interbank rate or curb rate on the unregulated segment of the capital market). It should be borne in mind that this approach was created to overcome the lack of appropriate data, and thus should not be discarded easily because of its shortcomings; the alternative would be not to measure capital mobility via return differentials. It is clear though that an approach based on covered interest rate differentials à la Dooley and Isard (1980) is preferable. This is what we turn to next.

9.3 The model of Dooley and Isard

The approach of Dooley and Isard is built on a simple portfolio balance model of the domestic private sector and of the non-residents, both of which optimize their portfolio, given the existing capital controls and the (individual) prospects of future capital controls.[6] It implicitly takes account of existing legal or illegal arbitrage possibilities. The Norwegian private sector can invest in Norwegian assets, with return i^d in Norway and i^e in the international market, and in foreign assets, with expected return $i^* + \Delta s$, where i, i^e, and i^* are the interest rate on domestic (kroner) deposits, the Eurokroner interest rate, and the Euro-interest

6 This and the following sections draw on Jansen and Schulze (1996a). I am very much indebted to my co-author, and to Birger Vikøren and many of his colleagues in Norges Bank, the Norwegian central bank for providing data and information, and to Gebhard Kirchgässner for helpful comments.

rate on foreign deposits, respectively; Δs stands for the expected depreciation of the kroner. Foreigners (both private and public sector) have the same option. The asset demand functions are given by

$$B^n = f(i - i^* - \Delta s, i - i^e, W^n, C) \tag{9.5}$$

$$B^* = g(i - i^* - \Delta s, i - i^e, W^*, C), \tag{9.6}$$

where B^n and B^* denote, respectively, the Norwegian private and the foreign holdings of kroner government debt, W^n and W^* the Norwegian and foreign financial wealth. C is a measure of capital controls already in place. Asset demand depends positively on both the return differentials and wealth. The total supply of kroner debt is B^s, so asset market equilibrium entails

$$B^s = B^n + B^*. \tag{9.7}$$

Since the covered interest parity holds in the Euromarket, we can write

$$\Delta s = i^e - i^* + \phi, \tag{9.8}$$

where ϕ is the exchange risk premium. Combining equations (9.5)–(9.8) and assuming equations (9.5) and (9.6) to be linear, leads to

$$i - i^e = \alpha_0 + \alpha_1 B^s - \alpha_2 W^n - \alpha_3 W^* + \alpha_4 \phi + \alpha_5 C \tag{9.9}$$

with α_i positive ($i = 1, \ldots, 4$) in the normal case. Equation (9.9) can be viewed as the sum of a political risk premium associated with *prospective* capital controls ($\alpha_0 + \alpha_1 B^s - \alpha_2 W^n - \alpha_3 W^* + \alpha_4 \phi$) and an effective tax caused by the *already existing* capital controls ($\alpha_5 C$). According to the simple portfolio balance model of the exchange rate (e.g., Branson *et al.* 1977) the exchange risk premium can be written as (adopting a linear specification)

$$\phi = \beta_0 - \beta_1 B^s + \beta_2 W^n + \beta_3 W^* \tag{9.10}$$

with β_i positive ($i = 1,2,3$) in the normal case. Substituting equation (9.10) into equation (9.9) and adding a disturbance term, yields our regression equation

$$i - i^e = \underbrace{\gamma_0 + \gamma_1 B^s + \gamma_2 W^n + \gamma_3 W^*}_{DIFF_{pol.risk}} + \gamma_4 C + \nu \tag{9.11}$$

where ν is assumed to follow a normal time-independent distribution with zero mean. $DIFF_{pol.risk}$ estimates the differential due to the political risk of future imposition of capital controls, whereas $\gamma_4 C$ measures the tax effect of the controls in place. Since the coefficients of B^s, W^n, and W^* have opposite signs in equations (9.9) and (9.10), the signs of γ_i

$(i = 1,2,3)$ are indetermined. The political risk premium and the exchange risk premium are negatively related. The sign of $\gamma_4 C$ depends on the type of control: it is negative in case of capital export restrictions and positive for capital import restrictions. The interest differential due to political risk depends on the gross stock of government debt and the distribution of total wealth among the Norwegian private sector and the foreigners.

9.4 A case study for Norway

9.4.1 Overview of Norwegian capital controls

The Eurokroner market has existed since the end of 1977, but it only really began to function in November 1978, after Norges Bank allowed the large Norwegian banks to borrow and lend freely on the international market, provided their combined net foreign exchange position (spot plus forward) was approximately zero on a daily basis. In April 1980 all banks were allowed access to the Euromarket (Grønvik 1991). In September 1980 the general price freeze including all lending rates was discontinued. It is only after this date that the comparison between onshore and off-shore rates becomes viable to measure the effectiveness of *capital* controls as such.[7]

Transborder portfolio investment was almost prohibited, borrowing abroad required restrictively granted licenses, and inward direct investment was made subject to concessions. The minor amount of outward direct investment was treated liberally. Banks had to balance their total foreign position (spot and forward) and non-residents were restricted from holding kroner accounts, just as residents were restricted from holding foreign exchange accounts. Only companies with foreign currency transactions were allowed to operate on the international deposit market, although their financial transactions were restricted in size, maturity, and currency denomination. In December 1981, the maturity restriction (set at 12 months) was lifted for those firms. There followed a period of gradual and cautious liberalization, especially with regard to inward portfolio investment (Spring 1982), but also outward portfolio investment and bank regulations were eased. A major liberalization package entered into effect in June 1984, affecting almost all types of transactions. Other residents were permitted access to the Euromarket

---

[7] For a chronology of Norwegian capital controls, cf. Brekk (1987), Norges Bank (1989), and Schulze (1992c).

in December 1989. Capital controls were completely abolished by July 1, 1990.

Since Norway pursued a low-interest rate policy, we focus on capital export restrictions. These were liberalized in December 1981 and in December 1989. The controls are represented by two dummies: D_{81} (equal to one for 1980.II–1981.IV and zero otherwise) and D_{89} (equal to one for 1982.IV–1989.IV and zero otherwise), for which we expect a negative sign in equation (9.11) as these controls inhibit the exploitation of more profitable investment opportunities in the Euromarket. In order to avoid a downward bias, capital control dummies should enter the regression equation only for those quarters in which the controls were actually binding, i.e., in which the desired capital outflow was larger than was permitted. Since this bindingness is not directly observable, we resort to an indirect measure and consider the restrictions to be non-binding if the private non-bank sector has actually been importing short-term capital on a net basis.

9.4.2 Data and empirical results

Like Dooley and Isard (1980), we calculate B^s, W^n, and W^* as linear combinations of government debt (DEBT), official foreign exchange reserves (RES), and the net stock of Norwegian claims on non-residents, equal to the accumulated current account surpluses ($\sum$ CAS) as follows

$$B^s = \text{DEBT} + \text{RES} \tag{9.12}$$

$$W^n = \text{DEBT} + \sum \text{CAS} \tag{9.13}$$

$$W^* = - \sum \text{CAS}. \tag{9.14}$$

Since this wealth concept does not include claims on real assets, world net wealth is zero. Government net wealth is –DEBT, so that $W^n + W^* = \text{DEBT}$.

As external interest rate (i^e) we use the 3-month Eurokroner rate; for the internal rate we could use the special 3-month deposit rate Norwegian commercial banks offer to large customers.[8] Due to data availability, our sample consists of quarterly data and runs from 1980.III to 1990.IV. The onshore and offshore interest rates are shown in figure 9.1. In the early

---

[8] We are grateful to Dr Birger Vikøren from the Norwegian Central Bank for giving us access to this data base.

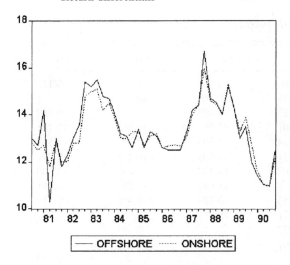

Figure 9.1 Covered interest rate differential in Norway

eighties the Euromarket rate is much more volatile than the domestic interest rate which indicates that capital controls denied at times short-term arbitrage. For the rest of the sample period both interest rates moved closely together implying that both markets have been effectively integrated.[9]

Equation (9.11) is estimated with OLS and the results are depicted in table 9.1.[10] The capital control dummy D_{81}, having an insignificant coefficient of the right sign, and D_{89}, having an insignificant coefficient of the wrong sign, imply that the effective tax is estimated to be zero. The political risk premium is also zero as the parameter estimates are all insignificant and the fit is very poor. An F-test on the joint significance of the coefficients of B^s, W^n, and W^* produced an $F(3,37)$ value of 0.96, below the 5 percent critical value of 2.86. In addition, the Durbin–Watson and Breusch–Godfrey statistics signal seriously autocorrelated residuals. The relation is dynamically misspecified. To remedy this we added a lagged interest rate differential as a regressor, on the assumption that the banks adjust the domestic deposit rate with some lag to changes in the Eurokroner rate. This conjecture is consistent with the somewhat lower variance of the domestic interest rate compared to the Eurokroner rate.

[9] Domestic deposit rates are typically lower than the corresponding Eurorates due to the minimum reserve requirement.
[10] The diagnostic tests are explained in appendix C.2.

Table 9.1. *CIP, 1980.III–1990.IV*

	(1)	(2)	(3)	(4)
constant	0.160	0.188	0.102	0.143
	(0.48)	(0.56)	(0.33)	(0.47)
B_t^n	7.783	8.095	0.313	0.969
	(1.50)	(1.58)	(0.06)	(0.18)
W_t^n	−12.784	−13.393	−1.337	−2.523
	(1.53)	(1.63)	(0.15)	(0.29)
W_t^*	13.702	14.132	−2.048	−3.000
	(1.61)	(1.68)	(0.23)	(0.34)
D_{8081}	−0.168	−0.189	−0.491	−0.515
	(0.77)	(0.88)	(2.08)	(2.20)
D_{89}	0.072		0.098	
	(0.60)		(0.90)	
$(i^d - i^e)_{t-1}$			0.468	0.454
			(2.77)	(2.71)
σ	0.319	0.316	0.290	0.289
$\bar{R}^2$	0.028	0.045	0.217	0.221
DW/Durbin-h	1.288	1.257	1.585	1.394
BG(1)	6.498	7.079	2.549	1.927
BG(2)	6.007	6.714	2.550	1.872
ARCH(1)	0.838	0.523	0.001	0.044
JB	2.649	3.091	2.108	1.754

Note: Durbin-h applies to regressions (3) and (4).
Source: Norges Bank, BIS; t values in parentheses.

The estimation results of the dynamic equation are much better and imply an estimated effective capital control tax of 0.9 percent in the long run on domestic deposits for the early years in the sample period. The dummy D_{89}, however, is still insignificant. Moreover, since all determinants of the political risk premium have small and highly insignificant coefficients, the estimated political risk premium associated with future capital controls is effectively zero. This is not startling because after liberalizing the money market, the Norwegian government was continuously dismantling capital controls in other areas in the course of the eighties. In such a climate a reversal of the money market liberalization was certainly considered unlikely. Compared to the static equation, the fit of the equation has increased considerably, while the test statistics do not indicate any autocorrelation, conditional heteroskedasticity, or non-normality.[11]

Although there were some capital controls in force, it seems fair to conclude that on the whole the Norwegian money market appears to have been well integrated into the international money market in the 1980s. The fact that some private agents were barred from the international market did not prevent interest rate equalization, presumably due to the competitive banking system. Only in the early 1980s did we find some weak evidence of binding capital controls. So it would make more sense to analyze the experience in the seventies, when the money market was highly regulated. Unfortunately, data unavailability constitutes a fatal stumbling block for such a venture.

9.5 Other return differentials

In the early eighties international portfolio investment, the cross-border trade of long-term bonds and stocks, was most severely regulated. We therefore turn our attention to the relative returns on bonds and stocks, employing the same theoretical framework as above: the expected return differential is explained by relative asset supplies, wealth and dummies representing capital controls. The actual return differentials (computed relative to US assets) include exchange rate changes and asset price changes. The portfolio balance model states that

$$E_t(r^n - r^u)_{t+1} = \delta_0 + \delta_1 A^n + \delta_2 A^u + \delta_3 W^n + \delta_4 W^u + \text{dummies}, \tag{9.15}$$

where A and W denote asset supply and wealth at the end of quarter t, r denotes the total return converted to kroner over quarter t, and superscripts n and u denote Norway and United States, respectively. E_t denotes

---

[11] We also estimated equation (9.11) (the static as well as the dynamic version) after scaling B^s and W^n by world wealth ($W^n + W^*$). This scaling is more in line with the international capital asset pricing model (CAPM), which connects relative yields to relative asset supplies, measured as shares of world wealth (see, e.g., Frankel 1982b). W^* was dropped from the equation to avoid linear dependence among regressors. The estimation results proved to be imperceptibly influenced by this data transformation.

As an alternative to the partial adjustment specification of the Dooley and Isard equation, we also estimated a simple Error Correction Model (ECM) linking i^d to i^e and capital control dummies. This approach solely focuses on the time series characteristics of the two interest rates. The interest differential due to the effective capital control tax was now estimated at -0.5 percent for D_{81} (t-value estimate 2.49) and zero for D_{89} (t-value estimate 0.07).

the expectation conditional on information available at the end of quarter t. Assuming rational expectations our regression equation reads

$$(r^n - r^u)_{t+1} = \delta_0 + \delta_1 A^n + \delta_2 A^u + \delta_3 W^n + \delta_4 W^u + \text{dummies} + \varepsilon_{t+1},$$

$$(9.16)$$

where ε_{t+1} is a white noise prediction error. The sample period is 1978.I–1990.IV (52 quarters). Returns are expressed as quarterly rates.

9.5.1 Bond returns

Until autumn 1980, market forces played no significant role in the bond market: the government controlled supply via restrictive issue regulations and demand through an investment obligation for banks, life insurance companies, etc. Low bond rates discouraged voluntary purchases (Norges Bank 1989, Næs and Winje 1993). Then, the issue regulations were eased and the investment obligation was gradually phased out by the mid 1980s.

Both the inward and outward trade of bonds were strictly regulated. The purchase of Norwegian bonds by foreigners was severely limited. Until 1980 the purchase of foreign bonds by Norwegian residents was practically ruled out; in the early 1980s some firms could buy foreign bonds, but only for narrowly defined hedging purposes. After January 1985 Norwegians were allowed to buy foreign bonds, but a ceiling was set on these transactions. Having been barred from the bond market since 1984, non-residents were allowed to purchase Norwegian bonds in May 1989.

We summarize the different regulations in one dummy for capital import and one for capital export. Both dummies are equal to one at the start of the sample period and decrease stepwise to zero at the end of the sample period. In order to observe the bindingness of the restriction we assign positive values to the capital import (export) dummy, only if there is net import (export) of bonds.

The bond yield consists of the coupon payment and the capital gain (in NKr). Quarterly yields are highly volatile: For 1978.I–1990.IV, the return on Norwegian bonds had a mean of 2.67 percent and a standard deviation of 2.43 percent; for American bonds the mean was 2.69 percent and the standard deviation 6.60 percent. The difference between the means is only 0.02 percent (less than 0.1 percent on an annual basis) and insignificantly different from zero (t-value 0.02). The time path of the bond return differential is rather erratic, its peaks and troughs reflecting the extremes of the volatile American bond return.

Table 9.2. *Differential bond returns, 1977.IV–1990.III*

Constant	B_t^n	B_t^u	W_t^n	W_t^u	D_{export}	σ	$\bar{R}^2$
0.092	−17.65	−1.555	10.33	0.497	−0.041	0.665	0.084
(1.64)	(1.91)	(2.02)	(0.85)	(1.55)	(1.67)		

Source: IFS, t-values in parentheses.

The estimation results (not reported) produced no significant values for the dummies representing capital controls and no discernable political risk premium. Since the import dummy performed especially badly and the Norwegian capital controls in general were targeted at restricting capital export, we dropped the import dummy from the equation. The export dummy represents only the period of severe controls on outward capital movements; it is one through 1984.IV, zero otherwise. It turned out to be significant at the 10 percent level (cf. table 9.2).[12] The estimated effect is 16.5 percent on an annual basis, which amounts however to only 0.6 times the standard deviation of the return differential. The determinants of the political risk premium still fail to exert a significant influence, the F(4,45) statistic reaching only 1.74 which is in line with the expectation of (gradual) liberalization, which is what actually took place.

9.5.2 Equity returns

Since Norway continuously experienced net capital import as to the trade in stocks (net selling of Norwegian stocks to abroad) over the whole sample period, regulations restricting outward capital movements are considered to have been non-binding by our classification criterion. Therefore we focus solely on the capital import restrictions. Until October 1979 foreigners could only purchase one million kroner of Norwegian quoted stocks. In February 1982 trade in quoted stocks became free, while there was licensing for non-quoted stocks. This licensing was abolished in January 1984.

Table 9.3 shows the estimation results when the three regimes are represented by three separate zero–one dummies. The values for the respective test statistics are: DW 2.218, BG(1) 1.158, BG(2) 2.214, ARCH(1) 1.791, and JB 0.521. It appears that the effective capital con-

---

[12] The values for the respective test statistics are DW 2.814, BG(1) 0.984, BG(2) 1.048, ARCH(1) 0.386.

Table 9.3. *Differential equity returns, 1978.I–1990.III*

Constant	A_t^n	A_t^u	W_t^n	W_t^u	D_1	D_2	D_3	σ	R^2
0.172	−123.6	5.989	17.89	−5.113	0.215	−0.059	0.161	0.150	0.158
(1.02)	(2.41)	(2.03)	(0.51)	(2.13)	(2.27)	(0.76)	(1.44)		

Source: IFS, Morgan, Stanley; t-statistics in parentheses.

trol tax was highest in the first subperiod when the controls were most severe. The estimated effect is fairly high and significant at the 5 percent level. The other two estimates of capital control effects are insignificant. The test that the coefficients of the political risk premium determinants are jointly zero yields an F(4,46) statistic of 2.73, which is significant at the 95 percent confidence level (critical F(4,46) is 2.57). So a risk premium associated with prospective regulations explains part of the observed share yield differential, albeit a small part as is indicated by the adjusted R^2 statistic of only 0.12.

9.6 Conclusion

The investigation of Norway's capital controls for the sample period of 1978–1990 has produced the following results: The controls had a significant effect on *stock returns* in the first subperiod, but have been ineffective from the mid eighties onwards when controls were increasingly dismantled. It has proved hard, however, to identify a systematic influence of the controls on *short-term interest rates* and *bond returns*, although there is some evidence that regulations on international portfolio investment systematically affected also these return differentials in the late seventies to early eighties.

That the results do not show a stronger impact of the capital controls may be partly due to data quality: the time series on stock and bond returns display a high variance; but especially the unavailability of data for the seventies constitutes a fatal stumbling block for a more comprehensive analysis. This period marks an era of really stringent capital controls, which should have produced more pronounced effects of capital controls on return differentials. Unfortunately, lack of data inhibits this venture.

It is also conceivable that results have been affected by our method of assigning (non)bindingness to the control dummies: although our method makes good sense, there is no guarantee that the assignment is entirely correct. An alternative approach, viz. endogenization of the regime clas-sification (though theoretically promising) seems unfeasible in the face of the poor data quality. It would be overdemanding to expect the data to determine both incidence and effects of capital controls.

These remarks notwithstanding, it seems obvious that the Norwegian capital controls have not been very effective in the eighties. At first glance this is very surprising, not only because the regulations were explicitly aimed at insulating the domestic credit markets: "The wish to pursue an autonomous Norwegian monetary and credit policy is at present the main reason for the foreign exchange regulations" (Brekk 1987: 28). That the controls effected so little is also surprising because the restric-tions were tight and covered a broad variety of transactions (inward and outward portfolio and direct investment, borrowing abroad, purchase of vacation homes abroad, and the like) and institutions (private non-banks, banks, insurance companies, other financial institutions).

Our result is, however, in line with an emerging body of evidence showing that for developed economies capital controls have been hardly effective in the medium and long term in the recent past. Controls became more and more leaky as time passed. This is shown by Browne and McNelis (1990) for Ireland, Spiegel (1990) for Mexico, and Gros (1992) for the EMS member countries.

A reason for this ineffectiveness of capital controls is that international trade provides ample opportunities to illicitly import and export capital via leading and lagging of trade payments and via misinvoicing of inter-national trade (see part II). Moreover, the mere growth and the rising sophistication of financial markets and the emergence of new financial instruments may have made it difficult for the authorities to keep track of these developments and to efficiently regulate and monitor the rising number and variety of transactions. A special Norwegian line of explana-tion lies in the dichotomous structure of the economy – and of the foreign exchange regulation. Since the shipping and the oil sector were unrest-ricted, the Norwegian economy possessed a window to the world finan-cial markets, despite the controls. Backward and forward linkages of these sectors to the rest of the economy provided – legal and illegal – channels for foreign-originated funding. In the end, it may not only have been a growing insight into the advantages of efficient capital allocation that has led to the abolition of capital controls.

10 The correlation of saving and investment

10.1 Introduction

The interest rate approach, discussed in the previous chapter, focuses on *financial assets*, i.e., claims on existing (and hence installed) capital at any given point in time, rather than on *new physical capital*. Net transfers of capital are effected through current account balances, which by national accounts identity amount to the difference between saving and investment. For this reason Feldstein and Horioka (1980) suggested that the international mobility of this new physical capital (defined in a broad sense)[1] be measured by the correlation of saving and investment. We will discuss this measurement concept for capital mobility, and thus for the effects of capital controls, in this chapter.

Feldstein and Horioka (1980: 317) state that "with perfect world capital mobility, there should be no relation between domestic saving and domestic investment: saving in each country responds to the worldwide opportunities for investment while investment in that country is financed by the worldwide pool of capital." However, in a cross-country regression using period-averaged saving and investment figures for 16 OECD countries, they obtain a significant coefficient close to unity and conclude that capital is rather immobile. This result constitutes the "Feldstein–Horioka puzzle," as it contradicts the widely held perception that capital is highly mobile across countries. The findings of Feldstein and Horioka (1980) have led to numerous theoretical and empirical papers on the close correlation between domestic saving and domestic investment, and its

[1] If we disregard statistical errors and omissions it is clear from the balance of payments identity that the difference between domestic saving and domestic investment amounts to net capital exports. These net capital exports, however, can be effected not only through the export of capital goods but also of consumption goods and services. For the sake of completeness it must be noted that net capital import need not increase the domestic capital formation, because it can be accompanied by an increased consumption (compared to the *ex ante* consumption plan). Besides, investment also includes inventory investments.

supposed implications for international capital mobility: They confirmed the close correlation, though its implication for the degree of capital mobility remains a moot point.[2]

This chapter contributes to the understanding of the puzzle on both theoretical and empirical counts.[3] After reviewing the state of the discussion we first discuss the possible usefulness of the estimates for detecting capital mobility and judging the effects of capital controls thereon. Second, we present a theory-based econometric specification for estimating saving–investment correlations. Third, we provide empirical results for the interesting case of Norway.

Apart from seeking reliable measures for the effectiveness of capital controls, our research is motivated by a methodological peculiarity: Various regression equations have been used to measure the saving–investment correlation, but none of them has a firm theoretical foundation! This in turn raises questions about the interpretation and comparability of the existing empirical results. In order to obtain reliable estimates of the saving–investment correlation, we propose an econometric specification that is founded in intertemporal general equilibrium models, in which agents optimize under intertemporal budget constraints. We are then able to show that studies reporting time series regressions have estimated misspecified equations and that studies reporting cross-section regressions are seriously flawed because they neglect dynamics. As a result the puzzle may turn out to be an artifact caused by measurement errors.[4]

Norway serves as a suitable example to cement our methodological arguments with empirical evidence, thanks to its system of capital controls, which were phased out during the 1970s and 1980s and eventually dismantled by 1990, the oil discoveries, and its small size. We demonstrate that the failure to take structural breaks into account seriously distorts the picture, making a strong case for careful diagnostic testing. Our main empirical results are that the "Feldstein–Horioka puzzle" does

[2] Tesar (1991: 76) concludes her survey article stating that "the correlation between national saving and domestic investment rates in the OECD countries remains an important empirical regularity to be explained, although it offers little evidence on the question of international capital mobility."

[3] This chapter draws heavily on Jansen and Schulze (1996b) and Schulze (1993).

[4] Whether the misspecification is grave enough to explain the puzzle is an empirical issue, of course. We are able to establish also empirically the superiority of our specification. The significance of reliable measurement of the saving–investment correlation goes beyond solving the "Feldstein–Horioka puzzle" and analyzing whether this correlation can serve to assess the impact of capital controls. Since current account dynamics are at the heart of open economy models, saving–investment correlations represent the stylized facts these models are to explain.

not exist for Norway and that the correlation will be able to measure capital mobility and thus the effects of capital controls only in a restrictive sense.

We proceed as follows. In section 10.2 we review the state of the discussion regarding Feldstein and Horioka's findings and interpretations. Here we discuss how to make inferences about capital mobility and the effects of capital controls. Section 10.3 is devoted to methodology: We derive our specification from the theory and compare it to the specifications previously used. Section 10.4 contains the case study for Norway, which underpins our theoretical arguments. First, we sketch major events in the post-war Norwegian economic history, notably the abolition of capital controls and the emergence of the important oil sector. Then we deliver the empirical results and, subsequently, attempt to assess the influence of the oil sector, which was not hampered by capital controls, on the estimates. Section 10.5 summarizes and concludes.

10.2 The "Feldstein–Horioka puzzle"

In a cross-section analysis for 16 OECD countries Feldstein and Horioka (1980) regress the investment rate (i.e., investment divided by GDP) on the savings rate: they obtain a regression coefficient of 0.887 (SE 0.074) for the figures averaged over 1960–1974 and similar values for the three subperiods.[5] Their regression equation is

$$IR_i = \tilde{\theta}_0 + \tilde{\theta}_1 SR_i + \tilde{\epsilon} \tag{10.1}$$

where SR (IR) denotes domestic saving (investment), divided by the gross domestic product, i is the country index and $\tilde{\epsilon}$ is a well-behaved error term. (The tilde is used to distinguish the parameters from the similar time series equation (10.7) introduced later.) Many authors have confirmed Feldstein and Horioka's result of a high and stable correlation of saving and investment for OECD countries, both in cross-country studies and in time series studies. This finding can be regarded as a robust empirical regularity; smaller countries, especially less developed countries, tend to display lower correlations.[6]

[5] Averaging over many years was intended to wash out cyclical phenomena. The coefficients are even higher if net figures are used, cf. Feldstein and Horioka (1980: 321). They run this regression also for changes in the respective ratios between subperiod averages and still obtain coefficients not significantly different from one (p. 327).

[6] Cf. *inter alia* Fieleke (1982), Feldstein (1983), Penati and Dooley (1984), Summers (1985), Dooley *et al.* (1987), Bayoumi (1990), Feldstein and Bacchetta (1991), Tesar (1991) for cross-country analyses and Frankel (1986), Obstfeld (1986b, 1989), Bayoumi (1990), Leachman (1991), and Tesar (1991) for time series studies. An exception is Frankel

These findings are puzzling on three counts. First, do the observed high correlations of saving and investment rates really indicate low capital mobility?[7] Second, why do coefficients remain relatively stable until the mid eighties, despite major deregulations of financial markets around 1974, for instance in the US, in Germany, and in the UK? Third, how can lower correlations for smaller, less developed countries be explained, although these countries tend to have stricter capital controls and less developed financial markets?

Several critiques have emerged on Feldstein and Horioka's claim that a regression coefficient of zero is necessary to conclude perfect capital mobility. This critique has been put forward mainly on econometric grounds (the large country effect and the endogeneity problem) and also on grounds of insufficient integration of goods markets leading to real interest rates disparities.

To see this we refer to the central regression equation (10.1) and note that following Feldstein and Horioka's interpretation, perfect capital mobility implies the covariance between SR and IR to be zero (for small countries). The meaning of this postulate can be made explicit in a simple model that includes functions for domestic saving rate (SR), domestic investment rate (IR), and net foreign investment divided by GDP (NR). Following Feldstein (1983),[8] these variables are functions of the domestic real interest rate (r). r^* denotes the world real interest rate and c, d, e the respective random shock terms.

$$IR = \mu(r) + c \quad \text{with} \quad \mu' < 0$$
$$SR = \lambda(r) + d \quad \text{with} \quad \lambda' \geq 0$$
$$NR = \eta(r - r^*) + e \quad \text{with} \quad \eta' \leq 0.$$

Disregarding central bank interventions and statistical discrepancies, the balance of payments identity gives us

---

Footnote 6 continued

(1991), who obtains in a time-series regression for the US a coefficient of 0.85 for the period 1930–1979, while for 1980–7 it is 0.15. due to the large current account deficits in the 1980s ("Reaganomics"). Obstfeld (1989) finds low correlations based on annual data for some countries. Murphy (1984), Summers (1985), Obstfeld (1986b), Dooley et al. (1987), Wong (1990) analyze correlations for smaller industrialized or developing countries, which are found to be lower on average. The literature is reviewed in Tesar (1991), Frankel (1992), and Schulze (1993).

[7] According to Feldstein and Horioka (1980: 328), low mobility of long-term capital is consistent with a high mobility of short-term liquid capital because most capital is not available for arbitrage among long-term investments owing to institutional rigidities and/ or portfolio preferences; foreign investment is predominantly made for marketing or tech-nology transfer reasons, and thereby insensitive to changes in domestic saving.

[8] Feldstein (1983: 139–144) regards levels of savings and investment instead of shares of GDP.

$$SR = IR + NR. \tag{10.2}$$

Hence it follows that

$$\text{cov}(IR, SR) = \text{cov}(c, SR) + \mu'(r)\,\text{cov}(r^*, SR) + \mu'(r)\,\text{cov}(r - r^*, SR). \tag{10.3}$$

Now it is seen that for $\tilde{\theta}_1 = 0$ three conditions have to be fulfilled simultaneously (cf. Dooley *et al.* 1987). First, domestic investment must not depend on any variable, which is correlated with domestic saving, other than the domestic real interest rate, i.e., $\text{cov}(c, SR) = 0$. In other words, this very strong condition requires that *any* other factor affecting investment must have an impact on the current account of the same magnitude and opposite sign, as equation (10.2) implies. The econometric difficulty arises because both the explanatory variable and the variable to be explained, IR and SR, are endogenous and simultaneously determined. Therefore, the regression coefficient may not only present a causal link between the two variables, but also the influence of a third factor, affecting both variables simultaneously – this is the so-called endogeneity problem.

Second, the world real interest rate must be independent of the level of domestic savings, i.e., $\text{cov}(r^*, SR) = 0$. Stated differently, if the country is large enough to influence world capital markets, a variation in domestic investment will feed back to the level of domestic savings through the altered real interest rate on the world market. Then $\tilde{\theta}_1$ will be different from zero even if capital is perfectly mobile (large country problem).

Third, $\text{cov}(r - r^*, S/Y) = 0$. This is the case if (expected) real interest rates are equal, $r = r^*$, which implies that η goes to infinity. However, real interest rate parity need not hold if claims on physical capital located in different national jurisdictions are imperfect substitutes.

To sum up, testing for $\tilde{\theta}_1$ being insignificantly different from zero means testing for the joint "validity" of the hypotheses that there are no common factors other than r influencing S and I, that the country is small, and that claims on (physical) capital are perfect substitutes and mobile across national borders. If any of those links is missing, the regression coefficient cannot be expected to be zero.

The point most frequently raised is the endogeneity of saving, implying that third factors can produce a substantial correlation of saving (S) and investment (I) in the presence of full capital mobility. Among the factors mentioned are the procyclicality of S and I and population growth (Summers 1985, Obstfeld 1986b). Saving is procyclical, following the permanent income hypothesis, and so is investment (accelerator hypothesis). Moreover, saving is a positive function of the labor force's growth rate in standard overlapping generations models because of the lower weight of the dissaving of the old (Modigliani 1970); also investment must increase with labor force growth to keep the rental rate of capital equal to the world's rate if labor is internationally immobile. Productivity and other shocks may also generate co-movement of S and I in the presence of full capital mobility. If a positive productivity shock is transitory and labor immobile, the resulting increase in the wage rate and stockholders' windfall profits will lead to increased saving as individuals will smooth consumption. If at the same time the shock is sufficiently persistent, investment will go up to restore equality of rental rates of capital (Obstfeld 1986b: 74–82). Finn (1990) shows that positively autocorrelated technology shocks produce high SI correlations. Shocks that are correlated across major countries inhibit large-scale consumption smoothing – additional domestic saving must result in additional domestic investment. Tesar (1991: 74–76) provides evidence for such correlations of shocks for the major economies. Persson and Svensson (1985) show how the effect of terms of trade shocks depend upon the degree of anticipation and the time needed to install capital.

Murphy (1986) and Wong (1990) show that the existence of non-traded goods may lead to a positive SI correlation. Murphy (1986) finds in an intertemporal Heckscher–Ohlin model that the response of the current account to productivity shocks in the tradeable or non-tradeable sector to depend on the relative factor intensity in the respective sector. Wong (1990: 63–66) demonstrates that whenever saving is increased, and thereby wealth, investment must go up if certain goods are not tradeable: The positive wealth effect will increase future demand, which in case of the non-tradeables can only be satisfied by increased domestic capital formation in that sector.[9]

This endogeneity problem can be tackled by averaging over longer periods to wash out business cycles and single shocks, as Feldstein and Horioka (1980), Feldstein (1983), Tesar (1991), and others have done, or by adding the respective variable to the regression (e.g., population growth; Summers 1985, Feldstein and Bacchetta 1991), or by using instrument variables in a two-stage least squares regression, as done by

---

[9] However, a statistically significant correlation requires a substantial variation in productivity (Murphy 1986) or saving (Wong 1990) over time. Saving behavior, at any rate, seems to change only gradually over time, and also productivity shocks do not occur very frequently. This casts some doubt on the empirical relevance of their theoretical findings.

Feldstein and Horioka (1980), Frankel (1986, 1991), Dooley *et al.* (1987).[10] Yet, none of these procedures alters the results considerably.

A special form of endogeneity may arise from a government's reaction to incipient current account imbalances; variations in public saving in particular may be used to offset fluctuations of private saving (*inter alia* Fieleke 1982, Tobin 1983, Westphal 1983, Summers 1985, Bayoumi 1990, Artis and Bayoumi 1991). However, an identification problem arises: The observed negative relationship between budget deficits and the private saving–total investment gap can be attributed to either endogenous government reactions coupled with high capital mobility (Summers 1985), or to a crowding out effect of private investment by public borrowing, presupposing less than perfect capital mobility (Feldstein and Bacchetta 1991).[11]

Frankel (1986) and Dooley *et al.* (1987) are the only papers which attempt to resolve the aforementioned problem by using military expenditure as an instrument variable for government saving (in addition to demographic variables as instruments for private saving). They do not obtain significantly differing results. Is this a convincing indication of the irrelevance of the endogenous policy argument? The gist of the argument (government reaction to incipient current account deficits) allows for much more than endogenous adjustment of the budget deficit to a widening saving–investment gap. The government could react with a reduction of public investment, alter tax or interest rate policy to stimulate saving or dampen investment, etc.; the external balance would be restored without changing public saving. Thus, the argument can still be valid even if the instrument variables approach does not exhibit results different from the traditional ones (i.e., without instruments). This deficiency in the Frankel (1986)–Dooley *et al.* (1987) approach (and any other approach) has not been noted so far. We will address this problem in our case study

---

[10] Feldstein and Horioka (1980) use demographic variables as intruments for private saving: ratio of retirees over 65 to the working age population (aged 20–65 years), the ratio of younger dependants to the same population, the benefit–earning replacement ratio under social security, and the labor force participation rate of older people.

[11] Summers (1985) regresses the budget deficit on the gap between private saving and domestic investment and obtains a coefficient of 0.715 ($R^2 = 0.77$). He concludes that governments set budget deficits such that the external balance is maintained. Since the political pressure to do so is by far less in LDCs, correlation coefficients are smaller for those countries. Feldstein and Bacchetta (1991) reorder Summers' equation and regress the investment rate on the private saving rate and the budget deficit divided by GDP. This yields coefficients of 0.699 (SE 0.112) and −0.865 (0.150); they conclude that "each dollar of gross private saving adds 70 cents to gross investment while each dollar of the budget deficit crowds out 87 cents of investment" (p. 19). The second coefficient is higher because public investment tends to be smaller when the deficit is larger.

of Norway (section 10.4) in which we assess the effects of capital controls, one of the most obvious policy tools that can be used to re-equilibrate the current account.

Another argument tries to reconcile the idea of high capital mobility with a high *SI* correlation: for large countries, an exogenous variation in domestic saving, say an increase, will feed back to an increase in investment demand via a lowered world interest rate (Murphy 1984).[12] Moreover, larger countries tend to be more self-contained, and regional shocks may cancel themselves out to a greater extent in larger entities (Harberger 1980, Tobin 1983). However, the first argument holds no force in cross-section studies since the world interest rate is given for all countries. For time series analyses Frankel (1986) shows that the large country effect is far from being responsible for the high correlation, even for the US: The variation in the US saving rate has a significantly larger effect upon the US investment rate than upon the rest-of-the-world investment rate.

As we have seen from equation (10.3), and as Frankel (1986) and Dooley *et al.* (1987) point out, for *SI* correlation close to zero the real interest rate parity must hold, a condition which is frequently violated (cf. *inter alia* Cumby and Obstfeld 1984, Mishkin 1984a, 1984b, Mishkin 1988, Fraser and Taylor 1990). Though ample empirical evidence rejects short-run equality of real interest rates, there are empirical indications that in the long run real interest rates converge (Modjtahedi 1988, Kugler and Neusser 1993).[13] The reason for this short-run inequality is the essentially insufficient integration of goods markets, leading to non-zero currency premia; the *ex ante* purchasing power parities in particular do not hold. This is demonstrated by decomposing the real interest differential as follows[14]

---

[12] This point is also raised by Obstfeld (1986b), Dooley *et al.* (1987), Baxter and Crucini (1993). In the model set out on pp. 185–186 this is portrayed by

$$\frac{\mathrm{d}I}{\mathrm{d}d} = \frac{\mu'}{\mu' + \eta' - \lambda'} + \frac{\mu'\eta'}{\mu' + \eta' - \lambda'}\frac{\mathrm{d}r^*}{\mathrm{d}d}.$$

Now assume perfect capital mobility, $\eta' \to -\infty$. Then the limit of the above equation is given by $\lim_{\eta' \to -\infty}(\mathrm{d}I/\mathrm{d}d) = \mu'[\mathrm{d}r^*/\mathrm{d}d]$. Domestic investment will increase to the extent to which the investment demand reacts to the worldwide changes in the cost of capital.

[13] There is, however, dissent about whether real interest rates are stable; e.g., Kirchgässner and Wolters (1993) and Kugler and Neusser (1993) for opposing views and a discussion of the literature.

[14] Note that we refer to *expected* real interest rates, which are relevant to international investment decisions. Equation (10.4) is an approximation commonly made; the exact formulation is $1 + r = (1 + i)/(1 + \pi^e)$.

$$r - r^* = i - i^* - (\pi^e - \pi^{*e})$$

$$= \underbrace{(i - i^* - fd)}_{\substack{\text{covered} \\ \text{interest differential}}} + \underbrace{(fd - \Delta s^e)}_{\substack{\text{exchange} \\ \text{risk premium}}} + \underbrace{(\Delta s^e - \pi^e + \pi^{*e})}_{\textit{ex ante } \text{PPP}}, \qquad (10.4)$$

where i is the domestic nominal interest rate, π^e the expected inflation rate, fd the forward discount, and Δs^e the expected rate of depreciation. Again, the asterisk indicates foreign variables.

The first component in equation (10.4) is the covered interest rate differential, or the political premium, as it captures the differences of assets in terms of the political jurisdiction, in which they are issued. The second and third component is referred to as currency premium, or real forward discount $(fd - \pi^e + \pi^{*e})$, as it accounts for differences due to the currency denomination. As we have seen in chapter 9.2, the covered interest rate differential is virtually zero in the absence of substantial transaction costs, capital controls, the risk of future capital controls, and default risk.

A substantial body of literature shows that the real forward discount is non-zero. The covered interest rate parity, together with a zero exchange risk premium, result in the uncovered interest parity (UIP, $i - i^* = \Delta s^e$). However, there is ample empirical evidence that UIP does not hold, due to non-zero and time-varying exchange risk premia.[15] This is not surprising as investors may be risk averse. The usual tests on UIP are *joint* tests on rational expectations *and* zero risk premia; in order to decompose these possible sources of deviations from UIP, survey data for exchange rate expectations have to be utilized, as in MacDonald and Torrance (1988) – they find both some irrationality and risk aversion. Frankel and Froot (1987) also reject risk neutrality in a study on UIP using survey data. While the usual studies refer to short-run UIP, there is some empirical evidence that in the long run UIP may hold: Frankel (1980), Gaab *et al.* (1986), Modjtahedi (1988).

Ex ante purchasing power parity (EAPPP)[16] posits that economic agents expect that the depreciation will reflect the future inflation differential or, in other words, the expected *real* depreciation will be zero and the real exchange rate will follow a random walk. Empirical evidence on

---

[15] The literature is too huge to be surveyed appropriately in this context. Since the literature on international parity conditions is well developed and easily accessible we decided not to review it in detail, and instead to name the main contributions and results. The vast majority of the studies on uncovered interest parity strongly reject UIP or zero exchange risk premium, among them are Hansen and Hodrick (1980), Cumby and Obstfeld (1981, 1984), Mishkin (1984b), Gaab *et al.* (1986), Frankel and MacArthur (1988); Boothe and Longworth (1986), Frankel (1988), and MacDonald and Taylor (1990) survey the literature.
[16] The concept of EAPPP was first put forward by Magee (1978) and Roll (1979).

EAPPP is mixed – some authors (like Roll 1979, Solnik 1982) fail to reject the random walk hypothesis of the real exchange rate, while others (e.g., Cumby and Obstfeld 1984, Huizinga 1986) document violations from EAPPP. Frankel and MacArthur's (1988) results even imply that the observed real interest rate differentials are by and large explained by deviations from the EAPPP. The failure to reject a hypothesis does not imply its acceptance; besides, this failure may be due to the low power of the tests (small sample size or high variability of the observations). Moreover, since the empirical evidence of the failure of (*ex post*) PPP to hold in the short run is so overwhelming,[17] there is little reason to believe that economic agents will *expect* PPP to hold in the future. Lastly, as Krugman (1978: 397) puts it, "Few international economists would deny that purchasing power parity holds in some sufficiently long run." Hence, it seems reasonable that individuals expect the long-run inflation rate differentials to predict depreciation rates. Indeed empirical evidence supports this notion (Gaab *et al.* 1986, Rogoff 1996 and the literature cited).

To summarize, even in the absence of capital controls there are good reasons to believe that real interest rates will not be equal across countries in the short term, but that differentials will fade as time goes by. This is exactly what Modjtahedi (1988) finds in his empirical analysis on the dynamics of real interest rate differentials: the differentials converge to a constant value after six months. This long-run value can be attributed to stable tax differentials. Hence, even if the large country problem and the endogeneity of saving and investment were irrelevant in practice, S and I could be significantly correlated in the presence of full capital mobility. Especially the failure of EAPPP to hold in the short run, owing to insufficient integration of goods markets rather than capital markets, will account for that. For these reasons we should expect a close correlation of I and S in the long run, but not in the short run. We will take up this point below.

Note that, unlike maintained by Frankel (e.g. 1991: 229), it is not the real interest differentials as such that matter, but the – smaller – *variations* thereof, as the real interest rates move in tandem (though not one-to-one, see Cumby and Mishkin 1986). Dooley *et al.* (1987: 506, equation (3)) show that, in order for the SI correlation to be zero, it is necessary that the covariance between the real interest rate differential and the saving rate is also zero (see also equation (10.3) on p. 186). This condition,

[17] Cf. for example Frenkel (1981) and Nessen (1992). See Rogoff (1996) for an extensive review of the empirical literature on the purchasing power parity; cf. also Goldberg and Knetter (1997).

however, is satisfied, not only if the real interest rates are equal across countries, but also if they are stable.

Though these papers shed light on the possible sources of positive *SI* correlations in the presence of full capital mobility, the basic questions remain unanswered. This remains true even though the correlation based on annual data has been found to be considerably lower and variable (Sinn 1992). For example, it is not clear whether endogenous government behavior effectively contributes to the high correlation observed. Before we address this point, we will turn to important methodological issues concerning the measurement of the correlation of saving and investment.

10.3 Measuring the correlation of saving and investment: Methodological issues

The regression of saving on investment explores an unusual relation, because the regression equation cannot directly be derived from a theoretical model. It can be viewed neither as structural relationship (it is not a behavioral relation in a model) nor as a reduced-form relation (it is not the solution of a system). Though there is no obvious candidate specification, surprisingly little attention has been devoted to the issue of specification. Instead, various econometric equations have been used to measure what is supposedly the same phenomenon, without a systematic evaluation of their relative merits. The empirical literature provides correlations between the levels of *S* and *I*, between changes of *S* and *I*, and between the levels of *S* and *I* averaged over varying time spans.

As will be demonstrated below, closer inspection of modern macroeconomic theory shows that the specifications used so far are incompatible with key theoretical insights. This incompatibility between theory and empirical practice has two consequences, which potentially invalidate the conclusions drawn from the existing empirical work. First, empirical estimates are probably biased due to misspecification. Second, it is not exactly clear what we can infer from estimates which come from different specifications, because we lack a theoretical guideline telling us how to interpret and to compare them (see also Genberg and Swoboda 1992). For instance, are studies using period-averaged data in a cross section as valuable for detecting capital mobility as studies using time series data? Without theory it is impossible to tell. We believe that the confusion about the merits of the *SI* correlation can at least partly be traced back to the mismatch of recent theoretical contributions and prevailing methods of measurement.

In this section we put forward a specification that *is* built upon modern macroeconomic theory and that is broad enough to cover opposing viewpoints concerning the factors producing the *SI* correlation. We then survey the econometric specifications used in the literature and show that they are special cases of our specification. Finally, we address the issue of what we can infer from the correlation for the degree of capital mobility.

10.3.1 Specification of the regression equation

Our theoretical frame of reference consists of the open-economy variants of modern macroeconomic theory, as expounded in Blanchard and Fischer (1989). In both the infinitely lived representative agent models and the overlapping generations models, agents maximize (expected) lifetime utility subject to an intertemporal budget constraint. Capital is assumed to be completely mobile, and hence agents can use the international capital market for smoothing their consumption.

We consider intertemporal general equilibrium models with steady states in which the current account, when suitably scaled (e.g., by output), is constant. Accordingly, saving and investment have a one-to-one relationship in the steady state. An example is the equality of saving and investment, implying that sustained current account deficits or surpluses are ruled out. In the short run, however, shocks to the system may push the economy out of the steady state and cause saving and investment to temporarily diverge from their steady state values. These models are able to produce non-zero short–run *SI* correlations despite perfect capital mobility. Examples are Buiter (1981), Persson and Svensson (1985), Obstfeld (1986b), Matsuyama (1987), Finn (1990), Leachman (1991), and Koch (1992). The modern analysis also shows that both the sign and size of this endogenously produced *SI* correlation depend on the nature and the size of the shock and the structure of the economy (see esp. Finn 1990). The same holds for the level of saving and investment in the new steady state.

The characteristics sketched above have important implications for the econometric specification. First, since the steady state value of investment and saving depends on exogenous variables, which may be non-stationary, they may be non-stationary variables too. Second, the theory implies that saving and investment have a one-to-one relation in the steady state, regardless of their value. In other words, saving and investment are cointegrated variables. Engle and Granger (1987) prove that variables that exhibit these two properties have an error correction representation. Stationary variables can also be described by an error correction model. Consequently, the saving–investment regression should be specified as an error correction model (ECM).

The simplest member of this class of specifications, which already serves our purpose, is

$$\Delta IR_t = \alpha + \beta \Delta SR_t + \gamma(SR_{t-1} - IR_{t-1}) + \delta SR_{t-1} + \epsilon_t, \qquad (10.5)$$

where IR and SR denote the share in output of investment and saving, respectively, and ϵ is a well-behaved disturbance. The analytically relevant SI correlation is the short-run correlation, defined between the changes of saving and investment, as measured by the parameter β. This parameter is the empirical counterpart of the short-run reaction of saving and investment on shocks in theoretical models. The long-run relation between saving and investment can be derived as the steady state solution

$$\alpha + \gamma(\bar{SR} - \bar{IR}) + \delta \bar{SR} = 0. \qquad (10.6)$$

If $\delta = 0$, the current account $(\bar{SR} - \bar{IR})$ equals some constant in the long run, while if $\alpha = \delta = 0$, it is zero. In both cases there exists a one-to-one long-run relation, as theory implies. Note that a one-to-one relation between SR and IR in the long run is perfectly compatible with full capital mobility. Testing parameter restrictions enables us to discern whether the steady state relations suggested by modern open macroeconomic models are consistent with the data.[18] An affirmative finding would lend support to our claim that an ECM reliably measures the saving–investment correlation.

Our theoretical frame of reference is broad enough to encompass (in principle) all explanations for zero and non-zero SI correlations, including limited capital mobility, endogenous government behavior and real interest rate differentials. All explanations are consistent with the idea that in the long run the current account is constant and that saving–investment dynamics are temporary phenomena. For example, Dooley et al. (1987) and Frankel (1991, 1992) assert that imperfectly integrated goods markets lie at the root of the positive SI correlation. Sluggish price adjustment creates the temporary real interest rate differentials, that are the driving force behind saving–investment dynamics. The real interest rate differentials decline in the course of time, and the long-run equilibrium of a balanced or constant non-zero current account is eventually reached.[19] Consequently, an ECM should be used for measuring the

[18] Note that the requirement that dynamic equations be consistent with the long-run equilibrium originates from Davidson et al. (1978), who introduced the influential error correction model.
[19] This is exactly what Modjtahedi (1988) finds in his study on real interest rate dynamics. His real interest differentials converge to a constant value after six months, which can be explained by stable tax differentials.

saving–investment correlation, no matter what the prior beliefs about the interpretation of this correlation.

Some of the explanations for non-zero *SI* correlations have already been incorporated in the intertemporal general equilibrium framework. Bacchetta (1992) introduces capital controls and a regulated domestic financial sector into an open economy model à la Matsuyama (1987) and investigates the consequences of liberalization and deregulation. The stochastic overlapping generations two-country model (one small, one large country) in Finn (1990) generates, in spite of perfect capital mobility, differences in expected real rates of return across countries.

When modeling saving–investment dynamics, care should be taken to detect structural breaks. It is a distinct possibility that different error correction models have governed the observed time series of saving and investment. Examples of events that may have caused structural breaks include the change in exchange rate regime (leading to higher exchange rate variability, which leads to real interest rate differentials; McKinnon 1987, Frankel and MacArthur 1988), reduction in capital controls and deregulation of domestic financial systems, large changes in the price of oil, sectoral shifts, and increased openness of economies. These considerations demonstrate the crucial importance of diagnostic testing in order to detect structural breaks. Yet, the empirical literature devotes little attention to diagnostic testing.[20]

10.3.2 Review of previous specifications

Empirical work on the saving–investment correlation has employed cross-section regressions as well as time series regressions. The cross-section studies use as observations the saving and investment rates for each country, either for a particular year (Tesar 1991, Sinn 1992) or averaged over some multi-year period (Feldstein and Horioka 1980 and other studies). Their regression equations are misspecified because they invariably concern a static relationship between saving and investment, instead of an ECM, suggested by intertemporal general equilibrium models.[21] Moreover, the common practice of using period-averaged data

[20] Feldstein (1983), Feldstein and Bacchetta (1991), and Leachman (1991) do not even report Durbin–Watson (DW) statistics. Bayoumi (1990) observes that satisfactory DW statistics were found for most regressions. Frankel (1986, 1991), estimating regressions in levels, finds low DW statistics. He proceeds by assuming first-order autocorrelated errors, but does not adjust his dynamic specification. Vikøren (1991) reports a full set of diagnostic statistics.
[21] The regression equation is equation (10.7) in the main text, with time index t replaced by country index i.

makes the estimated *SI* correlation unfit for assessing the degree of capital mobility on theoretical grounds. Sinn (1992) raises this point arguing that the intertemporal budget constraint implies that saving and investment are approximately equal when averaged over long periods of time. His empirical analysis shows that averaging over decades creates an upward bias in the estimated *SI* correlation.[22] This argument is reinforced by Jansen (1996a, 1997) who shows with the help of Monte Carlo simulations, that cross-section analyses in levels are biased considerably upwards if saving and investment are cointegrated variables. Moreover, he finds in a pooled time series cross-country analysis the *SI* correlation to vary across countries rather than over time, so that cross-section regressions are merely a (biased) estimate of average country-specific *SI* correlations. We are thus reserved about the explanatory power of cross-section studies and think instead that time series regressions might be more suitable to estimate meaningful saving–investment correlations.

The time series studies estimate the *SI* correlation per country on the basis of time series, employing four different specifications. Frankel (1986, 1991) estimates the static equation

$$IR_t = \theta_0 + \theta_1 SR_t + \epsilon_t .$$ (10.7)

Because this specification ignores the dynamic adjustment process, it cannot adequately capture saving–investment dynamics.

Feldstein (1983), Feldstein and Bacchetta (1991), and Bayoumi (1990) estimate the *SI* relation in first differences

$$\Delta IR_t = \phi_0 + \phi_1 \Delta SR_t + \epsilon_t.$$ (10.8)

Although equation (10.8) measures a short-run correlation, it has no static equilibrium solution in the sense that nothing is implied regarding the relation of the *levels* of saving and investment in the steady state. It is only correctly specified if there is indeed no long-run relationship between saving and investment. Since theory maintains the opposite, equation (10.8) is misspecified – it is overdifferenced. The reason Bayoumi (1990) differenced the time series was to make them stationary. However, Engle and Granger (1987) demonstrate that if saving and investment are co-integrated variables, equation (10.8) is misspecified.

---

[22] Sinn derives his result in a non-growth framework. The drift of his argument still holds when there is growth. The time-invariance of the intertemporal budget constraint also offers an explanation why the estimated correlation in the cross-section studies has decreased only slowly over time.

Feldstein and Bacchetta (1991) introduce a lagged adjustment of investment to changes in saving and posit that investment reacts to the gap between investment and saving in the previous period

$$\Delta IR_t = \psi_0 + \psi_1(SR_{t-1} - IR_{t-1}) + \epsilon_t. \tag{10.9}$$

This specification restricts the short-run correlation between IR_t and SR_t to zero and thus imposes limitations on the dynamic structure. Since it seems rather dubious that the data justify this restriction, equation (10.9) is also misspecified.

Summarizing, specifications (10.7)–(10.9) are all found wanting, and estimating them may result in unwarranted inferences. Note that equations (10.7) to (10.9) are contained in our ECM, equation (10.5), as special cases enabling us to test the validity of the parameter restrictions in section 5.[23] And in fact, for the Norwegian case, the parameter restrictions are rejected at very high significance levels, see table 10.2 on p. 207. Our theoretical framework also gives us clues as to what the parameter restrictions entail. The static equation (10.7) and the equation in differences (10.8), which is essentially static, are both compatible with theories which do not look on saving and investment as solutions of an intertemporal decision problem.

Recently cointegration techniques have been employed for the time series SI regressions. Examples are Miller (1988), Leachman (1991), Vikøren (1991), and de Haan and Siermann (1994). With the exception of Vikøren (1991),[24] they all use the conventional Engle–Granger (1987) two-step procedure. In the first step the static regression (10.7) is run, and its residuals are then tested on stationarity in order to detect cointegration. Leachman (1991) found that for none of the 23 OECD countries were saving and investment cointegrated, and, consequently, that the difference equation (10.8) could be used to estimate the saving–investment correlation. De Haan and Siermann (1994) challenge this result because of the low power of the cointegration test due to the short time series used (only 25 years). Using longer time series they detected cointegration for several countries.

In our approach we integrate the two steps of the Engle–Granger procedure. Both long-run and short-run dynamics are simultaneously estimated. Testing whether $\gamma = 0$ is equivalent to testing for cointegra-

---

[23] The restrictions are: $\beta - \delta = 1$, $\gamma = 1$ for (10.7), $\delta = \gamma = 0$ for (10.8), and $\delta = \beta = 0$ for (10.9).

[24] Vikøren employs an error correction model similar to ours. However, he does not allow for structural breaks. This leads to incorrect inferences concerning the dynamic behavior of S and I as we will show in section 10.4.2.

tion. Moreover, Kremers *et al.* (1992) show that this cointegration test has considerably more power than the conventional one.

10.3.3 What does the SI correlation say about capital mobility?

Before turning to the empirical part of this chapter, we address the crucial question whether the *SI* correlation contains information about capital mobility and, if so, in what sense. Feldstein and Horioka (1980) stated that full capital mobility implied a zero correlation whereas high positive correlations pointed to limited capital mobility. We argue that Feldstein and Horioka's basic idea that the *SI* correlation contains information about international capital mobility is correct, but that the interpretation of the estimated correlation value must be altered substantially in view of the results derived from modern macroeconomic models.[25]

Severely limited international capital mobility inevitably pins down the *SI* correlation at a high positive value, regardless of the size and nature of the shocks the economy is exposed to. Note that this is a sufficient, but not a necessary condition for high positive correlations. As has been pointed out repeatedly in the literature, high positive correlations can also be generated in the presence of full capital mobility. Consequently, we cannot ascertain which phenomenon a high correlation signifies without additional information: low capital mobility or a correlation due to shocks, imperfectly integrated good markets or the like under significant capital mobility. Relevant prior information comprises *inter alia* return differentials, direct measures of foreign exchange regulations, and structural breaks. On the other hand, small positive, zero, and negative correlations can only be generated if capital is sufficiently mobile. This implies that whenever we establish values of the *SI* correlation to be in this range, we can unambiguously conclude that there is significant capital mobility.

The arguments above make it clear that the correlation alone cannot be used to make inferences about the *degree* of capital mobility. For example, a correlation of 0.3 does not necessarily represent a lesser degree of

---

[25] It must be noted that the term "capital mobility" in this debate refers to actual capital movements, not to mobility as an unrestricted *possibility* to move capital across national borders (which need not be utilized). Capital can be perfectly mobile internationally but may hardly ever cross national boundaries because there is little incentive to do so – the (small) differences in the return to capital may be already eliminated through a small amount of foreign investment. The latter case is implicitly excluded (as unrealistic?) in the whole literature on the saving–investment correlation. Otherwise it would have been obvious right from the beginning of the debate that a correlation close to one goes along with perfect capital mobility.

capital mobility than a value of 0.1, since these values can (but need not) be produced under the same degree of (significant) capital mobility, reflecting different impacts of other factors. By the same token, it is not possible to associate a particular value of the correlation like Feldstein and Horioka's zero, or a range of values, with perfect capital mobility. Feldstein (1983: 130) claimed that, strictly interpreted, the Feldstein–Horioka test was on "the extreme hypothesis of perfect capital mobility," whereas we argue that such a test is not possible: At best we can reach the qualitative result that significant capital mobility prevails. Without additional information, the *SI* correlation can only be used to reject the hypothesis of capital immobility.[26]

When the *SI* correlation is high, meaningful conjectures about capital mobility can be derived only by consulting further sources of information. For instance, zero return differentials and the absence of institutional rigidities point to substantial capital mobility. Strict capital controls lead to the reasonable suspicion of restricted capital mobility; still we do not know *to what extent* the low capital mobility is responsible for the high correlation. However, if a reliable time profile of factors influencing the correlation, in this case capital controls, is available and the *SI* correlation reacts systematically and consistently to the varying restrictiveness of the regulations, we can conclude that the difference in the correlation value is caused by a different degree of interference in the free flow of capital. Only in this case a *difference* in the estimated *SI* value can be said to reflect a *difference* in capital mobility.[27]

10.4 A case study for Norway

10.4.1 Capital controls and oil discoveries – important Norwegian peculiarities

Norway offers several advantages for an empirical study. First, since it is a small country, the feedback effects of variations in domestic saving or investment via altered world market conditions can be neglected. Second, the system of Norwegian capital controls, which varied in the degree of tightness, allows us to *directly* measure the effect of government behavior on capital mobility. Since the *SI* correlation constitutes only an indirect

---

[26] We cannot reject the hypothesis of capital mobility and we must not regard high correlations in itself "as evidence that there are substantial imperfections in the international capital market" (Feldstein 1983: 131), because high correlations can have very different, complex causes, only one of which is low capital mobility.

[27] Argimón and Roldán (1994) have provided empirical evidence which points in the same direction: they test for long-run causality and show that investment is constrained by national saving for the EC countries with capital controls contrary to those without.

measure of capital mobility we can discern whether these two measures generate matching results.

By 1954, the beginning of our sample period, Norway had eliminated virtually all restrictions on current account transactions, while capital account transactions remained strictly regulated. Transborder portfolio investment was *de facto* prohibited, borrowing abroad required restrictively granted licenses,[28] and inward direct investment was made subject to concessions tied to certain conditions. The minor amount of outward direct investment was treated liberally. Narrow ceilings for banks' net foreign position were stipulated and non-residents were restricted from holding Kroner accounts, just as residents were restricted from holding foreign exchange accounts. The shipping sector (including shipbuilding) and, later, the oil sector were exempted from exchange regulations and denied access to the domestic credit market due to their large and fluctuating finance requirements.

It is impossible to describe accurately the actual restrictivenes of the regulations, because it depends on the varying use of the authorities' discretionary scope, on which no systematic information is available. Typically, the lifting of a restriction was preceded by a more liberal handling of this restriction. The first noteworthy liberalization including a formal change in the regulations took place in June 1973, when the prohibition to buy Norwegian stocks was eased. The Fall of 1978 marks the second important step: Banks had to balance only their combined (spot *and* forward) foreign exchange position instead of strict limits separately on both positions. It followed a period of gradual and cautious liberalization, especially with regard to inward portfolio investment (Fall 1979, Spring 1982), but also outward portfolio investment and bank regulations were eased. A major liberalization package entered into effect in June 1984, affecting almost all sorts of transactions. Controls were tightened somewhat in 1985/1986, but gradually dismantled thereafter. They were phased out by July 1, 1990. Regulations on the domestic credit market were dismantled with a time lead compared to foreign exchange regulations. The official stipulation of almost all interest rates was discontinued in December 1977, but reintroduced for two years in September 1978, when a general wage and price freeze included all lending rates.[29]

Third, the emergence of the oil sector has a substantial impact on our analysis since it marks an important structural break. The first oil field

---

[28] The ceiling for borrowing abroad was set in the national budget according to what was deemed "necessary" for the Norwegian economy and could therefore vary from year to year.

[29] For a more detailed description and further references see Jansen and Schulze (1994).

(Ekofisk) was discovered in December 1969; because of high production costs, however, oil field development became profitable on a large scale only after the first oil price shock of 1973/1974 when prices quadrupled. The build-up of oil and gas production facilities was financed to a large extent by foreign capital resulting in record net capital imports. The oil bonanza spilt over to the mainland economy and caused the whole economy to boom. The rising importance of the oil sector is demonstrated by figure 10.1, which plots the oil sector's share of gross investment and its share in GDP. All data were taken from OECD, National Accounts, as described in appendix C.1

Lastly, the shipping and shipbuilding sector was extremely outward oriented. Shipping contributed around 10 percent to GDP until 1968, when its share started to decline considerably. During 1983–1986 a dramatic flagging out took place for tax reasons until the International Shipping Register was established in 1987, which reversed the trend.[30]

10.4.2 Empirical results

We estimate our error correction model (10.5) on annual data for Norway over the period 1954–1989. Domestic investment is defined as the private sector's and government sector's net investment including the change in stocks; saving is the sum of private and government net saving. Both saving and investment are converted into rates by dividing them by net disposable income.[31] Our main data source is the OECD National

---

[30] Shipping accounted for 10 percent of the world tonnage in the peak year 1968 and about 8 percent in the following decade. For further reference see Hodne (1983), Galenson (1986), Schulze (1992c), and Jansen and Schulze (1994).

[31] Since the empirical part of our paper builds on Vikøren (1991), we employ the same definitions he did. However, using gross investment and gross saving expressed as shares of GDP hardly affects the results.

We examined the time series properties of IR and SR by carrying out the Augmented Dickey–Fuller (ADF) test. Addition of the one-period lagged first difference of the variable in question sufficed to make the residuals of the ADF regression appear white noise. The ADF (1) statistic for IR was -3.07 (almost significant at the 10 percent level) and for SR it was -4.30 (significant at the 1 percent level). Critical values for our sample size were calculated on the basis of MacKinnon (1991). In view of the low power of the ADF test in small samples, we conclude that the saving rate and the investment rate can be considered stationary in levels. This outcome concurs with Vikøren (1991), but Leachman (1991) found non-stationarity. We ascribe this difference to Leachman's shorter sample period (1960–1984) compared to ours (1954–1989).

Although the use of shares is standard practice in empirical work, Ronning (1992) points out that this may render OLS inefficient. The transformation into shares confines the values of the time series to a specific interval and this may give rise to non-normal and hetero-skedastic disturbances. However, our diagnostic tests always point to normality and homo-skedasticity of the residuals and hence the use of OLS is warranted.

Oil Sector's Weight in the Economy

— Share in Investment   ···· Share in GDP

ırce: OECD, National Accounts

Figure 10.1 The emerging oil sector

Accounts; for details see appendix C.1. Estimation of equation (10.5) is done by OLS, after testing for the exogeneity of ΔSR by means of a Hausman (1978) test; see appendix C.2. The test indicates that ΔSR can be treated as an exogenous variable, so we refrain from using Instrumental Variables methods.

The estimation results, shown in the first column of table 10.1, reproduce the results in Vikøren (1991), despite minor differences in sample period, specification, and estimation method. The estimate for the short-run coefficient is not significantly different from zero at any reasonable significance level. Furthermore, the hypothesis that $\alpha = \delta = 0$, or saving equals investment in the long run, could not be rejected (F(2,33) statistic yields 0.54). All diagnostic tests are passed.

The zero estimate of the short-run coefficient indicates significant capital mobility. This is a striking result as it amounts to an "inverted" Feldstein–Horioka puzzle: We estimate a zero coefficient, while expecting a highly positive one due to severe capital controls that were in place during the greater part of the sample period. Our finding that saving equals investment in the long run accords with our theoretical framework, thereby providing supportive evidence for our approach.

Next, we look into possible structural breaks. To facilitate their detection, figure 10.2 plots the time series for the saving and investment rate. Especially during the sixties they moved together, but the behavior of both variables changed dramatically in the early seventies, when investment jumped to an all time high and saving plummeted to an all time low. The opposite movements can be attributed to the combined effect of discoveries of large oil and gas deposits and the sharp rise in the oil

Table 10.1. *The correlation of saving and investment for Norway*

	(10.5)	(10.10)
constant	0.001	0.010
	(0.02)	(0.33)
ΔSR_t	−0.025	
	(0.13)	
$D_{(54-73)}\Delta SR_t$		0.655
		(2.02)
$D_{(74-78)}\Delta SR_t$		−1.257
		(2.75)
$D_{(79-89)}\Delta SR_t$		0.012
		(0.06)
$SR_{t-1} - IR_{t-1}$	0.281	0.401
	(2.19)	(3.30)
SR_{t-1}	0.029	−0.030
	(0.14)	(0.17)
σ	0.027	0.024
$\bar{R}^2$	0.174	0.372
DW	1.947	1.963
BG(1)	0.051	0.058
BG(2)	1.637	1.888
ARCH(1)	0.041	0.517
JB	0.555	1.327
H(ΔSR_t)	0.721	1.735

Note: Sample period: 1954–1989. Explanation of diagnostic statistics and data sources: see appendix C. t-statistics in parentheses.

price in 1973, which made the exploitation of the oil fields on a large scale profitable.[32] Intertemporal consumption smoothing in response to an unanticipated wealth increase can explain the observed saving pattern. Consumption went up in anticipation of revenues from a new source of income. Since measured actual income lagged behind (see table 10.1), the actual saving rate was temporarily driven down. In the course of time, the expected income rise materialized and the saving *rate* returned to normal. The temporarily increased investment rate can be explained by the huge investments needed to build up the oil sector and by the attendant spill-

[32] Dooley *et al.* (1987, fn. 7) mention the possibility of a negative *SI* correlation in case of oil discoveries. However, they do not explain this phenomenon.

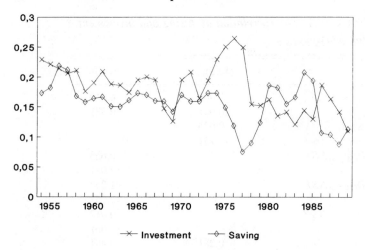

Figure 10.2 Saving and investment in Norway, 1954–1989

over effects of the oil investments on the mainland sector. Together with the increased consumption demand, this added up to a buoyant investment climate.

Judging by the graph, investment and saving were positively correlated until the oil boom and negatively correlated for the period 1974–1978, while thereafter there is no clear correlation. So it could well be that the zero correlation we have found masks structural shifts in the parameters. We have investigated this possibility by reestimating equation (10.5) allowing the parameters to vary. We specified three regimes: 1954–1973, 1974–1978, and 1979–1989.[33] The second column of table 10.1 reports the estimates of the ECM with time-variable short-run coefficients,

$$\Delta IR_t = \alpha + (\beta_1 D_1 + \beta_2 D_2 + \beta_3 D_3)\, \Delta SR_t + \gamma(SR_{t-1} - IR_{t-1}) + \delta SR_{t-1} + \epsilon_t, \tag{10.10}$$

where D_i $(i = 1, 2, 3)$ denote dummies that are one during subperiod i, and zero otherwise.[34] The hypothesis that the short-run coefficient is

[33] We also investigted other subdivisions of the sample period. The division for which results are reported generates the highest likelihood. Note that the second subperiod coincides with the first investment boom in the oil sector (cf. section 10.4.1), thereby also providing intuition for this split-up.
[34] We report a constrained version because the 12 parameter specification is overfitted for the second subperiod (4 parameters for 5 observations). The 6 parameter restrictions that equation (10.10) implies cannot be rejected at the 5 percent level as $F(6,24)$ is 2.14. The hypothesis of no structural break is rejected at the 1 percent level: $F(8,24)$ is 3.46.

constant is rejected at the 1 percent level ($F(2,30)$ is 6.05) and, again, we cannot reject that saving equals investment in the long run ($F(2,30)$ is 0.62). The fit is much better now and the diagnostic statistics do not indicate any trouble. We checked the stability of equation (10.10) by testing for structural breaks in the first and third subperiod. We specifically looked at whether the short-run coefficient changed after 1984, when a major liberalization package concerning foreign exchange regulations took effect, or after 1986, when the oil price collapsed. In all cases we are unable to reject our empirical model at the 5 percent significance level.[35]

The estimates show that the short-run correlation is 0.7 from the fifties to the early seventies, when indeed rather strict capital controls were in place. It is negative during Norway's structural adjustment to the oil discoveries, and zero after 1978. Accordingly, the Feldstein–Horioka criterion as set out in section 10.3.3 diagnoses significant capital mobility for the period after 1973. There exists corroborating evidence for this result. As argued in in the preceding chapter, the Norwegian money market was basically well-integrated in the world market during the 1980s. Moreover, the exchange controls were gradually being dismantled, while the shipping and the growing oil sector had free access to the world capital market to finance their huge and fluctuating investments. The freedom of the large oil sector to import capital effectively amounts to a lowering of capital controls for the nation as a whole.

Our finding of significant capital mobility does not imply that the restrictions on cross-border portfolio investment were necessarily ineffective, because the *SI* correlation relates to net total capital flows and not to net flows of a particular type of asset. We have merely established the existence of enough open channels between Norway and the world capital market to allow Norway to smooth its aggregate expenditure. Since the time pattern of the short-run correlation is consistent with other information on capital mobility, like asset return differentials and the historical evolution of the regulations, we conclude that the "Feldstein–Horioka puzzle" does not exist for Norway.

---

[35] We reject a different regime in 1954–1963 and 1964–1973: $F(4,20) = 0.95$. Likewise, we reject different β_3s between 1979–1984 and 1985–1989 or 1979–1986 and 1986–1989: the $F(1,29)$ statistics are 1.90 and 3.43, respectively. To assess the effect of the gradual dismantling of capital controls on β_3, we applied the Wilton–Reid technique, which specifies the parameter as an n-degree polynomial of time. We chose $n = 3$ to allow for an inflection point. Testing for the joint signifcance of the three additional parameters yields an $F(3,27)$ statistic of only 0.95. See Wilton (1975) and Reid (1977) for a description of this method and Dooley and Isard (1980) for an application to the analysis of the effects of capital controls on interest rate differentials.

We conclude this empirical section with an assessment of the empirical relevance of our criticism of other specifications, which is based on theoretical notions. Since our error correction model (10.5) encompasses the static equation (10.7), the equation in differences (10.8), and the partial adjustment equation (10.9), we are able to test these alternatives against our model. Each of the alternatives implies two restrictions on the ECM specification (see footnote 23). Since we have found structural breaks (cf. pp. 204–205), we use period-dependent parameters. Hence the ECM counts 12 parameters and the number of restrictions is 6 in each case. Table 10.2 presents the F-statistics.

The three incomplete regression equations are all rejected in favor of the ECM. The results for equation (10.8) reveal that neglecting the long-run equilibrium is particularly harmful. This outcome provides additional evidence that an ECM is the most suitable equation for measuring the saving–investment correlation.

10.4.3 The SI correlation and the oil sector

Since the emergence of the oil sector marks a structural break, an investigation into its influence on the *SI* correlation is warranted. There is a possibility that the non-oil economy is still rather insulated and that the low estimate of the *SI* correlation is chiefly caused by a large influx of foreign capital into the oil sector, which was dependent on the international capital market for financing of its investments.

It would therefore be illuminating to estimate an *SI* relation for the rest of the economy. However, this encounters problems, because data on saving are not available at the industry level; only the total for all industries are available. Data on net investment by industry are available.

We approach the data problem by estimating a two-sector system (oil and non-oil sector) along with a distribution of the net saving between the sectors. The sectoral *SI* relations are modeled as an ECM. Before 1974 only the non-oil sector existed. Hence, we have

$$\Delta IR_t^n = \alpha^n \Delta DFR_t^n + \beta^n IR_{t-1}^n + \gamma^n DFR_{t-1}^n + \epsilon_t^n \qquad [1954 - 73]$$

$$(10.11)$$

$$\left. \begin{array}{l} \Delta IR_t^n = \alpha^n \Delta DFR_t^n + \beta^n IR_{t-1}^n + \gamma^n DFR_{t-1}^n + \epsilon_t^n \\ \Delta IR_t^o = \alpha^o \Delta DFR_t^o + \beta^o IR_{t-1}^o + \gamma^o DFR_{t-1}^o + \epsilon_t^o \end{array} \right\} [1974 - 89],$$

$$(10.12)$$

where the superscripts o and n denote oil and non-oil sector variables and DFR^i $(i = o, n)$ denotes the pool of domestic funds available for financing

Table 10.2. *Test of alternative specifications against the ECM*

Static, eq. (10.7)	2.86
Difference, eq. (10.8)	5.47
Partial adjustment, eq. (10.9)	2.94
Critical $F_{0.05}$	2.51
Number of restrictions	6
Degrees of freedom	24

the sector i's investment, expressed as a fraction of net disposable income. The disturbance vector $(\epsilon_t^n \epsilon_t^o)'$ has a normal distribution with a zero mean and covariance Ω, while during 1954–73, ϵ_t^n has a normal distribution with a zero mean and variance ω^n, the element of Ω in the upper-left corner.

Since the oil sector was not allowed to borrow domestically, the pool of *domestic* funds available to this sector consists of its own retained profits (internal funding). The remainder of national saving is at the disposal of the non-oil sector. The oil sector is assumed not to invest in the mainland sector and vice versa. We can write the unobservable DFR^n and DFR^o as

$$DFR_t^o = \tau_{t-1}^o SR_{t-1}^p \qquad (10.13)$$

$$DFR_t^n = SR_t - \tau_t^o SR_t^p, \qquad (10.14)$$

where τ^o is the oil sector's share in private sector saving, SR^p. Equation (10.13) contains a lag because profits earned in the current period can be used to fund investment only from the next period on. We postulate that τ^o is a function of oil price and the oil sector's share in the total operating surplus (OS), as this is the variable that comes closest to saving. The difference between operating surplus and saving consists mainly of the remuneration of financial capital (interest and dividend payments) and taxes. We postulate a linear relation between τ^o and its determinants

$$\tau_t^o = v_0 + v_1(OS_t^o/OS_t) + v_2 p_{\text{oil}}, \qquad (10.15)$$

where p_{oil} denotes the oil price, quoted in US dollars. Combining equations (10.11)–(10.15) we obtain our system, which is estimated by maximum likelihood. Assuming serial independence of the disturbances, we can write the log likelihood of the whole sample as (ignoring constants)

$$\mathcal{L} = -\frac{1}{2}\left\{\sum_{t=54}^{73}(\epsilon_t^n)^2/\omega^n + 20\ln\omega^n + \sum_{t=74}^{89}(\epsilon_t^n\epsilon_t^o)\Omega^{-1}(\epsilon_t^n\epsilon_t^o)' + 16\ln|\Omega|\right\}.$$

(10.16)

The log likelihood prior to 1974 (20 years) refers only to the non-oil sector, while after 1973 (16 years), it refers to the two equation system. Table 10.3 shows the results for the system with time-dependent α^n and α^o, where the sample period is partitioned as in table 10.1. The estimates for the non-oil sector bear strong resemblance to those in table 10.1. Testing whether α^n is the same across subperiods (2 restrictions) gives us a likelihood ratio statistic of 11.19, so we can reject this hypothesis at the 1 percent level.

We have carried out a sensitivity analysis of our results by estimating equations (10.5) and (10.10) for the non-oil sector, assuming that the oil sector has financed its investment entirely from foreign sources. This leaves national saving as the pool of domestic funds the non-oil sector can draw from for its investment. This analysis is reported in appendix C.3. Since even under these extreme assumptions the results are comparable to those in table 10.1, we reach the same conclusion as for the total economy: The non-oil economy operates under conditions of significant capital mobility since 1973. This outcome is broadly consistent with other indicators of capital mobility.[36]

10.5 Conclusion

The correlation between saving (S) and investment (I) is at the core of modern macroeconomics since it represents important stylized facts theory is to explain. Reliable measurement of the correlation requires an econometric specification with a sound theoretical foundation in order to avoid biased results and to allow meaningful interpretations. Only error correction models (ECMs) meet this requirement because up-to-date intertemporal general equilibrium models imply a cointegrating relation between S and I. In the most obvious and most frequently analyzed case, saving equals investment in the steady state and deviations from this equality (current account imbalances) are temporary phenomena. The specifications used up until now are seriously flawed because they ignore the dynamics or the steady state relation between S and I. Drawing on Feldstein and Horioka (1980), we argue that the possibility of deriving inferences about capital mobility from the SI correlation is

---

[36] We have repeated all estimations for the economy excluding the oil *and* the shipping sector and obtain similar results (cf. appendix C.3).

Table 10.3. *ML estimates of the two-sector system: oil and non-oil*

	Non-oil sector		Oil sector
$\alpha_{(54-73)}$	0.07006		–
	(2.89)		
$\alpha_{(74-78)}$	−0.8657		−2.0991
	(1.94)		(2.81)
$\alpha_{(79-89)}$	0.0351		0.0855
	(0.14)		(0.68)
β	−0.5437		−0.1797
	(5.96)		(1.35)
γ	0.6149		0.0936
	(5.72)		(1.28)
v_0		−0.0893	
		(0.37)	
v_1		1.4791	
		(3.60)	
v_2		0.3703	
		(1.37)	
sdev	0.0264		0.0130
σ	0.0178		0.0110
DW	2.39		2.32
BG(1)	0.64		0.55
BG(2)	3.33		0.68
JB	1.04		2.63
ARCH(1)	1.00		2.14

Note: Sample period: 1954–1989. t-statistics in parentheses, for data sources and explanation of test statistics see appendix C.

asymmetric. While low or negative correlations presuppose significant capital mobility, high correlations can be produced under both low and high capital mobility. Without additional information it is impossible to identify which state prevails in the latter case.

Applying the ECM to Norwegian annual data for 1954–1989 underpins our methodological arguments. The long-run relation between S and I is consistent with the steady state equality and the ECM also outperforms previous specifications empirically. Moreover, we demonstrate the need for careful testing for structural breaks. We detect that the oil boom breaks the sample period into three regimes, for which the short-run correlation accords with the history of Norwegian capital controls. The correlation is positive and high in the times of tight controls prior to the oil boom, negative during the oil boom of 1974–1978, when Norway adjusted to the unanticipated increase in wealth and investment demand, and zero thereafter, when controls were gradually dismantled. This time pattern holds even if we exclude the oil and shipping sectors, which in contrast to the rest of the economy were not affected by capital controls. Analyzing the Norwegian example according to our new methodology has not only eliminated theoretical inconsistencies, it has also demonstrated that the "Feldstein–Horioka puzzle" does not hold for Norway: Capital has been shown to be mobile from 1974 onwards and we find a remarkable consistency of the tightness of capital controls and the value of the *SI* correlation. Indications have been provided for the liberalization of financial markets to drive down the correlation. These effects would have been buried in a traditional analysis.

In the meantime, after the publication of Jansen and Schulze (1996), corroborating evidence has emerged. Jansen (1996b) has applied the methodology presented in this chapter to an extended data set of 23 OECD countries for the period 1951–1991. His empirical estimates show, among other things, that saving and investment are cointegrated in the long run, as implied by the intertemporal budget constraint. Moreover, saving–investment correlations differ considerably between countries. Larger countries (USA, Japan, Germany, the EU as a whole, or total OECD) tend to display higher short-run correlations than the average of 0.57 and many small countries have low coefficients; nevertheless, there are also small countries with high coefficients and vice versa.[37] In addition, he confirms our result of the empirical superiority of an ECM over the traditional approaches. Finally, Jos Jansen shows that for many countries (14 out of 23) the short-run coefficient is significantly different from unity and that for half of the countries the short-run coefficient has decreased over time. The Feldstein–Horioka puzzle does not exist.

---

[37] See also Moreno (1997) for evidence on the *SI* correlation for Japan and the US estimated by an error correction model.

11 Finale

Restrictions on the freedom to move capital across national borders have been the concern of this book. We have analyzed the effects of capital controls, and named the reasons for politicians to implement them; we have demonstrated ways to circumvent the controls, and we have discussed methods and problems to measure their effectiveness.

In particular, our study has produced the following results: Capital controls ease or eliminate constraints to national governments (and bureaucracies) as they delink national from international markets through the denial of arbitrage activities. We have extensively argued that politicians are not benevolent planners striving for efficiency but rather act systematically as self-interested individuals (like anybody else) who maximize their political support through various means at their disposal, including prominently redistributive policies. Capital controls enhance the scope of feasible redistribution as they allow the government to tighten their grip on national resources. Residents can no longer escape the inflation tax through currency substitution, just as capital cannot flee from taxation or repressed interest rates through international reallocation. Capital controls not only affect income distribution through an increased budget and/or through a different distribution of the tax burden as they immobilize capital, they also alter relative factor endowments and thereby factor rewards. Income distribution is changed according to the relative factor ownership distribution and the influence the country has on international capital markets.

However, there is a variety of illegal channels to evade capital controls, the most important of which is the misdeclaration of international trade prices. The extent of misinvoicing (and thus evasion) is determined by the interest rate differential, the relative tax and tariff or subsidy rates, and the enforcement (probability of conviction and penalty). The effectiveness of capital controls thus becomes an empirical issue. It can be measured by covered interest rate differentials or the differences between onshore and offshore rates, as we have shown. The correlation of domestic saving (S) and domestic investment (I) may also provide indications on capital mobility, however not in the sense Feldstein and Horioka (1980) suggested. Only if the time pattern of the correlation is consistent with the history of capital controls and other major influences are absent, or controlled for, may the differences in the correlation be traced back to differences in capital mobility – the explanatory power of the SI correlation alone is limited.

What are the empirical findings on the recent past of capital controls and, more importantly, what will be the future of capital controls in the world? Although the effectiveness of capital controls depends on country-specific circumstances and has to be established on a case-by-case basis, they share one common feature: Controls tend to become leaky (Gros 1987) and to grow more complex and stringent (Bhagwati 1978, Krueger and Duncan 1993) with the passage of time. The situation is similar to an arms race: Individuals explore new possibilities to circumvent controls while the government tries to close loopholes and to enforce the restrictions; the opponents invest an increasing (and socially wasteful) amount of resources in their endeavor. Who will win the arms race?

Latest history provides some clues. In the last two decades, major industrialized countries have liberalized their capital account: For instance, the United States and Germany in 1974, the United Kingdom in 1979, Japan in 1980, Australia and New Zealand in 1983/84, and France and Italy in the late 1980s (cf. OECD 1990). On the other hand, capital controls remained a very important feature in many LDCs: only one developing country reached full convertibility in the period 1975–1990 (Mathieson and Rojas-Suarez 1992). It seems fair to conclude that the recent past has seen a strong movement of the industrialized countries toward integrating their financial markets into the world markets and toward the abolitition of capital controls. Contrastingly, developing countries have continued to control capital account transactions, some noteworthy liberalization attempts especially by threshold countries like Mexico notwithstanding.

We attribute this observable inverse relation between the stage of development and the intensity of capital controls to the following reasons. First, capital controls are less likely to be sustainable in more advanced countries. Rising sophistication in computer and telecommunication technology as well as in financial products facilitate international capital movements and make them harder for regulating bodies to monitor. Moreover, current account transactions are more numerous and more diversified and therefore open more possibilities to circumvent controls through misinvoicing and transfer pricing policies. Since we observe differences in diversification and sophistication not only across countries, but also across time, the empirical findings (reported in Mathieson and Rojas-Suarez 1992) that capital controls tended to be more effective in the 1960s and 1970s than in the 1980s underpin this argument.

Second, capital controls are less needed in advanced economies. Because they have a better tax system of direct and indirect taxes and a more efficient tax administration most industrial countries need not resort to an inflation-financed budget. In a few countries seigniorage gains are severely limited anyway as they have either imposed restrictive ceilings on government borrowing from the central bank or the central bank is (relatively) independent from the government. Industrial countries often offer more attractive investment opportunities because they guarantee property rights and economic and political stability so that capital flight is less of an issue. Because they attract capital through a relatively more consistent macroeconomic policy and a stable environment there is less need to lock-in capital via controls of capital movements. International capital movements exert a disciplining function on national economic policy; this constraint is less felt, the sounder the economic policy already in place.

Third, capital controls contradict the growing tendency among industrialized countries toward economic, political, and military integration. The European Union and the North American Free Trade Agreement are prominent examples: The EU member states have abolished all relevant capital controls with effect from 1992 and NAFTA includes a distinctive liberalization scheme for capital movements (Hufbauer and Schott 1993). The free trade area MERCOSUR between four Latin American states (Argentina, Brazil, Paraguay, Uruguay) and even APEC may follow this road. The formation of blocs is in part a reaction to the perceived growing impotence of national policies in the presence of highly integrated goods and factor markets. Inasmuch as this is true, the first reason is reinforced: Politicians face the choice of either insulating the domestic markets in order to exert some control over national variables or cooperating with other governments in order to influence world variables. As we have seen, the two alternatives are not equally feasible to all countries.

Last but not least, capital movements may be regarded as the lesser evil. Since capital exports may reduce the wage differential *vis-à-vis* abroad as they may alter the relative factor endowments they may also reduce the incentive for (illegal) immigration. Throughout this book we have regarded labor as immobile. This is justified as an approximation because labor is rather immobile *relative* to capital, restrictions on cross-border migration are even much more prevalent than capital controls and easier to enforce. However, mass migration is increasingly on the march.

This phenomenon is pronounced for instance between Mexico and the US or between the East European states and the EU (see OECD 1994). Since immigration is more controversial than capital exports are, policy-makers may choose to lift the capital export controls if they cannot effectively insulate the economy from international factor movements (Schulze 1996).

Immigration affects the income distribution through altered relative factor endowments, just as capital exports do. But because people move and are not just factors of production, immigrants affect the utility of the residents additionally through their contribution to, and consumption of, social capital, like social security systems, education facilities, infrastructure, etc. The net effect is an empirical question and cannot easily be answered (cf., e.g., Simon 1989). Moreover, it depends on the status of migration (legal versus illegal) and the ability and preparedness to discriminate between residents and immigrants (e.g., Ramaswami 1968, Jones et al. 1986). Since the theoretical and empirical issues involved are complex and go beyond the scope of the present book we just note the following observations. First, virtually no country in the world allows unrestricted immigration, most of the countries either strictly control immigration according to some criteria (income, education, or origin) or attempt to deny immigration entirely (Bhagwati 1984). Second, illegal immigration is growing; combating it becomes increasingly difficult (OECD 1994: part C). Third, the sad truth is that resentments against foreigners prevail among a considerable share of nationals of Western countries.[1] Immigration implies political costs to incumbents so that they may face the unpleasant choice of accepting illegal immigration or opening up the capital account and have capital exit the country. In such a situation politicians may trade off some of the political gains from capital export controls against reduced losses from smaller illegal immigration. The political-economic interdependence between capital movements and migration deserves a more thorough treatment though; it seems a promising line of future research.

Quo vadis, capital control?

As the economy advances, capital controls become less attractive: They are less effective and less sustainable, less needed, and the political-economic priorities shift as labor mobility increases internationally. However, given the widespread prevalence and strictness of controls, and the degree

---

[1] In an insightful study based on a Eurobarometer survey in 1988, Gang and Rivera-Batiz (1994) find that 36 percent of those interviewed thought that there were "too many" foreigners in their country, another 40 percent considered them "a lot," and still 11 percent of all Europeans interviewed found "their presence disturbing."

of regulations of economic activity in developing countries, which leaves their goods and factor markets far from being integrated into world markets, it will be a long way to go to the worldwide abolition of capital controls. Capital controls are here to stay for quite a while.

It is not only a matter of time, though, until capital controls will have disappeared on a large scale. For one thing, there is no consensus even among leading economists about the desirability of capital account convertibility. A recent symposium on the suggestion of the Interim Committee of the IMF to make liberalization of capital movements one of the Fund's purposes demonstrates that very clearly (Kenen, ed. 1998): While Stanley Fischer (1998) and Rüdiger Dornbusch (1998) support a well-designed dismantling of capital controls, Richard Cooper (1998) and Dani Rodrik (1998) are very reluctant to advise liberalization of capital movements. Yet another thing is public opinion on which political decision-makers depend. If in the course of globalization fears are mounting, however unfounded they may be, that sinister market forces act against the well-being of the nations, and that in particular the whims and fads of the international capital markets determine the nation's fate, the public outcry for the restriction of capital movements would not be long in coming. Empirical evidence shows that, although international capital mobility constrains the whims and fads of politicians and disciplines national policies, globalization of capital markets is by no means the end of the nation state nor does it establish a major obstacle to welfare state policies (see Schulze and Ursprung 1999b for a comprehensive review). On the contrary, capital account liberalization leads to higher growth rates as it enhances efficiency of factor allocation (cf. Pagano 1993 and Edwards 1998 for ample empirical evidence). It reduces the discretionary scope of politicians and bureaucrats and thus the scope for corruption and favoritism; it allows better portfolio diversification, secures property rights, and supports international trade as it opens up more channels for its financing. However, people have to realize this and politicians may not be supportive to this insight as globalization fears can be used to divert attention from own deficiencies to some anonymous and remote force.

Yet, there is light at the end of the tunnel: As trade liberalization, in the framework of the WTO or through regional agreements, becomes increasingly successful, more and more channels open up to the undermining of capital controls – the integration of goods markets sow the seed for capital market integration. Again, it is not the growing insight into the advantages of efficient resource allocation that will lead politicians to the removal of barriers but the stiffened constraints under which they operate.

Appendix A Notation and abbreviations

A.1 Notation used in part I

In the following list we survey the notation used in part I. The term "[section 3.5]" indicates parameters or variables used only in the specific factors model presented in section 3.5.

*	indicates a foreign variable
^	indicates a relative change of the respective variable
a_{lm}	quantity of factor l ($l = 1, 2, N$) required per unit of commodity m ($m = 1, 2$)
c	voting costs
F	(domestic) production function
i	indicates a value of a particular individual i
j	indicates a value of a particular individual j
k	capital–labor endowment ratio for the economy ($k = \bar{K}/L$)
k^i	individual i's capital–labor endowment ratio $k^i = K^i/L^i$
K	capital
K^*	domestically owned capital exported abroad
$\bar{K}$	total domestically owned capital stock
$\bar{K}^*$	capital stock owned by foreigners (and installed abroad)
K^h	domestically owned capital installed at home
K^i	individual i's capital endowment
L	actual labor force employed
$\bar{L}$	potential labor force (full employment)
L^i	individual i's labor endowment
p_1 (p_2)	domestic price for the first (second) commodity [section 3.5]
r	(domestic) rental rate of capital
r^*	foreign rental rate of capital
$\bar{r}$	rental rate of capital associated with the minimum wage
R_1	rental rate of (sector-one-specific) capital [section 3.5]

R_2	rental rate of (sector-two-specific) land [section 3.5]
R_N	wage rate of the intersectorally mobile labor [section 3.5]
t	(domestically levied) tax rate on proceeds from exported capital; in section 3.5: tax rate on proceeds to foreigners from imported capital
t_{opt}^i	individual i's income maximizing tax t (in the case of full employment)
$t_{opt^{ue}}^S$	individual i's income maximizing tax t (in the case of unemployment)
t_{opt}^S $(t_{opt^{ue}}^S)$	national income maximizing tax t in the case of full employment (unemployment)
T	total tax revenue
T^i	individual's share of total tax revenue
U^i	indirect utility function of individual i [section 3.5]
V_1	economy's endowment with (sector-specific) capital [section 3.5]
V_1^h	sector-specific capital installed at home [section 3.5]
V_1^*	sector-specific capital installed abroad [section 3.5]
V_2	economy's endowment with (sector-specific) land [section 3.5]
V_N	economy's endowment with sectorally mobile labor [section 3.5]
w	wage rate
$\bar{w}$	minimum wage rate
w^e	expected wage rate (in case of unemployment)
X	homogeneous good
X_1 (X_2)	commodity produced by the first (second) sector [section 3.5]
y^i	individual income
Y	national income
Δ	abbreviation for $\Delta = \lambda_{N1}\frac{\sigma_1}{\theta_{11}} + \lambda_{N2}\frac{\sigma_2}{\theta_{22}}$ see equation (3.32) [section 3.5]
θ_{kj}	distributive share of factor k $(k = 1, 2, N)$ in industry j $(j = 1, 2)$ [section 3.5]
λ_{N1} (λ_{N2})	share of labor used in the first (second) sector [section 3.5]
μ^*	proportion of capital stock that the foreign country has borrowed, $\mu^* = K^*/(\tilde{K}^* + K^*)$
ξ^*	factor price elasticity of foreign demand for (imported) capital
σ_j	elasticity of substitution between factors in sector j [section 3.5]
τ_1 (τ_2)	import tariff on the first (second) commodity [section 3.5]

Ψ^i individual share from factor ownership (cf. eq. (3.7) and (3.30) in section 3.5

A.2 Notation used in part II

$\star$	indicates optimal value
$\smile$	indicates a variable in chapter 7, similar to the one in chapter 6, but with different functional form or slightly altered definition
a	critical value for the absolute value of the price differential $\tilde{p}^t - p^d$ below which investigation is not rewarding
A	stands for $A = (P - k)(1 - t) - p^t$, cf. equation (6.13)
Cex	illegal capital export
$E(\cdot)$	expectation operator
Eva	the expected amount of net evasion
$f(p^d - p^t)$	detection function,
	denoting the probability to be investigated and convicted
g	gain from interest rate arbitrage per domestic currency unit via overdeclaration, cf. p. 128.
$\bar{g}$	costs for foreign exchange per domestic currency unit incurred by illicit underdeclaration, cf. p. 128
$i(p^d)$	investigation function
K	cost of production excluding the costs for the imported input
k	(constant) per unit cost of production excluding the imported input
$l(p^d - p^t)$	function describing the probability that investigation leads to conviction
p^t	true price for the imported input
p^d	declared price for the imported input
$\tilde{p}^t$	latent variable for the authorities for the true import price p^t (random variable)
$\tilde{p}^t_l$	lower bound for $\tilde{p}^t$: for $\tilde{p}^t < \tilde{p}^t_l$ the density function $q(\tilde{p}^t)$ is zero
$\tilde{p}^t_u$	upper bound for $\tilde{p}^t$
P	(domestic) price of the finished product
$q(\tilde{p}^t)$	the authorities' density function for $\tilde{p}^t$
$Q(\tilde{p}^t)$	primitive of $q(\tilde{p}^t)$
s	rate of penalty (surcharge)
S	penalty (per unit output)
t	(proportional) income tax
z	stands for $z = t(1 + \tau) - \tau$, cf. equation (6.14).

α	parameter ensuring that the penalty for tax and tariff evasion cannot become negative
β	parameter distinguishing illicitly borrowing foreign exchange at a black market premium from illicitly depositing capital abroad at the foreign rate, cf. equation (6.9).
γ	parameter ensuring that evading capital controls by over-declaration is punished
Π^t	the firm's true (but not stated) profit per unit of output
τ	*ad valorem* tariff on imported input

A.3 Notation used in part III

$*$	indicates a foreign variable
e	indicates an expected variable, unless otherwise indicated
n	indicates a Norwegian variable
u	indicates a US variable
B^n	asset demand for Kroner government debt by the Norwegian private sector
B^n	asset demand for Kroner government debt by foreigners
B^s	supply of Kroner government debt
C	measure of capital controls in place
CAS	(Norwegian) current account surplus
DEBT	(Norwegian) government debt
DFR	pool of domestic (loanable) funds
f	forward exchange rate
fd	forward discount
i	(nominal) interest rate
i^e	Euromarket interest rate
I	domestic investment
IR	domestic investment rate (divided by GDP)
NR	net foreign investment (i.e., capital export) divided by GDP
r	(expected) real interest rate
RES	foreign exchange reserves held by Norwegian monetary authorities
s	spot exchange rate
S	domestic saving
SR	domestic savings rate (divided by GDP)
t	time index
W	(financial) wealth
Δ	indicates first differences of variables (with respect to time)
π^e	expected inflation rate
ϕ	exchange risk premium (chapter 8)

τ oil sector's share in domestic private savings

All other greek parameters denote regression coefficients (or error terms) and are not listed as such. Abbreviations concerning test statistics in the tables are explained in appendix C.2.

A.4 Abbreviations

cet. par.	*ceteris paribus* (other things being equal)
cif	cost, insurance, freight
CIP	covered interest rate parity
EAPPP	*ex ante* purchasing power parity
ECM	error correction model
EMS	European Monetary System
FDI	foreign direct investment
fob	free on board
F.O.C.	first order condition
EU	European Union
GDP	gross domestic product
GNP	gross national product
iff	if and only if
IFS	*International Financial Statistics* (ed. by the IMF)
IMF	International Monetary Fund
LDC	less developed country
LHS	left-hand side
MVM	median voter model
NAFTA	North American Free Trade Agreement
NBER	National Bureau of Economic Research (Cambridge/ Mass.)
OECD	Organisation for Economic Cooperation and Development
PPP	purchasing power parity
RHS	right-hand side
UIP	uncovered interest rate parity
W.l.o.g.	Without loss of generality

Appendix B   Appendices to part II

B.1 Qualitative analysis of the importer's expected-profit function

B.1.1 Case I: Overdeclaration is optimal

First, we analyze the case of $z + g > 0$. Results apply *mutatis mutandis* for $z + \bar{g} < 0$. The function (recall (6.15))

$$E(\Pi^t(p^d)) = A + zp^d + (p^t - p^d)[z + \beta g]f + (p^d - p^t)\beta g$$
$$- s(p^d - p^t)\{\alpha z + \gamma\}f$$

can be decomposed into four additively connected functions. These functions are defined as follows[1]

$$h_1(p^d) := (p^t - p^d)[z + \beta g]f(p^d - p^t), \tag{B.1}$$

$$h_2(p^d) := -\{\alpha z + \gamma\}sf(p^d - p^t)(p^d - p^t)$$
$$\text{with} \quad \alpha = 1 \text{ if } z(p^d - p^t) > 0, \quad \alpha = 0 \text{ otherwise} \tag{B.2}$$
$$\text{and} \quad \gamma > 0 \text{ if } (p^d - p^t) > 0, \quad \gamma = 0 \text{ otherwise},$$

$$h_3(p^d) := A + zp^d, \tag{B.3}$$

$$h_4(p^d) := (p^d - p^t)\beta g$$
$$\text{with} \quad \beta = \bar{g}/g \text{ if } (p^d - p^t) > 0, \quad \beta = 1 \text{ otherwise}, \tag{B.4}$$

and

$$E(\Pi^t(p^d)) = h_1(p^d) + h_2(p^d) + h_3(p^d) + h_4(p^d). \tag{B.5}$$

---

[1] In what follows we give the argument of the detection function in parentheses: $f = f(p^d - p^t)$.

Since z is positive, h_1 is positive, downward sloping and convex for $p^d < p^t$, has an inflection point at $p^d = p^t$ for which $h_1(p^t) = h_1'(p^t) = 0$ and is negative and concave afterwards $(p^d > p^t)$; cf. equations (6.5)–(6.7). This can easily be seen by differentiating $h_1(p^d)$ and is shown in figure B.1.

We turn to the penalty function h_2 and assume for expositional simplicity that $z > 0$. We could also assume $z < 0$ with $z + g > 0$, which would not change the basic argument: also underdeclaration would be punished on the grounds of tax and tariff evasion, thereby making underdeclaration even more disadvantageous than it is anyway (given any positive value for $z + g$).[2] Because $z > 0$, $\quad \alpha = 0$ for $p^d \le p^t$ as seen from (6.12). Likewise, capital controls will be evaded, and thus the evader will possibly be punished, only when overdeclaration takes place (see p. 129). In other words, $h_2(p^d)$ equals zero for $p^d \le p^t$. For $p^d > p^t$, $\quad h_2(p^d)$ is a negative, concave and downward-sloping function since for $z > 0$ and $p^d > p^t$, $\quad \alpha = 1$ and $\gamma > 0$ and therefore

$$h_2(p^d) = s\frac{\alpha z + \gamma}{z + \beta g}\, h_1(p^d).$$

The function h_2 is shown in figure B.2.

The sum function $h_1 + h_2 := h_{12}$ is immediately derived from figures B.1 and B.2 since the sum of two concave functions is again a concave function and s is positive. Note that the inflection point $(p^t; h_{12}(p^t))$ is not altered because h_2 is strictly concave for $p^d \in (p^t; P]$ and zero otherwise. The function $h_{12}(p^d)$ plots as $h_1(p^d)$ in figure B.1, the only difference being that it is steeper for all $p^d > p^t$, i.e., $\forall p^d \in (p^t, P] : h_{12}(p^d) < h_1(p^d) < 0$.

This can also be calculated by differentiating

$$h_{12}(p^d) = (1 + s\frac{\alpha z + \gamma}{z + \beta g})\, h_1(p^d) = (p^t - p^d)[z + \beta g + s(\alpha z + \gamma)]$$

$$f(p^d - p^t)$$

(B.6)

and setting it equal to zero. We obtain

$$h_{12}(p^d)' = [z + \beta g + s(\alpha z + \gamma)][(p^t - p^d)f' - f] \overset{!}{=} 0. \qquad \text{(B.7)}$$

---

[2] Since our arguments hold for any positive sum $z + g$, the case of $z + g > 0 > z$ can be covered by an equivalent variation of z and g, starting from positive values for both parameters, such that their sum remains constant, but z becomes negative. The arguments are then identical to those for the initial state, which will be described below, with the only exception that h_2 becomes negative also for $p^d < p^t$. Since we will prove that the importer is worse off when underdeclaring even without this additional punishment, it is clear that in case of $z < 0$ but $z + g > 0$ underdeclaration will be to his or her disadvantage all the more.

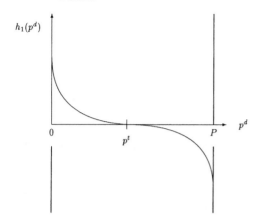

Figure B.1 $h_1(p^d) = (p^t - p^d)[z + \beta g]f$, depicted for $z + \beta g > 0$

It is immediately seen that $p^d = p^t$ solves (B.7) and establishes an inflection point because the second derivative

$$h_{12}(p^d)'' = [z + \beta g + s(\alpha z + \gamma)][(p^t - p^d)f'' - 2f'] \qquad (B.8)$$

calculated for $p^d = p^t$ is equal to zero as well.

As seen from equation (B.3), $h_3(p^d)$ is a linear function with the slope z. It can either be positive ($z > 0$) or negative, if $z < 0 < z + g$. $h_4(p^d)$ consists of two linear parts. It is negative with the constant slope of $\bar{g}$ for $p^d < p^t$, zero at $p^d = p^t$, and positive and increasing with the constant slope g thereafter. The sum of $h_3(p^d)$ and $h_4(p^d)$, h_{34}, is then straightforwardly derived: It is a positively sloped function, consisting of two linear parts with, first, the slope $\bar{g} + z$ for $p^d \in [0, p^t)$, with a kink at p^t, and, second, with the slope $z + g$. In figure B.3 we depict the case that $z > 0$, therefore h_3 is upward sloping. If h_3 was downward sloping because z was negative, h_{34} would still be a positive sloped function under case I since $\bar{g} > g > -z$.

By adding the function h_{34} to h_{12} the shape of the function is transformed from a monotonically decreasing function into a function that resembles a cubic one.[3] However, the inflection point at p^t becomes a kink of the graph of $E(\Pi(p^d))$, because h_{34} is not differentiable at $p^d = p^t$.[4] The necessary condition for an extremum of $E(\Pi'(p^d))$ is that

---

[3] This relies on the assumption that $z + g > 0$. We will see that for $z + g < 0 < z + \bar{g}$, $E(\Pi(p^d))$ will have a quite different shape. Note, however, that cubic functions are continuously differentiable, $E(\Pi(p^d))$ is not at $p^d = p^t$.

[4] The left-side limit of the difference quotient $\Delta h_{34}(p^d)/\Delta p^d = z + \bar{g}$, while the right-hand side limit equals $z + g$.

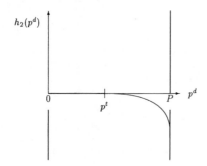

Figure B.2 $h_2(p^d)$, depicted for $z > 0$

$h'_{12} = -h'_{34}$. Due to the linearity of h_{34} in p^d for the two intervals $[0, p')$ and $(p', P]$, its first derivative is constant and equals $z + \bar{g}$ and $z + g$, respectively.

We consider the concave part of h_{12} first (i.e., the interval $[p', P)$). Because $h''_{12} > 0$, h'_{12} decreases strictly monotonically starting from zero at p^t (see above, equations (B.7)–(B.8)) and may reach $-(z + g)$ at some price $p^{d\star} > p^t$. Since the addition of a concave (convex) function and a linear one creates a concave (convex) function, it is clear that $E(\Pi^t(p^{d\star}))$ establishes an interior maximum, which is unique owing to the strict concavity of h_{12} in $[p^t, P)$.

Lowering p^d beginning with p^t the first derivative of h_{12} decreases strictly monotonically as a result of the convexity of h_{12} in $[0, p')$ starting from $h_{12}(p^t) = 0$. It may reach at most one $p^{d\star\star}$ for which $h_{12}(p^{d\star\star})' = -(z + \bar{g}) = -h_{34}(p^{d\star\star})'$. Thus $E(\Pi^t(p^{d\star\star}))$ is a unique local minimum. ∎

This is illustrated in figure B.4.

B.1.2 Case II: Honesty is optimal

Since the analysis of the case III, i.e., $z + \bar{g} < 0$, runs *mutatis mutandis* almost parallel to the one set out above,[5] we turn to the interesting case in which correct declaration is the optimal strategy. This is the case iff

---

[5] In that case, h_{34} is a similar, however decreasing, function with a kink at p^t. h_1 has similar geometrical properties, but the opposite sign. A major difference is found only with h_2: It takes on negative values in the range of overdeclaration due to the evasion of capital controls, but also in the range of underdeclaration because of tax and tariff evasion. But since we discuss this also for case II, the analysis of case III is straightforward, and therefore left to the reader.

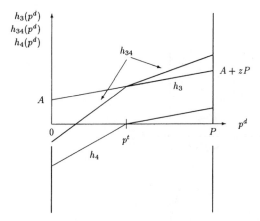

Figure B.3 $h_3(p^d)$, $h_4(p^d)$, and their sum $h_{34}(p^d)$ for $z > 0$

$z + \bar{g} > 0$, but $z + g < 0$. In order to minimize redundancies, we confine the exposition to the essential arguments that are different from case I.

We show that it is optimal to invoice correctly for this parameter constellation by proving that for any $p^d \neq p^t$ the gain from misdeclaration becomes negative. Recall equation (6.16) on page 130

$$E(\Pi^t(p^d)) - \Pi(p^t) = (p^d - p^t)(1 - f)(z + \beta g) - Sf.$$

This can be restated using (6.11) and (6.14) as

$$E(\Pi^t(p^d)) - \Pi(p^t) = (p^d - p^t)(z + \beta g)\left[1 - f(1 + s\frac{\alpha z + \gamma}{z + \beta g})\right].$$

$$(B.9)$$

First, consider $p^d > p^t$. This implies that $\beta = 1$ and because $z < 0$, $\alpha = 0$. Since $(z + g) < 0$, overdeclaration would only be rewarding if in equation (B.9) the term in square brackets was negative. We show that the opposite holds

$$1 - f(1 + s\frac{\gamma}{z + g}) \overset{?}{<} 0 \qquad (B.10)$$

yields after some standard manipulations (note that $z + g < 0$!)

$$(z + g)(1 - f) \overset{?}{>} fs\gamma. \qquad (B.11)$$

Since $z + g < 0$ and $1 - f \geq 0$, the LHS of (B.11) is non-positive. f, s, and γ are positive so that the inequality in (B.11) cannot hold.

Now consider $p^d < p^t$.

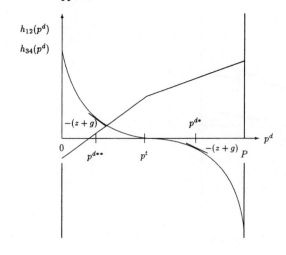

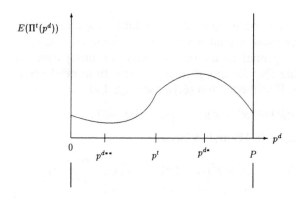

Figure B.4 Graphical derivation of $E(\Pi(p^d))$ for $z + g > 0$

In this case $\beta = \bar{g}/g$, $\gamma = 0$, and $\alpha = 1$ because z is negative. In equation (B.9) $(p^d - p^t)$ is now negative, but $(z + \beta g) = z + \bar{g}$ is now positive, so that underdeclaration is again only fruitful if the term in square brackets is negative. Taking the different parameter values into account and noting that now $z + \bar{g} > 0$, the inequality (B.10) is transformed into

$$(z + \bar{g})(1 - f) \overset{?}{<} fz. \tag{B.12}$$

Obviously this cannot hold: $f > 0$, $1 - f \geq 0$, $z + \bar{g} > 0$, but $z < 0$. The LHS of (B.12) is non-negative whereas the RHS is strictly negative.

Hence, for $p^d \neq p^t$ the gain from misdeclaration is negative. If $p^d = p^t$, the LHS of equation (B.9), $E(\Pi^t(p^d)) - \Pi(p^t)$, equals zero. Correct declaration maximizes expected profit.   ∎

For comparison we sketch the graphical representation of $E(\Pi(p^d))$ for this case. $h_1(p^d)$ depicts as shown in figure B.5; it cannot take on negative values as $z + \bar{g} > 0$ for $p^t - p^d > 0$ and $z + g < 0$ for $p^t - p^d < 0$. For $p^d < p^t$, $h_2(p^d)$ becomes $h_2(p^d) = sz(p^t - p^d)f(p^d - p^t)$ since underdeclaration is punished on the grounds that overall tax and tariff liabilities have been evaded (see equations (6.11), (6.12) on pages 129–130). For $p^d > p^t$, tax and tariff evasion is not punished (because the importer has paid too much), but the illegal capital export is. For $p^d > p^t$, h_2 becomes $h_2(p^d) = s\gamma(p^t - p^d)f(p^d - p^t)$.

h_{12} can have either sign in both intervals $[0, p^t)$ and $(p^t, P]$. For $p^d > p^t$ equation (B.6) can be written as

$$h_{12} = \underbrace{(p^t - p^d)}_{<0}[\underbrace{z + g}_{<0} + \underbrace{s\gamma}_{>0}]\underbrace{f(p^d - p^t)}_{>0},$$

$$\underbrace{}_{?}$$

while for $p^d < p^t$ equation (B.6) becomes

$$h_{12} = \underbrace{(p^t - p^d)}_{>0}[\underbrace{z + \bar{g}}_{>0} + \underbrace{sz}_{<0}]\underbrace{f(p^d - p^t)}_{>0}.$$

$$\underbrace{\phantom{(p^t - p^d)[z + \bar{g} + sz]}}_{?}$$

h_{34} is derived graphically as shown in figure B.6.

Some possible slopes of $E(\Pi(p^d))$ for the parameter constellation $z + \bar{g} > 0 > z + g$ are depicted in figure B.7. In any case $\Pi(p^t)$ establishes the maximum of $E(\Pi(p^d))$, as proven on pp. 224–227.   ∎

B.2 The effect of tax and tariff rates and the strictness of capital controls on misdeclaration and evasion

B.2.1 The effect of a variation in z on the amount of misdeclaration and evasion

B.2.1.1 The effect on misdeclaration

In this section we assume that the variation of z does not change the sign of $z + \beta g$, and that misdeclaration (as opposed to honest declaration in the case of $z + \bar{g} > 0 > z + g$) is optimal.[6]

We repeat the F.O.C. for a maximum of $E(\Pi^t)$, equation (6.27)

---

[6] For the analysis of a variation of the sign of $z + \beta g$ see pp. 130–131 and figure 6.3.

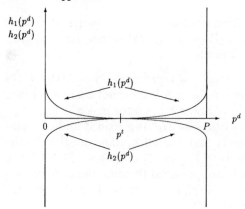

Figure B.5 $h_1(p^d)$ and $h_2(p^d)$ for the optimality of honest declaration

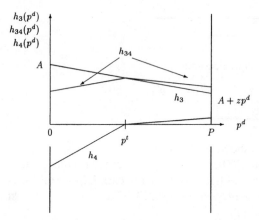

Figure B.6 Derivation of h_{34} for the optimality of honest declaration

$$0 = \left(1 + s\,\frac{\alpha z + \gamma}{z + \beta g}\right)[(p^t - p^{d\star})f' - f] + 1$$

and differentiate it totally with respect to $dp^{d\star}$ and dz. This yields after some standard operations

$$\frac{dp^{d\star}}{dz} = -\frac{1 + \{(p^t - p^{d\star})f' - f\}(1 + \alpha s)}{[(p^t - p^{d\star})f'' - 2f'](z + \beta g + s\{\alpha z + \gamma\})}\,. \tag{B.13}$$

The denominator is always negative: The term in brackets is positive for underdeclaration and negative for overdeclaration (cf. p. 137), as

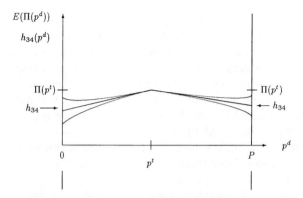

Figure B.7 Possible slopes of $E(\Pi(p^d))$ for the optimality of honest declaration

follows from the properties of the detection function f, whereas the term in parentheses carries the opposite sign since overdeclaration (underdeclaration) takes place only if $z + \beta g > 0$ (< 0).[7]

We compare the numerator of (B.13) with (6.27) and see that it is positive if $(1 + s\alpha) < (1 + s\frac{\alpha z + \gamma}{z + \beta g})$; cf. p. 137. In other words

$$\text{sign} \left(\frac{dp^{d\star}}{dz} \right) = \text{sign} \left(\frac{\alpha z + \gamma}{z + \beta g} - \alpha \right).$$

Now we can see that *misdeclaration increases if the penalty base decreases relative to the importer's gain from an undetected misdeclaration.* (We recall from (6.11) and (6.15) that the magnitude on which the penalty is based is $(p^d - p^t)(\alpha z + \gamma)$ and the gain of successful misdeclaration amounts to $(p^d - p^t)(z + \beta g)$.) The declared price increases with increasing z if the following inequality holds

$$\frac{\alpha z + \gamma}{z + \beta g} > \alpha. \tag{B.14}$$

Again we distinguish the three cases. For $z + g > 0$, the importer over-declares and therefore $\gamma > 0$. In the first case, $z > 0$. Inequality (B.14) reduces to $\gamma \overset{?}{>} g$. If this inequality holds and for instance z has risen, both the penalty base and the gain from unrevealed misdeclaration have risen by the same absolute amount, $(p^d - p^t)dz$, but since the penalty base is larger it has risen relatively less.

---

[7] The term in parentheses has the same sign as $z + \beta g$ because for $z + \beta g < 0$, $z < 0$ and due to underdeclaration $\gamma = 0$ whereas for $z + \beta g > 0$ overdeclaration is optimal and hence $\gamma > 0$ and either $z > 0$ or $\alpha = 0$, if $z < 0$.

The second case is characterized by $z + g > 0$, but $z < 0$. Since now $\alpha = 0$, (B.14) becomes $\gamma \overset{?}{>} 0$. If the evasion of capital controls is punished at all, an increase in z will raise the optimal declared price. Because for $z < 0$, the optimal overdeclaration implies that the importer pays taxes and tariffs exceeding his true liabilities, he or she will be punished if detected only on the grounds of his or her violation of capital export restrictions. Thus, the penalty base remains unaltered ($\gamma (p^d - p^t)$) while for increased z the gain is increased by $dz (p^d - p^t)$: z has become less negative thereby reducing the excess payments to the state necessary to realize illegal arbitrage gains. Once more the gain from misdeclaration has risen (relatively) more than the penalty base.

In the third case, $z + \bar{g} < 0$, underinvoicing is the profit-maximizing strategy. In this case ($z < 0$, $\gamma = 0$, $\alpha = 1$) the inequality (B.14) takes the form $\bar{g} \overset{?}{>} 0$. In other words, misdeclaration increases (i.e., p^{d*} diminishes) as a consequence of decreasing z if capital controls exist ($\bar{g} > 0$). Again, the penalty base ($p^d - p^t)z > 0$ decreases by the same amount as the gain from successful misdeclaration ($p^d - p^t)[z + \bar{g}] > 0$, but relatively less since $z < z + \bar{g}$ (< 0).

To sum up, in all three cases misdeclaration increases if the penalty base increases *relatively* less or decreases *relatively* more than the gain from the importer's undetected misdeclaration.

B.2.1.2 The effect on the amount evaded

In this section we analyze the variation of the expected net evasion caused by a variation in the (relative) tax and tariff rates. The expected evasion comprises the expected fines *for the evasion of taxes and duties*, but not for the evasion of capital controls. This is done for systematic reasons; however since the latter fines also contribute to the payments to the state affected by the described misinvoicing of international trade, we will note the alteration of the results when these penalties are included in a broader notion of evasion of liabilities to the state.

The change of the taxes and duties evaded is calculated by differentiating (6.26) with respect to z

$$\frac{dEva}{dz} =$$

$$\underbrace{(p^d - p^t)\{1 - f(1 + \alpha s)\}}_{\substack{\text{Change due to altered yield} \\ \text{per unit of misdeclaration}}} + \underbrace{z[1 + ((p^t - p^d)f' - f)(1 + \alpha s)]\frac{dp^{d*}}{dz}}_{\substack{\text{Change due to altered misdeclar-} \\ \text{ation and thereby altered detec-} \\ \text{tion probability}}}$$

$$(B.15)$$

A variation in the tax and tariff rates[8] affects the amount evaded threefold. First, for constant misdeclaration the expected yield (per currency unit of misdeclaration) varies. This is described in the first term underbraced of equation (B.15); since the term in braces is positive (cf. (6.18)) an increase in z increases the evasion in case of overdeclaration (or reduces negative evasion in case of $z < 0$) and decreases the evasion if underdeclaration is optimal. This is intuitively clear, because for a constant misdeclaration and thus a constant probability of detection the gain from successful overdeclaration rises if z rises, whereas the gain from underdeclaration diminishes if z becomes less negative.

The second underbraced term of (B.15) describes the effect of a changed misdeclaration: For a constant yield per unit of misdeclaration a variation in the amount of misdeclaration will alter the total profit from successful misinvoicing and will at the same time change the probability of detection as f is a function of the amount of misdeclaration. Note that the term in square brackets carries the same sign as $dp^{d\star}/dz$, which is seen from the comparison with (B.13) and the subsequent discussion on page 229. Therefore, the second underbraced term has the same sign as z.

We can now summarize the effect of a change in z on *Eva*. W.l.o.g. we assume that z increases.[9]

Case 1: $z > 0$ The gain per currency unit of overdeclaration increases, because z has become even more positive, i.e., more favorable to the evader. The gain from the price adjustment to the new and better parameter constellation is also positive, as described by the second term underbraced.

Case 2: $z + g > 0$ but $z < 0$ As in case 1 overdeclaration is optimal on an overall basis, but now evasion is negative. Once more the gain per currency unit of misdeclaration increases – it becomes less negative as z becomes less negative. However, the price adjustment effect works in the opposite direction, it decreases evasion and thereby tends to enlarge the loss to the importer. The reason for this is that the optimal declared price unambiguously rises if z rises (see page 229), since the loss in payments to the state has diminished per currency unit of misdeclaration. Though the loss per currency unit of misdeclaration

---

[8] From (6.14): $\partial z/\partial t = 1 + \tau > 0$ and $\partial z/\partial \tau = -\tau(1 + t) < 0$.

[9] To prevent confusion: Cases 1 and 2 refer to the case in which overdeclaration is optimal (case I on page 130), in case 3 underdeclaration is optimal (identical to case III on page 131). Obviously, we do not deal with honest declaration here (case II on page 131).

has shrunk the amount of misdeclaration has increased and the net effect is ambiguous.[10]

Case 3: $z + \bar{g} < 0$ An increase in z drives down the gain per currency unit of misdeclaration, as z becomes less negative and (a constant amount of) misdeclaration less profitable. Likewise, as we have seen on pages 230–231, misdeclaration decreases always if capital controls exist so that the price adjustment effect reduces evasion further.

If the penalties for evading *capital controls* are added, equation (B.15) will change into

$$\frac{\mathrm{d}\widetilde{Eva}}{\mathrm{d}z} = (p^d - p^t)\{1 - f[1 + s(\alpha + \gamma/z)]\}$$

$$+ \underbrace{z[1 + ((p^t - p^d)f' - f)[1 + s(\alpha + \gamma/z)]]}_{<0}\frac{\mathrm{d}p^{d\star}}{\mathrm{d}z}.$$

(B.16)

If γ/z is sufficiently small, so that the term in braces remains positive, the discussion of the change of the yield per unit of misdeclaration is analogous to the one above. Using the same technique as above, one can show that the term underbraced is always negative. This is easy to understand: If the declared price rises in case of overdeclaration not only the detection probability increases but also the penalties both for tax and tariff evasion and for the evasion of capital controls. Since (B.16) describes only part of the gain from overdeclaration, i.e., the expected tax and tariff evasion, but all of the costs (expected punishment for both offenses) and the gain from undetectedly evading capital controls rises with rising overdeclaration, this "gain" from the variation of the optimal declared price (the underbraced term) will become negative. It will be optimal to increase $p^{d\star}$ over the value that would be optimal if capital controls did not exist, since the additional gain offsets the additional penalty.[11] $\widetilde{Eva}$ however includes only the additional penalty, not the additional arbitrage gain. For the case of underdeclaration $\gamma = 0$ and the above analysis applies.

---

[10] Only if misdeclaration is not punished, $s = 0$, the optimal declared price does not shift and evasion is unambiguously driven down.

[11] This is shown in appendix B.2.2 in which we analyze the variation of $p^{d\star}$ as a consequence of an increase of the arbitrage gain.

B.2.2 The effect of varying tightness of capital controls on the amount of misdeclaration

Since we have already analyzed separately the effect of a variation of the penalty, on the one hand, and a variation of the arbitrage gain, on the other hand, we now combine the two opposite effects. We assume that the variation of the penalty is identical to the variation of the potential arbitrage gain: $dg = d\gamma$.

We totally differentiate the F.O.C., equation (6.27), and solve it with respect to $dp^{d\star}$ and $dg = d\gamma$. This yields for the case of overdeclaration

$$\left(\frac{dp^{d\star}}{dg}\right)\bigg|_{dg=d\gamma} = -\frac{\{(p^t - p^{d\star})f' - f\}(\beta + s) + \beta}{[(p^t - p^{d\star})f'' - 2f'](z + \beta g + s\{\alpha z + \gamma\})}.$$

(B.17)

We use the same technique as in appendix B.2.1.1 and therefore point out only the differences to the above procedure. Since the denominator is negative a comparison with (6.27) shows that for *over*declaration $(z + g > 0)$

$$\text{sign}\left(\frac{dp^{d\star}}{dz}\right)\bigg|_{dg=d\gamma} = \text{sign}\left(\frac{\alpha z + \gamma}{z + g} - 1\right).$$

In case 1 $(z > 0)$, overdeclaration increases if $\gamma > g$, in case 2 $(z + g > 0$, but $z < 0)$ overdeclaration increases if $\gamma > z + g$. Analogous to appendix B.2.1.1 this implies that if these conditions hold an equal increase in the gain from successful misdeclaration and in the penalty base increases the gain from misdeclaration *relatively* more, because it has been smaller than the penalty base.

Note that in case of underdeclaration $\gamma = d\gamma = 0$ and therefore the numerator of (B.17) is altered to $\{(p^t - p^{d\star})f' - f\}\beta + \beta$. This leads to the condition for a reduction of underdeclaration of $\bar{g} > 0$, i.e., capital controls have to exist at all. Then again the decrease in the potential gain is (relatively) greater than that of the penalty base: The latter remains unaltered.

Differentiation of (6.25) shows that an increased optimal declared price increases the illegal capital export

$$\frac{dCex}{dp^{d\star}} = 1 + [(p^t - p^{d\star})f'(p^{d\star} - p^t) - f(p^{d\star} - p^t)].$$

(B.18)

The comparison with (6.27) shows that the RHS of equation (B.18) is clearly positive, see also discussion on page 136. ∎

B.3 Qualitative analysis of the exporter's expected-profit function

In this section we will analyze the qualitative shape of $E(\Pi^t(P^d))$. It will be shown that no unambiguous general conclusion about the curvature of the exporter's expected-profit function can be drawn. Instead, we will point out under which conditions interior maxima will exist. The discussion will follow along the lines set out in appendix B.1 as far as possible and deviate where necessary; it is confined to the relevant interval $[0, P^t]$ since overdeclaration does not make any sense for the importer.[12]

We reformulate the expected-profit function $E(\Pi^t(P^d))$ from equation (7.1)

$$E(\Pi^t(P^d)) = \underbrace{P^t - k(1-t) - tP^d}_{:=\check{h}_1(P^d)} \underbrace{+g(P^t - P^d)}_{:=\check{h}_2(P^d)} \underbrace{-(t+g+s)(P^t - P^d)\check{f}}_{:=\check{h}_3(P^d)}.$$

(B.19)

Figure B.8 depicts the functions $\check{h}_1$ and $\check{h}_2$ and its sum, $\check{h}_{12}$.

Recall from the discussion on page 150 that the detection function $\check{f}$ is convex in $(P^t - a, P^t)$ and that it may have convex as well as concave parts in $[0, P^t - a)$. We show possible slopes of $\check{f}$, which are derived by multiplying $\check{i}$ and l in figure B.9. The upper part of figure B.9 (which is identical to figure 7.2 on p. 149) shows the geometrical properties of l and $\check{f}$: $l(P^t - P^d)$ is convex throughout the interval while $\check{i}(P^t - P^d)$ is convex for $P^d \in (P^t - a, P^t)$ and concave for $P^d < P^t - a$. The lower part of figure B.9 depicts possible slopes of the detection function, the product of different functions l and $\check{i}$ which have the properties pointed out above.[13]

This unpredictability concerning the curvature of $\check{f}$ carries over to the function $\check{h}_3$; hence we cannot make conclusive *general* statements about the existence and uniqueness of an interior maximum. Instead, we can formulate conditions under which at least one interior maximum will exist.

In order to derive these conditions, let us assume for now that the critical value a equals zero: this eliminates the convex part of $\check{i}(P^d)$. We assume furthermore that the concavity of the investigation function dominates the curvature of the function l signifying the probability that investigation leads to conviction. In other words, the detection function is assumed concave throughout the range of underdeclaration. Moreover, we have to assume that small evasion is also convicted (if investigated)

---

[12] This implies that $\beta = 1$ and $\alpha = 1$.
[13] Note that $\check{f}$ must lie below l.

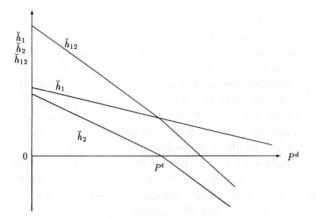

Figure B.8 Derivation of $\check{h}_{12}$

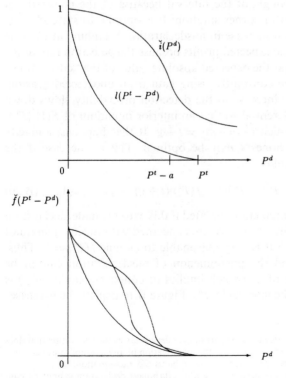

Figure B.9 Possible slopes of $\check{f}(P^t - P^d)$

with a probability distinctly greater that zero, i.e., $\lim_{\epsilon \to 0} l(\epsilon) >> 0$.[14] The latter assumption guarantees the convexity of $\breve{h}_3$ in the relevant interval. Two cases are possible: either $\lim_{\epsilon \to 0} \breve{h}'_3(P^t - \epsilon) = \lim_{\epsilon \to 0} \breve{f}'(\epsilon) < -\breve{h}'_{12}(P^t) = (t+g)$ or $\lim_{\epsilon \to 0} \breve{h}'_3(P^t - \epsilon) > -\breve{h}'_{12}(P^t)$.[15]

The function h_{12} describes the profits derived from *successful* misdeclaration through reduced taxes ($\breve{h}_1$) and realized arbitrage gain ($\breve{h}_2$) and $\breve{h}_3$ represents the expected value of the "corrections" being made in case of detection, i.e., correct taxation, seizure of the arbitrage gain, and punishment, all multiplied by the probability of detection. With rising misdeclaration both effects work in the opposite direction: While the gain from *undetected* misdeclaration rises at the constant rate $t+g$ as P^d diminishes, the (negative) "corrections" decrease further according to the increase of the misdeclaration and the increase in $\breve{f}(P^t - P^d)$.

In the first case ($\breve{h}'_3(P^t - \epsilon) > \breve{h}'_{12}(P^t - \epsilon)$), the increase in $\breve{f}$ owing to the rise in misdeclaration is so small from the outset that the additional profits from unrevealed misdeclaration outweigh the enhanced probability of being detected. If this is true for $P^d = P^t - \epsilon$ with $\epsilon \to 0$ and positive, it is true throughout the interval because of the convexity of $\breve{h}_3$. This first case yields a corner solution: It is optimal to state $P^d = 0$.

In the second case an increase in misdeclaration beginning at the true price P^t drives down the expected profits because the detection function $\breve{f}$ increases so rapidly that the expected absolute value of the "corrections" rises by more than the constantly rising gain from undetected evasion. Since $\breve{f}$ is concave the increase in the detection probability slows down with a rising price differential so that an interior minimum of $E(\Pi^t(P^d))$ may be reached, at which $\breve{h}'_3 = -\breve{h}'_{12} = t+g$. If that happens, audacity ($P^d = 0$) rather than honesty *may* be optimal. This is the case if the following inequality holds

$$E(\Pi^t(0)) - \Pi^t(P^t) = P^t[(1 - \breve{f}(P^t))(t+g) - s\breve{f}(P^t)] > 0. \quad \text{(B.20)}$$

Obviously, this requirement is violated if this extreme underdeclaration is detected with certainty. Since we are concerned with misinvoicing, not with smuggling as such it is very reasonable to assume $\breve{f}(P^t) = 1$. Thus, honesty is optimal and the phenomenon of misdeclaration cannot be explained if convexity of h_3 (which implies of course concavity of $\breve{f}$) is assumed throughout the interval $[0, P^t)$. Figure B.10 depicts the two cases

---

[14] These assumptions are made in a large part of the relevant tax evasion literature that does not use a threshold model and assumes that the investigation of any amount of evasion will always lead to conviction. We demonstrate how dubious these assumptions are.
[15] We have to use the lims formulation since $l(0) = 0$ (honest declaration cannot be convicted) but $l(\epsilon) >> 0$.

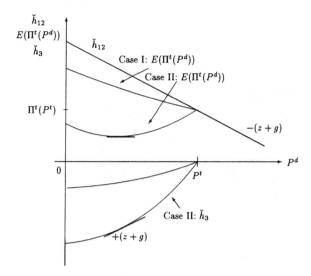

Figure B.10 Derivation of the expected-profit function for convex $\check{h}_3$

described above; for the second case we assume the optimality of honest declaration.

It is evident that the restrictive assumptions made on page 234 and in the relevant body of the tax evasion literature lead to a situation in which optimal authorties' behavior and optimal behavior of a potential evader produce unrealistic corner solutions.

"Sufficient concavity" in parts of $\check{h}_3$ is necessary for interior maxima. We replace the restrictive assumptions made on page 234 by the following non-restrictive assumptions.

1 Tiny misdeclarations will be detected with negligible probability only, to be more precise: $\lim_{\epsilon \to 0} \check{l}(\epsilon) = 0$. This assumption alone produces some concavity of $\check{h}_3$ since $\check{h}'_3(P^t) = 0$.

2 The critical value a for the misdeclaration, below which investigation is not rewarding (cf. pp. 124, 148,) can take on any non-negative value below P^t. This produces, as we have seen in section 7.2.1, a convex part of $\check{f}$ at least in $(P^t - a, P^t)$.

3 $l(P^t - P^d)$ is strictly convex in $[0, P^t)$. This may produce concavity of $\check{h}_3$ also in $[0, P^t - a)$. This assumption makes perfect sense as seen in section 6.1.2.

We have shown that for strictly convex $\check{h}_3$ only – unrealistic – corner solutions will exist. The analysis for strictly concave h_3 (i.e., strictly convex $\check{f}$) resembles very much the analysis of the importer's case as carried out in section 6.2 (see figure 6.5) and appendix B.1.1. Strict concavity of

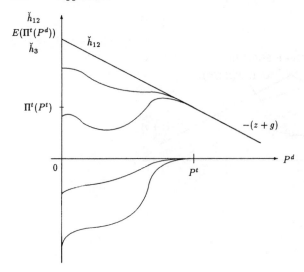

Figure B.11 Derivation of the expected-profit function for convex–concave $\check{h}_3$

$\check{h}_3$ will prevail if the convexity of l dominates the concave $\check{i}$ throughout the interval $[0, P^t)$. It is easy to see that in this case a unique interior maximum will exist in the range of underdeclaration if the inequality (B.20) does not hold, which is most likely since $\check{f}(P^t) = 1$ can be reasonably assumed (see p. 236). In our context the two cases mentioned are only boundary cases; the more general situation is one in which concave and convex parts succeed one another.

For expositional clearness we confine our analysis to a function $\check{h}_3(P^d)$ with two inflection points, i.e., two concave parts and one convex in between. An interior extremum is reached when $\check{h}_3'(P^d) = t + g = -\check{h}_{12}'(P^d)$. We lower the declared price beginning with $P^d = P^t$. At the true price the first derivative of $\check{h}_3$ is zero

$$\check{h}_3'(P^d) = (t + g + s)[\check{f}(P^t - P^d) - (P^t - P^d)\check{f}'(P^t - P^d)]$$

calculated for $P^d = P^t$ yields zero because $\check{f}(0) = \lim_{\epsilon \to 0}\check{f}(-\epsilon) = 0$ since $\lim_{\epsilon \to 0}\check{f}(-\epsilon) = 0$; cf. assumption 3.[16] With P^d decreasing, $\check{h}_3$ becomes steeper since the first part is convex. If it reaches a $P^{d\star}$ at which $\check{h}_3' =$

[16] Since we removed the restrictive assumptions on page 234, which we made to ensure concavity throughout $[0, P^t)$, there is no longer a discontinuity of $\check{f}$ at $P^d = P^t$. Hitherto it was produced by the assumption that also marginal evasion was detected with a probability distinctly greater than zero, i.e., $l(-\epsilon) >> 0$. Since $\lim_{\epsilon \to 0}\check{h}_3'(P^t) = \lim_{\epsilon \to 0}\check{f}(0)$ the assumption now removed was necessary to produce concavity of $\check{h}_3$ right from the beginning.

$t + g$ a local maximum of the expected-profit function exists. If a local maximum exists, the succeeding convex part of $\check{h}_3$ may produce a local minimum for $E(\Pi^t(P^d))$: Since with the declared price decreasing further the first derivative becomes smaller again and may take on the value $t + g$ once more. In the following – convex – part a local maximum may exist if no interior maximum exists so far or if a local minimum exists in the preceding part. This description could easily be extended to functions with more than two inflection points. Without knowledge of the concrete specifications of $l(P^t - P^d)$ and $\check{i}(P^d)$ it is impossible to know whether interior maxima of the expected-profit function will exist and, if so, how many and which one will be the global maximum. In addition we have to check whether the boundary values $E(\Pi^t(0))$ or $E(\Pi^t(P^t))$ constitute the global maximum. We can exclude the former case by calculating (B.20); the latter case will not emerge if an interior maximum exists in the first convex part of the expected-profit function (beginning with P^t). This is a sufficient, but not necessary condition. Two possible slopes of $\check{h}_3$ and $E(\Pi^t(P^d))$ are depicted in the subsequent figure B.11. ∎

Appendix C   Appendices to part III

C.1 Data sources

The main source of the data is the *OECD National Accounts, Volume II*,
published annually by the OECD. Table 1 (*Main aggregates*) contains all
the data needed to compute the investment and saving rate as defined in
the main text.

Gross investment for the oil sector is taken from table 3, line 7 (*Gross
fixed capital formation by kind of activity*) and depreciation and operating
surplus are taken from table 13, line 7 (*Cost components of value added by
kind of activity*). Comparable data for the shipping sector were made
available by the Central Bureau of Statistics in Oslo. Total operating
surplus is taken from table 1. The price of oil is taken from
International Financial Statistics, published by the International
Monetary Fund, table *Commodity prices*, line 456.

Concerning the instruments used in the Hausman exogeneity test,
defense spending is taken from *OECD National Accounts*, table 5
(*Total government outlays by function and type*), direct taxes from table
6 (*Accounts for general government*) and wage income from table 1. The
dependency ratio is defined as the ratio between the number of people
aged less than 15 or more than 65 years old and the number of people
aged 15 to 65 years old. Data are taken from the *Labour Force Statistics*,
published by the OECD, table 1. All instruments (except the demographic variable) are expressed as shares of net disposable income.

C.2 Explanation of the test statistics in the tables

We follow the idea of battery testing of economic models as set out by
Beggs (1988: 82): "subject the estimated model to a *large* number of
diagnostic statistical tests (including the common sense test) at conventional levels of statistical significance, and if it passes all these tests it is an

adequate model." Therefore, we have carried out tests on autocorrelation, heteroskedasticity, non-normality of the residuals, exogeneity of the explaining variables, and parameter instability. Since the tests applied have become state of the art in econometrics, we refrain from explaining test statistics and procedures and give references instead. Diagnostic tests are described in Beggs (1988), Godfrey (1988), Johnston (1985), Judge *et al.* (1988), among others.

σ is the standard error of the regression, $\bar{R}^2$ the coefficient of multiple correlation adjusted for degrees of freedom, DW the Durbin–Watson statistic and sdev the standard deviation of the dependent variable. BG(1) and BG(2) are Breusch–Godfrey statistics, testing for first and second autocorrelation in the residuals, respectively. Their distribution under the null hypothesis of zero autocorrelation is $\chi^2(1)$ and $\chi^2(2)$, respectively. ARCH(1) tests for first-order autoregressive conditional heteroskedasticity, see Engle (1982). Its distribution under the null hypothesis of homoskedasticity is $\chi^2(1)$. JB is the Jarque–Bera statistic testing for non-normality of the residuals. Its distribution is $\chi^2(2)$ under the null hypothesis of normality, cf. Jarque and Bera (1980).

$H(\Delta SR_t)$ denotes the Hausman test, which is conducted by regressing ΔSR_t on a set of instruments and using the residuals of that projection as an additional regressor in the original regression. In case of exogeneity the projection residuals have no additional explanatory power. The test statistic is the t-value of the added variable's parameter estimate, see Hausman (1978). As instruments we used one and two period lagged values of saving and investment, one period lagged wage income and direct taxes, current defense spending, and the dependency ratio. The latter two instruments were also employed by Dooley *et al.* (1987) and Frankel (1991).

C.3 Sensitivity analysis for the results on the oil sector

In section 10.4.3 we showed that since 1973 the non-oil sector (like the oil sector) has operated under conditions of significant capital mobility. This section demonstrates that this result is insensitive to assumptions on the distribution of national saving between the two sectors. Moreover, the result stands up if we exclude not only the oil sector but also the shipping sector.

We have estimated slightly rewritten versions of equations (10.5) and (10.10)[1] under the extreme assumption that all investment of the excluded

---

[1] We report only one coefficient for SR_{t-1}, which equals $\gamma + \delta$ of equations (10.5) and (10.10). The coefficient for IR_{t-1} is $-\gamma$ of (10.5) and (10.10). We ignore a constant term which was found to be not significantly different from zero.

Table C.1. *SI relations, for the non-oil and the mainland sector (equations (10.5) and (10.10))*

	Non-oil sector		Mainland sector	
ΔSR	0.0215		0.0417	
	(0.13)		(0.27)	
$D_{(54-73)}\Delta SR$		0.6307		0.7040
		(1.97)		(2.35)
$D_{(74-78)}\Delta SR$		−0.4300		−0.3537
		(0.98)		(0.85)
$D_{(79-89)}\Delta SR$		−0.0898		−0.0964
		(0.45)		(0.53)
IR_{t-1}	−0.2414	−0.2654	−0.2229	−0.2583
	(2.86)	(3.00)	(2.53)	(2.79)
SR_{t-1}	0.2465	0.2658	0.2100	0.2388
	(2.63)	(2.79)	(2.36)	(2.64)
σ	0.0252	0.0241	0.0238	0.0223
$\bar{R}^2$	0.142	0.215	0.103	0.211
DW	1.96	2.02	1.78	1.93
BG(1)	0.00	0.04	0.11	0.01
BG(2)	1.61	1.52	1.64	0.19
JB	0.22	1.15	0.46	0.47
ARCH(1)	0.34	1.27	0.24	0.03
H(ΔSR)	1.00	1.45	0.77	1.29

Note: Sample period: 1954–1989. t-statistics in parentheses. See appendices C.1 and C.2 for test statistics and data sources.

sectors is financed by borrowing abroad. In other words, the pool of savings for non-oil investment in the first case and mainland investment (total economy minus oil and shipping sectors) in the second case is then simply national saving.

Table C.1 reports the estimated *SI* relations for the non-oil sector and the mainland sector. The results are comparable to the estimates for the whole economy reported in table 10.1, although the fits are somewhat poorer. As for the βs, the estimated short-run correlation during the oil boom is again less than zero, but it is smaller in absolute value and no longer significantly negative. This can be explained by the fact that the lion's share of the increase in investment in 1974–1978 was absorbed by the build-up of the oil sector. All diagnostic tests are passed. Judged from

Table C.2. *ML estimates of the two-sector system, mainland economy,
and oil + shipping sector (equations (10.11)–(10.12))*

	Mainland		Oil + Shipping
$\alpha_{(54-73)}$	1.974a		−0.1361
	(2.12)		(0.39)
$\alpha_{(74-78)}$	−0.7700		−0.3606
	(2.02)		(0.71)
$\alpha_{(79-89)}$	0.0033		0.1667
	(0.01)		(0.59)
β	−0.4319		−0.3240
	(3.87)		(3.15)
γ	0.4681		0.2933
	(3.36)		(1.87)
v_0		−0.0119	
		(0.52)	
v_1		1.6547	
		(3.32)	
v_2		0.2293	
		(1.60)	
sdev	0.0243		0.0202
σ	0.0185		0.0178
DW	1.937		2.318
BG(1)	0.013		1.243
BG(2)	1.323		1.257
JB	0.52		0.543
ARCH(1)	0.199		0.928

Note: Sample period: 1954–1989. t-statistics in parenetheses, for data sources and
explanation of test statistics see appendices C.1 and C.2.

these estimates the short-run *SI* correlation was about 0.7 prior to 1974
and approximately zero thereafter.

For the sake of completeness we report the maximum likelihood estimates of the two sector system as described in section 10.4.3, now however the economy being split into the oil and shipping sectors, on the one
hand, and the mainland economy (non-oil non-shipping activities), on the
other.

References

Aarle, Bas van and Budina, Nina (1997) Financial Repression, Money Growth and Seigniorage: The Polish Experience, *Weltwirtschaftliches Archiv*, 133: 683–707.

Aizenman, Joshua and Guidotti, Pablo (1990) Capital Controls, Collection Costs, and Domestic Public Debt, Cambridge, MA: NBER working paper no. 3443.

Albert, Max (1994) *Das Faktopreisausgleichstheorem*, Tübingen: Mohr (Siebeck).

Albert, Max and Vosgerau, Hans-Jürgen (1990) Mobility, a Theoretical Analysis of the Key Factors of Structural Differences, in Willem Molle and Aad van Mourik (eds.), *Wage Differentials in the European Community: Convergence or Divergence?*, Aldershot: Avebury (Gower), 21–41.

Aldrich, John (1997) When is it Rational to Vote?, in Dennis Mueller (ed.), *Perspectives on Public Choice: A Handbook*, Cambridge: Cambridge University Press, 373–390.

Alesina, Alberto, Grilli, Vittorio, and Milesi-Ferretti, Gian Maria (1994) The Political Economy of Capital Controls, in Leonardo Leiderman (ed.), *Capital Mobility: Impact on Consumption, Investment and Growth*, Cambridge: Cambridge University Press, 289–321.

Alesina, Alberto and Tabellini, Guido (1989) External Debt, Capital Flight and Political Risk, *Journal of International Economics*, 27: 199–220.

Aliber, Robert (1973) The Interest Rate Parity Theorem, *Journal of Political Economy*, 81: 1451–1459.

Alleyne, Trevor (1987) Exchange Controls, Smuggling, and the Black Market for Foreign Exchange, Ph.D. dissertation, University of Maryland.

Allingham, Michael and Sandmo, Agnar (1972) Income Tax Evasion: A Theoretical Analysis, *Journal of Public Economics*, 28: 323–338.

Alm, James (1988) Compliance Costs and the Tax Avoidance–Tax Evasion Decision, *Public Finance Quarterly*, 16: 31–66.

Alm, James and McCallin, Nancy (1990) Tax Avoidance and Tax Evasion as a Joint Portfolio Choice, *Public Finance/Finances Publiques*, 25: 193–200.

Alm, James, McClelland, Gary, and Schulze, William (1992) Why Do People Pay Taxes? *Journal of Public Economics*, 48: 21–38.

Alworth, Julian (1988) *The Finance, Investment and Taxation Decisions of Multinationals*, New York: Basil Blackwell.

Andreoni, James, Erard, Brian, and Feinstein, Jonathan (1998) Tax Compliance, *Journal of Economic Literature*, 26: 818–860.

Appelbaum, Elie and Katz, Eliakim (1987) Seeking Rents by Setting Rents: The Political Economy of Rent Seeking, *Economic Journal*, 97: 685–699.

Aranson, Peter and Hinich, Melvin (1979) Some Aspects of the Political Economy of Election Campaigns Contribution Laws, *Public Choice*, 34: 435–461.

Aranson, Peter and Ordeshook, Peter (1981) Regulation, Redistribution, and Public Choice, *Public Choice*, 37: 69–100.

Argimón, Isabel and Roldán, José Maria (1994) Saving, Investment and International Capital Mobility in EC Countries, *European Economic Review*, 38: 59–67.

Arrow, Kenneth (1951, rev. edn 1963) *Social Choice and Individual Values*, New York: John Wiley.

Artis, Michael and Bayoumi, Tamim (1991) Global Financial Integration and Current Account Imbalances, in G. Alogoskoufis, L. Papademos, and M. Porter (eds.), *External Constraints on Macroeconomic Policy: The European Experience*, Cambridge and New York: Cambridge University Press.

Ashenfelter, Orley and Kelley, Stanley Jr. (1975) Determinants of Participation in Presidential Elections, *Journal of Law and Economics*, 18: 695–733.

Aumann, Robert and Kurz, Mordecai (1977) Power and Taxes, *Econometrica*, 45: 1137–1161.

Austen-Smith, David (1984) The Pure Theory of Large Two-Candidate Elections: A Comment on the Ledyard Paper, *Public Choice*, 44: 43–47.

(1987) Interest Groups, Campaign Contributions, and Probabilistic Voting, *Public Choice*, 54: 123–139.

Bacchetta, Phillipe (1992) Liberalization of Capital Movements and of the Domestical Financial System, *Economica*, 59: 465–474.

Bailey, Martin (1956) Welfare Cost of Inflationary Finance, *Journal of Political Economy*, 64: 93–110.

Baldry, Jonathan (1987) Income Tax Evasion and the Tax Schedule: Some Experimental Results, *Public Finance/Finances Publiques*, 22: 357–383.

Baldwin, Robert (1985) Trade Policies in Developed Countries, in Ronald Jones and Peter Kenen (eds.), *Handbook of International Economics*, vol I: *International Trade*, Amsterdam: North-Holland, 571–619.

(1986) *The Political Economy of US Import Policy*, Cambridge, MA: MIT Press.

(1992) Are Economists' Traditional Trade Policy Views Still Valid?, *Journal of Economic Literature*, 30: 804–829.

Baron, David (1994) Electoral Competition with Informed and Uninformed Voters, *American Political Science Review*, 88: 33–47.

Barzel, Yoram and Silberberg, Eugene (1973) Is the Act of Voting Rational?, *Public Choice*, 16: 51–58.

Baxter, Marianne and Crucini, Mario (1993) Explaining Saving–Investment Correlations, *American Economic Review*, 83: 416–436.

Bayoumi, Tamim (1990) Saving–Investment Correlations: Immobile Capital, Government Policy, or Endogenous Behavior?, *IMF Staff Papers*, 37: 360–387.

Becker, Gary (1968) Crime and Punishment: An Economic Approach, *Journal of Political Economy*, 76: 169–217.

(1976) *The Economic Approach to Human Behavior*, Chicago: University of Chicago Press.

(1983) A Theory of Competition Among Pressure Groups for Political Influence, *Quarterly Journal of Economics*, 98: 371–400.

(1991) *A Treatise on the Family*, Enlarged edition, Cambridge, MA and London: Harvard University Press.

Becker, Gary and Stigler, George (1974) Law Enforcement, Malfeasance and Compensation of Enforcers, *Journal of Legal Studies*, 3: 1–18.

Beggs, John (1988) Diagnostic Testing in Applied Econometrics, *Economic Record*, 64: 81–101.

Ben-Zion, Uri and Eytan, Zeev (1974) On Money, Votes, and Policy in a Democratic Society, *Public Choice*, 17: 1–10.

Bental, Benjamin and Ben-Zion, Uri (1975) Political Contributions and Policy – Some Extensions, *Public Choice*, 19: 1–12.

Bernheim, B. Douglas and Whinston, Michael (1986) Menu Auctions, Resource Allocation, and Economic Influence, *Quarterly Journal of Economics*, 101: 1–31.

Bhagwati, Jagdish (1958) Immiserizing Growth: A Geometrical Note, *Review of Economic Studies*, 25: 201–205.

(1964) On the Underinvoicing of Imports, *Bulletin of the Oxford University Institute on Statistics*, Nov. 1964, reprinted in Bhagwati (1974), 138–147.

(1965) On the Equivalence of Tariffs and Quotas, in Robert Baldwin *et al.* (eds.), *Trade, Growth and the Balance of Payments – Essays in Honor of Gottfried Haberler*, Chicago: Rand McNally, 53–67.

(1967) Fiscal Policies, the Faking of Foreign Trade Declarations, and the Balance of Payments, *Bulletin of the Oxford University Institute on Statistics*, Feb. 1967, reprinted in Bhagwati (1974), 66–83.

(1968) More on the Equivalence of Tariffs and Quotas, *American Economic Review*, 58: 142–146.

(1973) The Theory of Immiserizing Growth: Further Applications, in Michael Connolly and Alexander Swoboda (eds.), *International Trade and Money*, Toronto: University of Toronto Press.

(1978) *Foreign Trade Regimes and Economic Development: Anatomy and Consequences of Exchange Control Regimes*, Cambridge, MA: Ballinger.

(1984) Incentives and Disincentives: International Migration, *Weltwirtschaftliches Archiv*, 120: 678–701.

Bhagwati, Jagdish (ed.) (1974) *Illegal Transactions in International Trade*, Amsterdam: North-Holland and New York: American Elsevier.

Bhagwati, Jagdish and Brecher, Richard (1980) National Welfare in an Open Economy in the Presence of Foreign-Owned Factors, *Journal of International Economics*, 10: 103–115.

Bhagwati, Jagdish and Hansen, Bent (1973) A Theoretical Analysis of Sumggling, *Quarterly Journal of Economics*, 87: 172–187.

Bhagwati, Jagdish, Krueger, Anne, and Wibulswasdi, Chaiyawat (1974) Capital Flight from LDCs: A Statistical Analysis, in J. Bhagwati (ed.), *Illegal Transactions in International Trade*, Amsterdam: North-Holland and New York: American Elsevier, 148–154.

Bhagwati, Jagdish and Srinivasan, T.N. (1983) *Lectures on International Trade*, Cambridge, MA: MIT Press.

Bhandari, Jagdeep and Decaluwe, Bernard (1986) A Framework for the Analysis of Legal and Fraudulent Trade Transactions in "Parallel" Exchange Markets, *Weltwirtschaftliches Archiv*, Fasc. 3.

Black, Duncan (1948) On the Rationale of Group Decision Making, *Journal of Political Economy*, 56: 23–34.

(1958) *The Theory of Committees and Elections*, Cambridge: Cambridge University Press.

Blanchard, Olivier and Fischer, Stanley (1989) *Lectures on Macroeconomics*, Cambridge, MA and London: MIT Press.

Bloom, H. (1979) Public Choice and Private Interest: Explaining the Vote for Property Tax Classification in Massachusetts, *National Tax Journal*, 32: 527–534.

Blumers, Wolfgang, Frick, Jörg, and Müller, Lutz (1997) *Betriebsprüfungshandbuch einschließlich Zollprüfungen* (Handbook for Government Tax Audit Including Customs Investigation), including eighth supplement, Munich: C.H. Beck.

Bommer, Rolf and Schulze, Günther (1999) Environmental Improvement with Trade Liberalization, *European Journal of Political Economy*, 15, forthcoming.

Boothe, Paul and Longworth, David (1986) Foreign Exchange Market Efficiency Tests: Implications of Recent Findings, *Journal of International Money and Finance*, 5: 135–162.

Border, Kim and Sobel, Joel (1987) Samurai Accountant: A Theory of Auditing and Plunder, *Review of Economic Studies*, 54: 525–540.

Bovenberg, A. Lans (1986) Capital Income Taxation in Growing Open Economies, *Journal of Public Economics*, 31: 347–376.

(1994) Destination and Origin-Based Taxation under International Capital Mobility, *International Tax and Public Finance*, 1: 247–273.

Brady, Henry, and Sniderman, Paul (1985) Attitude Attribution: A Group Basis for Political Reasoning, *American Political Science Review*, 79: 1061–1078.

Branson, William, Halttunen, Hannu, and Masson, Paul (1977) Exchange Rates in the Short Run: The Dollar–Deutschemark Rate, *European Economic Review*, 10: 303–324.

Brecher, Richard and Choudhri, Ehsan (1982) Immiserizing Investment from Abroad: The Singer-Prebisch Thesis Reconsidered, *Quarterly Journal of Economics*, 97: 181–190.

Brecher, Richard and Diaz Alejandro, Carlos (1977) Tariffs, Foreign Capital and Immiserizing Growth, *Journal of International Economics*, 7: 317–322.

Brecher, Richard and Findlay, Ronald (1983) Tariffs, Foreign Capital and National Welfare with Sector-Specific Factors, *Journal of International Economics*, 14: 277–288.

Brekk, Odd Per (1987) *Norwegian Foreign Exchange Policy*, Norges Bank Skriftserie, no. 16, Oslo: Norges Bank.

Brennan, Geoffrey and Buchanan, James (1980) *The Power to Tax – Analytical Foundations of Fiscal Constitution*, Cambridge: Cambridge University Press.

   (1984) Voter Choice: Evaluating Political Alternatives, *American Behavioral Scientist*, 28: 185–201.

Brennan, Geoffrey and Pincus, Jonathan (1987) Rational Actor Theory in Politics: A Critical Review of John Quiggin, *Economic Record*, 63: 22–32.

Brock, Philip (1984) Inflationary Finance in an Open Economy, *Journal of Monetary Economics*, 14: 37–53.

   (1989) Reserve Requirements and the Inflation Tax, *Journal of Money, Credit, and Banking*, 21: 106–121.

Brock, William and Magee, Stephen (1980) Tariff Formation in a Democracy, in J. Black and B. Hindley (eds.), *Current Issues in Commerical Policy and Diplomacy*, London: Macmillan.

Brody, Richard and Page, Benjamin (1973) Indifference, Alienation and Rational Decisions, *Public Choice*, 15: 1–17.

Brooks, Michael and Heijdra, Ben (1989) An Exploration of Rent-Seeking, *Economic Record*, 65: 32–50.

Browne, Francis and McNelis, Paul (1990) Exchange Controls and Interest Rate Determination with Traded and Non-traded Assets: The Irish–United Kingdom Experience, *Journal of International Money and Finance*, 9: 41–59.

Bruno, Michael and Fisher, Stanley (1990) Seigniorage, Operating Rules and the High Inflation Trap, *Quarterly Journal of Economics*, 105: 353–374.

Buchanan, James (1949) The Pure Theory of Government Finance: A Suggested Approach, *Journal of Political Economy*, 57: 496–505.

   (1988) Public Choice: The Economic Theory of Politics Reborn, *Challenge*, 31: 4–10.

Buchanan, James, Tollison, Robert, and Tullock, Gordon (eds.) (1980) *Toward a Theory of the Rent-Seeking Society*, College Station, Texas: A and M University Press.

Buchanan, James and Tullock, Gordon (1962) *The Calculus of Consent*, Ann Arbor: University of Michigan Press.

Buiter, Willem (1981) Time Preference and International Lending and Borrowing in an Overlapping-Generations Model, *Journal of Political Economy*, 89: 769–797.

Bundesbank (1994) Deutsche Bundesbank, Aufkommen und ökonomische Wirkungen des steuerlichen Zinsabschlages, *Monatsberichte der Deutschen Bundesbank*, Frankfurt am Main, January 1994, 45–58.

Capron, Henri and Kruseman, Jean-Louis (1988) Is Political Rivalry an Incentive to Vote?, *Public Choice*, 56: 31–43.

Caves, Richard (1976) The Welfare Economics of Controls on Capital Movements, in Alexander Swoboda (ed.), *Capital Movements and their Control*, Leiden: Sijthoff, 31–46.

Chander, Parkash and Wilde, Louis (1998) A General Characterization of Optimal Income Tax Enforcement, *Review of Economic Studies*, 65: 165–183.

Checchi, Daniele (1996) Capital Controls and the Conflict of Interests, *Economics and Politics*, 8: 33–50.

Chinn, Menzie and Maloney, William (1996) Financial and Capital Account Liberalization in the Pacific Basin: Korea and Taiwan During the 1980s, NBER working paper no. 5814, Cambridge, MA: National Bureau of Economic Research.

Claassen, Emil-Maria (1985) Kapitalverkehrskontrollen und ihre Auswirkungen auf Ersparnisse und Investitionen, *Der volkswirtschaftliche Sparprozeß, Beihefte zu Kredit und Kapital*, no. 9, 715–733.

Claassen, Emil-Maria and Wyplosz, Charles (1982) Capital Controls: Some Principles and the French Experience, *Annales d'INSEE*, 47–48: 237–277.

Claessens, Stijn and Rhee, Moon-Whoan (1994) The Effect of Barriers to Equity Investment in Developing Countries, in Jeffrey Frankel (ed.), *The Internationalization of Equity Markets*, Cambridge, MA: National Bureau of Economic Research.

Clements, Benedict and Schwartz, Gerd (1993) Currency Substitution: The Recent Experience of Bolivia, *World Development*, 21: 1883–1893.

Clinton, Kevin (1988) Transaction Costs and Covered Interest Arbitrage: Theory and Evidence, *Journal of Political Economy*, 96: 358–370.

Condorcet, Marquis de (1785) *Essai sur l'application de l'analyse à la probabilité des décisions rendues à la pluralité des voix*, Paris.

Cooper, Richard (1974) Tariffs and Smuggling in Indonesia, in J. Bhagwati (ed.), (1974), 183–192.

(1998) Should Capital-Account Convertibility be a World Objective?, in Peter Kenen (ed.), *Should the IMF Pursue Capital–Account Convertibility?* Essays in International Finance, no. 207, Princeton: Department of Economics, Princeton University, 11–19.

Cowell, Frank (1985a) The Economic Analysis of Tax Evasion, *Bulletin of Economic Research*, 37: 163–193.

(1985b) Tax Evasion with Labour Income, *Journal of Public Economics*, 26: 19–34.

(1990a) Tax Sheltering and the Cost of Evasion, *Oxford Economic Papers*, 42: 231–243.

(1990b) *Cheating the Government: The Economics of Evasion*, Cambridge, MA: MIT Press.

Cowell, Frank and Gordon, James (1988) Unwillingness to Pay. Tax Evasion and Public Good Provision, *Journal of Public Economics*, 43: 305–321.

Cox, Gary and Munger, Michael (1989) Closeness, Expenditure and Turnout in the 1982 US House Elections, *American Political Science Review*, 83: 217–231.

Crane, Steven and Nourzad, Farrokh (1985) Time Value of Money and Income Tax Evasion under Risk-Averse Behavior: A Theoretical Analysis and Empirical Evidence, *Public Finance/Finances Publiques*, 20: 381–394.

Cremer, Helmuth and Gahvari, Firouz (1993) Tax Evasion and Optimal Commodity Taxation, *Journal of Public Economics*, 50: 261–275.

Cremer, Helmuth, Marchand, M., and Pestieau, P. (1990) Evading, Auditing and Taxing: The Equity–Compliance Tradeoff, *Journal of Public Economics*, 43: 67–92.

Cross, Rodney and Shaw, G.K. (1982) On the Economics of Tax Aversion, *Public Finance/Finances Publiques*, 37: 36–47.

Cuddington, John (1987) Macroeconomic Determinants of Capital Flight: An Econometric Investigation, in Donald Lessard and John Williamson (eds.), *Capital Flight and the Third World Debt*, Washington, DC: Institute for International Economics, 85–96.

Cumby, Robert and Levich, Richard (1987) On the Definition and Magnitude of Recent Capital Flight, in Donald Lessard and John Williamson (eds.), *Capital Flight and the Third World Debt*, Washington, DC: Institute for International Economics, 27–67.

Cumby, Robert and Mishkin, Frederic (1986) International Linkage of Real Interest Rates: The European–US Connection, *Journal of International Money and Finance*, 5: 5–23.

Cumby, Robert and Obstfeld, Maurice (1981) A Note on Exchange-Rate Expectations and Nominal Interest Differentials: A Test of the Fisher Hypothesis, *Journal of Finance*, 36: 697–703.

  (1984) International Interest Rate and Price Level Linkages under Flexible Exchange Rates: A Review of Recent Evidence, in J.F.O. Bilson and R. Marston (eds.), *Exchange Rates: Theory and Practice*, Chicago: University of Chicago Press for the NBER, 121–151.

Dani, Rodrik (1995) Political Economy of Trade Policy, in G. Grossman and K. Rogoff (eds.), *Handbook of International Economics*, vol. III, New York and Oxford: Elsevier, North-Holland, 1457–1494.

Davidson, James, Hendry, David, Srba, Frank, and Yeo, Stephen (1978) Econometric Modelling of the Aggregate Time-series Relationship Between Consumers' Expenditure and Income in the United Kingdom, *Economic Journal*, 88: 661–692.

Deardorff, Alan and Stolper, Wolfgang (1990) Effects of Smuggling under African Conditions: A Factual, Institutional and Analytic Discussion, *Weltwirtschaftliches Archiv*, 126: 116–141.

Dellas, Harris and Stockman, Alan (1988) Self-Fulfilling Expectations, Speculative Attacks and Capital Controls, Cambridge, MA: NBER working paper, no. 2625.

Delorme, Charles and Snow, Arthur (1990) On the Limits to Rent-Seeking Waste, *Public Choice*, 67: 129–154.

Dercon, Stefan and Ayalew, Lulseged (1995) Smuggling and Supply Response: Coffee in Ethopia, *World Development*, 23: 1795–1813.

Diamond, Peter and Mirrlees, James (1971) Optimal Taxation and Public Production I: Production Efficiency, *American Economic Review*, 61, 8–27.

Diewert, W. and Woodland, Alan (1977) Frank Knight's Theorem in Linear Programming Revisited, *Econometrica*, 45: 375–399.

Dixit, Avinash, Grossman, Gene, and Helpman, Elhanan (1997) Common Agency and Coordination: General Theory and Application to Government Policy Making, *Journal of Political Economy*, 105: 752–769.

Dixit, Avinash and Normann, Victor (1980) *Theory of International Trade*, Cambridge: Cambridge University Press.

Dooley, Michael (1976) Note on Interest Rate Parity, Eurocurrencies and Capital Controls, International Finance Discussion Papers, no. 80: The Federal Reserve System.

(1987) Comment on "Definition and Magnitude of Recent Capital Flight" by Robert Cumby and Richard Levich, in Donald Lessard and John Williamson (eds.), *Capital Flight and the Third World Debt*, Washington DC: Institute for International Economics, 79–81.

(1988) Capital Flight, a Response to Differences in Financial Risks, *IMF Staff Papers*, 35: 422–436.

(1995) Capital Mobility and Economic Policy, in Sebastian Edwards (ed.), *Capital Controls, Exchange Rates and Monetary Policy in the World Economy*, Cambridge: Cambridge University Press, 247–263.

Dooley, Michael, Frankel, Jeffrey, and Mathieson, Donald (1987) International Capital Mobility – What Do Saving–Investment Correlations Tell Us?, *IMF Staff Papers*, 34: 503–530.

Dooley, Michael and Isard, Peter (1980) Capital Controls, Political Risk, and Deviations from Interest Parity, *Journal of Political Economy*, 88: 370–384.

Dooley, Michael and Mathieson, Donald (1993) Capital Mobility in the Pacific Rim, in Reuven Glick and Michael Hutchinson (eds.), *Exchange Rate and Interest Rate Policy in the Pacific Rim.*

Dornbusch, Rüdiger (1983) Flexible Exchange Rate and Interdependence, *IMF Staff Papers*, 30: 3–30.

(1998) Capital Controls: An Idea whose Time is Past, in Peter Kenen (ed.) Should the IMF Pursue Capital–Account Convertibility?, Essays in International Finance, no. 207, Princeton: Department of Economics, Princeton University, 20–27.

Dornbusch, Rüdiger, Dantas, D., Pechman, C., Rocha, R., and Simoes, D. (1983) The Black Market for Dollars in Brazil, *Quarterly Journal of Economics*, 98: 25–40.

Downs, Anthony (1957) *An Economic Theory of Democracy*, New York: Harper and Row.

(1967) *Inside Bureaucracy*, Boston: Little, Brown.

Drazen, Allen (1984) A General Measure of Inflation Tax Revenues, The Foerder Institute for Economic Research, Tel Aviv University, working paper no. 37–84.

(1989) Monetary Policy, Capital Controls and Seigniorage in an Open Economy, in Marcello de Ceccho and Alberto Giovannini (eds.), *A European Central Bank? Perspectives on Monetary Unification after Ten Years of the EMS*, Cambridge: Cambridge University Press, 13–32.

Dubin, Jeffrey and Wilde, Louis (1988) An Empirical Analysis of Federal Income Tax Auditing and Compliance, *National Tax Journal*, 41: 61–74.

Edwards, Sebastian (1993) The Political Economy of Inflation and Stabilization in Developing Countries, Cambridge, MA: NBER working paper, no. 4319, April.

(1995a) Introduction, in Edwards (ed.), *Capital Controls, Exchange Rates, and Monetary Policy in the World Economy*, Cambridge: Cambridge University Press.

(1998) Openness, Productivity and Growth: What Do We Really Know? *Economic Journal*, 108: 383–398.

Edwards, Sebastian (ed.) (1995b) *Capital Controls, Exchange Rates, and Monetary Policy in the World Economy*, Cambridge: Cambridge University Press.

Edwards, Sebastian and Khan, Mohsin (1985) Interest Rate Determination in Developing Countries: A Conceptual Framework, *IMF Staff Papers*, 32: 377–403.

Enelow, James and Hinich, Melvin (1984) *The Spatial Theory of Voting*, Cambridge: Cambridge University Press.

Engle, Robert (1982) Autoregressive Conditional Heteroscedasticity with Estimates of the Variance of UK Inflation, *Econometrica*, 50: 987–1008.

Engle, Robert and Granger, Clive (1987) Cointegration and Error Correction: Representation, Estimation and Testing, *Econometrica*, 55: 251–276.

Ethier, Wilfred and Svensson, Lars (1986) The Theorems of International Trade with Factor Mobility, *Journal of International Economics*, 20: 21–42.

Eun, Cheol and Janakiramanan, S. (1986) A Model of International Asset Pricing with a Constraint on the Foreign Equity Ownership, *Journal of Finance*, 41: 897–914.

Falkinger, Josef (1991) On Optimal Public Good Provision with Tax Evasion, *Journal of Public Economics*, 45: 127–133.

Falvey, Rodney (1978) A Note on Preferential and Illegal Trade under Quantitative Restrictions, *Quarterly Journal of Economics*, 92: 175–178.

Feinstein, Jonathan (1990) Detection Controlled Estimation, *Journal of Law and Economics*, 33: 233–276.

Feldstein, Martin (1983) Domestic Saving and International Capital Movements in the Long Run and in the Short Run, *European Economic Review*, 21: 129–151.

Feldstein, Martin and Bacchetta, Phillipe (1991) National Saving and International Investment, in D. Bernheim and J. Shoven (eds.), *National*

Saving and Economic Performance, Chicago: University of Chicago Press, 201–220.

Feldstein, Martin and Horioka, Charles (1980) Domestic Saving and International Capital Flows, *Economic Journal*, 90: 314–329.

Ferejohn, John and Fiorina, Morris (1974) The Paradox of Not Voting: A Decision-Theoretic Analysis, *American Political Science Review*, 68: 525–536.

Fieleke, Norman (1971) *The Welfare Effects of Controls over Capital Exports from the United States*, Essays in International Finance, no. 82, Princeton University.

(1982) National Saving and International Investment, in *Saving and Government Policy*, Federal Reserve Bank of Boston Conference Series, no. 25, 138–157.

Filer, John and Kenny, Lawrence (1980) Voter Turnout and the Benefits of Voting, *Public Choice*, 35: 575–585.

Findlay, Ronald (1978) Relative Backwardness, Direct Foreign Investment and Transfer of Technology, *Quarterly Journal of Economics*, 92: 1–16.

(1984) Growth and Development in Trade Models, in R. Jones and P. Kenen (eds.), *Handbook of International Economics, vol. I: International Trade*, Amsterdam: North-Holland, 185–236.

(1990) The New Political Economy: Its Explanatory Power for LDCs, *Economics and Politics*, 2: 193–221.

Findlay, Ronald and Wellisz, Stanislaw (1982) Endogenous Tariffs, the Political Economy of Trade Restrictions and Welfare, in Jagdish Bhagwati (ed.), *Import Competition and Response*, Chicago: University of Chicago Press, 223–238.

Findlay, Ronald and Wilson, John (1987) The Political Economy of Leviathan, in Assaf Razin and Efraim Sadka (eds.), *Economic Policy in Theory and Practice*, London: Macmillan, 289–304.

Finn, Mary (1990) On Saving and Investment Dynamics in a Small Open Economy, *Journal of International Economics*, 29: 1–21.

Fiorina, Morris (1976) The Voting Decision: Instrumental and Expressive Aspects, *Journal of Politics*, 38: 390–415.

(1997) Voting Behavior, in Dennis Mueller (ed.), *Perspectives on Public Choice: A Handbook*, Cambridge: Cambridge University Press, 391–414.

Fischer, Stanley (1982) Seigniorage and the Case for National Money, *Journal of Political Economy*, 90: 295–313.

(1996) Why are Central Banks Pursuing Long-Run Price Stability?, *Achieving Price Stability*, Proceedings from a symposium sponsored by the Federal Reserve Bank of Kansas City, Kansas City, Mo, 7–34.

(1998) Capital Account Liberalization and the Role of the IMF, in Peter Kenen (ed.), *Should the IMF Purusue Capital–Account Convertibility?*, Essays in International Finance, no. 207, Princeton: Department of Economics, Princeton University, 1–10.

Fishburn, Geoffrey (1979) On How to Keep Tax-Payers Honest (or almost so), *Economic Record*, 55: 267–270.

(1981) Tax Evasion and Inflation, *Australian Economic Papers*, 20: 325–332.

Foster, Carroll (1984) The Performance of Rational Voter Models in Recent Presidential Elections, *American Political Science Review*, 78: 678–690.

Frank, Robert (1988) *Passions Within Reason*, New York, London: Norton.

Frankel, Jeffrey (1980) Tests of Rational Expectations in the Forward Exchange Markets, *Southern Economic Journal*, 46: 1083–1101.

(1982a) On the Franc, *Annales de l'INSEE*, 47–48: 185–231.

(1982b) In Search of the Exchange Risk Premium: A Six Currency Test Assuming Mean-Variance Optimization, *Journal of International Money and Finance*, 1: 255–274.

(1986) International Capital Mobility and Crowding-out in the US Economy: Imperfect Integration of Financial Markets or of Goods Markets?, in R. Hafer (ed.), *How Open is the US Economy?*, Federal Reserve Bank of St. Louis, Lexington: Lexington Books, 33–67.

(1988) Recent Estimates of Time-Variation in the Conditional Variance and in the Exchange Rate Premium, *Journal of International Money and Finance*, 7: 115–125.

(1991) Quantifying International Capital Mobility in the 1980s, in D. Bernhein and J. Shoven (eds.), *National Saving and Economic Performance*, Chicago: University of Chicago Press, 227–260.

(1992) Measuring International Capital Mobility: A Review, *American Economic Review*, 82: 197–202.

Frankel, Jeffrey and Froot, Kenneth (1987) Using Survey Data to Test Standard Propositions Regarding Exchange Rate Expections, *American Economic Review*, 77: 133–153.

Frankel, Jeffrey and MacArthur, Alan (1988) Political vs. Currency Premia in International Real Interest Differentials, *European Economic Review*, 32: 1083–1121.

Fraser, Patricia and Taylor, Mark (1990) Some Effciency Tests of International Real Interest Rate Parity, *Applied Economics*, 22: 1083–1092.

Frenkel, Jacob (1981) The Collapse of PPP during the 1970s, *European Economic Review*, 16: 145–165.

Frenkel, Jacob and Levich, Richard (1975) Covered Interest Arbitrage: Unexploited Profits?, *Journal of Political Economy*, 83: 325–338.

(1977) Transaction Costs and Interest Arbitrage: Tranquil versus Turbulent Periods, *Journal of Political Economy*, 85: 1209–1226.

(1981) Covered Interest Arbitrage in the 1970's, *Economic Letters*, 8: 267–274.

Frenkel, Jacob and Razin, Assaf (1992) *Fiscal Policies and the World Economy*, 2nd edn, Cambridge, MA: MIT Press.

Frey, Bruno and Eichenberger, Reiner (1994) The Political Economy of Stabilization Programmes in Developing Countries, *European Journal of Political Economy*, 10: 169–190.

Friedman, Milton (1971) Government Revenue from Inflation, *Journal of Political Economy*, 79: 846–856.

Fry, Maxwell (1982) Models of Financially Repressed Developing Economies, *World Development*, 10: 731–750.

(1995) *Money, Interest and Banking in Economic Development*, 2nd edn, London: Johns Hopkins University Press.

Fukuda, Shin-ichi (1995) The Determinantes of Capital Controls and their Effects on Trade Balance During the Period of Capital Market Liberalization in Japan, in Sebastian Edwards (ed.), *Capital Controls, Exchange Rates, and Monetary Policy in the World Economy*, Cambridge: Cambridge University Press, 229–245.

Gaab, W., Granziol, M.J., and Horner, M. (1986) On Some International Parity Conditions, *European Economic Review*, 30: 683–713.

Galenson, Walter (1986) *A Welfare State Strikes Oil*, Lanham, NY, London: University Press of America.

Gang, Ira and Rivera-Batiz, Francisco (1994) Does Familarity Breed Contempt? Unemployment, Attitudes and Foreigners in the European Union, Rutgers University, New Brunswick and Columbia University, New York, unpublished manuscript.

Gärtner, Manfred (1994) Democracy, Elections, and Macroeconomic Policy: Two Decades of Progress, *European Journal of Political Economy*, 10: 85–109.

Geeroms, Hans and Wilmots, Hendrik (1985) An Empirical Model of Tax Evasion and Tax Avoidance, *Public Finance/Finances Publiques*, 20: 190–209.

Gelb, Alan (1989) Financial Policies, Growth, and Efficiency, World Bank PPR working paper WPS 202, Washington DC: World Bank.

Genberg, Hans and Swoboda, Alexander (1992) Saving, Investment and the Current Account, *Scandinavian Journal of Economics*, 94: 347–366.

Genser, Bernd and Schulze, Günther (1997) Transfer Pricing under an Origin-based VAT System, *Finanzarchiv*, 54: 51–67.

Giavazzi, Francesco and Giovannini, Alberto (1986) The EMS and the Dollar, *Economic Policy*, 455–485.

Giavazzi, Francesco and Pagano, Marco (1985) Capital Controls and the European Monetary System, Capital Controls and Foreign Exchange Legislation, Occasional Paper, Milano : Euromobiliare, 19–38, reprinted in D.E. Flair and C. de Boissieu (eds.) (1988), *International Monetary and Financial Integration: The European Dimension*, Dordrecht: Martinus Nijhoff, 261–289.

Giovannini, Alberto (1988) Capital Controls and Public Finance: The Experience in Italy, in Francesco Giavazzi and Luigi Spaventa (eds.), *High Public Debt: The Italian Experience*, Cambridge: Cambridge University Press, 177–211.

(1989) National Tax System versus the European Capital Market, *Economic Policy*, 4: 345–386.

(1991) International Capital Mobility and Tax Avoidance, *Banca Nazionale del Lavoro Quarterly Review*, no. 177, June 197–223.

Giovannini, Alberto and Melo, Martha de (1993) Government Revenue from Financial Repression, *American Economic Review*, 83: 953–963.

Giovannini, Alberto and Turtelboom, Bart (1994) Currency Substitution, in Frederick van der Ploeg (ed.), *The Handbook of International Macroeconomics*, Oxford and Cambridge, MA: Basil Blackwell, 390–436.

Godfrey, L.G. (1988) *Misspecification Tests in Econometrics*, Cambridge: Cambridge University Press.

Goldberg, Pinelopi and Knetter, Michael (1997) Goods Prices and Exchange Rates; What Have We Learnt?, *Journal of Economic Literature*, 35: 1243–1272.

Gordon, James (1989) Individual Morality and Reputation Costs as Deterrents to Tax Evasion, *European Economic Review*, 33: 797–805.

(1990) Evading Taxes by Selling for Cash, *Oxford Economic Papers*, 24: 244–255.

Gordon, Roger (1992) Can Capital Income Taxes Survive in Open Economies?, *Journal of Finance*, 47: 1159–1180.

Gordon, Roger and Bo Nielsen, Søren (1997) Tax Evasion in an Open Economy: Value-added vs. Income Taxation, *Journal of Public Economics*, 66: 173–197.

Goulder, Lawrence (1990) Implications of Introducing Withholding Taxes on Foreigners' Interest Income, in Larry Summers (ed.), *Tax Policy and the Economy*, Cambridge, MA: National Bureau of Economic Research, 103–140.

Graetz, Michael, Reinganum, Jennifer, and Wilde, Louis (1986) The Tax Compliance Game: Toward an Interactive Theory of Law Enforcement, *Journal of Law, Economics, and Organization*, 2: 1–32.

Grant, Darren (1998) Searching for the Downsian Voter with a Simple Structural Model, *Economics and Politics*, 10: 107–126.

Greenberg, Joseph (1984) Avoiding Tax Avoidance: A (Repeated) Game-Theoretic Approach, *Journal of Economic Theory*, 32: 1–13.

Greenwood, Jeremy and Kimbrough, Kent (1987) Foreign Exchange Controls in a Black Market Economy, *Journal of Development Economics*, 26: 129–143.

Grilli, Vittorio and Milesi-Ferretti, Gian Maria (1995) Economic Effects and Structural Determinants of Capital Controls, *IMF Staff Papers*, 42: 517–551.

Grønvik, Gunnvald (1991) The Transition from Regulated to Free Credit Markets: The Norwegian Case, Norges Bank working paper no. 1991/8, Oslo.

Gros, Daniel (1987) The Effectiveness of Capital Controls, *IMF Staff Papers*, 34: 621–642.

(1992) Capital Controls and Foreign Exchange Market Crises in the EMS, *European Economic Review*, 36: 1533–1544.

Grossman, Gene (1983) Partially Mobile Capital: A General Approach to Two-Sector Trade Theory, *Journal of International Economics*, 15: 1–17.

(1984) The Gains from International Factor Movements, *Journal of International Economics*, 17: 73–83.

Grossman, Gene and Helpman, Elhanan (1994) Protection for Sale, *American Economic Review*, 84: 833–850.

(1995a) Trade Wars and Trade Talks, *Journal of Political Economy*, 103: 675–708.

(1995b) The Politics of Free Trade Agreements, *American Economic Review*, 85: 667–690.

(1996) Electoral Competition and Special Interest Politics, *Review of Economic Studies*, 63: 265–286.

Gulati, Sunil (1987) A Note on Trade Misinvoicing, in D. Lessard and J. Williamson (eds.), *Capital Flight and the Third World Debt*, Washington, DC: Institute for International Economics.

Gultekin, Mustafa, Gultekin, N. Bulent, and Penati, Alessandro (1989) Capital Controls and International Capital Market Segmentation: The Evidence from Japanese and American Stock Markets, *Journal of Finance*, 44: 849–869.

Gutowski, Armin (1972) Kapitalverkehrskontrollen – Eine Alternative zu größerer Wechselkursflexibilität?, *ORDO*, 23: 11–50.

Haan, Jakob de and Siermann, Clemens (1994) Saving, Investment and Capital Mobility: A Comment on Leachman, *Open Economies Review*, 5: 5–17.

Hansen, Lars and Hodrick, Robert (1980) Forward Exchange Rate as Optimal Predictors of Future Spot Rates: An Econometric Analysis, *Journal of Political Economy*, 88: 829–853.

Haque, Nadeem and Montiel, Peter (1990) Capital Mobility in Developing Countries – Some Empirical Tests, IMF working paper no. 117, Washington, DC: International Monetary Fund.

Harberger, Arnold (1980) Vignettes on the World Capital Market, *American Economic Revew*, Papers and Proceedings, 70: 331–337.

Hausman, Jerry (1978) Specification Tests in Econometrics, *Econometrica*, 46: 1251–1271.

Helpman, Elhanan and Krugman, Paul (1985) *Market Structure and Foreign Trade*, Cambridge, MA: MIT Press.

(1989) *Trade Policy and Market Structure*, Cambridge, MA: MIT Press.

Herring, Richard and Marston, Richard (1976) The Forward Market and Interest Rates in the Eurocurrency and the National Money Markets, in Carl Stem, J. Makin, and D. Logue (eds.), *Eurocurrencies and the International Monetary System*, Washington, DC: American Enterprise Institute for Public Policy Research, 139–163.

Hettich, Walter and Winer, Stanley (1990) The Positive Political Economy of Income Taxation, in Sijbren Cnossen and Richard Bird (eds.), *The Personal Income Tax – Phoenix from the Ashes?* Amsterdam: North-Holland, 265–289.

(1997) The Political Economy of Taxation, in Dennis Mueller (ed.), *Perspectives on Public Choice: A Handbook*, Cambridge: Cambridge University Press, 481–505.

Hewson, John and Sakakibara, Eisuke (1975a) *The Eurocurrency Markets and their Implications: A "New" View of International Monetary Problems and Monetary Reform*, Lexington, MA: Lexington Books.
(1975b) The Impact of US Controls on Capital Outflows on the Balance of Payments: An Exploratory Study, *IMF Staff Papers*, 22: 37–60.

Hillman, Arye (1982) Declining Industries and Political-Support Protectionist Motives, *American Economic Review*, 72: 1180–1187.
(1989) *The Political Economy of Protection*, Chur: Harwood Academic Publishers.
(1992) Comment on Schulze (1992a), "Capital Controls in Direct Democracies", in Hans-Jürgen Vosgerau (ed.), *European Integration in a Changing World Economy*, Berlin: Springer, 772–774.

Hillman, Arye (ed.) (1991) *Markets and Politicians*, Boston: Kluwer Academic Publishers.

Hillman, Arye, Hinds, M., Milanovic, B., and Ursprung, H. (1993) Protectionist Pressures and Enterprise Restructuring: The Political Economy of International Trade Policy in the Transition, paper presented at the Tel Aviv–Konstanz Conference on International Economics.

Hillman, Arye and Katz, Eliakim (1984) Risk-Averse Rent-Seekers and the Social Cost of Monopoly Power, *Economic Journal*, 94: 104–110.

Hillman, Arye and Riley, John (1989) Politically Contestable Rents and Transfers, *Economics and Politics*, 1: 17–39.

Hillman, Arye and Samet, Dov (1987) Dissipation of Rents and Revenues in Small Numbers Contests, *Public Choice*, 54: 63–82.

Hillman, Arye and Ursprung, Heinrich (1988) Domestic Politics, Foreign Interests, and International Trade Policy, *American Economic Review*, 78: 729–745.
(1993) Multinational Firms, Political Competition, and International Trade Policy, *International Economic Review*, 34: 347–363.

Hinrichs, H. (1966) *A General Theory of Tax Structure Change During Economic Development*, Cambridge, MA: The Law School of Harvard University.

Hirshleifer, Jack (1989) Conflict and Rent-Seeking Success Functions: Ratio vs. Difference Models of Relative Success, *Public Choice*, 63: 101–112.

Hirshleifer, Jack and Riley, John (1978) Auctions and Contests, UCLA working paper no. 118B.

Hodne, Fritz (1983) *The Norwegian Economy*, London and Canberra: Croom Helm, New York: St. Martin's Press.

Holcombe, Randall (1980) An Empirical Test of the Median Voter Model, *Economic Inquiry*, 18: 260–274.
(1989) The Median Voter Model in Public Choice Theory, *Public Choice*, 61: 115–125.

Holmes, Mark and Wu, Yangru (1997) Capital Controls and Covered Interest Parity in the EU: Evidence from a Panel Data Unit Root Test, *Weltwirtschaftliches Archiv*, 133: 76–89.

Horst, Thomas (1971) The Theory of the Multinational Firm: Optimal Behavior under Different Tariff and Tax Rates, *Journal of Political Economy*, 79: 1059–1072.

Hotelling, Harold (1929) Stability in Competition, *Economic Journal*, 39: 41–57.

Hufbauer, Gary Clyde and Schott, Jeffrey (1993) *NAFTA: An Assessment*, rev. edn., Washington, DC: Institute for International Economics.

Huizinga, Harry (1991) Law Enforcement and the Black Market Exchange Rate, *Journal of International Money and Finance*, 10: 527–540.

Huizinga, John (1986) *An Empirical Investigation of the Long-Run Behavior of Real Exchange Rates*, Chicago: University of Chicago Press.

IMF [International Monetary Fund (1975, 1980, 1985, 1990, 1992, 1993, 1997)] *Exchange Arrangement and Exchange Restrictions*, Annual Report, Washington, DC: IMF.

(various issues) *International Financial Statistics*, Washington, DC: International Monetary Fund.

Ito, Takatoshi (1986) Capital Controls and Covered Interest Parity Between the Yen and the Dollar, *Economic Studies Quarterly*, 37: 223–241.

Ito, Takatoshi and Krueger, Anne (eds.) (1996) *Financial Deregulation and Integration in East Asia*, Chicago: University of Chicago Press.

Jackman, R. (1987) Political Institutions and Voter Turnout in Industrial Democracies, *American Political Science Review*, 81: 405–423.

Jansen, W. Jos (1995) *International Capital Mobility and Asset Demand*, Rotterdam: Tinbergen Institute, University of Rotterdam.

(1996a) The Feldstein-Horioka Test of International Capital Mobility: Is It Feasible?, IMF working paper no. 100, Washington, DC: International Monetary Fund.

(1996b) Estimating Saving-Investment Correlations: Evidence for OECD countries based on an Error Correction Model, *Journal of International Money and Finance*, 15: 749–781.

(1997) Can the Intertemporal Budget Constraint Explain the Feldstein-Horioka Puzzle?, *Economics Letters*, 56: 77–83.

Jansen, W. Jos and Schulze, Günther (1994) The Effectiveness of Norwegian Capital Controls, University of Konstanz, Department of Economics Discussion Paper, series II, no. 242.

(1996a) A Note on the Effectiveness of Norwegian Capital Controls, *Aussenwirtschaft*, 51: 313–325.

(1996b) Theory-Based Measurement of the Saving–Investment Correlation with an Application to Norway, *Economic Inquiry*, 34: 116–132.

Jarque, Carlos and Bera, Anil (1980) Efficient Tests for Normality, Homoscedasticity and Serial Independence of Regression Residuals, *Economics Letters*, 6: 255–259.

Johnson, Harry (1953) Optimum Tariffs and Retaliation, *Review of Economic Studies*, 21: 142–153.

(1967a) The Possibility of Income Losses from Increased Efficiency or Factor Accumulation in the Presence of Tariffs, *Economic Journal*, 77: 151–154.

(1967b) Theoretical Problems of the International Monetary System, *Pakistan Development Review*, 1–28, reprinted in Richard Cooper (ed.) (1969), *International Finance*, Harmondsworth: Penguin, 304–334.

(1972) Notes on the Economic Theory of Smuggling, *Malayan Economic Review*, May; reprinted in Jagdish Bhagwati (ed.), (1974), 39–46.

Johnston, John (1985) *Econometric Methods*, 3rd edn, Auckland: McGraw-Hill.

Jones, Ronald (1971) A Three-Factor Model in Theory, Trade and History, in Jagdish Bhagwati *et al.* (eds.), *Trade, Balance of Payments and Growth, Papers in International Economics in Honor of Charles P. Kindleberger*, Amsterdam: North-Holland, 3–21.

Jones, Ronald, Coelho, Isaias, and Easton, Stephen (1986) The Theory of International Factor Flows, *Journal of International Economics*, 20: 313–327.

Jones, Ronald and Scheinkman, José (1977) The Relevance of the Two-Sector Production Model in Trade Theory, *Journal of Political Economy*, 85: 909–935.

Judge, G., Hill, R.C., Griffiths, W., Lütkepohl, H., and Lee. T.-C. (1988) *Introduction to the Theory and Practice of Econometrics*, 2nd edn, New York: John Wiley.

Kearl, J.R. (1983) Rules, Rule Intermediaries and the Complexity and Stability of Regulation, *Journal of Public Economics*, 22: 215–226.

Kemp, Murray (1964) *The Pure Theory of International Trade*, Englewood Cliffs, NJ: Prentice-Hall.

(1966) The Gain from International Trade and Investment: A New-Heckscher-Ohlin Approach, *American Economic Review*, 56: 788–809.

Kemp, Murray and Ng, Yew-Kwang (1979) The Importance of Being Honest, *Economic Record*, 55: 41–46.

Kenen, Peter (ed.) (1998) *Should the IMF Purusue Capital-Account Convertibility?*, Essays in International Finance, no. 207, Princeton: Department of Economics, Princeton University.

Kesselmann, Jonathan (1988) Income Tax Evasion, *Journal of Public Economics*, 38: 137–182.

Keynes, John M. (1924) Foreign Investment and National Advantage, *The Nation and Athenaeum*, August 9, 584–587.

Kindleberger, Charles (1958) *International Economics*, Homewood, IL: Richard Irwin.

(1967) The Pros and Cons of an International Capital Market, *Zeitschrift für die gesamte Staatswissenschaft*, 32: 600–617.

Kirchgässner, Gebhard (1980) Können Ökonomie und Soziologie voneinander lernen?, *Kyklos*, 33: 420–448.

Kirchgässner, Gebhard and Schimmelpfennig, Jörg (1992) Closeness Counts if it Matters for Electoral Victory: Some Empirical Results for the United Kingdom and the Federal Republic of Germany, *Public Choice*, 73: 283–299.

Kirchgässner, Gebhard and Wolters, Jürgen (1993) Are Real Interst Rates Stable?, in Hans Schneeweiß and Klaus Zimmermann (eds.), *Studies in Applied Econometrics*, Heidelberg: Physica, 214–238.

Kliemt, Hartmut (1986) The Veil of Insignificance, *European Journal of Political Economy*, 2(3): 333–344.

Koch, Karl-Josef (1992) Trade, Investment and Debt in a Two-Country Growth Model, in Hans-Jürgen Vosgerau (ed.), *European Integration in the World Economy*, Berlin: Springer, 344–373.

Koch, Karl-Josef and Schulze, Günther (1998) Equilibria in Tax Competition Models, in Karl-Josef Koch and Klaus Jaeger (eds.), *Trade, Growth, and Economic Policy in Open Economies, Essays in Honor of Hans-Jürgen Vosgerau*, Berlin: Springer, 281–311.

Kolm, Serge-Christophe (1973) A Note on Optimum Tax Evasion, *Journal of Public Economics*, 265–270.

Kopits, George (1976) Taxation and Multinational Firm Behavior: A Critical Survey, *IMF Staff Papers*, 23: 624–673.

Körber, Achim and Kolmar, Martin (1995) To Fight or not to Fight – An Analysis of Struggle, Submission, and the Design of Contests, University of Konstanz, mimeo.

Koskela, Erkki (1983) On the Shape of Tax Schedule, the Probability of Detection, and Penalty Schemes as Deterrents to Tax Evasion, *Public Finance/Finances Publiques*, 38: 70–80.

Kremers, Jeroen, Ericsson, Neil, and Dolado, Juan (1992) The Power of Cointegration Tests, *Oxford Bulletin of Economics and Statistics*, 54: 325–348.

Krueger, Anne (1974) The Political Economy of the Rent-Seeking Society, *American Economic Review*, 64: 291–303.

(1978) *Foreign Trade Regimes and Economic Development: Liberalization Attempts and Consequences*, Cambridge, MA: Ballinger.

Krueger, Anne and Duncan, Roderick (1993) The Political Economy of Controls: Complexity, Cambridge, MA: NBER working paper, no. 4351; also published in Stetting, Lauge, Svendsen, Knud-Erik, and Yndgaard, Ebbe (eds.), *Global Change and Transformation: Economic Essays in Honor of Karsten Laursen Series A: Copenhagen Studies in Economics and Management, No. 1*. Copenhagen: Handelshojskolens; distributed by Munksgaard International Copenhagen, 193–209.

Krugman, Paul (1978) Purchasing Power Parity and Exchange Rates: Another Look at the Evidence, *Journal of International Economics*, 8: 397–407.

(1987) Is Free Trade Passé?, *Economic Perspectives*, 1: 131–144.

Kugler, P. and Neusser, K. (1993) International Real Interest Rate Equalization: A Multivariate Time-Series Approach, *Journal of Applied Econometrics*, 8: 163–174.

Kurer, Oskar (1993) Clientelism, Corruption, and the Allocation of Resources, *Public Choice*, 77: 259–273.

Landsberger, Michael and Melijson, Isaac (1982) Incentive Generating State Depending Penalty System, *Journal of Public Economics*, 19: 333–352.

Laussel, Didier and Montet, Christian (1994) Strategic Trade Policies, in David Greenaway and Alan Winters (eds.), *Surveys in International Trade*, Oxford and Cambridge, MA: Basil Blackwell, 177–205.

Leachman, Lori (1991) Saving, Investment and Capital Mobility among OECD Countries, *Open Economies Review*, 2: 137–163.

Leamer, Edward (1984) *Sources of International Comparative Advantage*, Cambridge, MA: MIT Press.

Ledyard, John (1984) The Pure Theory of Large Two-Candidate Elections, *Public Choice*, 44: 7–41.

Leidy, Michael (1994) Trade Policy and Indirect Rent-Seeking: A Synthesis of Recent Work, *Economics and Politics*, 6: 97–118.

Leidy, Michael and Hoekman, Bernard (1994) "Cleaning Up" While Cleaning Up: Pollution Abatement, Interest Groups and Contingent Trade Policies, *Public Choice*, 78: 241–258.

Lessard, Donald and Williamson, John (eds.) (1987) *Capital Flight and the Third World Debt*, Washington, DC: Institute for International Economics.

Levi, Maurice (1977) Taxation and "Abnormal" International Capital Flows, *Journal of Political Economy*, 85: 635–646.

Levich, Richard (1985) Empirical Studies of Exchange rates: Price Behaviour, Rate Determination and Market Efficiency, in R. Jones and P. Kenen (eds.), *Handbook of International Economics*, vol. II, Amsterdam: North-Holland.

Levine, Ross (1997) Financial Development and Economic Growth: Views and Agenda, *Journal of Economic Literature*, 35: 688–726.

Lewis, Stephen (1984) *Taxation for Development: Principles and Applications*, New York: Oxford University Press.

Lizondo, José Saúl (1983) Interest Differential and Covered Arbitrage, in Pedro Aspe Armella, R. Dornbusch, and M. Obstfeld (eds.), *Financial Policies and the World Capital Market: The Problem of Latin American Countries*, Chicago: The University of Chicago Press, 221–240.

Long, Ngo van and Vousden, Neil (1991) Protectionist Responses and Declining Industries, *Journal of International Economics*, 30: 87–103.

McCormick, Frank (1979) Covered Interest Arbitrage: Unexploited Profits? A Comment, *Journal of Political Economy*, 87: 411–417.

MacDonald, Ronald and Taylor, Mark (1990) International Parity Conditions, in A. Courakis and M. Taylor (eds.), *Private Behaviour and Government Policy in Interdependent Economies*, Oxford: Clarendon Press, 19–51.

MacDonald, Ronald and Torrance, Thomas (1988) Some Survey Based Tests of Uncovered Interst Parity, in R. MacDonald and M. Taylor (eds.), *Exchange Rates and Open Economy Macroeconomics*, Oxford: Basil Blackwell, 239–248.

MacDougall, G.D.A. (1960) The Benefits and Costs of Private Investment from Abroad: A Theoretical Approach, *Economic Record*, 36: 13–35.

McEachern, William (1978) Collective Decision Rules and Local Debt Choice: A Test of the Median Voter Hypothesis, *National Tax Journal*, 31: 129–136.

McGuire, Martin and Olson, Mancur (1996) The Economics of Autocracy and Majority Rule: The Invisible Hand and the Use of Force, *Journal of Economic Literature*, 34: 72–96.

McKelvey, Richard and Ordeshook, Peter (1985) Elections with Limited Information: A Fulfilled Expectation Model Using Contemporaneous Poll and Endorsement Data as Information Sources, *Journal of Economic Theory*, 36: 55–85.

McKenzie, Richard and Tullock, Gordon (1975) *The New World of Economics*, Homewood, IL: Irwin.

MacKinnon, James (1991) Critical Values for Cointegration Tests, in R. Engle, and C. Granger (eds.), *Long-Run Economic Relationships: Readings in Cointegration*, Oxford: Oxford University Press, 267–276.

McKinnon, Ronald (1973) *Money and Capital in Economic Development*, Washington, DC: Brookings.

(1987) *Monetary and Exchange Rate Policies for International Financial Stability: A Proposal*, Stanford: Stanford University Press.

(1993) *The Order of Economic Liberalization*, 2nd edn, Baltimore: Johns Hopkins University Press.

Macedo, Jorge Braga de (1982) Exchange Rate Behavior with Currency Incovertibility, *Journal of International Economics*, 12: 65–81.

Macho-Stadler, Inés and Pérez-Castrillo, J. David (1997) Optimal Auditing with Heterogeneous Income Sources, *International Economic Review)*, 38: 951–968.

Magee, Stephen (1978) Contracting and Spurious Deviations from Purchasing-Power Parity, in J. Frenkel and H. Johnson (eds.), *The Economics of Exchange Rates*, Reading, MA: 67–74.

(1980) Three Simple Tests of the Stolper–Samuelson Theorem, in P. Oppenheimer (ed.), *Issues in International Economics*, Oriel: Stockfield, 138–153.

(1994) The Political Economy of Trade Policy, in David Greenaway and Alan Winters (eds.), *Surveys in International Trade*, Oxford and Cambridge, MA: Basil Blackwell, 139–176.

Magee, Stephen, Brock, William and Young, Leslie (1989) *Black Hole Tariffs and Endogenous Policy Theory*, Cambridge: Cambridge University Press.

Malinvaud, Edmond (1989) Comment on "National Tax Systems versus the European Market" by A. Giovannini, *Economic Policy*, 4: 374–377.

Markusen, James and Melvin, J.R. (1979) Tariffs, Capital Mobility and Foreign Ownership, *Journal of International Economics*, 9: 395–409.

Marston, Richard (1995) *International Financial Integration: A Study of Interest Differentials between the Major Industrial Countries*, Japan–US Center Sanwa Monographs on International Financial Markets; Cambridge, New York, and Melbourne: Cambridge University Press.

Martin, Lawrence and Panagariya, Arvind (1984) Smuggling, Trade, and Price Disparity: A Crime-Theoretic Approach, *Journal of International Economics*, 17: 201–217.

Mathieson, Donald and Rojas-Suarez, Liliana (1992) Liberalization of the Capital Account: Experiences and Issues, IMF working paper, WP/92/46, Washington, DC: International Monetary Fund.

Mathis, Jean (1981) L'évolution des mouvements de capitaux à court terme entre la France et l'extérieur de 1967 à 1978, *Économie et prévision*, no. 2: 27–58.

Matsuyama, Kiminori (1987) Current Account Dynamics in a Finite Horizon Model, *Journal of International Economics*, 23: 299–313.

Mayer, Wolfgang (1984) Endogenous Tariff Formation, *American Economic Review*, 74: 970–985.

    (1993) Lobbying for Tariff Policies, *Review of International Economics*, 1: 221–233.

Mayer, Wolfgang and Li, Jun (1994) Interest Groups, Electoral Competition, and Probabilistic Voting for Trade Policies, *Economics and Politics*, 6: 59–77.

Mbaku, John (1992) Bureaucratic Corruption as Debt-Seeking Behavior, *Konjunkturpolitik*, 38: 247–265.

    (1996) Bureaucratic Corruption in Africa: The Futility of Cleanups, *Cato Journal*, 16: 99–118.

Meckl, Jürgen (1994) Migration, Income Redistribution, and International Capital Mobility, University of Konstanz, Department of Economics Discussion Paper, series II, no. 230.

Melvin, Michael (1988) The Dollarization of Latin America as a Market-Enforced Monetary Reform: Evidence and Implications, *Economic Development and Cultural Change*, 36: 543–558.

Melvin, Michael and Schlangenhauf, Don (1985) A Country Risk Index: Econometric Formulation and an Application to Mexico, *Economic Inquiry*, 23: 601–619.

Merrifield, John (1993) The Institutional and Political Factors that Influence Voter Turnout, *Public Choice*, 77: 657–667.

Miller, Stephen (1988) Are Saving and Investment Cointegrated?, *Economics Letters*, 27: 31–34.

Mishkin, Frederic (1984a) The Real Interest Rate: A Multi-Country Empirical Study, *Canadian Journal of Economics*, 17: 283–311.

    (1984b) Are Real Interest Rates Equal Across Countries? – An Empirical Investigation of International Parity Conditions, *Journal of Finance*, 39: 1345–1357.

    (1988) Understanding Real Interest Rates, *American Journal of Agricultural Economics*, 70: 1064–1072.

Mitchell, William and Munger, Michael (1991) Economic Models of Interest Groups: An Introductory Survey, *American Journal of Political Science*, 35: 512–546.

Modigliani, Francesco (1970) The Life Cycle Hypothesis of Saving and Intercountry Differences in the Saving Ratio, in W. Eltis, M. Scott and J. Wolfe (eds.), *Induction, Growth and Trade: Essays in Honour of Sir Roy Harrod*, Oxford: Oxford University Press.

Modjtahedi, Bagher (1988) Dynamics of Real Interest Differentials: An Empirical Investigation, *European Economic Review*, 32: 1191–1211.

Moe, Terry (1997) The Positive Theory of Public Bureaucracy, in Dennis Mueller (ed.), *Perspectives on Public Choice*, Cambridge: Cambridge University Press, 455–480.

Mookherjee, Dilip and Png, Ivan (1989) Optimal Auditing, Insurance and Redistribution, *Quarterly Journal of Economics*, 104: 399–415.

Moreno, Ramon (1997) Saving–Investment Dynamics and Capital Mobility in the US and Japan, *Journal of International Money and Finance*, 16: 837–863.

Morgenstern, Oskar (1950) *On the Accuracy of Economic Observations*, Princeton: Princeton University Press; esp. ch. 9 on foreign trade statistics.

Mueller, Dennis (1987) The Growth of Government, *IMF Staff Papers*, 34: 115–149.

(1989) *Public Choice II*, Cambridge: Cambridge University Press.

(1997) *Perspectives on Public Choice: A Handbook*, Cambridge; New York and Melbourne: Cambridge University Press.

Mundell, Robert (1957) International Trade and Factor Mobility, *American Economic Review*, 47: 321–337.

(1965) Growth, Stability, and Inflationary Finance, *Journal of Political Economy*, 73: 97–109.

Munley, Vincent (1984) Has the Median Voter Found a Ballot Box He Can Control?, *Economic Inquiry*, 22: 323–336.

Murphy, Robert (1984) Capital Mobility and the Relationship between Saving and Investment Rates in OECD Countries, *Journal of International Money and Finance*, 3: 327–342.

(1986) Productivity Shocks, Non-Traded Goods and Optimal Capital Accumulation, *European Economic Review*, 30: 1081–1095.

Musgrave, Richard (1959) *The Theory of Public Finance*, New York: McGraw-Hill.

Mussa, Michael (1974) Tariffs and the Distribution of Income: The Importance of Sector Specificity, Substitutability, and the Intensity in the Short and Long Run, *Journal of Political Economy*, 82: 1191–1204.

Myles, Gareth (1995) *Public Economics*, Cambridge: Cambridge University Press.

Myles, Gareth and Naylor, Robin (1996) A Model of Tax Evasion with Group Conformity and Social Customs, *European Journal of Political Economy*, 12: 49–66.

Næs, Randi and Winje, Pål (1993) The Norwegian Bond Market, *Norges Bank Economic Bulletin*, 64: 132–138.

Naya, Seiji and Morgan, Theodore (1969) On the Accuracy of International Trade Data: The Case of Southeast Asian Countries, *Journal of the American Statistical Association*, June 1969, reprinted in Bhagwati (1974), 123–137.

Nayak, P.B. (1978) Optimal Income Tax Evasion and Regressive Taxes, *Public Finance/Finances Publiques*, 33: 358–366.

Neary, Peter (1985) International Factor Mobility, Minimum Wage Rates, and Factor-Price Equalization: A Synthesis, *Quarterly Journal of Economics*, 100: 551–570.

Neary, Peter and Ruane, Francis (1988) International Capital Mobility, Shadow Prices and the Cost of Protection, *International Economic Review*, 29: 571–585.

Nessen, Marianne (1992) Common Trends in Prices and Exchange Rates: Tests on Long-Run Purchasing Power Parity, Stockholm School of Economics working paper no. 37.

Nicolini, Juan Pablo (1998) Tax Evasion and the Optimal Inflation Tax, *Journal of Development Economics*, 55: 215–232.

Niehans, Jürg (1988) *International Monetary Economics*, Baltimore: Johns Hopkins University Press.

Niskanen, William (1971) *Bureaucracy and Representative Government*, Chicago and New York: Aldine, Atherton.

(1991) A Reflection on Bureaucracy and Representative Government, in Andre Blais and Stephen Dion (eds.), *The Budget-Maximizing Bureaucrat*, Pittsburgh: University of Pittsburgh Press, 13–32.

Nitzan, Shmuel (1994) Modelling Rent-Seeking Contests, *European Journal of Political Economy*, 10: 41–60.

Nordhaus, William (1975) The Political Business Cycle, *Review of Economic Studies*, 42: 169–190.

Norges Bank *Annual Report*, Oslo, various issues.

(1989) *Norwegian Credit Markets, Norwegian Monetary and Credit Policy*, Norges Banks Skriftserie, No. 17, Oslo: Norges Bank.

Norton, Desmond (1988) On the Economic Theory of Smuggling, *Economica*, 55: 107–118.

Norwegian Central Bureau of Statistics *Statistical Yearbook*, Oslo, various issues.

Nowak, Michael (1984) Quantitative Controls and Unofficial Markets in Foreign Exchange, *IMF Staff Papers*, 31: 404–431.

Obstfeld, Maurice (1986a) Capital Controls, the Dual Exchange Rate, and Devaluation, *Journal of International Economics*, 20: 1–20.

(1986b) Capital Mobility in the World Economy: Theory and Measurement, *Carnegie–Rochester Conference Series on Public Policy*, 24: 55–103.

(1989) How Integrated are World Capital Markets? Some New Tests, in G.A. Calvo, R. Findlay, and J. de Macedo (eds.), *Debt, Stabilization and Development, Essays in Memory of Carlos Diaz-Alejandro*, New York and Oxford: Basil Blackwell.

OECD (Organisation for Economic Co-Operation and Development) (1990) *Liberalisation of Capital Movements and Financial Services in the OECD Area*, Paris: OECD.

(1994) *Trends in International Migration: Annual Report 1993*, Paris: OECD.

Olson, Mancur (1965) *The Logic of Collective Action*, Cambridge, MA: Harvard University Press.

Ordeshook, Peter (1986) *Game Theory and Political Theory*, Cambridge: Cambridge University Press.

Ortiz, Guillermo (1983) Currency Substitution in Mexico: The Dollarization Problem, *Journal of Money, Credit, and Banking*, 15: 174–185.

Ortiz, Guillermo and Solis, Leopoldo (1979) Financial Structure and Exchange Rate Experience: Mexico, 1954–1977, *Journal of Development Economics*, 6: 515–548.

Otani, I. and Tiwari, S. (1981) Capital Controls and Interest Rate Parity: The Japanese Experience 1978–81, *IMF Staff Papers*, 28: 793–815.

Pagano, Marco (1993) Financial Markets and Growth: An Overview, *European Economic Review*, 37: 613–622.

Palfrey, Thomas and Rosenthal, Howard (1983) A Strategic Calculus of Voting, *Public Choice*, 41: 7–55.

Peltzman, Sam (1976) Towards a More General Theory of Regulation, *Journal of Law and Economics*, 19: 211–240.

Penati, Alessandro and Dooley, Michael (1984) Current Account Imbalances and Capital Formation in Industrial Countries, 1949–81, *IMF Staff Papers*, 31: 1–24.

Pencavel, John (1979) A Note on Income Tax Evasion, Labor Supply, and Non-Linear Tax Schedules, *Journal of Public Economics*, 12: 115–124.

Persson, Torsten and Svensson, Lars (1985) Current Account Dynamics and the Terms of Trade: Harberger–Laursen–Metzler – Two Generations Later, *Journal of Political Economy*, 93: 43–65.

Persson, Torsten and Tabellini, Guido (1990) *Macroeconomic Policy, Credibility and Politics*, Chur: Harwood Academic Publishers.

Persson, Torsten and Tabellini, Guido (eds.) (1994) *Monetary and Fiscal Policy, Vol. I: Credibility, Vol. II: Politics*, Cambridge, MA: MIT Press.

Petite, Pascal (1987) Exchange Control, in John Eatwell, Murray Milgate, and Peter Newman (eds.), *The New Palgrave*, London: Macmillan, corrected reprint 1991, vol, II, 207–210.

Phelps, Edmund (1973) Inflation in the Theory of Public Finance, *Swedish Journal of Economics*, 75: 67–82.

Phylaktis, Kate (1988) Capital Controls: The Case of Argentina, *Journal of International Money and Finance*, 7: 303–320.

(1990) Capital Controls in Argentina, Chile and Uruguay, in K. Phylaktis and M. Proudham (eds.), *International Finance and LDCs*, London: Macmillan.

(1992) The Black Market for Dollars in Chile, *Journal of Development Economics*, 37: 155–172.

Phylaktis, Kate and Wood, Geoffrey (1984) An Analytical and Taxonomic Framework for the Study of Exchange Controls, in John Black and Graeme Dorrance (eds.), *Problems of International Finance*, London and Basingstoke: Macmillan, 149–166.

Pinto, Brian (1991) Black Markets for Foreign Exchange, Real Exchange Rates and Inflation, *Journal of International Economics*, 30: 121–135.

Pitt, Mark (1981) Smuggling and Price Disparity, *Journal of International Economics*, 11: 447–458.

(1984) Smuggling and the Black Market for Foreign Exchange, *Journal of International Economics*, 16: 243–257.

Polinski, Mitchell and Shavell, Steven (1979) The Optimal Tradeoff between the Probability and Magnitude of Fines, *American Economic Review*, 69: 880–891.

Pommerehne, Werner (1978) Institutional Approaches to Public Expenditures: Empirical Evidence from Swiss Municipalities, *Journal of Public Economics*, 9: 163–201.

(1987) *Präferenzen für öffentliche Güter*, Tübingen: Mohr (Siebeck).

Pommerehne, Werner and Frey, Bruno (1976) Two Approaches to Estimating Public Expenditures, *Public Finance Quarterly*, 4: 395–407.

Pommerehne, Werner and Weck-Hannemann, Hannelore (1992) Steuerhinterziehung: Einige romantische, realistische und nicht zuletzt empirische Befunde, *Zeitschrift für Wirtschafts- und Sozialwissenschaften*, 112: 433–466.

Potters, Jan and Winden, Frans van (1994) Models of Interest Groups: Four Different Approaches, in Norman Schofield (ed.), *Social Choice and Political Economy*, Boston: Kluwer Academic Publishers.

Preiser, Erich (1950) Kapitalexport und Vollbeschäftigung, *Jahrbücher für Nationalökonomie und Statistik*, 162: 321–335.

Pyle, D.J. (1951) The Economics of Taxpayer Compliance, *Journal of Economic Surveys*, 5: 163–198.

Quinn, Dennis (1997) The Correlates of Change in International Financial Regulation, *American Political Science Review*, 41: 531–551.

Quinn, Dennis and Inclan, Carla (1997) The Origins of Financial Openness: A Study of Current and Capital Account Liberalization, *American Political Science Review*, 41: 771–813.

Ramaswami, V.K. (1968) International Factor Movement and the National Advantage, *Economica*, 35: 309–310.

Ramirez-Rojas, C.L. (1985) Currency Substitution in Argentina, Mexico, and Uruguay, *IMF Staff Papers*, 32: 627–667.

Ray, Alok (1978) Smuggling, Import Objectives, and Optimum Tax Structure, *Quarterly Journal of Economics*, 92: 509–514.

Razin, Assaf and Sadka, Efraim (1991a) International Tax Competition and Gains from Harmonization, *Economics Letters*, 37: 69–76. (Nearly identical in Jacob Frenkel, A. Razin, and E. Sadka, *International Taxation in an Integrated World*, Cambridge, MA: MIT Press, chapter 11.)

(1991b) Efficient Investment Incentives in the Presence of Capital Flight, *Journal of International Economics*, 31: 171–181. (Nearly identical in Jacob Frenkel, A. Razin, and E. Sadka, *International Taxation in an Integrated World*, Cambridge, MA: MIT Press, chapter 10.)

Reid, Frank (1977) Dummy Variables with a Transitional Phase, *Canadian Journal of Economics*, 10: 326–329.

Reinganum, Jennifer and Wilde, Louis (1985) Income Tax Compliance in a Principal-Agent Framework, *Journal of Public Economics*, 26: 1–18.

(1986) Equilibrium Verification and Reporting Policies in a Model of Tax Compliance, *International Economic Review*, 27: 739–760.

Reisen, Helmut and Yeches, Helen (1993) Time-Varying Estimates on the Openness of the Capital Account in Korea and Taiwan, *Journal of Development Economics*, 285–305.

Richter, H.V. (1970) Problems of Assessing Unrecorded Trade, *Bulletin of Indonesian Economic Studies*, March 1970, reprinted in J. Bhagwati, (1974), 172–182.

Riker, William and Ordeshook, Peter (1968) A Theory of the Calculus of Voting, *American Political Science Review*, 62: 25–42.

Rodrik, Dani (1998) Who Needs Capital-Account Convertibility?, in Peter Kenen (ed.), *Should the IMF Pursue Capital-Account Convertibility?*, Essays in International Finance, no. 207, Princeton: Department of Economics, Princeton University, 55–65.

Rogoff, Kenneth (1996) The Purchasing Power Parity Puzzle, *Journal of Economic Literature*, 34: 647–668.

Roll, Richard (1979) Violations of Purchasing Power Parity and Their Implications for Efficient International Commodity Markets, in M. Sarnat and G. Szego (eds.), *International Finance and Trade*, Cambridge, MA: Ballinger, 133–176.

Ronning, Gerd (1991) *Mikroökonometrie*, Berlin: Springer.

(1992) Share Equations in Econometrics: A Story of Repression, Frustration and Dead Ends, *Statistical Papers*, 33: 307–334.

Rose-Ackerman, Susan (1978) *Corruption*, New York: Academic Press.

Roth, Alvin (ed.) (1988) *The Shapley Value*, Cambridge: Cambridge University Press.

Rowley, Charles (1984) The Relevance of the Median Voter Theorem, *Zeitschrift für die gesamte Staatswissenschaft/Journal of Institutional and Theoretical Economics*, 140: 104–126.

Rowley, Charles, Tollison, R.D., and Tullock, G. (eds.) (1988) *The Political Economy of Rent-Seeking*, Boston: Kluwer Academic Publishers.

Ruffin, Roy (1984) International Factor Movements, *Handbook of International Economics*, vol. I, ed. R.W. Jones and P.B. Kenen, Amsterdam: Elsevier Science Publishers, 237–288.

Ruffin, Roy and Jones, Ronald (1977) Protection and Real Wages: The Neoclassical Ambiguity, *Journal of Economic Theory*, 14: 337–348.

Sachs, Jeffrey (1981) The Current Account and Macroeconomic Adjustment in the 1970s, *Brooking Papers on Economic Activity*, 12: 201–282.

Sandmo, Agnar (1977) Portfolio Theory, Asset Demand and Taxation: Comparative Statics with Many Assets, *Review of Economic Studies*, 44: 369–379.

(1981) Income Tax Evasion, Labour Supply, and the Equity-Efficiency Tradeoff, *Journal of Public Economics*, 16: 265–288.

Schmidt, Susanne (1977) *Kapitalverkehrskontrollen und ihre Wirkung: Eine Analyse der Maßnahmen in der Bundesrepublik Deutschland 1971–1973*, Hamburg: Verlag Weltarchiv.

Schulze, Günther (1992a) Capital Controls in Direct Democracies, in Hans-Jürgen Vosgerau (ed.), *European Integration in a Changing World Economy*, Berlin, Heidelberg and New York: Springer, 750–771.

(1992b) Stating Import Prices Wrongly – Possibilities of Tax and Tariff Evasion, University of Konstanz. Department of Economics Discussion Paper, series II, no. 138.

(1992c) The System of Norwegian Capital Controls, University of Konstanz, unpublished manuscript.

(1993) On the Correlation of Saving and Investment: What Can We Infer for the Degree of Capital Mobility?, University of Konstanz, unpublished working paper.

(1994) Misinvoicing Imports – The Interdependence of Tax and Tariff Evasion, *Public Finance Quarterly*, 22: 335–365.

(1996) Capital Export, Unemployment, and Illegal Immigration, CEPR working paper no. 1394, London: Centre for Economic Policy Research.

Schulze, Günther and Koch, Karl-Josef (1994) Tax Competition in a Bertrand Model, *Journal of Economics/Zeitschrift für Nationalökonomie*, 59: 193–215.

Schulze, Günther and Ursprung, Heinrich (1999a) Economic Integration and Environmental Policy: A Survey of the Political-Economic Literature, in Hans-Jürgen Vosgerau (ed.), *Institutional Arrangements for Global Economic Integration*, London: Macmillan (forthcoming).

(1999b) Globalization and the Nation State, *World Economy*, 22: 235–352.

Schumpeter, Joseph (1942) *Capitalism, Socialism and Democracy*, New York: Harper.

Schweinberger, Albert (1989) Foreign Capital Flows. Tariffs, and Welfare: A Global Analysis, *Canadian Journal of Economics*, 22: 310–327.

Seldon, Arthur (ed.) (1979) *Tax Avoision*, London: IEA Readings 22, The Institute of Economic Affairs.

Shaw, Edward (1973) *Financial Deepening in Economic Development*, New York: Oxford University Press.

Shea, Koon Lam (1997) The Welfare Impact of Tariff-Induced International Capital Movements, *Canadian Journal of Economics*, 30: 404–412.

Sheikh, Munir (1973) Economics of Smuggling: Theory and Application, Ph.D. dissertation, University of Western Ontario, Canada; chapter 4 reprinted in *Bulletin of Oxford University Institute of Statistics*, 36: 287–296.

(1974) Smuggling, Production and Welfare, *Journal of International Economics*, 4: 355–364.

(1976) Black Markets for Foreign Exchange, Capital Flows and Smuggling, *Journal of Development Economics*, 3: 9–26.

(1977) A Partial Equilibrium Model of Smuggling, *Weltwirtschaftliches Archiv*, 113: 268–283.

(1989) A Theory of Risk, Smuggling and Welfare, *World Development*, 17: 1931–1944.

Shleifer, Andrei and Vishny, Robert (1993) Corruption, *Quarterly Journal of Economics*, 103: 599–617.

Siegel, Jeremy (1981) Inflation, Bank Profits, and Government Seigniorage, *American Economic Review*, Papers and Proceedings, 71: 352–355.

Silberman, J. and Durden, G. (1975) The Rational Behavior Theory of Voter Participation, *Public Choice*, 23: 101–108.

Silver, M. (1973) A Demand Analysis of Voting Costs and Voting Participation, *Social Science Research*, 2: 111–124.

Simkin, C.G. (1970) Indonesia's Unrecorded Trade, *Bulletin of Indonesian Economic Studies*, March 1970, reprinted in: J. Bhagwati (ed.), (1974), 157–171.

Simon, Julian (1989) *The Economic Consequence of Migration*, Oxford: Basil Blackwell.

Singer, H.W. (1950) The Distribution of Gains between Investing and Borrowing Countries, *American Economic Review*, Papers and Proceedings, 40: 473–485.

Sinn, Stefan (1992) Saving–Investment Correlations and Capital Mobility: On the Evidence from Annual Data, *The Economic Journal*, 102: 1162–1170.

Skinner, Burrhus (1948) *Walden II*, New York: Macmillan.

Slemrod, Joel (1988) Effect of Taxation with International Capital Mobility, in Henry Aron, Harvey Galper, and Joseph Pechman (eds.), *Uneasy Compromise: Problems of a Hybrid Income-Consumption Tax*, Washington, DC: Brookings Institution, 115–155.

Smith, Adam (1776) *The Wealth of Nations*, Modern Library Edition, New York: The Modern Library, 1937, first published as *An Inquiry into the Nature and Causes of the Wealth of Nations*, published by Strahan and Cadell, 1776.

Solnik, Bruno (1982) An Empirical Investigation of the Determinants of National Interest Rates Differences, *Journal of International Money and Finance*, 1: 333–339.

Spicer, Michael (1986) Civilization at a Discount: The Problem of Tax Evasion, *National Tax Journal*, 39: 13–20.

(1990) On the Desirability of Tax Evasion: Conventional versus Constitutional Economic Perspectives, *Public Finance/Finances Publiques*, 45: 118–127.

Spicer, Michael and Becker, Lee (1980) Fiscal Inequity and Tax Evasion: An Experimental Approach, *National Tax Journal*, 33: 171–175.

Spiegel, Mark (1990) Capital Controls and Deviations from Proposed Interest Rate Parity: Mexico 1982, *Economic Inquiry*, 28: 239–248.

Squire, P., Wolfinger, R.E., and Glass, D.P. (1987) Residential Mobility and Voter Turn-Out, *American Political Science Review*, 81: 45–65.

Srinivasan, T.N. (1973) Tax Evasion: A Model, *Journal of Public Economics*, 2: 339–346.

Stephan, Joerg (1994) *A Political-Economic Analysis of Exchange Rate Movements*, Konstanz: Hartung-Gorre.

Stern, Nicholas (1978) On the Economic Theory of Policy Towards Crime, in J.M. Heineke, (ed.), *Economic Models of Criminal Behavior*, Amsterdam: North-Holland, 123–152.

Stigler, George (1970) The Optimum Enforcement of Laws, *Journal of Political Economy*, 78: 526–536.

  (1971) The Theory of Economic Regulation, *Bell Journal of Economics and Management Science*, 2: 137–146.

Stiglitz, Joseph (1982) Utilitarianism and Horizontal Equity: The Case for Random Taxation, *Journal of Public Economics*, 18: 1–33.

Struthers, John and Young, Alistair (1989) Economics of Voting: Theories and Evidence, *Journal of Economic Studies*, 16: 2–42.

Stulz, Rene (1981) On the Effects of Barriers to International Investment, *Journal of Finance*, 36: 923–934.

  (1994) International Portfolio Choice and Asset Pricing: An Integrative Survey, NBER working paper no. 4645, Cambridge, MA: National Bureau of Economic Research.

Summers, Lawrence (1985) Tax Policy and International Competitiveness, in Jacob Frenkel (ed.), *International Aspects of Fiscal Policies*, NBER Conference Report, Chicago: Chicago University Press, 349–375.

Sussman, Oren (1991) Macroeconomic Effects of a Tax on Bond Interest Rates, *Journal of Money, Credit and Banking*, 23: 352–366.

Svensson, Lars (1984) Factor Trade and Goods Trade, *Journal of International Economics*, 16: 364–378.

Swidrowski, Jozef (1975) *Exchange and Trade Controls*, Epping, Essex: Gower Press.

Tamagna, Frank (1965) *Central Banking in Latin America*, Mexico City: Centro de Estudios Monetarios Latinamericanos.

Taylor, Mark (1987) Covered Interest Parity: A High-Frequency, High-Quality Data Study, *Economica*, 54: 429–438.

  (1989) Covered Interest Arbitrage and Market Turbulence, *The Economic Journal*, 99: 376–391.

Tesar, Linda (1991) Saving, Investment and International Capital Flows, *Journal of International Economics*, 31: 55–78.

Tesar, Linda and Werner, Ingrid (1995) Home Bias and High Turnover, *Journal of International Money and Finance*, 14: 467–492.

Thurman, Quint (1991) Taxpayer Noncompliance and General Prevention: An Expansion of the Deterrence Model, *Public Finance/Finances Publiques*, 46: 289–298.

Thursby, Marie, Jensen, Richard, and Thursby, Jerry (1991) Smuggling, Camouflaging, and Market Structure, *Quarterly Journal of Economics*, 106: 789–814.

Tipke, Klaus and Lang, Joachim (1996) *Steuerrecht: Ein systematischer Grundriß* ([German, G.S.] Tax Law: A Systematic Survey), 15th edn, Cologne: Otto Schmidt.

Tobin, James (1978) A Proposal for International Monetary Reform, *Eastern Economic Journal*, 4: 153–159.

(1983) Comment on "Domestic Saving and International Capital Movements in the Long Run and in the Short Run", by M. Feldstein, *European Economic Review*, 21: 153–156.

Tollison, Robert (1982) Rent-Seeking: A Survey, *Kyklos*, 35: 575–602.

(1997) Rent-Seeking, in Dennis Mueller (ed.), *Perspectives on Public Choice: A Handbook*, Cambridge: Cambridge University Press, 506–525.

Tollison, Robert, Crain, Mark, and Paulter, Paul (1975) Information and Voting: An Empirical Note, *Public Choice*, 24: 43–49.

Tollison, Robert and Willett, Tom (1973) Some Simple Economics of Voting and Not Voting, *Public Choice*, 16: 59–71.

Tsebelis, G. (1986) A General Model of Tactical and Inverse Tactical Voting, *British Journal of Political Science*, 16: 395–404.

Tullock, Gordon (1965) *The Politics of Bureaucracy*, Washington: Public Affairs Press.

(1967) The Welfare Costs of Monopolies, Tariffs, and Theft, *Western Economic Journal*, 5: 224–232.

(1974) *The Social Dilemma: The Economics of War and Revolution*, Fairfax, VA: The Center for the Study of Public Choice.

(1980) Efficient Rent-Seeking, in J. Buchanan, R. Tollinson, and G. Tullock (eds.), *Toward a Theory of the Rent-Seeking Society*, College Station: Texas A&M University Press, 97–112.

(1987a) *Autocracy*, Dordrecht: Kluwer Academic Publishers.

(1987b) Public Choice, in John Eatwell, Murray Milgate, and Peter Newman (eds.), *The New Palgrave*, London: Macmillan, corrected reprint 1991, vol. III, 1040–1044.

(1989) *The Economics of Special Privilege and Rent Seeking*, Boston: Kluwer Academic Publishers.

Ursprung, Heinrich (1987) Die Einführung politischer Elemente in die Theorie der internationalen Handelspolitik, *Geld und Währung/Monetary Affairs*, 3: 28–44.

(1990) Public Goods, Rent Dissipation, and Candidate Competition, *Economics and Politics*, 2: 115–132.

(1991) Economic Policies and Political Competition, in Arye Hillman (ed.), *Markets and Politicians*, Boston: Kluwer Academic Publishers, 1–25.

Varman, Benu (1989) *Capital Flight: A Critique of Concepts and Measures*, Hamburg: Verlag Weltarchiv.

Velthoven, Ben van (1989) *The Endogenization of Government Behaviour in Macroeconomic Models*, Berlin: Springer.

Vikøren, Birger (1991) The Saving-Investment Correlation in the Short and in the Long Run, Norges Bank working paper 91/7, Oslo. Reprinted in Birger

Vikøren, *Interest Rate Differential, Exchange Rate Expectations and Capital Mobility: Norwegian Evidence*, Norges Banks Skriftserie No. 21, Oslo, 1994.

(1993) The Relationship Between Domestic and Foreign Money Market Rates: An Empirical Investigation, Norges Bank working paper no. 11/1993, Oslo. Reprinted in Birger Vikøren, *Interest Rate Differential, Exchange Rate Expectations and Capital Mobility: Norwegian Evidence*, Norges Banks Skriftserie No. 21, Oslo, 1994.

Virmani, Arvind (1989) Indirect Tax Evasion and Production Efficiency, *Journal of Public Economics*, 39: 223–237.

Vosgerau, Hans-Jürgen (1992) Migration als wirtschaftsethisches Problem, in Peter Koslowski (ed.), *Neuere Entwicklungen in der Wirtschaftsethik und Wirtschaftsphilosophie*, Berlin: Springer, 219–238.

Walter, Ingo (1987) The Mechanisms of Capital Flight, in D. Lessard and J. Williamson (eds.), *Capital Flight and the Third World Debt*, Washington, DC: Institute for International Economics, 103–128.

Wang, Jian-Ye (1990) Growth, Technology Transfer, and the Long-Run Theory of International Capital Movements, *Journal of International Economics*, 29: 255–271.

Wang, Jian-Ye and Blomstrøm, Magnus (1992) Foreign Investment and the Technology Transfer – A Simple Model, *European Economic Review*, 36: 137–155.

Waud, Roger (1986) Tax Aversion and the Laffer Curve, *Scottish Journal of Political Economy*, 33: 213–227.

(1988) Tax Aversion, Optimal Tax Rates, and Indexation, *Public Finance/ Finances Publiques*, 43: 310–325.

Webley, Paul, Cowell, Frank, Long, Susan, and Swingen, Judyth (1991) *Tax Evasion: An Experimental Approach*, Cambridge: Cambridge University Press.

Weck-Hannemann, Hannelore (1990) Protectionism in Direct Democracy, *Journal of Institutional and Theoretical Economics/Zeitschrift für die gesamte Staatswissenschaft*, 146: 389–418.

(1992a) Institutional Analysis of Protectionism, in Hans-Jürgen Vosgerau (ed.), *European Integration in the World Economy*, Berlin: Springer Verlag, 717–745.

(1992b) *Politsche Ökonomie des Protektionismus, Eine empirische und institutionelle Analyse*, Frankfurt a.M., New York: Campus.

Weck-Hannemann, Hannelore and Pommerehne, Werner (1996) Tax Rates, Tax Administration and Income Tax Evasion in Switzerland, *Public Choice*, 88: 161–170.

Weigel, Russel, Hessing, Dick, and Elffers, Henk (1987) Tax Evasion Research: A Critical Appraisal and Theoretical Model, *Journal of Economic Psychology*, 8: 215–235.

Weiss, Laurance (1976) The Desirability of Cheating Incentives and Randomness in the Optimal Income Tax, *Journal of Political Economy*, 84: 1343–1352.

Welch, W. (1980) The Allocation of Political Monies: Economic Interest Groups, *Public Choice*, 35: 97–120.

Wertz, Kenneth (1979) Allocation by and Output of a Tax-Administering Agency, *National Tax Journal*, 22: 143–156.

Westphal, Uwe (1983) Comment on "Domestic Saving and International Capital Movements in the Long Run and in the Short Run", by M. Feldstein, *European Economic Review*, 21: 157–159.

Wicksell, Knut (1896) *Finanztheoretische Untersuchungen und das Steuerwesen Schwedens*, Jena: Gustav Fischer Verlag.

Wijnbergen, Sweder van (1990) Capital Controls and the Real Exchange Rate, *Economica*, 57: 15–28.

Wilton, David (1975) Structural Shift with an Interstructural Transition Function, *Canadian Journal of Economics*, 8: 423–432.

Wintrobe, Ronald (1997) Modern Bureaucratic Theory, in Dennis Mueller (ed.), *Perspectives on Public Choice*, Cambridge: Cambridge University Press, 429–454.

Wong, David (1990) What do Saving-Investment Relationships Tell us about Capital Mobility?, *Journal of International Money and Finance*, 9: 60–74.

Wong, Kar-yiu (1995) *International Trade in Goods and Factor Mobility*, Cambridge, MA: MIT Press.

Woodland, Alan (1982) *International Trade and Resource Allocation*, Amsterdam: North-Holland.

Yaniv, Gideon (1990a) Tax Evasion under Differential Taxation, *Journal of Public Economics*, 19: 327–337.

(1990b) On the Interpretation of the Income Effect in Tax Evasion Models, *Public Finance/Finances Publiques*, 45: 235–239.

Yitzhaki, Shlomo (1974) A Note on Income Tax Evasion: A Theoretical Analysis, *Journal of Public Economics*, 3: 201–202.

(1987) On the Excess Burden of Tax Evasion, *Public Finance Quarterly*, 15: 123–137.

Young, Leslie and Magee, Stephen (1986) Endogenous Protection, Factor Returns, and Resource Allocation, *Review of Economic Studies*, 53: 407–419.

Index